Subject Learning in the Primary Curriculum: Issues in English, science and mathematics

The Open University MA in Education

This book has been prepared to support students studying the course E832 *Teaching and Learning in the Primary Core Curriculum*, which is a module in the Open University's taught MA in Education. The course also includes: a set book *Thinking Through Primary Practice*, Bourne, J. (ed.) (1994), London, Routledge; three Open University Professional Development courses (including text, video and audio materials): E628 *English in the Primary Curriculum: Developing Reading and Writing*, E625 *Science in the Primary Curriculum* and E627 *Mathematics in the Primary Curriculum*; and a Study Guide.

The selection of readings in this book reflects the concern to introduce and cover some of the key issues essential in understanding current thinking about what learning about subjects means for children and teachers. Hence balance of opinion has not been the central concern of this selection. A range of perspectives is, however, covered.

This Reader is part of an integrated teaching system: the selection is therefore related to other material available to students and is designed to evoke critical understanding. Opinions expressed are not necessarily those of the course team or of the Open University.

If you would like to study this course and receive a Professional Development in Education prospectus, giving information about the MA and other programmes of professional development in education, please write to the Central Enquiry Service, PO Box 200, The Open University, Walton Hall, Milton Keynes, MK7 6YZ. A copy of *Studying with the Open University* is available from the same address.

Subject Learning in the Primary Curriculum

Issues in English, science and mathematics

Edited by Patricia Murphy,
Michelle Selinger, Jill Bourne
and Mary Briggs
at The Open University

London and New York
in association with
The Open University

First published 1995
by Routledge
11 New Fetter Lane, London EC4P 4EE

Simultaneously published in the USA and Canada
by Routledge
29 West 35th Street, New York, NY 10001

Selection and editorial matter © 1995 The Open University

Typeset in Garamond by Florencetype Ltd, Stoodleigh, Devon

Printed and bound in Great Britain by
Biddles Ltd, Guildford and King's Lynn

British Library Cataloguing in Publication Data
A catalogue record for this book is available from the British Library

Library of Congress Cataloguing in Publication Data
A catalogue record for this book has been requested

ISBN 0–415–12537–5

Contents

Introduction
Patricia Murphy

Part I Curriculum influences

1 Introduction   3
   Patricia Murphy

2 The aims of primary education in member states of the
   Council of Europe   5
   Norman Thomas

3 Knowledge for the masses: world models and national curricula,
   1920–1986   20
   Aaron Benavot, Yun-Kyung Cha, David H. Kamens,
   John Meyer and Suk-ying Wong

4 Education, Majorism and 'the curriculum of the dead'   35
   Stephen J. Ball

5 The problem of good primary practice   50
   Robin Alexander

Part II English: literacy practices in the primary classroom

6 Introduction   73
   Jill Bourne

7 The schooling of literacy   75
   Joanna C. Street and Brian V. Street

8 What counts as reading in this class? Children's views   89
   Eve Gregory

9   Disciplining English: the construction of a national subject   102
     Jill Bourne and Deborah Cameron

10 Young children's writing: from spoken to written genre   114
     Frances Christie

11 Planning for writing across the curriculum   123
     Beverly Derewianka

Part III Science: views of the domain and learning

12 Introduction   141
     Patricia Murphy

13 Constructivism and quality in science education   144
     Joan Solomon

14 Young people's understanding of science concepts   158
     *Rosalind Driver, John Leach, Philip Scott and
     Colin Wood-Robinson*

15 Progression in investigative work in science   184
     *Richard Gott, Sandra Duggan, Robin Millar
     and Fred Lubben*

16 Learning about physics through peer interaction   197
     Christine Howe

Part IV Mathematics: teaching strategies, perspectives on numeracy

17 Introduction   207
     Michelle Selinger

18 Scaffolding in mathematics, science and technology   209
     Mike Askew, Joan Bliss and Sheila Macrae

19 A proposed framework for examining basic number sense   218
     Alistair McIntosh, Barbara J. Reys and Robert E. Reys

20 Learning through problem-solving: a constructivist approach
     to second grade mathematics   232
     Paul Cobb, Terry Wood and Erna Yackel

21 Telling and asking   252
     Eric Love and John Mason

Part V Approaches to knowledge in the future curriculum?

22 Introduction   271
    Patricia Murphy

23 Expert knowledge and the processes of thinking   274
    Robert Glaser

24 The thinking curriculum   289
    John Nisbet

25 Situated cognition and the culture of learning   301
    John Seely Brown, Allan Collins, and Paul Duguid

    Notes on sources   320

    Author index   322

    Subject index   325

Introduction

Patricia Murphy

The emphasis on subject knowledge in primary curricula is a world-wide phenomenon. In the UK this has led to the introduction of subject co-ordinators in primary schools – staff with a particular responsibility for the development of practice in a subject area. Even where policy refers to cross-curriculum themes as additional elements within the 'whole curriculum', which is the case in the UK, it is clear that it is separate subjects that are the perceived power base of the curriculum.

The advocacy of a 'traditional' subject perspective has been constant throughout the history of curriculum development and reform. The perspective has prevailed even after intense periods of reform which directly challenged the view of knowledge enshrined in it.

What is at issue for teachers is how best to address such a curriculum in practice to equip children in the best way possible for their future lives. For teachers then the concern is with 'good' practice. Yet the notion of 'good' practice is a construction determined by subjective views of the nature of knowledge, the purposes it is seen to address in society and perceptions and beliefs about human nature and learning (Alexander, Chapter 5).

It is essential that teachers be able to engage critically with the curriculum in order to evolve their practice. To achieve this critical engagement they need to be aware of the way subjects become defined, the key influences on this and alternative perceptions of these influences. Teachers also need access to current thinking about the nature of knowledge and how children acquire and use domain-specific knowledge and the cognitive benefits of this. Whilst much has been revealed through research and practice, much also remains uncertain. Hence what constitutes a subject and its practice remains controversial and dynamic. It is this information that enables teachers to go beyond subject labels to select learning activities that allow children to develop the conceptual tools and practices they need to make sense of their worlds.

In any discussion of specialist knowledge in the curriculum the common terms used are 'subject' and 'academic discipline'. However, if the focus is on subject learning which involves an examination of the nature of knowledge and children's acquisition of it, more common terms include 'domains', 'practices', 'domain-specific knowledge', 'strategic knowledge' and 'thinking skills'. These terms are used in a variety of ways. For example, 'domain' is often used to describe an epistemological perspective or way of knowing and can incorporate both the knowledge, the practices and the culture of groups of practitioners. At other times its use can apply to specific aspects of a more general domain, for example a sub-set of phenomena in science such as the structure of matter or particular forms of literacy. In general it is a term used to denote knowledge structures and organizations. The different uses of terms is not a small matter and demonstrates the dynamic nature of the debate about the nature of knowledge and its acquisition.

The texts in this book have been selected to enable a critical examination of aspects of subject knowledge in the primary curriculum, the relationship of these to views about learners and learning and the teaching strategies that follow as a consequence of both. The intention is to go beyond labels to examine the processes by which children acquire ways of knowing and acting that they can use outside of school.

The book is organized into five parts. Part I looks first at the general aims of primary education as they have emerged in policy statements in Western Europe and worldwide. These are reviewed to provide the background for a more detailed exploration of UK curriculum development. The focus on the UK reflects in part the focus in the associated professional development courses but is also justified because of the close parallels between current developments and controversies in the UK and elsewhere in the world.

The next three parts pick up the subject areas of English, science and mathematics. In the English section, Part II, the texts focus on literacy (reading and writing) – that part of the English curriculum which is sometimes referred to as the 'basic skills'. Reading and writing practices as they take place in the social context of the classroom are related to wider debates on the nature of literacy, standard English, and the relationship between spoken and written English.

In Part III, science, the emphasis is on learning issues, in particular the emerging emphasis on social constructivism in science education. The chapters look at the implications of this view for what children should learn and how they should learn, and examines research into progression in children's conceptual and procedural understanding. Connections to the previous part are evident in terms of the changing definition and value placed on aspects of the primary science curriculum.

The selection of texts in Part IV focuses on teaching strategies which reflect the issues already covered and enable further examination of them but this time in the context of the mathematics curriculum. Social constructivism in learning and assessment is examined by consideration of the metaphor of scaffolding, what it means in practice for teachers and what it depends on. Views of domains are further explored in the context of learning about number. How investigative learning is set up and reinforced through the role of classroom talk and informal recording methods is also discussed.

A look across the detail provided in the texts of the three subject parts reveals commonalities of concern and emphasis. For example each part shares a common thread of constructivism; the child is consistently perceived to be the active meaning-maker. Another common theme following from this emphasis is that of the social nature of learning – the entering into a community of practices. Associated with this, each part stresses the need for utility in learning outcomes, on equipping children with ways of knowing and acting that they can use outside of school. In each part, though to varying degrees, the school culture is seen to be problematic in this regard. This concern with the school culture is evident in the discussions about the nature and purposes of learning activities in school. Perhaps the most obvious commonality emerging across the parts is the continuing concern about what should be taught, the definition of each of the curriculum areas remains unresolved and in a state of flux. Central to these debates are differing views about the purpose of education and the nature of knowledge.

In the final part of the book key debates about approaches to knowledge are introduced. Perspectives on domain knowledge are discussed and implications for practice drawn out. The issue of strategic knowledge (i.e. whether domain-independent knowledge exists) is examined in a review of current developments about thinking skills and their place in the curriculum. The final reading focuses on the view of domain learning as a process of enculturation. The entering into the culture of a subject domain is judged to be the essence of learning. To achieve this process it is argued that learning activities have to be authentic, i.e. coherent, meaningful and purposeful within the context of the ordinary practices of the domain culture. This raises questions about the future organization of the curriculum and the selection of tasks to achieve successful domain learning.

Part I

Curriculum influences

Chapter 1

Introduction

Patricia Murphy

In this first part of the book the focus is on the aims and nature of primary curricula. Numerous hypotheses exist to explain how educational curricula evolve, each of which point to different determining factors. If teachers are to adopt a critical stance to curricula it is necessary for them to understand these different perspectives and to relate them to their own positions and those of their schools, local communities and wider national contexts. The texts in this part of the volume are a limited selection intended to introduce readers to some of these perspectives. As such they take a general look across primary curricula and then consider in more depth a specific perspective on curriculum construction in the context of recent UK developments. The focus then shifts to consider how the differential status of groups within the education community, particularly primary teachers, might impact on policy-making. Teachers' own views of practice and hence of the curriculum are considered and applied to a framework for analysing practice.

Chapter 2 is an abstract from Thomas's wider overview of the aims of primary education in Western European countries. In the abstract he highlights some of the commonalities between the aims of different countries but also indicates the ways in which different conceptions of apparently common aims appear to operate and to affect practice. As Thomas notes, differences between statements of aims are those of 'degree, emphasis and balance'. However, differences in the interpretations of aims are more significant and alter the education that children receive.

The timetable is used to organize and define the curriculum and allocate time to various aspects of learning. Thomas cautions against using the timetable as the 'single means of prescribing and analysing the curriculum'. In his view the separate parts do not add up to the whole, and prevent connections being made between strands of children's learning.

The next chapter is abstracted from an article by Benavot *et al.*'s study of primary curricula worldwide. The abstract considers alternative approaches to curriculum study. The functionalist perspective, which views the curriculum as a product of the functional requirements of society, and the historical perspective, which sees it as a reflection of existing power relations in society. The authors propose an added dimension, that of the influence of worldwide polity. They looked at three hypotheses in testing their view of a worldwide model of mass education. The abstract focuses on two of these hypotheses – that primary curricula exhibit categories independent of national development, and that these categories exhibit increasing similarity. The notion that official primary curricula reflect a world educational order was supported by the study, but, as the authors argue, this does not negate other perspectives, it merely modifies and extends them.

Ball's chapter (4) would be located in the historicist tradition of curriculum study. In this strongly argued chapter, Ball describes the influences that affect national educational policy-making and focuses on the interactions of conflicting forces in England in the period of development and modification of the National Curriculum. His concern is with the ways that subject definitions evolve and are manipulated by powerful interests groups. The value of Ball's analysis of curriculum is the clarity with which views of epistemology, pedagogy and learners are linked. To achieve this clarity he presents polarized perspectives. Whilst his allegiance to one polarized view is made abundantly clear, this does not detract from the power of his analysis.

The final chapter by Alexander focuses on an analysis of primary practice. In the chapter, Alexander develops a framework for conceptualizing primary practice which takes account of observable practice in terms of what children should learn, how they learn and how teachers teach; and the values and beliefs about children, societal needs and knowledge that underpin this observable practice.

He goes on to develop a framework for the analysis of practice which attempts to determine what constitutes 'good' practice. He argues that in such a framework 'ethical and empirical questions need to be pre-eminent, and with both dependent on a prior conceptualization of the nature of educational practice itself'.

Chapter 2

The aims of primary education in member states of the Council of Europe

Norman Thomas

The definition of educational *aims* used in this chapter is as follows: they are statements about the directions in which one wishes to go. They may be broad or narrow, general or specific. For example, it may be an aim that children should use and develop their powers of communication; or that they should spell in conventional ways. Aims are different from objectives, which identify either a final or an intermediate level of achievement. Aims do not, for instance, propose which or how many words should be spelt conventionally at a given stage of a child's education; but an objective may.

It is tempting to think of primary education as though it were innocent and pure so that it could be conducted in the unsullied interests of children and without being stained by those of the outside world. The temptation should be avoided. If the context within which primary education operates is taken as given, there may be too little critical examination of its effects. Primary education's purposes are conditioned by and, to different degrees, condition both its conduct and its circumstances. To expand on one part of the interrelationship: the purposes of primary education are constrained by what is feasible, and what is feasible depends upon the talents of the adults and children engaged in it and the support they receive from the community. Furthermore, while primary schools should be regarded as providing a distinct stage of education, their effectiveness also depends upon what is done with children before they are first admitted, upon their experiences outside the school, and on how secondary schools build upon what they have done.

CHILDREN AS INDIVIDUALS

Widely held tenets of society in Western Europe in the 1980s include respect for the uniqueness and rights of individuals. It is not surprising that these are reflected in the aims of primary education by member states of the Council of Europe. They are treated in a number of different aspects. In particular, the rights of individual children are recognized in the determination of countries to make primary schools places to which children wish to go. Ways of achieving that goal include: Portugal's intention that children 'discover and develop their interests'; Norway's requirement that children should be participants in their education; Denmark's insistence that daily life in the school must be based on intellectual freedom and democracy; and the trend in a number of countries to involve children in the assessment of their own progress.

At its most idealistic, concern for individuality leads to the view that provision should be made so that each child, though different, can develop to the full. The requirement has led some to question whether more specialist teaching needs to be introduced into primary schools (e.g. Italy: Ghilardi, 1988), while others such as Liechtenstein are strengthened in their intention to provide 'more security for the pupils' through improvement of the system of class teachers. We shall come to some restraints on the meaning of 'full' later on, but the general intention has some profound implications for primary education. Most are positive, though there are negative outcomes also, at least potentially, especially if the notion leads to a supposition that there are predetermined limits to learning: a point where the individual is full.

Full can be understood in two senses. It can refer to the range of activities and learning on which a child is engaged, or it can mean that each child should make as much progress as he or she possibly can. We begin with the first.

The range of the educational programme

In most of the countries, . . . the expressed aim is to provide a wide-ranging education at the primary stage, covering children's intellectual, social, moral and spiritual, emotional and physical development. None of the member states excludes any of those as being irrelevant, though the spiritual element may relate to knowing about religious ideas, rather than believing in them, or be chosen to fit with the beliefs of parents, as in Spain. All want children to be informed about their place in history and in today's world, and to acquire knowledge of the natural world. Liechtenstein reports some difference of opinion over whether such an all-pervading ambition as full development is realizable in a small country. Some – including Spain, Cyprus and Belgium – place more emphasis than others on the development of the imagination, aesthetic and artistic appreciation and expression . . ., and the French . . . refer to 'sustained efforts to promote *musical* and *artistic* education'.

The overall aim, then, is to provide an education service that touches all aspects of human development that are capable of being educated. The contributory aims may be stated in broad and in specific terms. For example, it may be thought to be enough to acknowledge the importance of physical development and well-being; or there may be specific reference also to teaching children about a balanced diet. The encouragement of aesthetic response usually includes reference to music as well as to the visual arts, but may or may not include mention of the use of musical instruments. Views about the priority that should be given to some parts of the curriculum as compared with others are sometimes revealed by making some activities compulsory and others voluntary. For example, choral singing is an extra or voluntary activity in Austria. The availability of options may also stem from a view about differences in the talents of children – for example, provision for exceptional interest and skill in playing a musical instrument. Otherwise, differences of detail in the [policy] documents may be indications of what was at the front of the mind of a writer rather than a real difference in day-to-day practice in schools.

The balance between first-hand and second-hand sources

Looked at from a child's point of view, the development of breadth implies a curriculum that allows access to and the use of knowledge about what people believe and what they do; about the characteristics of the environment (living and non-living, near and far – in both distance and time); and about the part he or she might play in the circumstances of life. It is difficult to envisage how these aims could be satisfied unless children have opportunities to test out their growing skills and concepts. If the trialling process is to fit such a broad set of aims, it needs to encompass social behaviour and the exercise of social influence. It must also incorporate practical investigations and use of the environment, including the materials and objects of which it is composed. Certainly, the ways in which aims are expressed usually imply that children learn at first hand as well as at second hand, as in Malta's expressed intention to help children acquire an active attitude towards problems; Austria's determination to encourage independent judgement; and Denmark's aim to give children the chance to make independent assessments, evaluations and form personal opinions. Ghilardi (1988) comments on the Italian 1985 Act No. 104, noting that the role of the teacher has 'undergone a deep transformation' in which he or she is 'asked to organize a "learning environment in which each pupil is able to gradually develop his own field of action, of planning and testing, of exploration, of thinking and of individual study" '. But the roots of primary schooling may so bias practice as to make it desirable that the case for a non-sedentary education is made even more strongly.

Literacy and numeracy

The history of compulsory formal education is short – even in countries such as Norway, where compulsory basic education has existed since the eighteenth century. Its traditions everywhere have ensured that special emphasis is, rightly, placed on teaching children to read, write and calculate, skills that are often referred to as *basic*. The purpose has been to widen children's opportunities to learn and to engage in social life, especially but not only in paid employment. The needs of the children and of society have been and remain in tune in these respects as the operations of society have become increasingly complex. In the early years of compulsory education it was plainly absurd to expect illiterate parents to be responsible for teaching their children to be literate. Teaching children to read was a job for the school. Attitudes, once struck, have a way of persisting. For example, in England and Wales it has only been during the last dozen years, and after more than a century of compulsory education, that a significant number of teachers have begun to suppose that parents might have a part to play in the process.

The seizure of the words *basic* and *elementary* by the educational establishments for the early stages of reading, writing and arithmetic has been powerful, and generally accepted by the lay public. Yet the usage hardly stands examination if one thinks about the prior requirements of speech, motor control and social interchange, for all of which parents continue to be the informal teachers in the earliest stages.

Social development

The question of when children are ready for school is decided in light of perceptions of their social maturity as well as of their capacity to learn. Contextual questions relating to social aims will be considered in the next section, but there is no escaping the fact that a child entering school – even if he or she has experienced pre-school education – engages in a major shift of social experience and learning. In Switzerland it is recognized that 'during the 1st school year pupils must progress from play to a set activity and submit to a certain discipline'. Teachers of young children must pay a lot of attention to their pupils' need to accommodate to their new circumstances, and there is no shortage of aims reflecting upon children's social attitudes and competencies. The Spanish signal the importance of 'developing the ability to coexist', and the Portuguese argue for a balance between school culture and everyday culture; for the development of individual and team work; for the acquisition of positive attitudes, habits and co-operation conducive to good family relationships and thoughtful, responsible involvement with the environment.

Yet one seldom has the impression on visiting schools that this aspect of children's learning is thought of positively as a part of the curriculum. The stress is on persuading children to behave in ways that conform with the requirements of the school. Behaviour is more likely to be discussed with children at length when it is aberrant than for the purpose of making explicit the variety of ways in which co-operation can profitably take place, the kinds of roles that group members may adopt, and the ways in which individual initiative can best contribute.

The common approach, necessary but not sufficient, is that the teaching and learning are *about* social behaviour and organisation through subjects such as the local environment, geography, history, social studies, civics and notions of democracy, at least two of which form part of what is taught in the primary schools of each member state. These are, of course, important routes through which children learn about their cultural heritage, are helped to understand how the past has shaped the present and something of the complexity of the modern world. The learning needs to be linked to daily life inside and outside the school.

Some countries, for example Portugal, require specifically that schools should 'bring about a national awareness of the world situation, from a standpoint based on universalist humanism, solidarity and international understanding'. In many Western European primary schools the actual teaching is more mundanely concerned with bringing the children's attention to the extent to which they rely on the efforts of people in their own country and elsewhere to provide raw materials, including food, and manufactured goods for daily life. The stories of people who behave in commendable fashions provide models of good behaviour. The sympathies of children for others worse off than themselves are often aroused and may lead to positive attempts to compensate, for example through fund-raising for charities or the 'adoption' of a child in a Third World country.

On the other hand, much learning is on an impersonal, even grand scale. Teachers in France are more encouraged than they were to help children to relate their learning to everyday experience. Nevertheless, by the end of the primary stage they are expected to have covered pre-history, pre-Roman Gaul and the Gallo-Roman period, the High Middle Ages, the twelfth- and thirteenth-century renaissance, the Ancien Régime, the French Revolution and the Empire, the changes brought about during the nineteenth century, the two world wars, and the period since 1945 (Lewis, 1985).

The place of foreign languages

The teaching of languages introduced by recent immigrants raises two main considerations. The first concerns integration. It is the experience, for example in the Federal Republic of Germany, that many post-1939 immigrants arrived believing they would stay for a few years and then return to their former homes, and that the intention to return permanently often fades with time. If the in-comers and their children, more and more of them born in the new country, are to become settled, is it not best that they should forget their foreign language and ways and be integrated as soon and as completely as possible? The opposing and prevailing view welcomes the enrichment of the national character the newcomers bring and worries that too large a proportion of immigrants and their families are in lower-paid forms of employment or none, and that their condition is exacerbated by low expectations of them by the indigenous population, and also by low expectations the children may have of themselves. Everything should be done to raise expectations, to acknowledge the worth of the home language and culture, and to make sure that children know of people from their culture who have made significant contributions to mathematics, science, music and art – to learning generally – and who have succeeded in their new countries.

In *Länder* of the Federal Republic of Germany and in the Netherlands, as examples, teaching uses the home language as a medium of instruction. In those Swedish schools where there are 'many immigrant children of the same origin in a school at the junior and the middle level they often form bi-lingual classes'. The practical difficulties of providing home-language teaching in some schools are formidable: there are schools in the United Kingdom where more than ten languages, even more than 40 languages, are spoken by the pupils. Supplementary schools are supported financially, but run by members of the ethnic-minority group. They help children to acquire both literacy in their home language and knowledge of their religion and culture. In some ordinary schools, teachers familiar with both the national and the home languages are members of staff, either full time or on a visiting and advisory basis. There may also be ancillary workers, from the children's language groups, employed to work under the general direction of teachers. They use the national and the home language inter-changeably. It is very doubtful whether the practices best suited to these children have yet been fully evolved in any country.

Some countries, such as Sweden and the Netherlands, have responded more positively than others to the notion that a second, widely spoken language should be introduced. Worry in Italy, shared by others, was that it is difficult for children to learn a second language before they have sufficiently mastered their own (Mallinson, 1980), but Law No. 104 of 1985 requires the teaching of a foreign language from 1987. In the United Kingdom, uncertainty stems also from the effort that was made in the 1960s to teach French in primary schools (Burstall, 1974). Doubts have less to do with desirability than with practicality, for the indigenous population has not been renowned for learning modern languages other than its own and there may be difficulty in staffing the teaching of a modern foreign language for all even in secondary schools when the national curriculum is introduced.

Physical development

Some aspects of motor control have already been acquired by normal children well before they come to school. They can sit, walk, run, jump. In countries where they begin school at 7, most children can control scissors, a pencil, a paint brush or crayon when they are first admitted. Some can by 5.

Teachers continue to be interested in children's control of tools and equipment. Handwriting is an important skill and the aim may simply be to develop legibility and reasonable speed, though it may extend to settling on a chosen style. Drawing and painting are universal activities that call on the imagination as well as on manual skill. In some countries more than others, children are encouraged to make things because they will be attractive to look at (e.g. figures or pots from clay); or because they might be useful (e.g. a book to write in, a meal to eat or an item of clothing); or because they are part of an investigation being undertaken in the curriculum (e.g. a model of an old house, or working traffic lights to aid the understanding of traffic movement); in places, microcomputers are used to control models.

Opportunities for improving gross motor control continue to be of wide interest in European schools. They are directed at enhancing balance, speed and variety of movement, and the encouragement of climbing, jumping, ball control, and team games. The teaching of swimming is thought of as a school responsibility in some places and not in others.

There is also concern for healthy living in other senses. Sex education is part of the curriculum in some countries and may deal with human sexual relations, or with the study of plants and animals, or both. Diet, road safety and, more recently, the dangers of abusing drugs are of increasing interest.

A child should achieve as much as he or she can

The other sense of fullness relates to the depth of children's achievement and itself has two aspects. One relates to the appropriateness of what children are taught day by day: is what they do taking them into new ground or merely allowing them to exhibit what they already know? The second relates to their long-term achievements and contains a notion of potential, which may have some use when selecting aims but carries a dangerous infection leading to suppositions of ultimate limitation when attached to objectives.

Taking children as far as they can now go

It is obvious that the aims adopted should be appropriate to the children to whom they are applied; it is not always so easy to apply the truism in practice. Teachers have experience of the range of achievement exhibited by children of a given age, yet it is widely thought that teachers' expectations more often underestimate than overestimate children's competence. That might be too simple an interpretation of what researchers observe. Children can sometimes do both more and less than teachers suppose – more if the children have had the background experience and opportunities to examine its implications critically; less if they are asked to interpret events without knowledge of the underlying factors, and are accustomed to remembering standard explanations rather than arguing ideas through on the basis of personal and general experience. The importance of taking account of what children comprehend and can do is undeniable, and acknowledged ... Sweden [for example], warns of the importance of feeding back to schools the results of experience and research.

Earlier in this chapter it was argued that the emphasis on literacy and numeracy in primary education is partly due to the development of primary schools from basic or elementary schools. The message on the obverse of the coin is that children of primary school age are at a stage in their development when they can make a formal beginning to learning to read, write and calculate: progress in an aim should be realizable as well as desirable. Assumptions vary about exactly when it is best to start teaching children to read and write, and the choice made has an effect on the entry age for formal education. In the United Kingdom, the belief is that most children can make a start by 5 and increasing numbers of children are enrolled at 4 plus. Changes in the Netherlands in recent years have brought together nursery and primary education and have been accompanied by the view that children can achieve literacy earlier than was supposed. Across the member states, the age of admission to primary school and the beginning of the formal teaching of reading ranges in practice from 4 to 8 plus.

The problem is not simply to decide when to begin one aspect of teaching. It is also necessary to form a view about how the different aspects relate to each other. The issue may seem to be more a question of objectives than of aims, using the definitions adopted here, but the issue crops up in papers submitted to the Council of Europe. That from Greece refers to the matter explicitly when it expresses the need for a *harmonious and balanced* development of the intellectual and psycho-physical abilities of pupils, and refers to the importance of developing pupils with integrated personalities. These intentions are highly significant in deciding what to do and when, day by day, in the classroom. At the simplest of levels: should this child be given more practice in measuring to an accuracy of 2mm, or is the priority to introduce the child to an author whose work will give insight into dealing with conflict in a small group? What differences of perception led the government in the United Kingdom, unusually at the time, to stimulate the use of microcomputers in primary schools; and the *Land* of North-Rhine-Westphalia in the Federal Republic of Germany to argue that 'the principle of teaching "according to age" makes a systematic examination of the new technologies inadvisable at the primary level'. In this case it must surely have been a difference of view about the purposes of introducing children to microcomputers: (a) to aid learning generally, and (b) to teach children how computers work and how to program them. It could hardly have related to real differences in the children.

One's opinion about balance in the curriculum is based on perceptions about what children can do, about what it is now important for them to get better at, and about the resources available and their use. The allocation of time is one means by which balance might be achieved; it does not, in itself, provide a definition of balance. The essential problem is to identify the stages of learning in the various aims and to relate them to one another. The search for balance across the curriculum calls for the description of these stages against which children's achievements can be assessed. Anyone who supposes that can be managed with high precision will be defeated by human nature and the complexity of what must be learnt.

Individual differences

Expressions of aims in the various countries recognize individual differences. 'Full' is not the same for everyone. Allowances should be made for differences due to children's age, ability and aptitude, in their interests and beliefs, in their preferred techniques and methodologies. These differences should, within limits, be fostered. Differences of language and culture should be provided for; but negative attitudes concerning race, culture and gender should be corrected. Greece stresses that educational provision has to be available irrespective of a child's sex or social class.

Some children, on grounds of maturity, may be admitted to school in Austria and the Federal Republic of Germany at earlier or later ages than apply to the majority. The decision is taken by the headteacher, on advice from a doctor and in consultation with parents. Parents in any country need to be unusually strong-minded to withstand the combined might of the doctor and the head. Nevertheless, this permitted flexibility of response to individual differences is by no means repeated in all member states, and the starting age may be closely defined and applied.

Even moderate differences between children, well within what may be regarded as a normal range of achievement at a given age, have implications for the organization of teaching and learning within a primary school. The practice of requiring children to repeat a year is said to be diminishing in some countries where it has long been prevalent. In Austria's report of 1988, 13 per cent of children started school later than most of their age group. In North-Rhine-Westphalia the corresponding figure in 1984/5 was 8.6 per cent (House of Commons, 1986), and the age-range in a reception class may be as much as 2 years 6 months; in 1982/3 the percentages of children not moved up at the end of the 2nd, 3rd and 4th years were, respectively, 3.4 per cent, 2.6 per cent and 2.1 per cent.

Where schools arrange children more strictly according to age, there may be special arrangements for teaching some children in small groups by employing a teacher additional to the class teachers. In Sweden, approximately 25 per cent of the state grants are distributed per capita and can be used mainly for two purposes: for extra support to pupils with difficulties; and for teaching small groups of pupils to facilitate individualization. Whatever organizational solution is adopted, ordinary primary school classes contain children of a wide range of abilities, aptitudes and interests. The aim to provide for them according to individual need puts a considerable burden upon teachers, even in countries such as Luxembourg, which can claim that most primary school classes have fewer than 20 pupils and not many have more than 25.

Unless special support is provided, meeting individual differences is made more complex by the trend, in many countries, to admit to general primary schools some children who would a few years ago have been separated off into special schools for the handicapped. Many member states now share the view that the requirement is not to identify the mental or physical handicap and provide a label for the child accordingly; it is to identify any special educational need and provide for it with as little disruption to a child's ordinary life as possible – preferably in a mainstream school.

The balance between personal need and community membership

The papers provided by the member countries leave no doubt that there is wide agreement that it is important to encourage a sense of community and an awareness of how society is organized. The question is: how does one balance the two aims, one of which stresses the servicing of individual differences, and the other of which gives pride of place to membership of a community? The practicalities of teaching may count as much as principle in the chosen solutions.

THE REQUIREMENTS AND CONSTRAINTS OF SOCIETY

The previous section discussed the aims of primary education mainly from the points of view of the teachers and children. In this section, the main consideration will be: what does society require of primary education and its pupils?

The first point to be made is that there is less stress on development to the full, and more on accepting priorities and constraints characteristic of the society that provides the education. This is not reprehensible in principle: one's view in any particular case depends upon one's opinion of the society making the requirement. The principle is illuminated in many of the reports from member states. That from Iceland quotes an Act of Parliament on the needs for co-operation between home and school and for preparation for life in a modern democratic state. The Act requires that schools should 'endeavour to widen the children's horizon and develop their understanding of their environment, social conditions, the characteristics and history of Icelandic society and the obligations of the individual to society'. The already quoted periods of history to be covered in French primary schools have an understandably French bias. The Norwegian Basic School Act of 1969, as amended in 1975, requires the basic schools 'to help give the pupils a Christian and moral upbringing'. The Swedish curriculum 'reflects the view of the democracy on society and man, the implication being that human beings are active and creative and that they both can and must assume responsibility and seek knowledge in order to co-operate with others . . .'. The official aims of primary education in Turkey require schools to 'enable every Turkish child to acquire all the necessary basic knowledge, skills and habits required for effective citizenship and to raise him in a manner commensurate with national ethical concepts'. Children need to know that they must obey the rules of society as well as use them; contribute to social well-being as well as draw from it.

There are complications. No society is static, though some – world-wide – are more stable than others. It is not sufficient simply to act in accord with today's social practices and ambitions: everyone who can should assist in improving the general lot, socially and materially. As seen by the current providers – and there is no intention here to imply that any other stance could reasonably be expected at government level – the changes should be within limits that are acceptable to current society. In the words of the Icelandic Act: 'the school must foster independent thought *and* co-operative attitudes' (emphasis added).

Change may be on an individual or wider scale. The stimuli for change stem from different sources:

The acceptance and promotion of modern scientific and technological developments

It is no accident that the national curriculum introduced in England and Wales in 1989 includes science as well as English and mathematics among its core subjects, and technology among its foundation subjects for primary schools. It is unlikely that science would have been given the same priority or technology have appeared at all for the primary stage even as recently as 20 years ago. Portugal requires schools to keep pupils abreast of new knowledge. Section 9 of the Netherlands Primary Education Act requires that science, including biology, is taught in primary schools, and Mr van Eijndhoven at the Vaduz Conference heralded the arrival of microcomputers in Netherlands' primary schools. In Malta, 'it is a fact that innovation . . . was prompted by radical changes in contemporary society and the challenge children have to cope with owing to new discoveries in science and technology'.

Changes in the cultural, racial and religious make-up of the community

The populations of many countries of Western Europe have, in recent years, become far more mixed in culture, race and religion than they were. They contain a substantial number of families who speak languages and, to a marked degree, retain life-habits they brought with them from afar. Some children may speak little or none of the national language of the country when they first enter school. . . .

The main issues referred to in the aims of primary education in countries experiencing these changes relate, on the one hand, to the indigenous population and, on the other, to the ethnic minority groups. . . .

The minimum aim with regard to the indigenous population is, usually, that its members should exercise tolerance towards and understanding of the newcomers. They were, after all, permitted and even encouraged to enter the country to fill gaps in the existing workforce. Better still, the indigenous population should welcome the presence of the minority ethnic groups because of the skills and cultures they bring, not only in music, art and food, but also in richness of language. The presumption is that tolerance will grow as knowledge grows and contact between groups increases.

For the minority groups the issues are often sharper. Maintenance of one's religion, culture and language contributes to one's sense of identity. Acceptance of the principle that home languages should be maintained was discussed earlier, though it is not always realized as well as it should be.

Providing for the home language is not enough. Individuals do not have a full range of opportunities open to them, in either education or employment, unless they can speak and write the national language in its standard form. Generally speaking, provision is made, although there can be difficulties for children who enter the education system late. In Luxembourg, as in a number of other countries, special classes in the local language are set up for new entrants. In the United Kingdom, teachers may be specially funded and employed to assist children who have little or no English. In the Federal Republic of Germany, Turkish supplementary teachers are employed both to help children with their own language and to assist them when German is the language of instruction.

Political change

Where there have been marked changes in the political beliefs underpinning the government of a country, they are reflected in the strength of expression in some educational aims. In Spain and Portugal, recently emerged from authoritarian and nationalistic regimes, there is more than ordinary stress on children as citizens of the world and on the freedom of individuals and their rights, including the right to participate in decisions about their own lives as soon as they are ready.

SOME REFLECTIONS

One should not be surprised that the member states of the Council of Europe agree so closely in their statements of aims for primary education. They have, after all, come together in the Council because they share common interests; they also share interlocking histories. Even more today than formerly, their populations intermingle and have drawn in others from outside. The moral and religious beliefs that underlie the behaviour of their peoples recognize the uniqueness of individuals and that an individual has responsibilities to others. Their populations engage in a mixture of agricultural, industrial and commercial undertakings and require complex organizations of government that call for a literate and numerate population. They are going through a period of rapid change in technology, in their access to information and of material expectations. Some of the activities require a high level of specialist education, for which a primary school foundation is vital.

The differences between them are differences of degree, emphasis and balance. The differences in the primary education received by their children occur not because the aims are different but because they cannot all be applied at once with equal strength. Sometimes the needs of an individual can take priority; sometimes they must give way to the needs of the group; sometimes aims can be held in balance. The Irish paper of 1988 makes a distinction between enabling the child to live a full life as a child, and equipping 'him to avail himself of further education'. While the two aims may be in accord, they may not always seem so to a child practising handwriting on a warm summer day. There are teachers who would seize such an opportunity to walk their pupils by the river, get them to use their eyes and ears and to stretch their tongues; but the handwriting must take priority on enough days if the children are not to be at a disadvantage later.

Some children would be surprised to hear that their teachers and even the government thought they should develop to the full. Why, if so, should anyone stop them playing tricks or fighting for their rights? Full development, not surprisingly, turns out to apply only to those parts of development of which the teacher approves; and here the different levels of tolerance between teachers within a country may be more pronounced than the general differences between nations. Nor is it wise to guess what the level might be from the pedagogical model used.

In a more particular sense, the intention to extend a child's competence in one aspect of learning may have to be set against the search for progress in another. The more time and effort that teacher and children spend singing and playing musical instruments, the less time there is to manipulate paint and clay. So choices have to be made at national, local or school level about time allocations and about how the levels of achievement in different curricular areas match.

But caution is needed. The timetable is a way of organizing learning: of bringing together materials, facilities, teachers and children. It may be finely or broadly defined. It is often used also as the single means of prescribing and analysing the curriculum. Unfortunately, that is a practice that encourages the belief that it is possible to establish a taxonomy in which each aspect of the curriculum can be and is dealt with separately in its own periods and, even worse, that these separate parts add up to the whole. Opportunities for reinforcing one strand of learning by connecting it with others are diminished and may even be lost: children need to develop their powers of language, spoken and written, in a wide variety of contexts, whenever they occur during the school day. Where the timetable is used to define the curriculum, proper recognition and prominence are seldom given (to use an earlier example) to teaching children the broader lessons to be drawn from the social changes experienced on entering school. The process of social adjustment seems to get in the way of learning rather than being an opportunity for learning. The effect on teachers' attitudes and probably on children's attitudes to formal education are considerable: the uni-dimensional analysis of the curriculum creates the so-called hidden – and thus unexamined – curriculum.

Opportunities for an idiosyncratic interpretation of aims arises if there is often a confusion between aims and objectives. That leads to aims being end-weighted. But if an aim is a direction, then it is as important to be on course in the early stages as in the later, perhaps more so. More thought given to where one is at the current stage ought to strengthen the chance of achieving the desired improvement over time, and has immediate relevance in judging what is being achieved and what should be done. The confusion is seen at work strongly when it is supposed that children should learn how to perform a skill before they learn how to apply it, as though a toddler should learn the tongue and lip movements and to synchronize its breathing before being allowed to try to communicate through speech. It is not that the processes of acquiring a skill and applying it should be approached the other way round, but that the two go hand in hand, sometimes one predominating and sometimes the other.

There are many reasons why aims may be interpreted differently at the level of states, local communities, schools and classrooms. Not least, they are interpreted differently because individual men and women of singular temperaments and capacities have to apply them minute by minute in the busy circumstances of the classroom. Perhaps it is just as well that the certainty of variety exists, for none of us can be sure what is best for all children and all conditions of society, now and in the years to come.

NOTE

This chapter is based on the account of the conference on 'Primary Education in Western Europe: Aims, Problems and Trends' [DECS/EGT [83] 64] held in Vaduz in 1982, on papers the member states produced later in the lifetime of Project No. 8, on the sources referred to in the References, and on the writer's personal experience.

REFERENCES

Burstall, C. (1974) *Primary French in the Balance*, Slough: NFER.
Ghilardi, F. (1988) 'Dynamics of curriculum reform in primary education in Italy', unpublished paper.
House of Commons (1986) *Parliamentary Papers 1985–1986*, London: Chadwyck-Healey.
Lewis, H.D. (1985) *The French Education System*, London: Croom Helm.
Mallinson, V. (1980) The Western European Idea in Education, Oxford: Pergamon Press.

Chapter 3

Knowledge for the masses
World models and national curricula, 1920–1986

Aaron Benavot, Yun-Kyung Cha,
David H. Kamens, John Meyer and Suk-Ying Wong

Classical theorists in the sociology of knowledge such as Marx, Durkheim, Mannheim and Scheler sought to establish that the content and validity of ideas are ultimately tied to the social and economic interests in society (Mannheim, 1936; Durkheim, [1912] 1954; for reviews, see Coser, 1968; Kuklick, 1983; Eisenstadt, 1988). Subsequent research has focused on how socio-historical conditions influence the production, validation, and justification of different types of knowledge. Few scholars have examined an important corollary: *how knowledge is selected, organized, and transmitted by social forces* (see Wuthnow, 1987).

This neglect was forcefully stated by British sociologists of education (Young, 1971). Sociologists, they argued, should treat 'the knowledge ("transmitted" in education) as neither absolute, nor arbitrary, but as "available sets of meanings" which in any context do not merely "emerge" but are collectively "given"' (Young 1971: 3).

> How a society selects, classifies, distributes, transmits and evaluates the educational knowledge it considers to be public, reflects both the distribution of power and the principles of social control. From this point of view, differences within and change in the organization, transmission and evaluation of educational knowledge should be a major area of sociological interest.
>
> (Bernstein, 1971: 47)

National educational institutions – which presently enrol about one-fifth of the world's inhabitants (United Nations Educational Social and Cultural Organization, 1987) – have become the most important mechanism for organizing and transmitting knowledge to the young. Although sociologists have shown great interest in the expansion, improvement and equalization of educational opportunity, they have had little to say about the nature and social basis of the formal knowledge transmitted by these institutions, especially from a comparative vantage point. The types of socially approved knowledge taught in mass and elite educational institutions and the official endorsement of that knowledge as reflected in national school curricula deserve more attention from sociologists.

We tackle these issues by analysing, from a longitudinal and cross-national perspective, the changing nature of knowledge intended to be transmitted by schools to the mass population. . . .

Our main goal is to rethink and add to previous hypotheses about the rise and nature of the modern curriculum. In previous work, the educational curriculum has been viewed either as the product of the functional requirements of society (for example, the economies of advanced, industrialized countries require more instruction in mathematics and science) or as a reflection of existing power relations in society (for example, an emphasis on academic subjects such as classical language, literature, or laboratory science serves the political and economic interests of the 'dominant classes' or powerful elites). School curricula, according to these views, are nationally patterned collections of socially approved knowledge that, if compared cross-nationally, should show considerable diversity.

We propose an added dimension: The structure of school curricula – especially mass curricula – is closely linked to the rise of standardized models of society (see Meyer, 1980; Thomas et al., 1987) and to the increasing dominance of standardized models of education as one component of these general models (see Boli et al., 1985; Ramirez and Boli, 1987). These modern models of society and education and their interrelation, are similar around the world and generate educational systems and curricular structures that are strikingly similar. As a result, a new culture or set of cultural categories is being promulgated by mass educational institutions. If we are to understand this emergent world cultural system, the structure of the mass educational curriculum is an important place to start.

Many characteristics of societies or time periods can affect the content of school curricula, but their characteristics do not predict the rapid worldwide expansion of primary education (Meyer et al., 1977; Boli et al., 1985; Meyer et al., 1992). World educational expansion has outpaced most national indicators of political or economic development and is rather poorly predicted by such variables. Thus, the same worldwide processes that were involved in the spread of primary education may also have generated similarity in its curricular outline. This theme is useful for understanding both the character and the stability of curricular policies in primary education during the twentieth century.

BACKGROUND

The formal content of the school curriculum was a more central sociological concern in earlier historical periods. Durkheim ([1938] 1977), in his penetrating analysis of French educational history, highlighted the succession of political battles over the officially prescribed curriculum during the nineteenth century. Waller discussed the social and psychological consequences for teachers and students of the parcelling out of human knowledge into school subjects and 'nicely graded' courses ([1932] 1965: 335ff.).

In the early reports of educational leaders, issues of content – the textbooks used, the questions asked on tests, and classroom pedagogical practices – were a primary focus (for example, see Barnard, 1854; Klemm, 1889; Prince, 1897). Later, academics debated which languages to teach, at what age to introduce new topics in the natural or social sciences, and whether to allot instructional time to physical or aesthetic education.

In recent decades, however, the basic outline of the curriculum has become surprisingly uncontroversial. Conflicts arise, but they centre on specialized issues (for example, teaching of evolution, gender biases in textbook illustrations, bilingual instruction). These 'controversies' bespeak the taken-for-granted character of the basic structure.

HYPOTHESES

There is little comparative historical research on school curricula. Springer (1977) noted the paucity of comparative studies in the area of pedagogy and the curriculum. . . . Lacking basic comparative descriptions, there has been a tendency to apply general theories about the origins and significance of mass education to questions about the curriculum.

Early theoretical statements on the sources of educational expansion were functionalist in character, with ideological variations. The modern differentiated society (or its elites) created and required primary education to equip the masses with technical skills and hegemonic culture and to enhance their integration into society. Ideological variations revolved around who benefits from the system rather than the origins of mass education. . . .

Since the modern functionalist literature offers few specific hypotheses on curricular content or categories, we suggest several taken from the classic literature:

1 The more developed a society, the greater the emphasis in the curriculum on modern skills and values. Instruction in mathematics, the natural sciences, social science and a national language will be stressed more in developed societies than in less developed societies. Instruction in local languages, the arts, physical education, and vocational subjects like agriculture, manual training, and domestic science, will be emphasized less.

2 With increased modernization and development around the world, modern subjects like mathematics, natural science and social science will be increasingly emphasized.

3 Because international differences in socioeconomic development are relatively stable, national curricular differences will also be relatively stable.

In reaction to the failures of functionalism and its variants, a growing body of curriculum research has moved toward descriptive studies of individual nations that emphasize case-specific historical explanations (for example, Young, 1971; Goodson, 1987; Goodson and Ball, 1984). Much of this historical work traces the spread of mass education and curricular content to competition among different status and political groups (Collins, 1979; Goodson, 1987). ... In some arguments, the content of the curriculum is seen as reflecting the interests and advantages of dominant status groups (for example, professionals, political elites, capitalist social classes); in others, the content is less important than the competitive advantages groups may gain through particular curricular arrangements (Collins, 1979).

The historicist perspective argues that the interactions of conflicting forces in particular settings – rather than general functional imperatives – best explain the nature and development of school curricula. ... Two basic hypotheses follow:

4 Considerable curricular diversity exists among national educational systems.
5 National educational systems, each with its own trajectory, show consistent curricula over time.

Neither historicist approaches nor the variants of functionalism have come entirely to terms with the rapid spread of standardized mass education. To account for this spread, arguments about the importance of a wider world polity have developed. ...

If mass education is a worldwide model, or one component of a larger standardized nation-state model, its curricula should also evidence standardization at the world level. The institutionalized ideologies of society, and the specific ideologies of education as socializing individuals for society, should carry institutionally standardized content. Thus:

6 National primary curricular categories will generally reflect modern values, independent of national development;
7 Primary curricular categories in national societies will exhibit increasing similarity;
8 National differences in curricular emphases will show little consistency over time because all national systems derive from prevailing world conventions.

It is important to note that the propositions of the world polity model are not directly inconsistent with much of the earlier functionalist or historicist theorizing. . . . Ideas about the importance of the world polity [however] focus on the rise of very general subject categories, and on explaining their location in official policy.

DATA

. . . Many groups, frequently linked to UNESCO, have attempted to bring together standard descriptions of national school curricula. As a consequence, curricular standards and policies in sovereign states and dependent territories have been explicitly formulated and collected in a great many comparative reports. . . .

From each official curricular timetable obtained, we coded two items of information: the required subject categories to be taught during the elementary school cycle (usually a five- to six-year period), and the number of periods (or hours) to be devoted to each subject during a typical week. This information was transformed into two dependent variables: one indicating the presence or absence of basic school subject categories in the official curriculum and the second indicating the relative emphasis on each category.

Specific topics were classified into general categories according to the following scheme: *language* (national, local, official, and foreign languages); *mathematics* (arithmetic, geometry); *natural sciences; social sciences* (history, geography, civics, social studies); *religious and moral education* (religion, moral education); *aesthetic education* (art, handicrafts, singing, dance); *physical education; hygiene/health education; vocational education/practical subjects* (manual training, agriculture, domestic science, industrial arts, gardening); and *other* (recreation, extracurricular activities, miscellaneous subjects, recess and elective subjects). National language refers to an indigenous language, spoken by over 50 per cent of the population, that is also an official language. Official language refers to a metropolitan or world language that is given national standing but is not indigenous in origin or use. Local language is spoken by a minority of the population and not given official standing. Foreign languages are those that are neither official nor indigenous.

DATA FRAME AND COVERAGE

The data refer primarily to nations with state-administered educational systems. . . . Curricular information was assigned to one of three historical periods: the interwar period, 1920–44; the decolonization period, 1945–69; and the current period, 1970–86. Data coverage for each period, while extensive, does not constitute a representative sample. Data coverage is sparsest for the interwar period (1920–44) and tends to overrepresent countries in Europe and the Americas, whereas the sample of countries for the 1970–86 period is more complete.

[Limitations of the data] . , .

1   Our curricular measures indicate the percentage of total curricular time devoted to each subject, not the instructional hours each subject was supposed to be taught during the annual school term.
2   We have no information on the specific content of the subjects taught. Differences among countries or over time in such categories as 'history' or 'social studies' may or may not represent real differences in curricula. This is an important point, since many prevailing theories (particularly in the more historical and case study traditions) focus primarily on explaining variations and forms in the actual content or materials or syllabi used in instruction, rather than the general rhetorical categories we study. A scholar committed to the view that local interests dominate curricular design could reasonably argue that our data – covering very general official curricular categories – are biased toward our theoretical view, and that more detailed information would show the operation of local forces and interests. Our view is that the historical approach would benefit from considering the role played by wider changes that affect the curricular category system – in short that there may be some reasons to consider the broader frame, as well as detailed curricular information.

. . . Policy rhetoric and practice respond to different resource constraints. For example, great curricular visions may not be attainable by teachers and students with few educational resources; policy-makers may wish to impress national and international audiences more than teachers and local administrators do; or local educators may have to adapt to local requirements, and so on. Such processes might generate official curricula that are in greater conformity to world models than are subjects implemented in local practice. This could produce some distortions in our inferences from results.[1]

RESULTS

Table 3.1 reports basic trends in the percentage of countries offering instruction in specified categories. To permit comparisons across historical periods, Table 3.1 is based on a constant set of countries for adjacent time periods. (Because data coverage is more complete in the recent period, information on the middle period is included twice.)

Core subject categories – language, mathematics, natural science, social science, the arts, and physical education – have appeared in most official curricula through the time periods studied, and have become even more widespread over time. A few countries, for instance, adopted science instruction only during the periods covered by our study . . . But by the most recent period, the core subjects appear in practically all curricula, and may suggest the operation of processes of world educational standardization.

Table 3.1 Percentage of countries offering specified subjects in the primary school curriculum: 1920–86

Subject	Panel A			Panel B		
	1920–44	1945–69	N	1945–69	1970–86	N
Language:	100.0	100.0	43	100.0	100.0	73
National, local	97.7	97.7	43	92.0	92.0	75
Official, foreign	18.8	47.9	48	59.5	60.8	74
Mathematics	100.0	100.0	48	100.0	100.0	82
Natural science	81.3	93.8	48	92.3	100.0	78
Social sciences	97.9	97.9	47	96.1	100.0	76
History, geography, civics	91.5	85.1	47	76.3	52.6	76
Social studies	10.9	28.3	46	28.9	60.5	76
Aesthetic education	86.4	97.7	44	97.4	98.7	76
Religious or moral education	77.8	73.3	45	77.3	74.7	75
Physical education	89.4	95.7	47	97.4	96.1	76
Hygiene/health education	34.8	28.3	46	38.2	42.1	76
Practical subjects/ Vocational education	86.4	75.0	44	72.0	68.0	75

Note: Each panel refers to a constant set of countries for which data were available for the two time periods.

Little change occurred in the prevalence of religious or moral education and in health education. These subjects are not part of a universal core. Vocational education is declining through the period (as fewer countries treat primary education as a terminal stage).

Within two core areas, some changes appear. Instruction in official (or foreign, more rarely) languages is more common in the later periods, a finding that turns out to reflect the development of primary educational systems in former colonies .. And within the general social science category, there has been a strong trend toward instruction in a general social studies category and away from instruction allocated to history, geography, and civics. . . .

The most important finding in Table 3.1 is the rise to universality of a set of core categories across the diverse countries of the world. This result provides some support for ideas that educational curricula reflect standardizing world processes. And it runs against the predictions of more diversity that might be suggested by functional or historicist arguments.

Table 3.2 presents the average percentage of instructional time allocated to each subject category during the primary school cycle, along with the standard deviation around the average. Overall, there is a good deal of consistency over time in the allocation of instructional time. For the universally required subjects, standard deviations are relatively small and tend to decline

Table 3.2 Average percentage of total instructional time allocated to subjects in
the primary school curriculum: 1920–86

Subject	Panel A			Panel B		
	1920–44	1945–69	N	1945–69	1970–86	N
Language:	35.3	36.4	31	36.0	33.9	70
	(9.2)	(7.9)		(9.2)	(8.3)	
National, local	31.0	32.4	31	26.0	25.1	72
	(9.4)	(9.6)		(12.4)	(10.2)	
Official, foreign	3.5	4.6	45	9.5	8.3	73
	(9.3)	(8.2)		(13.3)	(11.6)	
Mathematics	15.4	17.3	37	16.5	18.2	80
	(4.2)	(4.6)		(4.0)	(3.3)	
Natural science	5.2	7.0	42	7.1	7.9	75
	(4.0)	(4.3)		(4.6)	(3.7)	
Social sciences	8.8	8.6	36	8.1	8.1	73
	(4.0)	(4.0)		(4.0)	(3.7)	
History, geography, civics	8.0	6.2	37	5.9	3.2	74
	(4.3)	(4.1)		(4.5)	(3.9)	
Social studies	0.5	2.5	45	2.1	4.8	74
	(2.4)	(4.6)		(4.2)	(5.2)	
Aesthetic education	9.2	10.5	39	10.0	10.2	71
	(5.9)	(4.5)		(3.9)	(4.4)	
Religious or moral education	6.9	5.2	37	6.1	5.2	68
	(7.5)	(4.9)		(6.0)	(5.3)	
Physical education	6.0	7.2	39	6.9	7.1	72
	(4.2)	(3.3)		(2.7)	(3.3)	
Hygiene/health education	0.9	1.0	40	1.4	1.2	70
	(1.9)	(2.6)		(2.8)	(1.9)	
Practical subjects/ Vocational education	6.2	5.8	34	6.3	5.1	73
	(4.8)	(5.5)		(6.9)	(5.3)	

Note: Standard deviations in parentheses. Each panel refers to a constant set of countries
for which data were available for the two time periods.

over time, indicating more standardization in the time devoted to the
subjects. The other categories – religious education, health education, and
vocational education, as well as subcategories of the core – show more
variation (distributions, in addition, tend to be more skewed).

Language instruction – reading, writing and grammar – is the dominant
curricular category in primary education. In each time period, about one-
third of total curricular time is devoted to language education. Variation
is relatively small, and tends to decline. Almost all language instruction is
in national or official languages. ... There has been a slight increase in
the amount of prescribed instruction in foreign languages or in official
languages that are exogenous in origin, resulting from the addition of more

developing countries to the data set (and to the world of primary education). These patterns support functionalist or worldly polity theories, which emphasize the primacy of the nation-state, and may run against (at least the most general) historicist perspectives. The unimportance of local languages, however provides little support for functionalist theories, which emphasize the importance of these languages in peripheral economies and societies.

There have been slight increases in the percentage of time that is to be devoted to mathematics education, and some movement toward increased similarity among countries in this measure. The percentage of instructional time devoted to natural science increased during the period under study, and (the rather low) variability declined overall. Similarly, there are modest increases in time allocated to aesthetic and physical education. Variability here is also fairly low, but does not show consistent declines.

The percentage of time allocated to combined social science instruction shows little change over the period of the study. Variation is low, but unchanged over the period. Within this category, the percentage of time devoted to history, geography, or civics declines sharply, while that devoted to 'social studies' increases sharply. This striking worldwide trend toward a more integrated notion of society could have a functionalist interpretation, for example, greater public involvement in, and control over, social life produced a stronger conception of society as a 'social system'. . . .

Aside from the common core of categories, the main finding in Table 3.2 is the low percentage of time allocated to the less universal ones. Religious or moral education is still required in primary schools in about three-quarters of the countries, but the time allocated to it is low and declining. This is also true of practical or vocational subjects. Health or hygiene receives very little time. The fact that such less universal subjects are not more prevalent in primary school curricula speaks against more extreme historicist theories of educational development, which predict a wide range of distinctive patterns even in curricular outlines.

Overall, Tables 3.1 and 3.2 suggest that an increasingly similar world curricular structure takes up most of the instructional time. These findings suggest that during much of the twentieth century a standard world scheme for primary education has been in operation. They provide some support for functionalist arguments suggesting that primary school curricula should move in a 'modern' direction over time. But they call into question some assumptions of more historicist theories, which often tend to view the evolution of national school curricula in terms of distinctive national trajectories.

. . . Table 3.3 presents the average percentage of instructional time devoted to subjects for major world regions for the most recent period (1970–86). Results for other periods (not shown) are similar. Countries are classified in the following world regions: Sub-Saharan Africa; the mainly Islamic countries of the Middle East and North Africa; Asia; Latin (Iberian)

Table 3.3 Average percentage of total instructional time allocated to subjects in the primary school curriculum, by world region: 1970–86

Subject	Sub-Saharan Africa	MidEast North Africa	Asia	Latin America	Carib-bean	Eastern Europe	West[1]
Language	38.2	36.8	36.7	24.4	34.7	37.4	34.1
	(29)	(15)	(18)	(14)	(9)	(9)	(19)
National, local	13.5	31.8	27.3	18.1	18.1	30.3	27.7
	(29)	(15)	(18)	(16)	(9)	(9)	(19)
Official	24.2	0.0	7.0	3.8	14.2	1.9	3.5
	(29)	(15)	(18)	(16)	(10)	(9)	(22)
Foreign	0.5	4.9	2.4	0.4	0.7	5.1	2.2
	(29)	(15)	(18)	(16)	(10)	(9)	(21)
Mathematics	17.7	16.6	17.5	18.6	20.7	20.5	18.5
	(32)	(18)	(20)	(18)	(10)	(9)	(21)
Natural science	7.0	6.7	8.1	11.3	7.5	7.5	6.4
	(32)	(17)	(19)	(18)	(9)	(9)	(19)
Social sciences	7.8	6.4	8.7	13.1	12.0	6.3	9.0
	(29)	(15)	(18)	(15)	(9)	(9)	(19)
History, geography, civics	4.5	2.6	2.6	4.3	4.3	6.3	3.3
	(29)	(15)	(18)	(15)	(10)	(9)	(20)
Social studies	3.3	3.8	6.0	8.7	7.2	0.0	5.0
	(29)	(15)	(18)	(15)	(9)	(9)	(19)
Aesthetic education	8.5	7.7	9.5	8.0	7.4	10.4	13.5
	(28)	(15)	(18)	(14)	(9)	(9)	(19)
Religious or moral education	4.6	12.0	6.1	3.4	2.5	0.0	5.0
	(29)	(13)	(17)	(14)	(9)	(9)	(18)
Religious education	3.8	11.8	3.0	2.2	2.2	0.0	4.7
	(29)	(15)	(18)	(14)	(9)	(9)	(18)
Moral education	0.8	0.7	2.9	1.0	0.8	0.0	0.2
	(29)	(13)	(17)	(16)	(10)	(9)	(20)
Physical education	5.9	6.3	5.8	7.4	5.3	9.4	9.2
	(28)	(15)	(18)	(15)	(9)	(9)	(19)
Hygiene/ health education	0.9	1.8	1.5	2.5	2.9	0.3	0.5
	(28)	(15)	(18)	(17)	(10)	(8)	(21)
Practical subjects/ vocational education	7.3	2.4	4.1	9.5	3.2	6.6	0.7
	(28)	(15)	(17)	(15)	(10)	(9)	(22)

Note: Number of cases in parentheses.
[1] West includes Western Europe, North America, Australia and New Zealand.

America; the non-Iberian Caribbean; Eastern Europe; and West (which includes Western Europe, the US, and the former British dominions of Canada, Australia and New Zealand).

Latin American countries allocate significantly less instructional time to language education (in total) than countries in other world regions. . . . In general, however, regional differences in the time devoted to language education are small: most regions allocate, on average, about one-third of total curricular time to some type of language instruction.

In the other core categories of the curriculum – mathematics, natural science, and social science – curricular emphases are rather similar across regions. Mathematics receives slightly more emphasis in Caribbean and Eastern European nations (a pattern that predates the establishment of socialist regimes). Emphasis on natural science and social science is stronger in Latin American countries . . . emphasis on social science is also strong in Caribbean nations.

The percentage of time allocated to religious or moral education exhibits considerable regional variation. Muslim countries in the Middle East/North Africa region place great emphasis on the teaching of the Koran and the religious principles of Islam in the elementary schools. This is reflected in their relatively high average percentage of instructional time devoted to religious education. Western countries, some of which maintain a state religion, also allocate more time to religious instruction than do countries in other regions. Among Asian countries, many of which lack an established national religion, moral education receives more emphasis than elsewhere . . .

Overall, interregional variation in the amount of time allocated to different subject areas appears, but this variation does not suggest radically different notions of appropriate subject matter for primary school children.[2] Apart from the differences noted, regional variation in the allocation of curricular time are small. The similarity of emphasis in the primary curriculum especially in the core categories of language, mathematics, natural science, social science and the arts, is the dominant feature of the regional breakdown.

SUMMARY AND DISCUSSION

The idea that the curricula of mass education are closely tied to standardized worldwide models of social and educational progress suggests that instruction in such 'modern' topics as mathematics, natural science and social science will diffuse throughout the world, that national primary curricular categories will be increasingly similar, and that stability over time will be modest. Most of our findings support this line of argument. While there is some variation concerning minor subjects – whether they are included and how much time they are allocated – core subject area categories appear in practically all national curricula and there is a great deal of similarity in the amount of time devoted to these core categories. National characteristics are only weakly related to curricular categories. Only the expectation of sharply increased similarity over time receives limited support; change is modest, though most countries include all the standard subjects in the curriculum.

The notion that official primary curricula reflect a world educational order modifies, rather than eliminates, functionalist and historicist hypotheses. Theorists can retain the notion of the modern curriculum as functional: they need simply to understand that functionalist models hold at the world level and are often adopted in peripheral areas as models rather than as responses to changed national, political or social realities.

Similarly, a historical perspective can still view the curriculum as a contested historical product, but by shifting the argument to two distinct levels of analysis. First, the history involved in such changes as the shift from rhetorical categories of history and geography to social studies needs to be understood as the playing out of power and interest at the global arena. Most scholarship in this area sees history as the product of specific interactions, but there is no logical reason to insist that these be primarily local or national in character.

Second, historicists can easily continue to see national and local interactions as generating unique patterns of detailed content, and unique implementations of general categories. It is quite plausible – and often convincing – to see the rise of new curricular categories as providing the occasion for the working out of class and interest forces in particular settings (Goodson, 1987; Holmes and McLean, 1989).

Our data suggest that historical and functional processes may operate at a global level. The categories being selected, organized and transmitted by different systems have a good deal of worldwide standardization. The modern pattern – much of it already in place at the beginning of our study – seems to involve the expansion of a language-focused curriculum to include mathematics, natural science, social science and physical and arts education. The spread of this curricular pattern around the world – mostly independent of regional and developmental factors – effectively incorporates modern functional theory as a broad ideological base and a general legitimating system. The rise and spread of this ideology can well be seen as a product of great historical forces – among them, certainly, the interests of class and professional groupings. And it can well be seen as providing the grounding frame on which further class and professional interests gain enhanced standing.

In one respect, the standardization of national school curricula is not a complete surprise. Our period is one in which local and primordial cultures are undergoing wholesale destruction, in part as a result of mass education. Local languages die out or are circumscribed, as are local gods and spirits. Local political divisions are undercut, usually in the name of a national polity, along with parochial technologies and customs. Every aspect of the modern world-system builds conformity of economic, or political or familial and cultural rules to regional, ethnic or national standards (Thomas *et al.*, 1987). Similarly, schools claim to be laid out in standard ways at national levels regardless of gender, class, tribe, region and locality. (In practice, however, there may be much curricular variation across such subgroups that is not acknowledged in the official rules of mass educational systems.)

The real surprise of our findings lie not in the unimportance of local influences, but in the relative unimportance of national influences on curricular structure. Similarities clearly outweigh differences. The few differences observed tend to be unstable and seem to arise as a matter of chance in national societies differing dramatically in wealth, political structure, and cultural and religious tradition. We may speak with some confidence about a relatively standard world curricular category scheme. The rise of this scheme as a legitimating frame by no means eliminates the power of local interests. Some such interests (for example, British elites linked to both education and the state, as well as the class system) may indeed gain power from the new system, and may use this power to embed further their position in the curriculum, education and society (Goodson, 1987). Our point is that they do so within the broad outlines of a modern cultural system.

NOTES

1   It is a mistake, however, to *assume* that while national officials seek to comply with international educational models, local school teachers and principals follow curricular standards that, by and large, reflect local constituencies and constraints. Given the growth of national and international networks of teacher-training institutes and professional associations, it is hard to imagine that teachers and school administrators in developing countries follow entirely distinctive curricular conventions. It is also difficult for local interests to develop distinct curricular themes. It is much more likely that they draw from similar curricular content frames, though in a less effective manner, as their national bureaucratic elites. In any case, it is interesting to see whether the official statements of national educational leaders reflect world standards of educational policy.

It seems most likely that local constituencies and interests are able to manipulate the specification, detailed content and implementation of general curricular categories under some restrictive conditions. They need to have strong enough and modern enough local cultural traditions to provide the needed resources, and to have power and authority enough to carry such projects out. These conditions would be least likely to be met in typical Third World countries (though such world movements as Islamic revival might provide enough support and direction). They would be more likely to be met in highly developed alternative policies (the Eastern bloc suggests examples). And they may be most likely to be met in the old European centres: in this respect, it is significant that much of the best historicist research stressing local power and cultural structures has been carried out in England – the old and long-dominant hegemony (Young, 1971); Bernstein, 1971; Goodson, 1987; see also Holmes and McLean, 1989).

2   The number of countries that maintain an extreme emphasis (or lack of emphasis) on a particular subject over time is very small. Typically, delay in requiring new subjects or dropping old subjects that have lost their value accounts for many of the 'deviant' curricular patterns. The one subject area in which we noted a distinctive curricular pattern is religious and moral education.

There are few distinctive elementary school curricula, a striking finding in view of the fact that many countries – for example, China, Korea, Japan, and Islamic countries – had unique systems of instruction entirely outside the modern orbit at the time of their incorporation into the modern world educational system.

REFERENCES

Barnard, H. (1854) *National Curriculum in Europe*, 3rd edn, Hartford, CT: Frederick Perkins.

Bernstein, B. (1971) *Class, Codes and Control*, vols 1 and 3, London: Routledge & Kegan Paul.

Boli, J., Ramirez, F. and Meyer, J. (1985) 'Explaining the origins and expansion of mass education' *Comparative Education Review* 29(2): 145–77.

Collins, B. (1979) *The Credential Society*, Orlando, FL: Academic Press.

Coser, L. (1968) 'Sociology of knowledge' *Encyclopedia of the Social Sciences*, New York: Macmillan and Free Press.

Durkheim, E. (1954) [1912] *The Elementary Forms of the Religious Life*, Glencoe, IL: Free Press.

—— (1977) [1938] *The Evolution of Educational Thought*, London: Routledge & Kegan Paul.

Eisenstadt, S.N. (1988) 'Explorations in the sociology of knowledge' in S.N. Eisenstadt and I.F. Silber, *Cultural Traditions and Worlds of Knowledge*, vol. 7 Newhaven, CT: JAI Press.

Goodson, I. (1987) *School Subjects and Curriculum Change*, London: Falmer Press.

Goodson, I. and Ball, S.I. (1984) (eds) *Defining the Curriculum: Histories and Ethnographies*, London: Falmer Press.

Holmes, B. and McLean, M. (1989) *The Curriculum: A Comparative Perspective*, London: Unwin Hyman.

Klemm, L. (1889) *European Schools*, New York: Appleton Company.

Kuklick, H. (1983) 'The sociology of knowledge: retrospect and prospect' *Annual Review of Sociology* 9: 287–310.

Mannheim, K. (1936) *Ideology and Utopia*, New York: Harcourt Brace & World Inc.

Meyer, J. (1980) 'The World Polity and the Authority of the Nation State', in A. Bergensen (ed.) *Studies of the Modern World-System*, New York: Academic Press.

Meyer, J., Ramirez, F.O., Rubinson, R. and Boli-Bennett, J. (1977) 'The world educational revolution 1950–1970' *Sociology and Education* 50(4): 242–58.

Meyer, J., Ramirez, F.O. and Soysal, Y. (1992) 'World expansion of mass education 1870–1980' *Sociology of Education*.

Prince, J. (1897) *Methods of Instruction and Organization of the Schools of Germany for the use of American Teachers and Normal Schools*, Boston, MA: Lee & Shephard.

Ramirez, J. and Boli, J. (1987) 'The political construction of mass schooling', *Sociology of Education* 60(2): 2–18.

Springer, U. (1977) 'Education, curriculum and pedagogy', *Comparative Education Review* 21: 358–70.

Thomas, G., Meyer, J., Ramirez, F.O. and Boli, J. (1987) *Institutional Structure: Constituting State, Society and the Individual*, Beverley Hills, CA: Sage.

Waller, W. (1965) [1932] *The Sociology of Teaching*, New York: John Wiley.

Wuthnow, R. (1987) *Meaning and Moral Order*, Berkley, CA: University of California Press.

Young, M. (1971) *Knowledge and Control*, London: Collier Macmillan.

Chapter 4

Education, Majorism and 'the curriculum of the dead'

Stephen J. Ball

In this chapter I want to consider the policy dominance of 'cultural restorationism' in UK education. Cultural restorationists being the 'hard line, old humanists of the New Right' (Ball, 1990: 6) within the British Conservative Party, whose main policy preoccupation is with the re-valorization of traditional forms of education (Wexler and Grabiner, 1986). . . .

While this chapter deals with the specifics of restorationist influence in UK education, the project of educational restoration is clearly evident in education systems across the English-speaking world. . . . The restorationist agenda has its basis in what Jones (1989: 32) calls 'cultural rightism':

> It could trace its philosophy back to Hobbes and the political ideology of Burke. It emphasizes the importance of a strong state to control the evils that an unregulated society is prey to. It regards custom and tradition as vital properties of an established order. Without them, the state is weakened, and subversion can grow in strength. Thus, it regards cultural cohesion as an essential prop of state authority.

Writing of the US education system Aronowitz and Giroux (1991) describe a similar restorationist impetus as militating around a 'cultural crisis' in education. They see the work of US restorationist writers like Bloom (1987) and Hirsch (1987) as representing:

> a frontal attack aimed at providing a programmatic language with which to defend schools as cultural sites, that is as institutions responsible for reproducing the knowledge and values necessary to advance the historical virtues of Western culture.

(p. 25)

In their analysis Aronowitz and Giroux see textual authority and political authority as tied tightly together within restorationist education. The aim of these 'aristocratic traditionalists', as they call them, is 'to restore knowledge as a particular form of social authority, pedagogy and discipline' (p. 39).

RESTORATIONISM AND POLICY INFLUENCE IN THE UK

There is a further complication involved in the analysis of the current dominance of restorationism. To fully appreciate what has been achieved we must consider what (and who) it was that the restorationists managed to replace in the 'context of influence' over policy. Under Major [Prime Minister] and Clarke [Secretary of State for Education], the losers in the policy-making arena were a coalition of educational 'modernisers'. A loosely constituted group made up of 'new progressive' educators, especially from the science and mathematics education communities, and 'progressive vocationalists' representing the educational concerns of many of the UK's largest multi-national companies (see Ball, 1990, for a full discussion of these groups). In the displacement of these influences a massive shift has taken place in the signification of education and education reform. The 'theoretical' and the 'innovative' in education have been replaced, as the signifiers of reform, by 'tradition'. . . . The reform process set in train by the 1988 Education Reform Act (ERA) has been wrestled away from the modernizers and reworked as a reassertion of traditional forms of education and curriculum. In some ways this is more than a little surprising given the strength of the industrial lobby in UK education during the 1980s. . . . But what this turn around in influence points up is the more general contradictions that exist within Conservatism between the traditionalist and modernizing tendencies. Within education this is, in crude terms, a contradiction between the emphasis on continuity within the former as against an emphasis on planned change within the latter. Jones (1989: 82) puts it like this:

> Thus, while no opponent of selection, the modernizing tendency has no time for the grammar school tradition. Unlike the cultural right, it considers it to be part of the problem, not the solution. It is thoroughly critical of the anti-industrial values of a liberal education.

. . . The changes in policy and policy influence since 1990 can be plotted very clearly. In the first phases of the post-1988 reform process the 'educational establishment' was clearly 'part of the game'; liberal professors, HMI (Her Majesty's Inspectorate of Schools), DES officials local educational authority (LEA) figures were all in evidence working in and around the two newly created agencies of educational change: the National Curriculum Council (NCC) and the Schools Examination and Assessment Council (SEAC). The former chaired by an ex-LEA person (Duncan Graham), the latter by an ex-DES official (Philip Halsey). For the cultural restorationists who had argued for and supported the ERA this looked like defeat snatched from the jaws of victory. Those people whose views and influence they had sought to supplant by the strictures and requirements of the ERA were the very people given the task of filling in and implementing the reform agenda.

> the main source of trouble has been successive Ministers allowing the crucial committees, commissions and working parties charged with the detailed implementation of the Act to be dominated by the same sort of people, and sometimes the very same people, as have been responsible for reducing our maintained school system to the catastrophic condition which that 1988 Act was supposed to remedy. These 'progressive egalitarians' remain more or less openly resolved to frustrate the reforming purposes of the 1988 Act. It is significant that among the original appointees to the National Curriculum Council (NCC) and the Schools Examinations and Assessment Council (SEAC) there was not even one person who had been prominent among the long-time critics calling for radical reform of the previous establishment. [In other words, not one of 'us' – SJB.]
>
> (Flew, 1991: 43)

One indication of the effect of this kind of critique on Major and Clarke came in July 1991 when Philip Halsey, Chairman and chief Executive of SEAC, and Duncan Graham, Chairman of the NCC, were both removed from their posts, the latter to be replaced by Lord Griffiths of Fforestfach. ... When appointed to the NCC, Lord Griffiths, a former professor of economics at City University, was chairman of the Centre for Policy Studies; absolutely 'one of us'. David Pascall, former adviser to Margaret Thatcher, became Chairman of the NCC. By mid-1992 it could be said that the cultural restorationists of the Conservative New Right, members of the CPS in particular, were well entrenched as the 'new' 'educational establishment'.

In effect, the implementation of the ERA has become the terrain for policy in-fighting over the determination of the three basic message systems of schooling (Bernstein, 1971): curriculum, assessment and, more recently, pedagogy. Representing this struggle for control of the definition of 'what it means to be educated' are two contrasting images of the school. The cultural restorationist image of the Victorian schoolroom and the modernisers' image of the flexible, post-Fordist school. But before I go on to unpack these images further I want to spend some time illustrating the issues at stake in each of the three areas of struggle.

The curriculum

The most visible aspect of the Conservative government's educational reform is the development and installation of the National curriculum. Not since the nineteenth-century Revised Codes has a UK government attempted to assert direct control over the school curriculum; although the examination system and university entrance requirements have always served as significant forms of surrogate control. But during the 1970s and 1980s it became the received wisdom within the Conservative Party that the school curriculum was out of control; that 'real' knowledge was being replaced, especially in comprehensive secondary and progressive primary schools, by an 'ideological curriculum'. Mrs Thatcher took up this concern in her speech to the 1987 Party Conference.

> Too often our children don't get the education they need – the education they deserve. And in the inner cities – where youngsters must have a decent education if they are to have a better future – that opportunity is all too often snatched from them by hard-left educational authorities and extremist teachers. Children who need to be able to count and multiply are learning anti-racist mathematics – whatever that may be. Children who need to be able to express themselves in clear English are being taught political slogans. Children who need to be taught to respect traditional moral values are being taught that they have an inalienable right to be gay.

The National Curriculum then is intended to put 'real' knowledge back into school and to discipline teachers. But the 'will to truth' underlying the reform has not been easy to realise, despite the enormous range of new powers accruing to the Secretary of State for Education from the 1988 ERA. Even a very careful selection of members of the Subject Working Groups (one for each of the 10 National Curriculum subjects), has not prevented the occurrence of several very public disagreements over the contents and orientation of the Working Group Reports. On a number of occasions the *process of curriculum specification* has been reduced to the assertion of a set of personal prejudices held by the incumbent Secretary of State . . . over and against the best judgement of Working Group members and subject practitioners (see Ball, 1990: 198–204, on the Mathematics Working Party). The political agenda for the National curriculum has never been very far from the surface in these encounters. I want to present three brief examples of these struggles, each of which highlights aspects of cultural restorationism; they relate to music, geography and history.

Music

Music has always been a subject backwater in the school curriculum, a matter of little interest to most students and hardly a focus of political controversy. The cultural restorationist response to the Music Working Party Report and the Secretary of State's subsequent intervention changed all that. The reaction to the Report was orchestrated by two newspaper articles both written by cultural restorationist philosophers, . . . Anthony O'Hear (1991) and Roger Scruton (1991). The report was described as 'a betrayal of the nation's children' and of 'the classical tradition . . . the highest achievement of European culture'. The focus of the philosophers' ire was the proposal that one of three main attainment targets for music should be 'performance'. What the writers of the Report had [done] was to represent school music as having elements of both knowledge and participation. That is, to attempt to write into the National curriculum the idea (already a well-accepted approach in school classrooms), that learning music could involve making music as well as learning *about* music. By devoting one attainment target to the musical experience of the student, their musical efforts were, in the eyes of the critics, being equated somehow with the products of the European canon. The restorationist response reduced a set of complex issues to a matter of Beethoven (always Beethoven) versus steel bands. Two key aspects of the restorationist project are touched upon here. The distrust of experience and relevance, and the eurocentric, cultural racism that informs their aesthetic judgements. The former is illustrated in a passage from Scruton's article which suggests an extraordinary personal alienation.

> But when I was 15, playing bass guitar and piano with my mates, I already knew that what I did could be of no lasting value to me. This knowledge came to be because I had been taught to value *music.*

The point here is that *music* is defined solely in terms of product, in terms of what others, listed in the canon, do. For the restorationists music is not a putting together of sounds to create effect or a shared activity, it is not a matter of creativity but rather a lonely appreciation, a . . . tradition, a mental abstraction divorced from the here and now and from the possibility of engagement. Education and learning here are founded upon alienation, a negation of self; knowledge is valued precisely for its irrelevance, esotericism, detachment, élitism and intrinsic difficulty; learning is an act of abasement, of passivity, of deference. The learner comes to knowledge naive and incorrect and leaves that which is learned untouched and unchanged. This is the curriculum as museum. Significantly Scruton's approved repertoire fails to name a single living composer. Daringly, O'Hear includes Duke Ellington in his list . . .

The Secretary of State's personal response to the Working Party Report and the subsequent NCC Consultation Report left little doubt as to who's views counted when the National curriculum was at stake. An editorial in the practitioner's journal *Music Teacher* (February 1992: 5) reported.

> The publication of the NCC Consultation Report on Music has caused fury among music teachers and educationalists . . . [it] alters its balance away from performing and in favour of factual knowledge and suggests that western classical music be given prominence over music of other cultures . . . The NCC has merely implemented the Education Secretary's desire for simplification, factual learning and an emphasis on the western

classical heritage . . . The report acknowledges that not only is it rejecting the main thrust of the Working Group's report, it is also discounting
the support it received . . . 80% of respondents agreed with the
Attainment Targets proposed.

The NCC Consultation Report on Music has concluded that:

> Council does not consider that the Working Group's proposals for three
> attainment targets place sufficient emphasis on the History of Music, on
> diverse musical heritage and on the appreciation of a variety of other
> musical traditions.

In the case of music the cultural restorationists saw the subject as having
been captured by progressive educators. In the case of geography, progressive educators (and many other practitioners) saw the initial working party
report as having been captured by or strongly influenced by the cultural
restorationist agenda.

Geography

The controversies over the Geography Working Group Report cover similar
ground, particularly the Secretary of State's concern for more emphasis on
factual learning. But in this case the initial draft of the Report was the
object of practitioners' concerns. . . . School geography was to be fragmented, as they saw it, with the effect that spatial, economic, political and
ecological aspects of the subject would be divorced from one another
(Huckle and Machon, 1990). Commentators discerned a strong
Conservative political agenda embedded in the Report.

> Why should California feature so strongly, without any requirement to
> undertake a serious study of China? The naming of the Falkland Islands
> could be seen as one instance of highlighting detail for its own sake and
> the re-establishment of Capes and Bays which had taken 50 years of hard
> campaigning to disestablish in the late sixties; alternatively its inclusion
> might be seen as political statement which reifies our Imperial Tradition,
> which is symbolically out of keeping with our economic future within a
> European community. Is Colonel Blimp to haunt us forever either
> through the specification of factual knowledge as an end in itself, or of
> particular places which are tombstones of the past?
>
> (Hall, 1990: 314)

What is striking again in these proposals is the backward lookingness of
the conception of subject knowledge. The Report appears to aim at a
repositioning of the UK in some mythical golden age of empire. Geography
is tied into an unstated politics of space. . . . The emphasis is upon the
subordination of the learner to place and space rather than on analytical

control. . . . National Curriculum geography isolates students in time and space, cutting them off from the realities of a single European market, global economic dependencies and inequalities, and ecological crisis.

History

Similar comments can be addressed to history, although the emotive background to the History Report is stronger. In the 1988 Conservative Party Conference, the then Secretary of State Kenneth Baker, announced his determination to ensure that in future all children would learn the key events in British history, including 'the spread of Britain's influence for good throughout the world' and added that 'we should not be ashamed of our history, our pride in our past gives us our confidence to stand tall in the world today'. Again the restorationist crusade against the curriculum reforms of the 1960s and 1970s, in this case 'new history', provided a driving force of assertion and critique (Beattie, 1987; Kedourie, 1988; Deuchar, 1989) to underpin National Curriculum History. Thus in a CPS publication *Errors and Evils of the New History*, Kedourie (1988: 6) explains:

> The purpose of this paper is to disclose to the general reader some of the ways in which, under the guise of history, which is one of the foundation subjects of the proposed national curriculum, secondary schoolchildren are being introduced to a subject very different to anything their parents are likely to have seen taught; which indeed resembles traditional history not at all. The situation is serious; many children are now leaving school with no historical knowledge at all (p. 5). History itself is to be understood in terms of concepts such as cause and effect, change and development, progress and continuity. Students are to feel that they can take part in history and that they have an active part to play. Their comprehension of the subject is to be fostered through empathy.

The coincidence of pedagogical and political critique here hardly needs comment. The shock and horror which run through all of the restorationist criticisms of 'new history' are a reaction against the possibility that students could or should be encouraged to see their lives and experiences as linked to, part of history, or to see themselves as makers of history. Restorationist history is a set of facts about the past made up of key events and famous people; it has its own passive momentum. There is no room for theory or analysis. . . . History is there to be learned, known about. Such a conception does profound political and pedagogical work. It 'effectively abolishes any practical sense of the future and of the collective project, thereby abandoning the thinking of future change to fantasies of sheer catastrophe and inexplicable cataclysm' (Jameson, 1984: 65). Restorationist history is 'the reconstruction of the past for its own sake' not a 'prelude to current affairs' (Beattie, 1987: 4). It is a value-free history that divorces fact from interpretation and interpretation from interest. We are left with the 'impersonal authority of tradition' (Jones, 1989), and it is in these terms that we can interpret the Secretary of State's response to the History Working Group's Interim Report. He (John MacGregor on this occasion) asserted that:

1 chronology deserves greater emphasis;
2 the proportion of British History be increased;
3 knowledge should be included as a separate Attainment Target.

Across these three subjects the assertion of the restorationist curriculum has a striking uniformity both in form and content. In each case, the starting point is the deconstruction of the comprehensive, modernist curriculum and thence its replacement with a political but depoliticized, authoritative curriculum of tradition. This employs what I have called else-where 'the discourse of derision' (Ball, 1990). Simple polarities are deployed within this discourse based upon the certainties of 'good' and 'evil', the sacred and profane, and sanity and lunacy. Foucault's (1971: 11) second principle of exclusion – division and rejection – is very much in evidence here. The language, style and tone of moral outrage leaves no grounds for professional judgement in these areas. There is no doubt, no compromise, no relativism. *This is curricular fundamentalism* . . . The modernist project of comprehensive education is damned and rejected root and branch. In each case, the attempt to recognize the pluralism and multiculturalism of late twentieth-century Britain is derided and replaced by a regressive 'little Englandism'. . . . The links between pedagogy and knowledge, experience and understanding are severed and replaced by authoritative texts and authoritative teaching. The student is to learn from history and about music and geography but is separate from them. The possibilities of analytical or political consciousness or of participation in 'culture' are excluded. Not surprisingly this curriculum of transmission is neatly packaged with equally uncompromising and traditionalist visions of assessment and pedagogy. The terrain of dispute over pedagogy and assessment is, not surprisingly, established across the contending versions of the nature of knowledge adumbrated above. It is to these I now turn, although again briefly.

Assessment

Here the issue at stake is superficially very simple; how best to assess the student? But as ever this simplicity makes for a set of difficult philo-sophical and psychological debates (see Troman, 1989). . . . The battle lines between the 'old' educational establishment – in favour of diagnostic, problem-solving, open-ended, process-oriented, teacher assessments – and the cultural restorationists – in favour of publishable, measurement-based, competitive, pencil and paper, externally-set tests and examinations – are well established. The original basis for National Curriculum assessment (the TGAT Report, DES, 1988) was fairly firmly on the former model. Subsequent changes recommended by SEAC or made unilaterally by Secretaries of State signal a decisive move towards the latter. Secretary of State Clarke summed up the restorationist position in his Westminster Lecture of 1991 (Clarke, 1991).

> The British pedagogue's hostility to written examinations of any kind can be taken to ludicrous extremes. The British left believe that pencil and paper examinations impose stress on pupils and demotivate them. [Note the casual juxtapositioning of 'pedagogues' and 'the left' – SJB.] We have tolerated for 20 years an arrangement whereby there is no national testing or examination of any kind for most pupils until they face GCSE at the age of 16 . . . This remarkable national obsession lies behind the more vehement opposition to the recent introduction of 7 year old testing. They were made a little too complicated [The TGAT model – SJB.] and we have said we will simplify them . . . The complications themselves were largely designed in the first place in an attempt to pacify opponents who feared above all else 'paper and pencil tests' . . . This opposition to testing and examinations is largely based on a folk memory in the left about the old debate on the 11-plus and grammar schools.

Here then *complex* assessment is seen as designed to obscure. *Simple* tests are revealing. Complexity is 'soft', misleading, product-based. Simplicity is 'hard', clear, unequivocal and commonsensical. For the restorationists, testing is a way of differentiating between students and identifying 'poor' schools. . . . In part also the restorationist attacks upon coursework and teacher assessments rest on a fundamental distrust of the teacher. ' "Pupil profiles" constructed by the pupils' own teachers are not to be relied on save in so far as they can be and are cross-checked against the findings of independently assessed public examinations' (Flew, 1991: 29). Assessments are seen to have little or no pedagogic value, rather they must serve as performance indicators of teacher effectivity. Thus, coursework assessment is taken as 'a call to abandon a fundamental principle of natural justice – that no one should be judge of their own cause' (Flew, 1991: 29). . . .

Pedagogy

The previous Secretary of State, Kenneth Clarke, reserved his particular views and concerns about teaching and learning for an assault upon the progressive movement in primary education. In a lecture to the Tory Reform Group (Clarke, 1991), . . . Clarke mounted a critique of 'progressive' and 'child-centred' education and the 'trendy progressive views of "expert" educationalists'. In particular, ... he argued that educational theory, and especially the theories of Rousseau and Dewey, had led to a neglect of knowledge in primary schools and a sentimental idealization of the child.

> Rousseau is the root of much of the position of the left on this as on so many other things. Rousseau's philosophy has been developed by John Dewey to form a basis for an ideology of modern education and one which has taken root in some of our schools, colleges and departments of education. His ideas are symptomatic of a whole philosophy of life which tends to be dismissive of what has been learned in the past.
>
> Dewey's hostility to traditional learning and to tradition in general stems from his belief that the child is or should be primarily concerned with working out his own answers to his own problems. Hence the so-called child-centred approach to teaching that he advocates. The child will be taught to discount custom and tradition. Dewey and his followers overlook the way in which any field of human activity (including the scientific incidentally) will contain a mass of customary and traditional knowledge and skills.
>
> (Clarke, 1991: 5)

Now [it] is questionable whether this [is] a recognizable account of Deweyian thought, but within this discourse accuracy is irrelevant. It is *effect* that counts – the destabilization of commitment and of respect. What is central here again is the deification of tradition and of the past and a trenchant opposition to any recognition of the child as active within the learning process. This discursive intervention into primary school teaching methods was followed up in December 1991 by the announcement by the Secretary of State of a 'debate among primary teachers about how children can most effectively be taught' (Letter, 11 December 1991). . . . His earlier *Statement on 'Primary Education'* (3 December 1991) explained:

> Let me be quite clear, however, that questions about how to teach are not for the Government to determine. I have no intention to seek to extend my powers in that direction. My purpose is to initiate a discussion, not to impose solutions . . . I am asking every primary head teacher and every primary classroom teacher to join in the radical rethinking now needed as to how best to teach children in our schools.
>
> (p. 2)

What is unclear in the statement is how the debate should progress. How would teachers make their views known? How would the outcomes be decided? Why should the debate be constrained to a 'radical rethinking'? No recourse to tradition and custom for teachers! The point is of course that this is no 'real' debate, it is a language game. . . . It all depends upon the ability to make oneself heard. Thus, the anti-educationalist media joined in with gusto. *The Evening Standard* (9 December 1991: 9) announced . . . that:

> Last week Her Majesty's Inspectors of Education declared that British primary school teachers could learn much from their French counterparts. Blackboards, desks, formal disciplined teaching and the return of streaming could soon become permanent features of our classrooms, concludes the report . . .

. . . . The Secretary of State summed up the HMI report referred to in the *Standard* article:

> HMI are publishing this week a report on primary education in France. Teachers worked through a highly centralised National Curriculum, with classes of similar size to those in England. Whole class and didactic teaching was used extensively. HMI found that such teaching was thoroughly planned, effectively implemented and challenging, and that children progressed well. Pupils concentrated on the task set and responded positively to demanding work.
>
> (Clarke, Statement: 5)

Also in his statement Secretary Clarke accounted that

> To help focus the debate and inform policy on the training of primary teachers, I have commissioned a report from Professor Robin Alexander, Chief Inspector Jim Rose of HMI and Christopher Woodhead, Chief Executive of the National Curriculum Council, on primary teaching methods and classroom organisation.
>
> (Clarke, Statement: 9)

In effect, the debate was opened, judged and closed in the same document. . . . Indeed, . . . there was no need for debate. It follows clearly from the fundamentalist approach to knowledge that learning is ritual, an initiation into heritage, a means of preserving and reproducing the canon.

COMMON SENSE AND VICTORIANISM

Running through all of this is a set of key themes and images. One of the themes . . . is an *anti-intellectualism.* That is, a distrust of theory and research and over and against these the assertion of common sense. . . . The discursive privileging of common sense also underwrites the unimpeachability of the canon. The *natural* superiority and status of the canon are part of common sense, and the gatekeepers and arbiters thus remain invisible. To question the canon is to go against common sense, is irrational, is destructive and mad. A second theme is *nostalgia,* an educational Victorianism which represents education, to parents in particular, in terms of familiar images of 'traditional' pedagogic forms. This is a form of cultural popularism organized around notions of discipline, authority and learning. The Victorian schoolroom and the grammar school are the lost objects of desire, standing for a time when education was simple, when learning meant doing and knowing what you were told by your teacher. . . . Of course, this is not what traditional classroom were actually like most of the time for most people. . . . Thus, 'traditional education' (and traditional values) here are a pastiche; a policy simulacrum – the identical copy for which no original has ever existed. UK education policy is now set within what Jameson calls 'the nostalgia mode', 'the desperate attempt to appropriate a missing past' (1984: 66), to return education to a state of naivety and innocence before special learning needs, worksheets, problem-solving, investigations, reading readiness and constructivism. Here learning is based on teaching and intelligence; teaching is about fixed and agreed knowledges (and knowledge is also constituted by the past) and intelligence is measured by tests. Not surprisingly this simulacrum coincides perfectly with the broader agenda of restorationism and the neo-conservative project to re-establish *order and place*. This is an education of deference, to the teacher, to the past, to the nation, and to your 'elders and betters' – the traditional values of Victorian middle-class childhood. Hierarchy and differentiation are naturalized within this discourse of 'authority'. . . .

. . . The ontology of restorationism is opposed to any conception of human nature as social (except in the narrow senses of family and nation) and conceives instead of private, self-sufficient competing individuals: this is founded on the politics and economics of Adam Smith and Fredrich Hayek. The belief in the Victorian *laissez-faire* economy (and its peculiar mercantile naturalism – realized in tradition and history – and notions of market-driven economic Darwinism) is paralleled in the idea of intellectual natural selection in the classroom. Teaching is not so much a pedagogic intervention as the most effective method for identifying and realizing inevitable intelligence-based differences between students.

And knowledge in the traditional schoolroom is realized via the traditional curriculum. The preservation and transmission of the 'best of all that has been said and written'; itself a pastiche, an edited, stereotypical, unreal, schoolbook past. It comprises a curriculum which eschews relevance and the present, concentrating on 'the heritage' and 'the canon', based on 'temporal disengagement'. A curriculum suspicious of the popular and the immediate, made up of echoes of past voices, the voices of a cultural and political elite. A curriculum which ignores the pasts of women and the working class and the colonized – *the curriculum of the dead*. Reverence and detachment are the acceptable educational stances within this pantheon approach to knowledge; rather different from any sense of 'critical distance'. This 'effectively abolishes any practical sense of the future and the collective project' (Jameson, 1984: 85). The canon is unchallengeable. The selections are done elsewhere, at other times, they are 'handed down' by the unassailable 'judgement of generations'. The Plowdonian child as active learner is replaced by the silent reader and patient listener. The schoolroom is a place of hush and the pupil is rendered incapable of fashioning representations of his or her own current experience.

REFERENCES

Aronowitz, S. and Giroux, H. (1991) *Postmodern Education: politics, culture and social criticism*, Minneapolis: University of Minnesota Press.
Ball, S.J. (1990) *Politics and Policy Making in Education*, London: Routledge.
Beattie, A. (1987) *History in Peril: many parents preserve it*, London: Centre for Policy Studies.
Bernstein, B. (1971) On the classification and framing of educational knowledge, in M.F.D. Young (ed.) *Knowledge and Control*, London: Collier-Macmillan.
Bloom, A. (1987) *The Closing of the American Mind*, New York: Simon & Schuster.
Clarke, K. (1991) *Education in a Classless Society*, Westminster Lecture to the Tory Reform Group, 12 June 1992.
Department of Education and Science (DES) (1988) *National Curriculum: the Task Group on Assessment and Testing: a report*, London: HMSO.
Deuchar, S. (1989) *The New History: a critique*, York: Campaign for Real Education.
Flew, A. (1991) Educational services: independent competition or maintained monopoly, in D.G. Green (ed.) *Empowering the Parents*, London: Institute of Economic Affairs.
Foucault, M. (1971) *L'Ordre du Discours*, Paris: Gallimard.
Hall, D. (1990) The national curriculum and the two cultures: towards a humanistic perspective, *Geography*, 22: 310–20.
Hirsch, E.D. (1987) *Cultural Literacy: what every American needs to know*, Boston: Houghton-Mifflin.
Huckle, J. and Machon, P. (1990) Geography and political education in the National Curriculum, *Teaching Geography*, 15(2): 53–7.
Jameson, F. (1984) Postmodernism or the cultural logic of late capitalism, *New Left Review*, 147: 61–84.
Jones,K. (1989) *Right Turn*, London: Radius.
Kedourie, H. (1988) *Errors and Evils of the New History*, London: Centre for Policy Studies.
Music Teacher, Editorial, February 1992.
O'Hear, A. (1991) Out of sync with Bach, *The Times Educational Supplement*, 22 February.
Scruton, R. (1991) Rock around the classroom, *Sunday Telegraph*, 10 February.
Troman, G. (1989) Testing tensions: the politics of educational assessment, *British Educational Research Journal*, 15: 279–96.
Wexler, P. and Grabiner, G. (1986) America during the crisis, in R. Sharp (ed.) *Capitalism, Crisis and Schooling*, South Melbourne: Macmillan.

GLOSSARY

Actors

Kenneth Baker. Secretary of State for Education 1986–89, architect of the 1988 Education Reform Act, was promoted to Home Secretary.

Kenneth Clarke. Secretary of State for Education 1990–92, also promoted to Home Secretary.

Professor Anthony Flew. Philosopher of education and member of the Education Group of the Centre for Policy Studies, has also written for the neo-liberal Institute of Economic Affairs and the Social Affairs Unit. He is also on the council of the Freedom Association.

Duncan Graham. Ex-LEA Chief Officer and first Chairman of the NCC, deposed in 1991 soon after John Major became Prime Minister.

David (Lord) Griffiths. Appointed as Chairman of SEAC in 1991, was previous long-time head of Mrs Thatcher's Policy Unit, and one time chair of CPS.

Philip Halsey. Ex-DES senior civil servant and first chairman of SEAC, deposed in 1991 soon after John Major became Prime Minister.

Keith (Lord) Joseph. Secretary of State for Education 1981–86, Conservative neo-liberal intellectual, political guru of Margaret Thatcher in the 1970s.

John MacGregor. Secretary of State for Education 1989–90, became Leader of the House and, in 1992, Minister of Transport.

John Major. Conservative Prime Minister 1990–

Professor Anthony O'Hear. Philosopher and CPS pamphlet writer, *Daily Telegraph* columnist, government appointee for the Council for the Accreditation of Teacher Education.

David Pascall. Executive of British Petroleum, appointed as Chair of NCC in 1991, was a member of Mrs Thatcher's policy unit 1983–84.

Roger Scruton. Professor of Aesthetics at Birkbeck College, editor of the High Tory journal *The Salisbury Review*, and writer for and member of several restorationist groups including the Educational Research Centre and Institute for European Defence and Strategic Studies.

Margaret Thatcher. Conservative Prime Minister 1979–90.

Agencies

CPS: Centre for Policy Studies, founded in 1974 after the Conservative election defeat to 'think' radical ideas, Margaret Thatcher and Keith Joseph were co-chairs.

CRE: Campaign for Real Education was founded in the wake of the suspension (and eventual 'buying out') of Headteacher John Honeyford in Bradford. In part the suspension had resulted from the publication of an article by Honeyford, critical of multiculturalism, in *The Salisbury Review* (see under Roger Scruton). Stewart Deuchar is vice-chairman of the CRE.

DES: Department of Education and Science, renamed Department for Education in 1992 with responsibility for science hived off.

HMI: Her Majesty's Inspectorate, a semi-autonomous 'quality control' unit based in the DES, identified by restorationist critics as part of the 'old' educational establishment and recently much reduced in size and reorganized within a new agency OFSTED, the Office for Standards in Education.

LEAs: Local education authorities, indirectly elected local government committees which until recently had considerable power and influence over local education policy and provision. Since the 1988 Education Reform Act, both power and influence have waned considerably and the 1992 Education White Paper proposes further reductions in LEA powers and responsibilities.

NCC: National Curriculum Council, established by the 1988 Education Reform Act, responsible for advising the Secretary of State on all aspects of the school curriculum, for carrying out research and development and for publishing and disseminating information relating to the curriculum for schools.

SEAC: Schools Examination and Assessment Council, established by the 1988 Education Reform Act to advise the Secretary of State and promote the new developments in assessment required under the Act.

Chapter 5

The problem of good primary practice

Robin Alexander

THE QUEST: PRACTITIONER VIEWS

What is 'good primary practice'? Is it really as elusive and problematic as we claimed on the basis of the Leeds evidence?[1]

The words of practitioners themselves provide one obvious starting point for our quest. Consider, for example:

> Why do we do it this way? Well, it's good primary practice, isn't it?

Here, immediately, we encounter one of the most prominent features of the discourse: the easy assumption of consensus, which pre-empts any further discussion. If one does pursue it, however:

> In this school we adopt best practice and approach the National curriculum thematically. We don't adopt the old-fashioned method of keeping it in little boxes. It's unnatural – children don't see the world that way, so why should we impose our adult views on them?

Thus, good practice *is* definable, but strictly in terms of certain canons. Where do these come from?

> By dividing the curriculum into subjects the government is sabotaging all the good practice established by primary schools since Plowden.

> I have no problem about good practice: Plowden is still my Bible, whatever the government or any airy-fairy academics say. They are not the practitioners – I am!

So the centre of gravity would seem to be the Plowden Report of 1967 or at least those ideas and practices which can claim descent from this famous document. Note next the characteristic use of buzzwords, slogans and shibboleths:

> The curriculum isn't subjects: it's a walk through autumn leaves.

> We apply all the basic principles of good practice here – a stimulating environment with high quality display and plenty of material for first

hand exploration; a flexible day in which children can move freely from one activity to the next without the artificial barriers of subjects; plenty of individual and group work.

We encourage freedom, flexibility, spontaneity, discovery. These are the watchwords of good primary practice.

With this is frequently combined a tendency to set up simple – and usually false – dichotomies, with no middle ground deemed possible or admissible:

We don't believe in teaching here. The job of the teacher is to create the environment in which children can find things out for themselves, not to tell them what they should know.

It isn't what the children learn that matters, but how.

To be fair, this is a tactic used by the opposition too:

Forget the trendy Sixties. The child cannot find it all out for himself. He needs to be told, he needs to be taught.

Note in the antepenultimate quotation above, the reference to *belief* as the basis for action, still more graphically put in the earlier assertion that 'Plowden is my Bible' and frequently illustrated in job advertisements:

The successful candidate will be familiar with good primary practice. A belief in a child-centred approach is essential.

Candidates should be committed to a child-centred approach to learning via first-hand experience.

We are looking for committed, enthusiastic child-centred teachers who believe in activity, a cross-curricular approach and enquiry-based learning.

Conviction, of course, can frequently breed intolerance of alternative viewpoints, including (and perhaps especially, because they are more threatening) those which are grounded in evidence of some kind:

Plowden is still my Bible, whatever the government or any airy-fairy academics say. They are not the practitioners – I am!

Six-year olds can't understand the past, so what's the government playing at bringing in history at Key Stage One? It just shows how out of touch they are.

I don't care what the ILEA research shows: the integrated day is right for me and right for my children.

But then, as the press coverage of the Leeds report showed, dismissiveness and intolerance are deployed at least as frequently by the counter-culture.

Thus, Prime Minister John Major stated in October 1991:

> I will fight for my belief, and my belief is a return to basics in education. The progressive theorists have had their say.

By this stage in our analysis, however, other cracks are beginning to show, as the old seeks to accommodate itself to the new:

> Don't worry about the National Curriculum – if you look at the attainment targets and programmes of study you'll find that we do all that already. In fact they just confirm good primary practice.

> The SATs will be cross-curricular and activity-based so as to be in line with good primary practice.

> I have terrible problems planning, because we're all supposed to use topic webs and show them to the head, and I'm not very good at them, and find them impossible to use, especially as now I have to add all the attainment targets. So what I do is a topic web to satisfy the head, and my own planning for me.

This brings us squarely to the context of power, and perhaps even patronage, within which the good primary practice issue is sometimes located (the first quotation below nicely capturing the authoritarianism with which, somewhat paradoxically, child-centredness is sometimes associated):

> When I go into one of my classrooms I don't expect to see all my children sitting down. I expect movement, I expect them to be busy. A quiet classroom is a dull classroom.

> If it's Authority policy to do it this way, you have to do it, at least when the advisers are around.

> I won't get this job, because the adviser thinks my practice is too formal. Actually, she only came in once, and even then didn't see me teach.

> I give my children the occasional spelling test, but I daren't tell the head.

> If you don't have drapes and triple mounting, you won't get on here.

This in turn can present the teacher (or in these two examples, the student teacher) with considerable dilemmas:

> On my first teaching practice I wasn't allowed to class teach – everything had to be done in groups, and I found it very difficult, especially when there were things that could most sensibly be discussed with the class as a whole and I had to repeat them six times.

> My class teacher tells me that good practice is a topic-based curriculum with lots of group and individual work. That's all very well – she's

experienced enough to make it work. But I'm not. Anyway, my tutor says there's no one right way, and good practice is finding what works best for me, so who do I believe, and if I want to pass this teaching practice what on earth am I to do?

THE QUEST: THE APPEAL TO AUTHORITY

Clearly, while statements such as those above begin to uncover the scope of the problem, they do not take us very far in what should be an open debate, a quest in which we ought to be able to follow any path which might seem promising. Are there other starting points?

A second possibility is to go not to practitioners but to those official documents which purport to define the characteristics of good practice in an authoritative way and which are free, one assumes, of particular foibles, preferences or prejudices.

In 1967, the Plowden Report adopted the device of describing rather than prescribing. It portrayed three schools 'run successfully on modern lines', whose characteristics tellingly endorse some of the assumptions we encountered and questioned in the Leeds research, as the following extract shows:

> The children . . . spread into the hall, the corridors and the playground. The nursery class has its own quarters and the children are playing with sand, water, paint, clay, dolls, rocking horses and big push toys under the supervision of their teacher. This is how they learn. . . . Learning is going on all the time, but there is not much direct teaching. . . . The class of sevens to nines had spread into the corridor and were engaged in a variety of occupations. One group were gathered round their teacher for some extra reading practice, another was at work on an extraordinary structure of wood and metal which they said was a sputnik, a third was collecting a number of objects and testing them to find out which could be picked up by a magnet and two boys were at work on an immense painting of St Michael defeating Satan. They seemed to be working harmoniously according to an unfolding rather than a preconceived plan. . . . As he leaves the school and turns into the grubby and unlovely street onto which it abuts, the visitor passes a class who, seated in a quiet, sunny corner, are listening to their teacher telling them the story of Rumpelstiltskin.
>
> (CACE, 1967: 103–5)

Twenty years later, the agenda had changed somewhat, though its antecedents were still discernible, as the following extracts from HMI's direct encounter with the good practice problem show.

First impressions were of an informality which typifies many primary classrooms. Closer investigation revealed that the freedoms were not there merely by chance. . . . The children were keenly interested in their work. Their commitment to what they were doing extended beyond the more obviously enjoyable aspects of their practical activities. . . . The children were being taught to listen carefully and speak clearly and articulately. . . . Their written work caused them to use a variety of styles. . . . The high quality of teaching was the strongest feature common to all the examples . . . there were variations in the teaching styles reflecting the needs of the situation and the personality of individual teachers. . . . Teachers had a sound knowledge of their pupils' social and cultural backgrounds. . . . A dominant factor in the achievement of high standards was the strength of commitment on the part of the teachers to ensure that pupils were making progress. . . . Challenges were set so that the work was neither too difficult nor too easy. . . . The overriding characteristic is that of agreed, clear aims and purposeful teaching.

(DES, 1987: 32–4)

Thus, the appearance might be that of a Plowden classroom, but the teacher had by now become considerably more prominent, and – crucially – the organic model of an unfolding sequence of intrinsically educative experiences had been replaced by a firm emphasis upon detailed prior planning. This theme was also taken up at school level, underscoring the way that serendipity was to be replaced by management, and individualism by collective endeavour:

In each school the head and staff had agreed aims . . . a shared sense of purpose . . . curricular guidelines which had been carefully thought out. . . . These guidelines had been written after staff discussions. . . . Schools were exploring ways of deploying the staff so that more effective use was made of their abilities and curricular strengths. . . . Schools were making positive efforts to strike the delicate balance which is involved in making the best use of the curricular expertise of a primary school staff as a combined teaching unit.

(DES, 1987: 31–2)

Two years later, the Plowden–HMI synthesis was reasserted by the National Curriculum Council, but expanded to leave no ambiguity about the re-emergence of traditional values:

The aims of the National Curriculum are more likely to be achieved where . . . pupils are properly equipped with the basic tools of learning. In particular, where numeracy, literacy and oracy are given highest priority by teachers and are soundly taught. These skills form the basis of a proper and rigorous education to the highest standards which parents and public expect. . . . Due recognition is given to the importance of first-hand experience and practical tasks. . . . Pupils are led to ask questions and seek answers. . . . Teachers' expectations of what pupils are capable of achieving are high and pupils' learning is structured, relevant and stimulating. . . . Pupils are encouraged to become self-confident, self-disciplined and courteous.

(NCC, 1989: 2)

Yet the key assumptions of the Plowden era in respect of classroom practice remained intact. In 1990, the School Examinations and Assessment Council's guidance to teachers about to embark on Key Stage One assessment offered a check list which appeared to presume both grouping and multiple-curriculum focus teaching:

Is the classroom organised to enable children to work independently or in groups without disturbing others? . . . Is there a balance in the activities you have planned so that all children will not need all your attention at the same time?

(SEAC, 1991)

THE INVISIBLE CRITERION PROBLEM

A notion of good practice presupposes criteria for judgement. While the 1987 HMI and 1989 NCC extracts make criteria explicit, they remain tacit or only partly explicated in the Plowden extract, and in some of the quotations from practising teachers there is even an assumption that criteria are not needed at all – either because good practice is about belief rather than justification, or because the (pseudo) consensus makes their explication unnecessary.

In general, good primary practice discourse is strong on assertion and weak on justification. As a result, the necessary task of defining and defending criteria is frequently neglected. Regrettably, this is a tendency to which even HMI – who have probably been more influential than any other group in shifting primary discourse away from purely 'process' pre-occupations to matters of curriculum content and management – are not wholly immune. Thus, for example, the Senior Chief Inspector's annual report:

33% of the work was judged to be good to very good, about 36% satisfactory and about 30% poor. . . . About 70% of English lessons were judged satisfactory or better with examples of good practice again occurring in the early years. . . . About 75% of mathematics lessons were satisfactory or better, but work of any distinction was rare . . .

(DES, 1991a: 6)

THE NOTION OF GOOD PRACTICE: WHAT DO WE MEAN BY 'GOOD'?

Our brief reference to the problem of criteria in good practice statements takes us from our initial desire to discover the characteristics of those classroom practices defined as good, to the much more fundamental question of what the notion of 'good practice' actually means. This, then, after consideration of the views of teachers and official sources, is the third possible starting point for our quest. It is qualitatively different from the other two in that it is concerned with a meta-level of analysis.

When we say of something we do, see or wish to commend 'this is good educational practice', what are we *really* asserting? there seem to be four possibilities:

1 This is the practice which I like, and which accords with my personal philosophy of education.
2 This is the practice which works for me, and which I feel most comfortable with.
3 This is the practice which I can prove is effective in enabling children to learn.
4 This is the practice which I (or others) expect to see, and it should therefore be adopted.

The status of each of these statements is significantly different:

Statement 1 is a statement of *value* or *belief.*
Statement 2 is a *pragmatic* statement.
Statement 3 is an *empirical* statement.
Statement 4 is a *political* statement.

If we now return to the teacher views with which the chapter started, we see that they can fairly readily be classified. However, it will also be noted that the statements cited are mostly statements of value or belief (what the teacher believes is right) or political statements (what the teacher is obliged by others to do). Many of them combine both attributes, being expressions of belief which one group imposes on another. For a profession generally much preoccupied with the 'nitty-gritty' or practical, surprisingly few of the statements are concerned with what works (pragmatic), or with what can be shown to be educationally effective (empirical). On the contrary, some (for example those from teachers teaching in ways to which they are not committed but to which they feel themselves compelled to conform) show how pragmatic considerations are overruled by power and belief; and others touch on empirical issues (the reference to academics and the ILEA research) but only to dismiss such sources as of no account.

So we appear to have a situation – strongly reinforced in the Leeds data – in which the 'good' in 'good primary practice' tends to be asserted but seldom demonstrated; where educational justifications for practice may be tacit rather than articulated; where those with power may assume the right to impose their preferred versions of good practice on those without; and where the front of consensus has to be maintained at all costs in order that the whole edifice does not come crashing down.

Good practice, then, becomes a matter more for decree than discussion. The climate of debate about good practice then becomes partisan and adversarial, rather than open, considered and reasoned. The discourse becomes tautologous: we do it this way because we do it this way.

THE NOTION OF 'GOOD PRACTICE': WHAT DO WE MEAN BY 'PRACTICE'?

There is a further difficulty. So far, we have considered one word in the phrase 'good practice' – the epithet 'good'. What of the other one, the notion of 'practice' itself? Is it reasonable to assume that when we speak of good primary practice we are all talking of the same phenomenon, and the only problem concerns the basis on which we rate practice as good, bad or indifferent?

To answer this we need to return once again to the earlier quotations. The Plowden extract, and that report's discussion of teaching in general, was preoccupied with the following:

- the use of time;
- the use of space;
- relationships;
- children's motivation, attitude and behaviour;
- the school and classroom context;
- pedagogic processes;
- the whole rather than the parts;
- evolution rather than structure;
- the needs of the child, defined developmentally and motivationally.

In contrast, the HMI extracts, and the many HMI documents since the seminal 1978 survey, imply a very different agenda:

- aims;
- planning;
- curriculum content;
- staff expertise and deployment;
- challenge in learning experiences;
- diagnosis and assessment;
- matching child and curriculum task;
- structure, progression and continuity;
- the parts as well as the whole;

- the needs of the child, defined in relation to societal realities and expectations.

If we place alongside these fairly dramatic differences of emphasis the teacher views with which the chapter started, we find a recurrent concern with:

- the whole rather than the parts;
- flexibility rather than structure;
- the visual impact of the classroom;
- curriculum integration;
- organizational principles rather than strategies.

In general, the quotations suggest a stronger sense of affiliation with Plowden than HMI, and this was certainly the case in the Leeds data referred to earlier. I have suggested elsewhere that there was a general tendency to highlight the visible features of practice like display and grouping, to focus on the environment of learning rather than learning itself, and to imply that securing the former would guarantee the latter.

The issue here, however, is not the reiteration of our earlier critique of certain aspects of the view of good primary practice which prevailed in Leeds during the period of our research [see Alexander, 1992] but to point out the more general *conceptual* problem raised by every single account of good practice discussed thus far: namely that they are all, in one respect or another, incomplete.

Consider, for example, the following statement from a recent HMI report on an initial teacher-training institution:

> The college declares publicly its philosophy of good primary practice. This is stated in all substantial course documents. The philosophy has several key elements. These are stated to include:
> - the recognition of the uniqueness of the individual child
> - the importance of first-hand experience
> - the value of an attractive and stimulating learning environment.
> (DES, 1991b: 1)

The problem here is not so much the *substance* as the *scope* of this statement. Few would dissent from the three principles thus enunciated, and many would applaud them. But as a *philosophy* of good primary practice this is surely woefully deficient. It is rather like a play with scenery but no actors or text, or a concert with orchestra but no music, or the National Gallery's Sainsbury Wing bereft of its pictures. It provides the context for education and gently hints at its conduct, but it indicates nothing of its purposes, scope, content or outcomes.

The problem with many accounts of good practice is that not only do they leave vital questions of value and evidence unexplored, and not only do they sometimes tend towards the authoritarian, but they also focus in a frequently arbitrary way upon particular aspects of practice which are then elevated to the status of a complete and coherent 'philosophy'. More often than not they are merely philosophical fragments or preliminary clearings of the throat.

In its everyday usage, therefore, the phrase 'good primary practice' is deeply flawed, both ethically and conceptually. Some who use the phrase are intuitively aware that this is so, and in writing adopt the apologetic device of placing the words in inverted commas, providing the digital equivalent in conversation. This is rarely more than a tic, since having made this passing acknowledgement that the phrase is problematic they invariably go on to treat it as though it were not.

A FRAMEWORK FOR CONCEPTUALIZING PRACTICE

In order to judge the adequacy of a good practice claim, therefore, we need not only to test the criterial and evidential basis on which practice is judged, but also to be clear about which aspects of practice are defined in this way and which aspects are ignored. There is of course no reason why a good practice statement should not be selective and sharply focused, and indeed every reason why sharpness of focus is desirable: it is difficult to talk meaningfully about teaching unless we engage with its specifics. The problem comes when, over time, or within a statement purporting to stand as a complete educational rationale, some aspects of practice are consistently emphasized while other aspects are consistently ignored. The underlying message of selectivity in this context is that *what is emphasized is all that matters*. That, essentially, was the problem in Leeds.

How can we begin to draw up a map of the vast territory of educational practice? In absolute terms it is an impossible enterprise. However, there may be a level at which such a map is not only possible but might also serve as a useful prompt to those involved in the examination, execution and judgement of practice.

My own shot at such a framework starts, as did the Leeds model, with what one encounters on entering a classroom: a *context* comprising first the physical and organizational features of furniture, resources and participants, and second the relationships observable as existing among and between these participants. This, then, is the setting.

Looking closer, one notes that most of the relationships and interactions are not random, but are framed by *pedagogic process*: teachers adopt particular strategies, particular combinations of class, group and individual work, particular patterns of interaction; and pupils are organized so as to facilitate these.

Next, we note that these processes are focused upon specific tasks and the acquisition of specific knowledge, skill, understanding or attribute: the *content* of teaching and learning.

Finally, we recognize that what we see and what the participants experience is subject to the teacher's *management*: it is planned, implemented and evaluated.

Thus far, we are dealing with what can be observed. However, to make sense of what we see we need to encounter the educational ideas and assumptions in which the observable practice is grounded. Without them practice is mindless, purposeless and random. It is reasonable to assume that although we may not necessarily agree with such ideas as an explanation and justification of what a teacher does, ideas of some kind are the basis for all observable practice. Talking with teachers about their practice in the context of the Leeds research and an earlier study of professional thinking (Alexander, 1989) and in my day-to-day work in initial teacher-training (ITT) and INSET, I find I can group such ideas under three broad headings.

The first concerns *children*. Most teaching rests on assumptions about what they can or cannot do, what they need, how they develop, how they learn, how best they can be motivated and encouraged.

The second collection of ideas concerns *society*. Teachers usually have some sense of the demands and expectations which emanate from outside the school, of the needs of society or particular sections of it, and of the needs of the individual in relation to that society. Reconciling and balancing these is one of the central challenges of every teacher and every school, and many primary teachers have a powerful sense of having moved from the era of Plowden in which the needs of the individual were paramount to one in which these are made subservient to, or are redefined in terms of, economic and political imperatives.

Finally, all teaching rests upon ideas about the nature of *knowledge*: its structure, its character, its source (whether newly created by each individual and culturally evolved or handed on from one generation to the next), and its content.

It will probably be apparent that at this point I have telescoped a line of analysis which deserves to be greatly extended, and indeed it derives from a conceptual framework which I have developed for a higher degree course on primary education which I run at Leeds University. However, for present purposes the intention is not to provide in fine detail a fully comprehensive framework for analysing and exploring classroom practice, but simply to illustrate that some such framework is perfectly feasible.

Thus my own framework has two main dimensions and seven main components, as shown in Figure 5.1. The categories are of course not discrete but are simply presented as such for analytical purposes. More important, the two dimensions, here presented as a sequential list, interact: each aspect

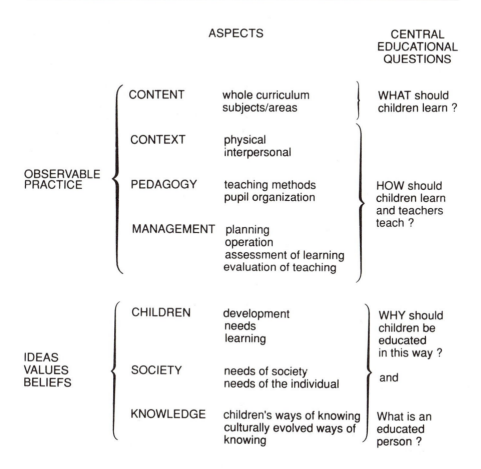

Figure 5.1 Educational practice: a conceptual framework

of practice is to a greater or lesser extent informed by one, two or all of the areas of ideas, values and beliefs.

These seem to constitute not so much the totality as the minimum: whatever else classroom practice encompasses, it contains these elements.

Armed with such a framework we can return to any good practice statement, test its emphasis and scope, and examine the thrust of the ideas and justifications, if any, in which it is rooted. The model, incidentally, has its parallel version at whole-school level. There the *observable practice* components include *context, management,* and *external relations,* but because the focus of this discussion is the classroom I am not elaborating that part of the framework in the same way.

Applying such a framework to the various examples given earlier, and to the wider contexts of the Leeds research and the emergence of the National curriculum, we can venture some basic propositions. Plowden, for example, tended to fixate on *context* and *pedagogy* and neglect *content* and *management*. Its vision was firmly grounded in views of *the child*, especially the child's development and learning. About *society* and its needs it had little to say; while its view of *knowledge* was an extension of its view of the child.

In contrast, from 1978 HMI developed a view of practice which dealt with all four elements, but focused particularly on *content* and *management*, with a relatively subsidiary interest in *pedagogy*. The justificatory basis had less to do with children's development than with their entitlement to breadth, balance and challenge in the curriculum, and was firmly guided by a sense of *knowledge* as cultural artefact, handed on from one generation to the next and providing an essential tool for the individual to make sense of, participate in, and act upon *society* and to respond to its needs.

The National Curriculum is even more distant from Plowden. The emphasis here (at least until the interventionist rumblings of late 1991) is almost exclusively on *content* and *management* – or rather those aspects of management which are concerned with delivery of content and proof of such delivery, *planning* and *assessment*. (The postal nuances of the language of the National Curriculum are startlingly pervasive, and have built remorselessly on former Secretary of State Keith Joseph's initial concept of the curriculum as educational package.) The justificatory basis is unambiguously societal, or rather economic.

The Leeds model was nearer to Plowden than to HMI. It focused on *context* and *pedagogy*, and only began to attend to content and management when this was dictated by the arrival of the National curriculum. The justificatory basis was tacitly Plowdenesque, though in fact, as we have seen, as a model it tended to be particularly deficient in the area of ideas and justifications, albeit fairly strong on values.

Analysed in this way, we can see the extent of the gulf, or culture clash, between the established view of primary education and the new regime; between the ideology of progressivism and the 1980s/90s emphasis on economic imperatives; between the mainstream culture of primary education and the new, tougher and much more instrumental educational culture legitimated by the 1988 Act. We can see, too, how at a time when the bedrock ideas and values of the education system were undergoing revolution, for an LEA to neglect ideas and concentrate on the external features of practice was particularly debilitating to its teaching force.

WHERE IS GOOD PRACTICE TO BE FOUND?

To take stock: 'good practice' statements come in different forms. Some are statements of *value or belief*, some are *pragmatic* statements; some are *empirical* statements; some are *political* statements; some combine more than one of these characteristics; and all presuppose a *concept* of practice itself.

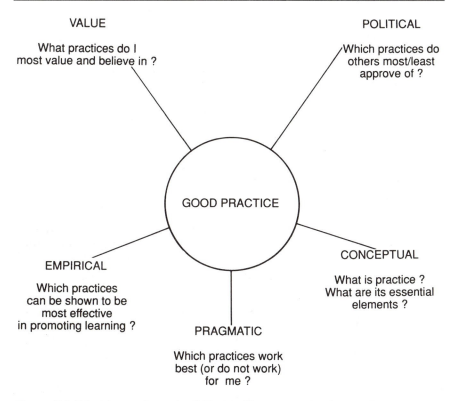

VALUE

What practices do I
most value and believe in ?

POLITICAL

Which practices do
others most/least
approve of ?

GOOD PRACTICE

EMPIRICAL

Which practices
can be shown to be
most effective
in promoting learning ?

CONCEPTUAL

What is practice ?
What are its essential
elements ?

PRAGMATIC

Which practices work
best (or do not work)
for me ?

Figure 5.2 What is good practice? Reconciling competing imperatives

Pursuing our quest for good primary practice in this way, therefore, we can see that while in a physical sense it resides in primary schools and classrooms, to know what we are looking for and to begin to understand how we might define and judge it, we need to recognize that it lies, *conceptually*, at the intersection of the five considerations or dimensions which we have explored: value, pragmatic, empirical, political and conceptual. Figure 5.2 represents this relationship.

The quest for good primary practice, then, is as much a conceptual as a geographical one. Before we can ask an LEA or a head to show us schools or classrooms in which good practice is to be found we need to be clear what we, and they, mean by good primary practice, and whether there is sufficient agreement to make the journey worthwhile. 'What do we mean by good practice?' must precede 'Where is good practice to be found? In other words, to provide a reasonably defensible view of good practice we need to be able to answer the following questions:

Conceptual. Am I clear what practice I am talking about? Is my version of practice as balanced and as comprehensive as it ought to be, or am I operating on the basis of a rather limited view of practice, missing out some aspects and over-emphasizing others?

Value. Why do I value or believe in this particular practice? Can I defend my value-position in terms of basic ideas and principles about what it is to be educated? Are these sustainable values or are they merely blinkered prejudices? Do I value this practice not so much because I have good reasons but because I've always done it this way – do I like what I know rather than know what I like?

Pragmatic. Does the practice work for me? Why? Is it reasonable to assume that it will work for others? If not, should I be commending it in this form? What are the necessary classroom conditions for making this practice practicable?

Empirical. Do I actually have evidence that the practice I am commending or adopting promotes learning? What kind of evidence? My own experience? Research findings? Am I prepared to allow for the possibility that there might be contrary evidence? Am I prepared to allow for the empirical perspective or am I going to press my view of good practice regardless?

Political. (a) Am I expecting people to adopt this practice not so much on its merits but because I say they should? Am I taking refuge in my authority because I haven't really thought through the arguments for the practices I am pressing for (or against)? Am I pressing for (or opposing) particular practices for other than educational reasons? Is this, in effect, an abuse of my power? (b) Does the view of good practice *x* is expecting me to adopt have good arguments and evidence to sustain it? Or if I am simply expected to adopt the practice because *x* says so, what can I do about it? Assuming *x* to be reasonable, am I prepared to argue the toss? How far am I prepared to compromise my own judgements in order to gain approval and advancement? When I achieve similar eminence how will I use the power I shall then have to influence the practice of others?

GOOD PRACTICE: THE PRIMACY OF VALUES AND EVIDENCE

It will be evident that in very few instances can we satisfy all of these conditions when determining classroom strategies. Our own values may lead us in one direction; alternative values in another; practical constraints may make neither course of action in its pure form possible without modification; we may know of evidence which makes us doubtful about the wisdom of adopting the compromise position to which we find ourselves being steered; our decisions may be further shaped by external pressures or expectations; and so on.

Primary practice – any educational practice – requires us to come to terms with and reconcile competing values, pressures and constraints. If this is so of practice in general, it must also be the case, *a fortiori*, with practice we wish to define as 'good'. Far from being an absolute, therefore, as it has been treated for decades, good primary practice requires us to compromise. Beliefs and actions are rarely congruent with each other.

However, there has to be a qualitative difference between practice and good practice if the latter notion is not to become redundant. Or is it the case that good practice is no more than the best we can do in the circumstances? Is our quest for educational quality to run into the morass of relativism?

I believe not. Though I have presented and discussed the five considerations or dimensions as if they have equal weight, the pursuit of good practice has to move beyond a mere balancing of competing imperatives. There have to be superordinate reasons for preferring one course of action to another, which enable education to rise above the level of the merely pragmatic.

The five considerations, therefore, are not in any sense equivalent. Each set of questions is wholly different from all the others. However, it is possible to order and group them.

Thus, the conceptual questions stand apart from all the rest as being concerned with the scope and comprehensiveness of our definition of practice: before we consider judgements of quality we must be clear what it is that we are talking about.

Next, the political and pragmatic questions remind us of the pressures and constraints of the circumstances in which practice takes place. Such pressures and constraints cannot be ignored, and they may yield practice which is as likely to be bad as good.

There remain the value and empirical dimensions. In the end, it seems to me, close attention to these two is what distinguishes *good* practice from *mere* practice. Education is inherently about values: it reflects a vision of the kind of world we want our children to inherit; a vision of the kinds of people we hope they will become; a vision of what it is to be an educated person. Values, then, are central: whatever the other ingredients of good practice may be, they should enable a coherent and sustainable value-position to be pursued.

Yet values alone are not enough. They provide no recipe for action, only the broad criteria by which we judge what we do is right. The methods we choose must also be *effective* as means to our chosen ends. We need, therefore, knowledge of a range of practical strategies together with evidence about their viability and effectiveness, and especially about their capacity to deliver learning of the kind which accords with the goals we have set or adopted.

Some go so far as to argue that the good practice problem is resolved at a stroke by talking of 'effective' practice (or the effective teacher/effective school) instead. This is mere sleight of hand: effective in relation to what? In relation, of course, to a notion of what it is to be educated. Good practice, then, is intrinsically educative as well as operationally effective. Effectiveness as a criterion existing on its own is meaningless.

Equally, some argue that value and belief alone should guide our action. Quite apart from the dangers of assuming that we have a right to impose our beliefs on the children we teach, I suspect that it is the excessively single-minded pursuit of belief in primary education which has made some of its professional community blind to the limitations of some of the methods they have commended and adopted. Yet how often does one hear practices justified by statements which begin 'We believe. . . .'?

In any event, while beliefs and actions need to be consistent, they are not synonymous. Thus, a belief in cooperation and a distaste for competition might imply and seem to justify group work, but does the belief of itself make such a strategy effective as a tool for the acquisition of knowledge, understanding and skill? Or a belief in the unity of knowledge might imply and appear to justify an integrated curriculum, but does it follow that this is the most effective way for children to come to know? Or a belief in the importance of an enquiring mind might imply and justify asking questions but never providing answers, but does it follow that through this strategy children themselves will learn to question what they experience?

Classroom strategy can never be merely an enacting or an extension of educational belief. Yet this is exactly how good practice has frequently been defined in primary education. First work out your 'philosophy', then construct your practice to fit it: if the philosophy is right, the practice will be sound. In this version of good practice, faith alone provides the justification and evidence becomes irrelevant. As one of our earlier-quoted respondents retorted: 'I don't care what the ILEA research shows: the integrated day is right for me and right for my children.'

We are now in a position to sum up. Figure 5.2 represented good practice as existing at the intersection of the five considerations and as a matter of reconciling competing imperatives. I have now suggested that this approach does not take sufficient note of what the 'good' in 'good practice' might dictate, and that although all the considerations are important, they are not equivalent. The pursuit of good practice sets the considerations in a hierarchical relationship with ethical and empirical questions pre-eminent, and with both dependent on a prior conceptualization of the nature of educational practice itself. This alternative relationship is shown in Figure 5.3.

Using this framework, we can see fairly readily the extent to which the various protagonists in primary education may pursue very different versions of quality, each of them in their own way somewhat restricted. Indeed, it is instructive visually to locate on the framework typical prescriptive statements about what counts as quality in primary education from different sources – from, say, a politician, an administrator, an adviser,

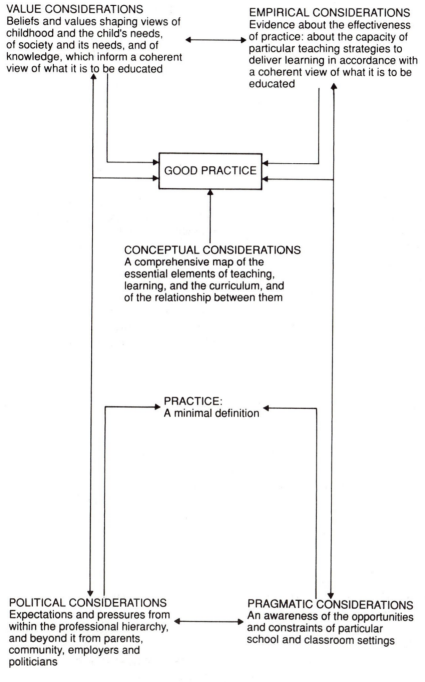

VALUE CONSIDERATIONS
Beliefs and values shaping views of
childhood and the child's needs,
of society and its needs, and of
knowledge, which inform a coherent
view of what it is to be educated

EMPIRICAL CONSIDERATIONS
Evidence about the effectiveness
of practice: about the capacity of
particular teaching strategies to
deliver learning in accordance with
a coherent view of what it is to be
educated

GOOD PRACTICE

CONCEPTUAL CONSIDERATIONS
A comprehensive map of the
essential elements of teaching,
learning, and the curriculum, and
of the relationship between them

PRACTICE:
A minimal definition

POLITICAL CONSIDERATIONS
Expectations and pressures from
within the professional hierarchy,
and beyond it from parents,
community, employers and
politicians

PRAGMATIC CONSIDERATIONS
An awareness of the opportunities
and constraints of particular
school and classroom settings

Figure 5.3 What is good practice? Beyond relativism

a teacher educator, a head, a teacher, a parent, a child – and note the different kinds of incompleteness which each reveals.

For some, especially at present, pragmatic considerations are all-important; but the proper concern with operational viability can become a distorting lens through which the whole educational enterprise is reduced to the question 'Does it work?' and the rest is dismissed as 'mere theory'. In a country notably unimpressed by intellectual endeavour, the stance has considerable popular appeal.

On the other hand, there are contexts in which the 'mere theory' charge is amply justified as the analysis of practice spirals upwards into the stratosphere of conceptual or ethical debate but never addresses pragmatic and empirical questions.

The pragmatic preoccupation tends to be shared by politicians, whose powerful value-orientations may be offered to a more or less gullible electorate as 'plain common sense'. The alliance of political and pragmatic calculations, however, yields a somewhat minimalist version of good practice; also a dangerous one, since the only partly explicated values can then be imposed on child, teacher and parent alike.

Or again, the researcher's proper preoccupation with the effectiveness of a teaching strategy in terms of learning outcomes may result in a counsel of perfection which no teacher can possibly expect to emulate because it takes so little account of the particular context of constraints and opportunities within which he or she has to work.

Finally, the prevailing culture of primary education, as we have seen, tends to demonstrate its particular bias towards a combination of no-nonsense pragmatism and high-sounding belief, with, necessarily, a weather eye open to two kinds of political pressure – from governments and from the professional hierarchy of primary education itself.

Similarly, we can apply the analysis not just to constituencies of opinion but to the practices themselves, and show how challenging the reconciliation of the various considerations becomes.

Consider, for example, the laudable commitment to individualized learning, never easily reconciled with the reality of large classes, and so often frustrating the very diagnosis it claims to promote by forcing the teacher into a crisis management mode.

Or consider curriculum integration and the tensions between powerful holistic and anti-subject values, the legal requirement that subjects be delivered in the classroom, the empirical evidence that, covertly or otherwise, they are there anyway, yet the pragmatic problem that without some degree of integration the National curriculum (in its early days at least) is undeliverable in the time available.

Or consider the collaborative ethic, its manifestation in group work, the empirical evidence that such group work is not particularly collaborative and may well frustrate the individual learning tasks of which much primary teaching is constituted, the organizational challenges it poses, yet at the same time the pragmatic counter-argument that the only way a teacher stands a chance of delivering a whole curriculum to a large class is through group work.

Or take the curiously contradictory notion of the integrated day, in which the fact that different areas of the curriculum are pursued simultaneously is taken to demonstrate that they are integrated, which self-evidently they are not, and in which the holistic intentions can give way to a much more serious fragmentation of teacher-time, energy and attention.

Good primary practice, like education itself, is as much an aspiration as an achievement; but at least we can try to become clearer about what it is we aspire to, and why; and in confronting the various considerations which bear upon classroom practice we can inject a greater degree of honesty and realism into professional discourse and thereby make the gap between achievement and aspiration a diminishing one. Moreover, thus armed we may be able to counter the journalistic and political hijacking of the debate about pedagogy rather more convincingly than we have hitherto.

NOTE

1 Leeds City Council initiated a Primary Needs Programme (PNP) in 1985 and commissioned an independent evaluation of the programme. This evaluation was conducted by a team at Leeds University directed by the chapter author Robin Alexander.

REFERENCES

Alexander, R. J. (1989) 'Core subjects and autumn leaves: the National Curriculum and the languages of primary education', *Education 3–13*, 17(1).
—— (1992) 'The problem of good primary practice', in R. Alexander *Policy and Practice in the Primary Curriculum*, London: Routledge.
(CACE) (1967) *Children and their Primary Schools* (Plowden Report), London: HMSO.
DES (1987) Primary Schools: Some Aspects of Good Practice, London: HMSO.
—— (1991a) *Standards in Education 1989–90: The Annual Report of HM Senior Chief Inspector of Schools*, London: HMSO.
—— (1991b) Bishop Grosseteste College: A Report by HMI, London: DES.
NCC (1989) *Curriculum Guidance 1: A Framework for the Primary Curriculum*, York: NCC.
SEAC (1991) *School Assessment Folder*, London: SEAC.

Part II

English: literacy practices in the primary classroom

Chapter 6

Introduction

Jill Bourne

> How comfortable we are in our specialised manuscript and print litera-
> cies, with our preferred texts and our certainty as we approach them.
> Reading, did I hear you say? Well, its just reading.
>
> (Meek, 1992: 227)

This part of the Reader focuses on the social practices of the primary
classroom. It draws its examples from the teaching of the 'basic skills' of
reading and writing: literacy as it occurs within the curriculum. But first,
what does it mean to be literate?

> A person is literate when he [sic] has acquired the essential knowledge
> and skills which enable him to engage in all those activities in which lit-
> eracy is required for effective functioning in his group and community,
> and whose attainments in reading, writing and arithmetic make it possi-
> ble for him to continue to use these skills towards his own and the com-
> munity's development.
>
> (UNESCO, quoted in Oxenham, 1980: 87)

The UNESCO definition suggests that there is not simply one single
form of literacy but that, just as there are multiple contexts in which
written texts in some form or another play a part, so there are multiple
literacies. This definition is *functional*: it focuses on what a person *does*
with written texts within the society, recognizing that this may be different
depending on the text and context. The definition is also *relative*,
recognizing that in different societies there are different literacy demands
made upon different people depending on the historical and political
structure of that society. It indicates that there is not one single 'cut off'
point where one can say someone can read or write effectively, but that
literacy is a continuum, with a range of levels of functioning from the most
simple to the most sophisticated. Such a definition requires an examination of the sorts of reading and writing practices that are customary and
that are valued in each society, and the access to them that different groups
are given.

Such definitions of literacy extend the focus of study from the mental plane, examining the cognitive strategies for processing text, to the plane of social activity: from the isolated individual reader or writer to social inter-action *between* people.

In this part we have chosen five chapters which encourage the reader to look critically at orthodoxies in primary practice, and which draw on a range of contexts, including classrooms in the UK, USA and Australia. The areas examined are commonplace: reading and writing events in school and at home, the 'hearing of reading', the debate around the role of standard English in the curriculum, the setting of a writing task and the planning of work in English across subject areas. In each of the chapters the aim is 'to make the familiar strange': to stand back and reflect on primary practice in order to reveal the ways of thinking about English and literacy that underlie routine classroom events.

The chapter by Street and Street explores reading and writing as it took place in one particular school context. It situates such 'schooled literacy' practices as co-existing among a variety of unschooled, informal literacies, and considers how far home and school should be seen as separate domains of literacy, concluding that for some middle-class children, parents have taken on a teacher's role, making the home context very similar to that of the school. In the next chapter, Eve Gregory also looks at the differential transmission of literacy. She examines in detail what goes on in specific 'hearing reading' episodes between teachers and children, and discusses how such events can construct different understandings about what reading is all about for different children. The third chapter focuses on the concepts of standard English and grammar. Bourne and Cameron argue that definitions of literacy and policies for English teaching are never politically neutral, and attempt to locate current debates within their historical and ideological context. The final two chapters in this part examine writing events in the classroom. In a highly edited version of her original paper, we show how Christie uses a transcription of teacher talk with a class to investigate the role and influence of the teacher in setting up expectations and standards for a writing task, which are then reflected in the shape of the written texts the children produce. While Christie describes an example of an approach which limits children's achievements, Derewianka moves the discussion forward by describing and analysing the way in which one teacher went about planning and teaching literacy through an approach which focused explicitly on extending the children's writing range for educational purposes.

REFERENCES

Meek, M.S. (1992) *New Readings: Contributions to the Understanding of Literacy*, London: A & C Black.
Oxenham, J. (1980) *Literacy*, London: Routledge & Kegan Paul.

Chapter 7

The schooling of literacy

Joanna C. Street and Brian V. Street

The meanings and uses of literacy are deeply embedded in community values and practices, yet they tend to be associated in many accounts simply with schooling and pedagogy. Recent approaches to literacy, however, have come to focus upon the varied social and cultural meanings of the concept and its role in power relations in contemporary society (Cook-Gumperz, 1986; Heath, 1985). Literacy is not a given, a simple set of technical skills necessary for a range of educational competencies, as much of the earlier literature would suggest. Literacy practices are neither neutral nor simply a matter of educational concern: they are varied and contentious and imbued with ideology. There are different literacies related to different social and cultural contexts rather than a single Literacy that is the same everywhere (Street, 1985). This raises the question of how it is that one particular variety has come to be taken as the only literacy. Among all of the different literacies practiced in the community, the home, and the workplace, how is it that the variety associated with schooling has come to be the defining type, not only to set the standard for other varieties but to marginalize them, to rule them off the agenda of literacy debate? Nonschool literacies have come to be seen as inferior attempts at the real thing, to be compensated for by enhanced schooling.

We are interested in exploring the ways in which, both at home and at school, dominant conceptions of literacy are constructed and reproduced in such a way as to marginalize alternatives and, we would suggest, to control key aspects of language and thought. We hypothesize that the mechanism through which meanings and uses of 'literacy' take on this role is the 'pedogogization' of literacy. By this we mean that literacy has become associated with educational notions of Teaching and Learning and with what teachers and pupils do in schools, at the expense of the many other uses and meanings of literacy evident from the comparative ethnographic literature. We use *pedagogy* not in the narrow sense of specific skills and tricks of the trade used by teachers but in the broader sense of institution-alized processes of teaching and learning, usually associated with the school but increasingly identified in home practices associated with reading and writing. Whether we are observing parent–child interactions, the development of educational toys and 'software' in the home, or the procedures associated with classroom learning, *pedagogy* in this sense has taken on the character of an ideological force controlling social relations in general and conceptions of reading and writing in particular . . .

LITERACY WITHOUT SCHOOLING

We begin by establishing what is meant by the notion of different 'literacies' and of conceptualizing literacy outside schooling and pedagogy. Literacy is so embedded within these institutions in contemporary society that it is sometimes difficult for us to disengage and recognize that, for most of history and in great sections of contemporary society, literacy practices remain embedded in other social institutions. While Ogbu's definition of *literacy* as 'synonymous with academic performance', 'the ability to read and write and compute in the form taught and expected in formal education' (Ogbu, 1990), would probably receive general agreement in contemporary society, it is put into perspective by a recent account by Reid (1988, p. 218) of literacy in pre-sixteenth-century South East Asia:

> The old Indonesian ka-ga-nga alphabet . . . was taught in no school and had no value either vocationally or in reading any established or secular literature. The explanation for its persistence was the local custom of *manjan*, a courting game whereby young men and women would gather in the evenings and the youths would fling suggestive quatrains written in the old script to the young women they fancied.

Many cultures in this region adopted writing systems originally introduced from India, and 'women took up writing as actively as men, to use in exchanging notes and recording debts and other female matters which were in the domestic domain' (Reid, 1988, p. 218). . . . The widespread use of literacy by women, in non-educational contexts prior to the introduction of Western schooled literacy, is becoming attested for a range of times and places: Yin-yee ko (1989), for instance, describes how, in seventeenth-century China, educated middle-class women wrote poetry as a means of constructing a private female culture against the homogenizing male character of late Imperial Chinese culture. Mickulecky (1985, p. 2) records the uses of literacy by women from the rising gentry in fifteenth-century England to write letters 'concerned with business affairs of the family, personal intrigues, duty and death'. . . . The invisibility of women's literacy (along with much of their social activity) is a product not only of patriarchal society but also of dominant definitions and concepts of literacy.

Similarly, the literacies of non-European peoples have been ignored by developers bringing Western institutions and schooling to different parts of the world. Only recently has it been recognized that many writing systems have been developed outside of the Western context. . . . More significant for the current argument has been the variety of "literacies' that are being documented by ethnographers, in which a script brought by outsiders such as missionaries or teachers has been 'taken hold of' by local people (Kulick and Stroud, 1991) and adapted to indigenous meanings and uses. In the village in New Guinea that Kulick and Stroud studied, missionary literacy was incorporated into local conventions of language use rather than being used for the purposes intended by teachers. Skills developed in speech-making, involving the avoidance of self-assertion or of putting others down, were also prominent in the ways that letters came to be written. As literacy is added to the rich communicative repertoire that already exists in the receiving societies, they adapt and amend it to local meanings, concepts of identity, and epistemologies: as Kulick and Stroud express it, the question is not what 'impact' literacy has on people but how people affect literacy. . . . Much, then, of what goes with schooled literacy turns out to be the product of Western assumptions about school- ing, power, and knowledge rather than being necessarily intrinsic to literacy itself. The role played by developmental perspectives in schooling, for instance, means that the acquisition of literacy becomes isomorphic with the child's development of specific social identities and positions: their power in society becomes associated with the kind and level of literacy they have acquired.

These examples of the relationship of variations in literacy to relative power and knowledge are not confined to the 'Third World' or to techno- logically simpler societies: recent ethnographies of literacy in the United States provide similar evidence of the rich varieties of literacy outside of school and formal learning processes and their significance for people's identities and positions in society. . . .

. . . Fishman's account [1991] of Amish literacy demonstrates the close association of literacy practices with identity, authority, and concepts of knowledge that are not necessarily those of schooled literacy. When she arrived in the community, she asked the girls of the family she was staying with to keep 'dialogue journals' as a way of observing their literacy practices and establishing communication with them. But they refused, and it later became obvious that their conceptions of literacy were at variance with those that underlie the use of such journals. Amish communicative con- ventions require an 'other-centredness' that involves downplaying the self and focusing on the community. As in the New Guinea case, self-assertive- ness was considered improper, and this became reflected in written conven- tions as these were added to the communicative repertoire: for the Amish girls to write of their own experience and feelings would be wrong – a challenge to Amish conceptions of identity and knowledge. The conven- tions associated with current writing practices and pedagogy in American schooling are not simply matters of technique and of neutral learning skills but may be associated with deep levels of cultural meaning and belief: other literacies exist alongside the dominant, school-oriented versions . . .

Literacy, then, need not be associated with schooling or with pedagogy: Ogbu's definition with which we began is inappropriate if we are to understand the full and rich meanings of literacy practices in contemporary society. Research needs, instead, to begin from a more comparative, more ethnographically based conception of literacy as the *social* practices of reading and writing and to eschew value judgements about the relative superiority of schooled literacy over other literacies.

LITERACY IN THE COMMUNITY AND IN THE SCHOOL

The school on which we focused [in a small pilot project] was set in an upper-middle-class suburb of a major American city that suffered from gross poverty, social inequality, and inner-city decline. Many of those who lived in this suburb had fled there to avoid these problems. The school was one of the few state schools that enjoyed a high reputation in middle-class and professional circles, and many families made considerable financial efforts to buy themselves into the area. House prices were high, and, in most families, both partners were obliged to work to meet mortgage costs and so on. They would frequently leave for work in the city early in the morning, leaving their children at the day-care centre at the school, and returning in the evening to pick the children up from the centre, which remained open well after school closing time. The school had classes from first grade through fifth with about 20 pupils per class and two or three classes in each year. We observed and taped classroom practices, in the first and fifth grades, each of us spending three mornings or afternoons in each class. We also taped discussion sessions with each of the teachers in which we asked about their conceptions of literacy. Outside of the school, we conducted interviews with half a dozen parents of children who attended the school and the classes we were observing, asked them to keep a 'Literacy Diary' by recording literacy events in their homes, and asked some families to tape-record the speech around these events. This focus upon literacy in middle-class, suburban homes is an aspect of literacy in the 'community' that has not received much research attention. Shirley Brice Heath's *Ways with Words* (1985), for instance, makes reference to it but she does not research it in any detail, appearing to assume that we all know what middle-class life and literacy are like.

We began the project by assuming a distinction between literacy practices in the community and in the school. We wanted to explore the ways in which the particular variety of literacy that we labelled 'school literacy' comes to dominate other forms of literacy in contemporary society. Our experience forced us to refine these ideas, particularly those regarding home and school literacies, and to recognize that the extent of similarity between practices of literacy in the community, in the home, and in the school make our earlier dichotomy unhelpful. Underlying literacy in all of these contexts is a common thread, derived from wider cultural and ideological processes. We focus here on one particular aspect of this common thread, the processes of pedagogization.

PROCESSES OF PEDAGOGIZATION

We found that one way of answering our questions about the pedagogization of literacy was to break it down into a number of specific processes and then to examine these processes in both home and school. In this chapter, we are particularly concerned with the processes that help construct an 'autonomous' model of literacy – in which many individuals, often against their own experience, come to conceptualize literacy as a separate, reified set of 'neutral' competencies, autonomous of social context – and with the procedures and social roles through which this model of literacy is disseminated and internalized.

The construction and internalization of the autonomous model of literacy is achieved by a number of means, some of which we will briefly attempt to illustrate from our data: the distancing of language from subjects – the ways in which language is treated as though it were a thing, distanced from both teacher and learner and imposing on them external rules and requirements as though they were but passive recipients; 'metalinguistic' usages – the ways in which the social processes of reading and writing are referred to and lexicalized within a pedagogic voice as though they were independent and neutral competencies rather than laden with significance for power relations and ideology; 'privileging' – the ways in which reading and writing are given status vis-à-vis oral discourse as though the medium were intrinsically superior and, therefore, those who acquired it would also become superior; and 'philosophy of language' – the setting of units and boundaries for elements of language use as though they were neutral, thereby disguising the ideological source of what are in fact social constructions, frequently associated with ideas about logic, scientific mentality, and so on.

Among the institutional processes that contribute to the construction and internalization of the pedagogic voice in school, we focus on 'space labelling' and 'procedures'. The institutionalization of a particular model of literacy operates not only through particular forms of speech and texts but in the physical and institutional space that is separated from 'everyday' space for purposes of teaching and learning and that derives from wider social and ideological constructions of the social and built world. 'Procedures' represent the way in which rules for the engagement of participants as teachers and learners are continuously asserted and reinforced within practices supposedly to do simply with using and talking about literacy:

while apparently simply giving instructions about handling a text, for instance, teachers and parents are also embedding relations of hierarchy, authority, and control.

A 'mix' of oral and literate media, sometimes referred to as an 'oral–literate' continuum, is to be observed in all of these processes: participants employ both oral and literate discursive strategies as they interact, in both home and school. But this interactive aspect of literacy and orality tends, within actual practice, to be disguised behind prescriptions and linguistic conventions that represent the linguistic modes as entirely separate, as though there were a 'great divide' between orality and literacy. This conception of literacy appears to be one of the major means whereby an autonomous model of literacy is internalized and disseminated in contemporary society. . . .

OBJECTIFYING LANGUAGE

Much classroom discourse turns upon explicit attention to language and what it means for children. The contemporary literature on learning to read places great emphasis on the achievement of metalinguistic awareness and frequently presumes that the development of this highly valued ability is associated with the acquisition of literacy. . . . Self-awareness about language and the development of specific terms for describing it are seen as part of cognitive development, leading to critical thought, detachment, and objectivity, and it is taken as self-evident that the writing down of language facilities these processes. . . . Given the powerful pressure in favour of this model of language within teacher training institutions in both the United Kingdom and the United States, it is not surprising to find it underpinning much classroom practice. However, while recognizing the significance of metalinguistic awareness, we would reject the claim that it is peculiarly associated with literacy and also question the tendency to focus on certain syntactical and formal features of language at the expense of other aspects as though language awareness were a matter of specific grammatical terminology.

In the classroom we observed, teachers appeared to treat language as though it were something outside both the students and themselves, as though it had autonomous, non-social qualities that imposed themselves upon its users. The language of instruction presupposed and helped to construct distance between children and their language. Writing is one way of creating that distance – putting it on the blackboard serves as one technique for enabling children to see and objectify that process of learning. Once the language is on the board, on the worksheet, in the book, and so on, it becomes a separate problem for the teacher and children to work on together. In the sessions we observed, the teacher made an effort to get the children to identify with her as she worked out a problem in grammar or expression, as though they were commonly struggling against an outside authority to which they were both subject. The aim was to get children to follow her own work processes and mimic them. There was little discussion of the meaning of language, of alternative interpretations of texts, or of how the teacher arrived at her sense of what they meant. This was so even after library reading: views might be elicited before reading but responses were not called for afterward. Similarly, book reports, in which students were asked to read a book and then present orally a structured report on it to the whole class, took on a ritualized and nonsemantic character in which the aim appeared to be to develop schooled language rather than to actually discuss the books. In contexts such as these, it would seem, the final object is to achieve mastery and authority over the text, whose meanings are not negotiable. The book reports are modelled on written language, as conceived within this subculture: planning, the use of topic sentences and paragraphing, and explicitness are carried over from how written language has been learned into spoken language. The school presentation of the text is, then, unproblematized regarding its meaning and content, focusing on form. Technical problems are set, to do with grammar and syntax, and solutions once given are assimilated to a general list of rules and prescriptions about the nature of language itself.

There were a number of ways in which this process operated collectively, so that the whole class was constructing a collective voice in ways that excluded exploration of the meanings of what was being uttered: the pledge of allegiance in which teacher and students chanted formulaic phrases together, certain question-and-answer sessions, some circle games. Similarly, diagnostic and evaluative tests were used as a way to create distance between the children and their own perception of their knowledge. The teacher identified with them and helped them through the process. This identification exacerbates the notion of the objective, neutral status of the text and reduces the role of speaker/reader to passive recipient rather than active negotiator of meaning. While the aims of language learning were spelled out in school documents as being based upon 'communication', the practice was frequently concerned with learning formalized uses of language and subjecting oral to written conventions.

We observed similar processes in the children's homes, although they did not necessarily carry over directly from school as we at first imagined. Parents in middle-class homes are indeed frequently concerned about structuring learning for their children in the ways legitimized by the school. Similarly, from our observations, it appeared that attention to children's school exercises played a dominant part in everyday life: book reports, in particular, could take over the weekend as parents helped their child to spot 'topic sentences', develop links, and work up endings for their presentation to the class on Monday morning. Project work could take the whole family to the local library, which would be filled with teams of family researchers scanning encyclopedias and the non fiction section for accounts of shells, electricity, fish, and so on. Acquisition of proper literacy was perceived as a 'problem' to be solved, a task to be accomplished: rules were set from outside and the child and parent were collaborators in responding to this hegemony. Tests were as much part of home practice as school.

From these practices, it at first appeared that home was simply dominated by school and that this would explain the pedagogization of literacy there. But the extent of the internalization of the pedagogic voice for literacy acquisition and dissemination suggests it is part of wider social and cultural currents. It is produced and reinforced through newspaper discussions on literacy, labelling on educational toys, political debates, and parental discourses. In our interviews with parents of the children whose classes we observed, we found an ambivalence toward the school as an institution but a ready adoption of the pedagogized view of literacy that we identified there. These parents did not always see the school as the source of value and legitimacy in this area; they were developing their pedagogic voice from other sources too.

A number of parents had formed a Parent's Information Committee (PIC) to put pressure on the school where they thought it was failing to develop the appropriate model of literacy. At these meetings, it appeared that parents, not teachers, were the guardians of proper literacy. An example of this activity was parents pressuring school to adopt 'Writing Process' approaches, and the PIC supported and lobbied for developments already taking place in the school district that involved in-service days on these ways of teaching literacy. Our findings suggest that the shift was not as radical as they believed because the same pedagogy underlay the focus on writing as process rather than as product. As Rudy (1989) demonstrated through research on Collaborative Learning of Writing in secondary classrooms in a nearby city, new approaches are frequently assimilated to traditional assumptions and ways of relating to students. We are not concerned here with evaluating these different approaches – collaborative, process-oriented writing instruction and traditional product-oriented writing instruction – but with demonstrating how both may be subsumed under the more general principle of the pedagogization of literacy. The reason the change from one to another is not always as significant as exponents of the different approaches would hope may be that they both persist in reducing reading and writing to particular social practices associated with 'learning', thereby missing the range of literacy practices associated with non-schooled purposes and concepts. In the classrooms we studied, the methods of teaching and learning associated with product-oriented teaching did not alter much as process approaches were introduced: literacy was still 'out there', an objective content to be taught through authority structures whereby pupils learned the proper roles and identities they were to carry into the wider world. . . .

Similarly, in their own homes, the parents were claiming authority to direct their children's learning and thereby challenging the sole dominance of the school while at the same time marginalizing the alternative literacies that children may have encountered in the context of home, peer group, and community in favour of a 'schooled' literacy. Homes were full of toys, games, and videos that were explicitly directed toward school achievement and readiness, but the definition of that achievement became as much the property of the parent as the teacher. The labels in which these toys and the like were packaged and the accompanying leaflets used academic language, frequently derived from psychological literature, to legitimize and reinforce their educational value, and some of this language had crept in to parents' discussions around literacy. . . .

A perception of literacy as the major source of Western supremacy, scientific achievement and so on lay behind the willingness to engage in specific literacy tasks. An 'autonomous' model of literacy was thus crucial to the commitment parents showed, which they also expected of their children. Home interest in the use of tests, concern with formal features of literacy and language, the treatment of language as an external force with rules and requirements to be learned, and the intertwining of conventions associated with literacy and the management of texts with assertions of authority and control, including the organization of other people's time and space – all of these features of home literacy practice indeed complement the uses of literacy apparent in the children's school. The source, however, may not be the school itself but derived from larger cultural and ideological currents that influence both home and school. Just as in the Amish example (Fishman, 1991), it may be more fruitful to focus on continuities between home culture and school culture rather than on the discontinuities with which much of the research has been concerned. To do so, we argue, requires us to theorize literacy practices differently – to develop not only ethnographies of home and school but also ethnographies of literacy, of the kind being attempted in this chapter.

SPACE LABELLING

In popular discourse, *the school* refers perhaps to the people who run or attend it, perhaps to the building in which it is situated that symbolizes its presence. But the school as an institution finds its main form of expression through a particular form of language, in evidence not only in the speech of teachers and the text of the written materials but in the classroom, on the walls, and in the stream of bureaucratic paperwork though which it constantly signifies and reproduces itself. The language of the teacher and of the text positions the subject (whether student or researcher), pins them to their seats, locates them in a socially and authoritatively constructed space. How this space is constructed is crucial to our understanding of the particular linguistic and literacy processes with which this chapter is concerned.

The main building of the school we were investigating is large and square and breathes public importance. It is part of a whole genre of public architecture representing the state. Above the doorway in large letters, embedded in the wall, as part of the permanent structure, are the words X Elementary School. Inside the school, space is designated by authority and authority is expressed in signs: rooms are numbered and labelled, they have designated functions that are likewise labelled. The first notice one sees as one enters the building is 'All visitors must report to the office'. When one enters the building, one is situating oneself physically inside a particular universe of signs. Within a classroom, the pictures and notices on the walls continue this process of situating the individual within a sign system. This is particularly evident in the first-grade classroom. The children sit at the centre of a system of codes through which their experience is to be transformed. It is as though the walls themselves were a filtering screen through which the world outside the school is transformed and translated into various discrete sets of analytic concepts: lists of numbers, the letters of the alphabet, shapes and colours, lists of measurements – all the devices by which the experience of the senses can be filtered and then transformed into discrete social and analytic concepts, tabulated, and measured. The five senses themselves dangle on separate little labels from a mobile. Time is filtered through a grid of days of the week, seasons, birthday charts, and clock faces. The birthday chart situates the child herself within this catalogue of time, just as she is situated within space. The classroom's four walls are labelled 'south', 'east', 'north', and 'west', right and left hang on the wall – the room is framed as a signifying space with the child at the centre, making sense of things. These spatial categories only make sense when oriented to the child at the centre of the classroom, and they indicate in a very powerful way the contract between the individual and the institution that underpins the ideology of language within the school. This process of writing down and labelling experiences incorporates them into a visual system that is external to the child. The organization of the visual environment itself helps to construct and provide a model of the child's relationship to language and to the written word. The walls of the classroom become the walls of the world. The maps of the United States and the world on the wall at the front of the classroom indicate the system of signs through which that world may be attained.

PROCEDURES

Procedures for organizing classroom time, work practices, and literacy materials dominate the classroom and form a major part of the pedagogic voice. One teacher told her students explicitly that they had to speak differently in class: 'Now you are in school, use your inside school voice'. Thereby school is separated from other times and places, and familiar everyday processes of speaking, reading, and writing are given a distinct character and a special authority. A session is divided into phases by means of linguistic markers that have illocutionary force in actually constructing the separate times and spaces. The teacher continually interrupts students' work with statements about where the class are in her time frame and what to do next: 'Journals now: write how the group work went'; 'close your scripts up, all the pages inside. You're going to be putting them inside'; 'the first thing you're going to do when everyone gets back is go over the homework so this would be a marvellous time to get it finished'; 'get out last night's reading assignment'; 'break now, have a snack now'. 'Now we're running overtime. Quick, reading groups. Get your maths papers out'. 'We'll finish now. A new book on Monday'. These interjections are not simply practical features of classroom activity, although they do have specific surface functions in organizing the day where only one teacher takes a class right through. They also, however, help to define what literacy is: they define the organizations of texts, papers, and reading and writing materials as the organization of cultural time and space. While they appear to be teaching strategies, they in fact set the boundaries of literacy itself and assert its place within a culturally defined authority structure. The teacher has the authority to bound time and space for the students, and this authority reinforces her control over the definition and bounding of linguistic practices: literacy is placed in relation both to oral discourse and to specific material practices with which it becomes entwined and defined.

In the same voice as she marks phases of time during the day, the teacher sets out procedures for this material practice of literacy: 'When you've finished, put all the papers in the folder I gave you. You're going to be responsible for finding all the things when we're going through it. That's why you have the folder'; 'If you want to write the sentences on lined paper, then take some from your book'. 'Turn over on the back of the paper'. The ending of a session is defined by a combination of linguistic markers and literacy practices: 'Put your scripts in a folder. You may fold it in half once to get it in'.

Oral procedures for finding their way around a written text also combine teacher authority over texts with a 'mix' of oral and written conventions that is not explicitly addressed. It is as though the words were not being spoken but assimilated to the written form:

TEACHER: Top of page 62. What does C's mother do about that? . . .
           Let's look at page 66 now. I'm sorry, page 64. Read to me
           the third sentence. That's the third sentence not the third
           line. How can you find a paragraph? It starts in.
STUDENT: It starts with a capital letter.

TEACHER: Yes, but it also starts in. . . . Can you tell me the last word of the sentence? What was that word? Page 59 now. So D. was going home . . . what was the friend's name? . . . the last two lines tell you. Page 60 now. Read what Steve says . . . Bob says that.

Much of this discourse depends upon shared assumptions about the visual perception of a text, its layout and organization – a paragraph 'starts in', page numbers mark the physical boundaries of written material, 'sentences' are visual presences whose opening and closing words can be easily identified (unlike in much oral discourse). The oral representation of the materiality of the written medium becomes a means of organizing actual social relations in the classroom. . . .

HOMOGENIZATION OR VARIATION?

There is not space here to extend the analysis in this degree of detail of literacy practices in the home, although our experience was that there were many similarities, particularly in the link between literacy and linguistic practices, on the one hand, and the organization of time and space, on the other. A key question for future research in both contexts is how the assertion of authority and the allocation of participants to specific roles and relationships are inscribed within particular literacy events and practices. At first, this may lead us to conclude that the conception of literacy associated with schooling and pedagogy, in particular the emphasis on Teaching and Learning, is transforming the rich variety of literacy practices evident in community literacies into a single, homogenized practice. Mothers and children in the home adopt the roles of teachers and learners; a toy is treated not as a source of 'play', to be used according to the cultural conventions associated with leisure, relaxation, childhood, and so on, but instead is located within a framework of teaching and learning, scaffolding the child to future academic achievement; reading a story aloud is transformed by the pedagogic voice from a context of narrative, character, and morality to a prescribed role for the listening child in the achievement of school 'readiness'.

However, as ethnographies of literacy in the community proliferate, a more complex picture may emerge, and we expect to find forms of resistance and alternative literacies alongside 'schooled' literacy. . . .

The new ethnographies of literacy tell us that people can lead full lives without the kinds of literacy assumed in educational and other circles. The reconceptualization of literacy suggested there involves moving away from the dominant view of literacy as having distinctive 'autonomous' characteristics associated intrinsically with schooling and pedagogy. It also entails a shift away from the characterization of the literate person as intrinsically civilized, detached, logical, and so on in contrast with 'illiterates' or those who communicate mainly through oral channels. If the qualities of logic, detachment, abstraction conventionally associated with the acquisition of literacy turn out to be available in oral discourse, . . . or rather in some mix of channels that does not require the conventions and rules usually associated with literacy-in-itself, as we have been suggesting here, then literacy loses some of the status and mystification that currently underpin the investment of vast resources in both teaching and measuring it. . . .

CONCLUSION

We have suggested that research in this area should not focus on the school in isolation but on the conceptualization of literacy in the 'community'. In rethinking concepts of literacy associated with pedagogization, particularly focused around the language of literacy, procedures for its dissemination, and the construction of an autonomous model of literacy, we have come to recognize how they derive not so much from the school itself as from wider cultural and ideological patterns. Within school, the association of literacy acquisition with the child's development of specific social identities and positions; the privileging of written over oral language; the interpretation of 'metalinguistic' awareness in terms of specific literacy practices and grammatical terminology; and the neutralizing and objectification of language that disguises its social and ideological character – all must be understood as essentially *social* processes: they contribute to the construction of a particular kind of citizen, a particular kind of identity, and a particular concept of the nation. The community in its wider sense, including the 'nation' itself, participates in these ideological constructions through processes that are equally represented as politically neutral, simply educational matters.

Parents, whether helping their children with school tasks or challenging school control of literacy through local lobbies, reinforce the association of literacy with learning and pedagogy; the construction and filling of the home space with literacy materials are associated with specific theories of learning; the kinds of literacy children might be acquiring from peer groups and the community are marginalized against the standard of schooled literacy. This reinforcement of schooled literacy in the community contributes, alongside that of the school itself, to the construction of identity and personhood in the modern nation-state. The home and community practices feed back in turn into school practice, helping to assert and refashion there too the pedagogization of literacy. These, then, are the characteristic social processes and values through which literacy is construed and disseminated in mainstream America today, very different processes and values than those evident from the ethnographies of literacy currently emerging from research in the Third World, in the history of America, and in sections of contemporary American society itself. If we wish to understand the nature and meanings of literacy in our lives, then, we need more research that focuses on literacy in the community – in its broadest sense – and on the ideological rather than the educational implications of the communicative practices in which it is embedded.

REFERENCES

Cook-Gumperz, J. (1986) *The Social Construction of Literacy*, Cambridge: Cambridge University Press.

Fishman, A. (1991) 'Because this is who we are: Writing in the Amish community'. In D. Barton and R. Ivanič (eds), *Writing in the Community*, London: Sage, pp. 14–37.

Heath, S.B. (1985) *Ways with Words*, Cambridge: Cambridge University Press.

Kulick, D. and Stroud, C. (1991) 'Conceptions and uses of literacy in a Papua New Guinea village' in B. Street (ed.), *Cross-Cultural Approaches to Literacy*, Cambridge: Cambridge University Press.

Mickulecky, B. (1985) 'The Paston letters: An example of literacy in the 15th century'. Unpublished manuscript.

Ogbu, J. (1990) 'Cultural mode, identity and literacy', in J.W. Stigler (ed.), *Cultural Psychology*, Cambridge: Cambridge University Press.

Reid, A. (1988) *South East Asia in the Age of Commerce: 1450–1680: Vol. 1. The Lands Below the Winds*, New Haven, CT: Yale University Press.

Rudy, M. (1989) 'The dynamics of collaborative learning of writing (CLW) in secondary classrooms: Control or cooperation?' Unpublished doctoral dissertation, University of Pennsylvania (UMI Dissertation Information Services).

Street, B. (1985) *Literacy in Theory and Practice*, Cambridge: Cambridge University Press.

—— (1993) (ed.) *Cross-cultural Approaches to Literacy*, Cambridge: Cambridge University Press.

Yin-yee Ko, D. (1989) 'Toward a social history of women in seventeenth century China'. Unpublished doctoral dissertation, Stanford University.

Chapter 8

What counts as reading in this class? Children's views

Eve Gregory

Gillian is sharing a simple picture book with her teacher. It is a story she knows well from class shared-reading sessions. Here, the children are apprenticed to the teacher as skilled practitioner, listening first, then gradually taking over the role of reader themselves:

GILLIAN: I can't even read yet. You read it and I'll listen to yer.
TEACHER: We'll read it together.
               'If you were a bird . . .'
GILLIAN: I can't do it. I can't even see the words.

Why has five-year-old Gillian already decided that she cannot read? she has not yet even been asked to decode individual words. Her Bangladeshi class-mate, Tajul, responds very differently. He brings numerous stories from the book-corner to share with his teacher and he actually reads some of them word for word. Yet he is still unable to speak more than a few phrases of English. Gillian, on the other hand, speaks English fluently, is an interesting conversation partner and easily retells her own life stories. Neither child comes from a bookish or school-oriented home. Neither attended nursery school. How might the very different progress of children from non-school-oriented homes be accounted for as they begin reading in school? This chapter focuses on this apparent puzzle and paradox and offers one approach to explaining it.

Children like Gillian and Tajul are often called exceptional. Yet most classes have a number of exceptions. They puzzle teachers because they defy paradigms of what beginning reading entails. These paradigms are largely informed by linguistic and psycholinguistic theories which centre on the role of language, on the story or text or book, in learning to read. Thus, children need to bring experience of language, life and culture as well as a familiarity with stories and books to enable them to predict a text. Within this frame, the Gillians and Tajuls escape our expectations and remain a paradox.

But if we were to step outside these paradigms, might the reading task look somewhat different? In this chapter I shall argue that a psychosemiotic approach to beginning reading in school provides some explanation for what appears to be paradoxical. This approach shifts the emphasis from the language and text of linguistic theories to the role of the classroom as a cultural site and the children's cognitive and linguistic interpretation of it. What follows is a brief outline of the approach I propose. . . .

Within a psychosemiotic framework the shared reading lesson is viewed as an ideological construct where events are played out. Thus, children need to learn to position themselves in three interlocking contexts:

1   The situational context: a positioning within a context-specific discourse in a social and cultural site and the interpersonal relationships attached to it. Here, the site is the classroom and the relationships that of teacher and pupil. The focus is on the features and the rules of the site itself.
2   The interpretational context or the context of the mind: a positioning within the appropriate mental frame of knowledge which is relevant to the situation. Here, the frame of knowledge in question is what counts as reading in the minds of the teacher and pupils. The focus is on the mental processes of individuals within the site.
3   The textual context: a positioning within the text and the actual language and words or code it is expressed in. Here, the texts are the classroom story books. The focus is on the language, story and book as a specific site within the wider frame of the shared-reading lesson in school.

These layers or contexts can be exemplified through the word 'reading' itself. Reading is the code (textual context) conjuring up a mental image or interpretation (interpretational level) within the cultural site and the corresponding relationships within the school (situational context). Thus, taking a psychosemiotic approach to learning to read looks like this: beginning reading in school involves learning to position oneself as a reader within the context of the classroom as an institutional site and the corresponding relationships within it, internalizing and adopting the appropriate frame of knowledge which counts as reading within the site and learning to express this in terms of a linguistic response to the text offered. These linguistic expressions I term a 'code' to signify their exclusive nature.

The following sections show how different children are able to position themselves in these contexts and suggest why this might be. I then offer reasons why a demystification (Freire and Macedo, 1987), in the sense of access to the code, might be easier for some bilingual children from non-school-oriented homes than for their monolingual peers. Examples are drawn from a corpus of data collected over two years in an urban multilingual classroom. How do each of the above contexts fit into linguistic paradigms on learning to read? . . . I shall briefly examine how each of the above contexts is viewed in [linguistic] studies, before going on to introduce the psychosemiotic approach proposed.

The situational context

Within linguistic theory on beginning reading the cultural site for early acculturation into stories and books is usually assumed to be the home environment. Within this environment it is axiomatic that there is a shared cultural context between care-giver and child. Story-reading takes place as a collaborative enterprise. This often takes the form of the bed-time story, where the adult is able to link the culture of the child with events in the text and relate the story to real-life experiences and vice versa. . . . Young children learning to position themselves in the situational context model themselves on the adult as skilled practitioner. They are apprenticed, but not as subservient workers to a stranger, consciously working to master the separate skills of a trade. Rather, the apprenticeship takes place unconsciously and naturally, by immersion. The social relationship between the participants is one of equal status, where the adult acts as facilitator.

Importantly, the social site itself and the relationships within it are unproblematic. Child and adult share cultural values and expectations mediated by and through the story and the book. There are no barriers between the text and the participants' interpretation of it. The shared experience of the text is central, and everything radiates from it.

Crucially, I suggest, many studies imply that the shared interpretation of the social site, equality of relationship and collaboration between participants can be transplanted from home to school without changes necessarily taking place. . . . Here is the crux of the difference between linguistic studies and the psychosemiotic approach proposed.

The interpretational context

Through modelling themselves on the adult within a shared cultural context, children learn a specific interpretation of reading. Thus, reading is not simply the labelling of packages in a supermarket or a magazine; it belongs to stories and books, '. . . when my baby brother's hands are big enough to hold a book, he'll be able to read', (Scollon and Scollon, 1981).

The textual context

Within the shared interpretation of reading, children learn both how to position themselves in the words of the text and to fictionalize themselves by seeing themselves as a third person in relation to the text and the characters within it. . . . They see how life experiences can be brought to bear on the text . . . and how far the meaning and words of the text are not arbitrary and are unchanging. They learn how to focus on the text itself . . . and to realize that texts can 'speak to each other'. . . . Through the repeated sharing of stories, children learn both semantic and syntactic prediction of texts as well as the formal aspects of written language, e.g. collocations, ellipsis and lexical cohesions. . . .

Thus, a direct relationship between adult, child and text within a shared cultural framework is assumed. There are no barriers between the participants and the text, and the role of the text itself is central. Decisively, it is often implied that learning to read in school retains the same characteristics and can be learned in the same way as at home. By immersing non-school-oriented children in the cultural practice of story-reading in school and through the provision of 'good books', they become acculturated into literacy in the same way as young school-oriented children are at home. But is this necessarily so? By overlooking or rendering unproblematic the situational context and believing she is modelling a cultural practice as it exists at home, the teacher may be teaching something very different from what she intends. Later in this chapter I shall show how this takes place. The vital question is: can cultural practices be transplanted from home to school without change? If not, what changes ensure and what consequences might such changes have?

An unproblematic transfer of some cultural practices from home to school has been seen as possible within a psychosemiotic approach to the development of abstract thought (Walkerdine, 1981). Starting from theories of developmental psychology, Walkerdine sees learning the situational context as part and parcel of the signification process itself. Convincingly, she rejects the notion of context as an extra grafted on to children's already developed schema, as in the Piagetian model, and argues instead that language, thought and context must be viewed as interlocking parts of the signification process. For example, Walkerdine shows how understanding the language alone is not sufficient to interpret a couple's words in reaction to their baby's cries. We need to be able to position their discourse within both a social and historical dimension of behaviour and events surrounding child care, as well as within other discourses.

Walkerdine offers a number of examples to show how, by dint of participating in everyday cultural practices as they occur in school, children are able both to position themselves in relation to others within thepractice and master the appropriate discursive practices relevant to them. One example from a nursery school shows how two girls are able to call up appropriate relations and discourse patterns to suit the cultural practice of tv watching in the home corner. Crucially, she claims that it is the metaphor itself – tv watching – which triggers off a switching into the appropriate set of relations and discourse.

Walkerdine's argument for the fusion of thought, language and context as essential parts of signification itself is important here, for she places context in a central role, so that thought itself is fused with context. Context exists within the cultural practice itself, which can remain unchanged when transferred into the site of the school. Everything depends, therefore, upon children's ability successfully to participate in everyday cultural practices. Thus, Walkerdine assumes that a cultural practice and the social relationships within it can be taken over in its original form into the institution of school. This assumption means she can then go on to imply that an essential starting-point for the teaching of young children is the provision of familiar cultural practices within which they can position themselves.

This approach fits well with the theory of beginning reading discussed earlier. Following the tv example, immersion alone in the cultural practice of story-reading in school by and alongside the already initiated should enable newcomers to learn to position themselves within it. But can vital practices really enter the institutional site of the school and remain unchanged, or is the tv example rather the exception, because it is within the frame of socio-dramatic play? What might be the case if the site itself were to change the original nature of the practice and the relationships within it?

Walkerdine's argument about the importance of a knowledge of the social and historical background for understanding discourse is obviously vital. Volosinov (1976) provides a similar and poignant example of this. A group of people are sitting in the doctor's waiting-room in Moscow. Suddenly, one looks out of the window and says with a sigh, 'Well!'. Fully to understand this word, Volosinov claims, knowledge of the Russian word for 'well' is not enough. One needs to feel the culture of the situation, that it is snowing outside, and that it is May, the month when finally the long Russian winter should be over. Everyone feels disappointed. In this context, the actual inner site of the doctor's waiting-room is obviously unimportant, for the focus is outside, on the wider culture and relationships within it. However, we can imagine many situations where this is not the case. Let us take Walkerdine's own example: a knowledge of the historical and social context might not be enough to understand a baby's cries. But imagine that the couple and their baby are suddenly placed under scrutiny in the psychologist's laboratory. How might this affect the practice, relationships within it and the corresponding discourse?

Foucault (1972) provides a framework which centralizes the situational context as the institutional site which determines both the body of discourse and the relationships or positions individuals are able to take up within it. Applied to shared-reading lessons in school, his model means we shall need to examine the status of the individuals, as seen within a historical perspective, the institutional site – in this case, the school from which the discourse derives its source and application – also within a historical perspective, the situation the subject occupies in the discourse, as questioner or listener, the group of relations, for instance, or how schools and teachers are viewed in a historical perspective. In other words, the school discourse will affect the relations between all the participants; who is qualified to speak, for instance. Taking this perspective implies that cultural practices cannot simply be transplanted from one site to another; that shared-reading will take an essential part of its substance from the site in which it takes place.

Is it, then, at all possible to transplant a cultural practice and its corresponding discourse into school? Some argue strongly that it is not. Willes (1983) brings longitudinal data to show that even very young children starting school quickly learn the rules of a special discourse of school which is different from any other setting. In a more formal model, Bernstein (1990) argues that pedagogic discourse distorts discourse as it exists in its original field and, in so doing, changes the nature of the practice itself. For example, physics in the classroom bears little comparison to physics in the laboratory.

SHARED READING: MODELLING OR MYSTIFICATION?

I am proposing that a similar distortion may take place in reception classes as teachers introduce children to shared reading in school. The examples given take place in an urban, multilingual reception class. The children are five years old. Most enter school unfamiliar with story books. Aware of this, the teacher regularly reads with the class, groups and individuals, and encourages the children to share reading with her. Thus, she often introduces the lesson by saying, 'Today, we're going to *read . . .* together'. She aims to show the children that reading is about knowing the story and enjoying and gaining meaning from good stories and books. Aiming at a role similar to that of care-giver with a young child, the teacher intends to model the fluent reader, a skilled practitioner, showing the children as apprentices what they should be doing as future readers.

What might be the effect of the site upon the teacher's initiation of the shared-reading practice and how does this affect children's ability to position themselves in it? This particular story is a simple picture-book version of *The Elves and the Shoemaker*. The following examples are typical of the exchanges between the teacher and non-school-oriented monolingual children:

TEACHER: [points to illustration of shoemaker's house]
            Do you like that house?
CHILDREN: Yeah.
TEACHER: He [the shoemaker] was very poor. If you're very poor,
            what can't you do?
CHILD: Can't buy bubble-gum.
TEACHER: Yes. What else?
CHILD: Sweets.
TEACHER: Yes. What else?

What is being modelled here? The teacher is asking the children explicit questions about their own lives. Rather than immersing children in the story and the text, these examples show the teacher hardly allowing the children to enter the text at all. They are being confined to life. This lesson is a typical one, where almost all interactions between teacher and non-school-oriented children are outside the text. So the teacher is not actually modelling what she intends: knowing what a story is and enjoying it. At the same time, she jumps in and out of the text, reading a little, then questioning the children on their lives; but she never makes explicit what actually belongs to the text and what does not. However, her responses to different children's answers show that she implicitly assumes that the children understand they are reading a story and that life-sense answers are not required. For example, during *Rosie's Walk*:

CHILD: [referring to fox] He's strong, just like Big Daddy! [chants] Big Daddy! Big Daddy!

TEACHER: Shh! You must sit quietly when we're reading a story together.

In fact, such life-modelling is following the explicit pattern set by the teacher.

Interestingly, the school-oriented children in the group who are familiar with home shared-reading do not allow themselves to be taken away from the story. They largely ignore life-sense questions or attempt to bring the teacher back to the text. Above all, unlike those above, their interruptions are met with support:

CHILD: I know that story!

TEACHER: Well, you can help us tell the story then.

I shall return to this in more detail later. Already we begin to see how non-school-oriented children might find it difficult to position themselves in the situational context. The teacher aims to model the proficient reader and convey enjoyment and interest in the story, but her explicit teaching takes the children away from it and questions them on their lives. How might this contradiction be accounted for?

A focus on the situational context and the social relationships it determines provides one explanation. The transfer of the shared-reading practice from home to school means that the teacher is not in the role of caregiver but has a job to do, i.e. to teach. In her professional role as teacher, she wants to involve all the children in the lesson in whatever way possible. However, she is aware that some of the children are not familiar with the story. She therefore involves them in the only way she can, which is to call upon their own life experiences.

Thus, the main point of the sharing is no longer story-focused as between a young child and caregiver at home, but teaching-focused. The teacher uses the non-school-oriented children's own lives as a starting-point; but, in doing so, unconsciously excludes them from the story. At the same time, a parallel lesson takes place within the story for those who are familiar with it and refuse to be drawn outside. The site of the school, therefore, changes the cultural practice from its original site, but the social relationships are not as simple as those proposed in Foucault's model, where we might expect the teacher to praise the children who follow her explicit instruction. The teacher's actual aim is for the children to get to know and enjoy the story, and it is consequently the children who show they can do this who receive praise, even if her explicit teaching is ignored. Such is the nature of the distortion of a social practice transferred from home to the institution of school.

However, an interesting pattern emerges in individual shared-reading lessons between the teacher and some bilingual children. With these beginners in the English language the teacher does not attempt to engage in a conversation about their own lives. Instead, the reading is similar to examples given between a care-giver and a very young monolingual child (Gibson, 1989). The focus is on a very simple text; no expectations or demands are made of the child's response. Positioning within the situational context as a stranger might, therefore, be easier than for some children who are assumed to share the language and culture of the school. Whether or not this is the case will, I argue, depend upon the expectations and interpretations that these children bring to reading in school. It is to these I now turn.

CHILDREN'S EXPECTATIONS AND INTERPRETATIONS

I now want to consider how different children are able to switch into certain areas of knowledge and discourse which are appropriate for the shared-reading lesson. The extent to which they do this depends upon the way in which they position themselves within the interpretational context or the 'context of the mind' (Cazden, 1982). Walkerdine's reference to a cultural practice in terms of a metaphor which calls up a pattern of shared interpretations is valuable here. The question is, how far do different children share the school interpretation of reading? How do they position themselves in the school metaphor of reading and its corresponding areas of knowledge?

. . . . The teacher uses the metaphor of reading to introduce her lessons, usually saying, 'We're going to read a story together.' she then goes on to assume that the children share her metaphor of what reading is without explicitly teaching it: that it calls up a frame of stories and books, an area of knowledge of stories generally and this story particularly, as well as calling upon 'story' rather than 'life-sense' during readings.

The children from school-oriented backgrounds are able to position themselves within her metaphor. Exactly how they do this is discussed later. However, some children from non-school-oriented backgrounds are likely to call up a very different interpretation of reading in school and consequently do not understand the task they are presented with in early reading lessons. Studies show how school reading may have little meaning for these children and how they are likely to make poor progress in class (Schieffelin and Cochran-Smith, 1984). Their families may well actually 'read' just as much. Longitudinal emic data from the USA provides evidence that lower socio-economic indigenous and ethnic minority families spend just as long on reading activities as their middle-class counterparts, but these are of a non-book nature (Anderson and Stokes, 1984). A study of mothers and their children with reading difficulties in London's docklands shows that reading is not interpreted as enjoyable but as hard work, not sharing stories but learning the words, not encouraged by a teacher as facilitator but con-sciously and explicitly taught (Gregory, 1988).

Thus, a common interpretation of reading and its appropriate area of knowledge is not brought by all children to the school site. In this class of children, Tony, a Cantonese speaker from Hong Kong, quickly rejects attempts by the teacher to share reading. He seems unable to choose a book, and when one is chosen for him he tries to repeat every word the teacher says. His interest is in collecting words rather than in the story itself. Tony's grandfather refuses the books he brings home with the explanation, 'First, he must learn to read, then he may have the book.' The pain of learning to read is rewarded by the pleasure of possessing the esteemed book. To give the child a book before he is worthy of it degrades its value. Tony is just one child who is finding difficulty in 'positioning' himself within the context of the mind of reading in school. Bernier (1982) refers to these basically different interpretations as the 'ideological mapping' reflecting our socialization within ideological groups which, as teachers or pupils, we bring to tasks in school. It is in the nature of schooling, argues Bernier, that auto-matic reward is given to those whose life-space is characterized by a narrow parallelism, which just happens to coincide with schooling folkways.

In what ways might being a stranger to the language and culture of the school possibly help children? . . . If some individual shared-reading lessons between teacher and bilingual child take on the pattern of the cultural prac-tice as it exists between care-giver and young child, we may assume that the child is learning to associate new English words and discourse patterns with the appropriate boundaries or areas of knowledge of 'reading' as interpreted by the teacher. Put simply, by learning that the semantic boundaries for 'aunt' and 'uncle' are different in English from the first language (where in some languages different words may exist according to whether the relative is on the maternal or paternal side, etc.) a young bilingual child is develop-ing a cognitive flexibility . . . which may well be useful in sorting out the boundaries between story and reading and life.

If certain 'boundary rules' do exist – and if we accept that rules can be learned – why have they bypassed children such as Gillian, who say 'I can't

do it'? To say, 'I can't read' means that a child has already made the important discovery that rules do exist, that required answers are somehow within
the book and the text and that printed words are not arbitrary, but part of
a secret code from which the child feels excluded. What is the nature of this
code within which children must position themselves?

I want to argue here that the text acts as a code to which children have
greater or lesser access, and to ask how different children learn to 'position'
themselves within the story, text and words of the book and how trans-
parent the teacher makes their task.

I have demonstrated how the situational context influences the teacher to
'teach' the children and how she goes about this by questioning non-school-
oriented children on their lives rather than on the unfamiliar text. I have
also shown how school-oriented children largely ignored these life references and kept within the text. What is the result of this teaching on
the non-school-oriented children's positioning? Gillian's reaction is one
typical example. The teacher begins reading the story, and Joanna, a
school-oriented child, joins in, 'Once upon a time, there was a poor shoemaker . . .'. Gillian interrupts and points to the shoemaker in the picture,
'That your grandad?' The teacher's answer is significant, 'Mmm . . .' (she
then points to the shoemaker in the illustration) 'Can you see the shoemaker?' A similar pattern is often repeated with other non-school-oriented
children.

Gillian's answer would be perfectly logical within life-sense knowledge.
There is evidence, too, that other text-sense does not escape her and similar children. For instance, she does not confuse the name of one brand of
crisps with another, neither does she think that any old name she might
invent from life-sense will do. What she is doing here is copying the
teacher's pattern of instruction and returning a life-sense answer. However,
this is not what is required, as is clearly shown by the teacher's reaction.
Children who offer knowledge on the text, on the other hand, are given
both feedback and praise: 'You can help us tell the story', for example.
Yet nowhere is it made explicit that this is required, nor are non-school-
oriented children shown how to go about doing this. Two different reading
lessons are, therefore, taking place; one on life and one on the story and
text. We can conclude that children like Gillian are not being given the
criterial knowledge or shown the rules of the game, which require staying
within this and other stories and within the appropriate text. . . . What
we see here is a partnership extended to some children but remaining a
secret to others.

The bilingual children, too, have as yet little access to the story or the
text it is expressed in. Nor, however, do they have enough understanding of
English to confuse life and story sense during group reading lessons. In their
individual reading lessons, the whole event is in a new language or code.
How might this help them? In the last two sections, I have suggested ways

in which bilingual children might be better able to position themselves in the situational and interpretational contexts. One way of cracking the textual code is through a mastery of the words themselves. Two five-year-old Sylheti speakers reading together show what this might look like. They are reading *Each, Peach, Pear, Plum*, a simple rhyming picture book. The less advanced child is being helped by her peer. This child points to each word for the other to read. When the second child stumbles, the first quickly switches out of the code into Sylheti to tell her, 'Look at the picture'. We see that the code is sometimes learned in a parrot-like fashion, where one child simply repeats the text word-for-word. Sometimes, however, it is learned in a more analytic way: for example, when similarities are noticed between the code and the first language ('Gosh!' – 'That word's like "ten" in Sylheti').

These children appear to be consciously positioning themselves in the words of the text as a code, and, in so doing, attaching the words to the appropriate mental and situational contexts. They may not yet be able to point to the 'plum pudding' when asked, but they are consciously rule-making: 'Is it "D/Gosh" (Sylheti) or "Oh my gosh, my golly/Gosh" (English)'. In this, they are sorting out criterial knowledge for specific tasks. This awareness gives them a firm basis for mastering the appropriate criterial knowledge for school reading, which escapes some of their monolingual peers. They learn the non-arbitrary nature of the written word and are able to possess individual words before they even fully understand them. This is one way of positioning themselves within the text. It questions what is really meant within our paradigm of reading for meaning. Meaning may be different for each child, and possession of words may be a way forward for some.

The teaching of reading has a special role in school; for reading needs to be learned first for school success. Everything else depends upon it. . . . Many studies stress that the school should build upon early home learning in literacy teaching. But *whose* home learning is it to be? How far can the real world of reading conform with what takes place in classrooms, when different children have different real worlds of reading? . . .

If this is the case, an obvious question is whether all children can naturally be acculturated into reading in school through participation in a practice which is only real for some. If not, we might need to widen our interpretation of the term 'apprenticeship' to include a greater consciousness of teaching and learning of the sort which is involved in an apprenticeship to a skilled trade. Brown, Collins and Duguid (1989) refer to this in the school context as a 'cognitive apprenticeship' and cite examples of a teacher who pursues very definite strategies in mathematics teaching in her aim to authenticate the activities for the children. We might also call this a 'conscious apprenticeship', where we aim to empower children as readers through heightening their awareness of how and why they learn to read, as well as building on their knowledge of what print is and the functions it may serve. . . .

These factors may begin to explain the paradox with which I began, though they do not solve the problem. When Gillian and others say, 'I can't do it', we may deduce that they feel powerless before the task as they perceive it. Brief examples indicate that these children are confused and disempowered by the teacher, who unconsciously excludes them from reading as it is validated in school. For Gillian to feel she 'can' will involve a 'demystification' (Freire and Macedo, 1987) or a 'demythologising' (Fairclough, 1989) of the reading process. One way towards this may be the conscious teaching of important boundaries to children from non-school-oriented homes about how to position themselves in reading in school. In so doing, we may begin to give children access to the basic tool with which 'to interrogate and selectively appropriate those aspects of the dominant culture that will provide them with the basis for defining and transforming . . . the wider social order' (Giroux and McLaren, 1986).

REFERENCES

Anderson, A.B. and Stokes, S.J. (1984) 'Social and institutional influences on the development and practice of literacy' in H. Goelman, A. Oberg and F. Smith (eds), *Awakening to Literacy*, Heinemann Educational.

Bernier, N. (1982) 'Beyond instructional context-identification – some thoughts for extending the analysis of deliberate education' in D. Tannen (ed.), *Spoken and Written Language: Exploring Orality and Literacy*, Advances in Discourse Processes vol. 9, Ablex.

Bernstein, B. (1990) 'The grammar of pedagogy', lecture given at University of London Institute of Education, 16 February.

Brown, J.S., Collins, A. and Duguid, P. (1989) 'Situated cognition and the culture of learning', *Educational Researcher*, Jan–Feb.

Cazden, C. (1982) 'Contexts for literacy: in the mind and in the classroom', *Journal of Reading Behaviour*, 14(4).

Fairclough, N. (1989), *Language and Power*, Longman.

Freire, P. and Macedo, D. (1987) *Literacy: Reading the Word and the World*, Routledge & Kegan Paul.

Foucault, M. (1972) *The Archaeology of Knowledge*, Tavistock.

Gibson, L. (1989) *Literacy Learning in the Early Years: Through Children's Eyes*, Cassell.

Giroux, A. and McLaren, P. (1986) 'Teacher education and the politics of engagement: the case for democratic schooling', *Harvard Educational Review*, Aug.

Gregory, E. (1988) 'Reading with mother: a dockland story' in M. Meek and C. Mills (eds), *Language and Literacy in the Primary School*, The Falmer Press.

Schieffelin, B.B. and Cochran-Smith, M. (1984) 'Learning to read culturally: literacy before schooling' in H. Goelman, A. Oberg and F. Smith (eds), *Awakening to Literacy*, Heinemann Educational.

Scollon, R. and Scollon, B.K. (1981) *Narrative, Literacy and Face in Interethnic Communication*, Ablex.

Volosinov, V.N. (1976) *Freudianism: A Marxist Critique*, Academic Press.

Walkerdine, V. (1981) 'From context to text: a psychosemiotic approach to abstract thought' in B. Beveridge (ed.), *Children Thinking through Language*, Edward Arnold.

Willes, M.J. (1983) *Children into Pupils*, Routledge & Kegan Paul.

Chapter 9

Disciplining English: the construction of a national subject

Jill Bourne and Deborah Cameron

In 1987, a Committee of Inquiry into the Teaching of the English Language was announced by the Secretary of state for Education, Kenneth Baker. It was commissioned as part of a wider government initiative to construct a national curriculum for schools. However, the Committee, chaired by a mathematician, John Kingman, had a more specific, preliminary role. In announcing the committee, Mr Baker said:

> I am working towards national agreement on the aims and objectives of English teaching in schools in order to improve standards. But I have been struck by a particular gap. Pupils need to know about the workings of the English language if they are to use it effectively. Most schools no longer teach old fashioned grammar. But little has been put in its place. There is *no common ground* on teaching about the structure and workings of language, about the way it is used to convey meaning and achieve other effects. We need to equip teachers with a proper model of the language to help improve their teaching.
>
> (DES Press Notice, 16 January 1987, our stress)

The Kingman brief was to recommend a model of the English language, knowledge of which would form one element of the English subject curriculum whilst also informing programmes of teacher training.

Soon after the Committee began work, major legislation on the English education system was introduced into Parliament. A new committee, the National Curriculum English Working Group, was formed to begin work immediately following the Kingman Committee's report in 1988. If Kingman was to set the agenda with its 'model' of the English language, the English Working Group was to work out the 'nuts and bolts' of delivery within a wider focus on the full English curriculum, including literature, drama and media studies. The Working Group's report, not Kingman's, was to be the basis for statutory orders in Parliament setting out what is to be taught in schools.

In the event, the Kingman Committee's Report (DES, 1988a, here-after 'Kingman') met with faint praise from the Secretary of State, as 'an interesting report which will contribute to discussion about the grammatical structure of the English language and the correct use of the spoken word' (DES Press Notice, 29 April 1988. However, if the Kingman Report failed to please, the English Working Group's first report (DES, 1988b) actively contested the concept of 'correct' English. It presented a critical analysis of 'Standard English' as part of the recommended programme of study for pupils, while reserving a place for the use of 'linguistic terminology' in schools. In response, the Secretary of State did not engage with the Working Group's discussion of Standard English, but called for them to give 'greater emphasis to pupils' mastery of the grammatical structure of the English language'. Even as we write, the struggle continues! [Yet another set of proposals for English (SCAA, 1994) has been sent out for consultation and new legislation on the English curriculum is expected in 1995].

The Secretary of State's response to the English Working Group's proposals, however, was nothing compared to the furore anticipated by the media. Columnist Simon Jenkins (*Sunday Times*, 20 November 1988) summed up: 'Grammar is the fastest rising topic in the Tory policy firmament, now almost on a par with hanging and dole fraud. No matter that most constituency chairmen hated the subject. The nation's grammar stirs the political juices.'

In this chapter, we propose to examine the earlier Kingman Report, not for its practical application to English teaching, but as a historical event, as a battlefield around which ideological assumptions have been paraded and contested. Our reading of Kingman is intended to provide perspectives from which the meanings of the English Working Group Report, later proposals, and the responses to them, as they emerge, might also become clearer. We will focus on Kingman as a key ideological text about the state of the language and its relation to the state of the nation.

The domain of Kingman is marked out in the phrase 'English grammar', and both these words are significant if we seek to understand the meaning and context of the report. We will deal, accordingly, with the question of 'grammar' and the question of 'English'.

KINGMAN AND THE QUESTION OF GRAMMAR

Right from the start, the setting up of the Kingman Committee was perceived as contentious. The Committee put back on the agenda something – 'knowledge about language' or, less coyly, grammar – which, it was thought, had been largely abandoned in educational practice, with some theoretical support from modern linguistics as well as educational theory, under pressure from the 'liberal' ideas of the 1960s and 1970s.

The move away from grammar had never gone unopposed, however. When Kingman publicly reopened the question the rumble of discontent from traditionalist quarters turned into a roar; and their progressive opponents were equally vocal in deploring the return of grammar. What was crucial, though, was that the context for this familiar debate had changed dramatically since the 1970s. [See Ball, this volume].

It is, of course, a commonplace observation that people do feel strongly about language and correctness in language: perceptions of 'falling standards' and 'sloppiness' are pervasive (and have been for around 300 years). But this fact in itself does not explain why the teaching of *grammar* is so often seen as a panacea – nor indeed why grammar is so vehemently opposed by many people (linguists and teachers, for instance) who by no means deny the importance of clarity and elegance in the use of language.

To understand the peculiarly violent responses that grammar inspires we need to examine its social significance in our culture. Arguably, grammar is an innocuous concept in itself, but has become inextricably linked with less innocuous concepts such as authority, hierarchy, tradition, order and rules. Attitudes to grammar are connected with attitudes to authority; anxieties about grammar are at some deeper level anxieties about the breakdown of order and tradition, not just in language but in society at large. This point, on the face of it quite startling, is spelt out in an article written for the *Observer* newspaper in 1982 by independent school headmaster John Rae under the heading 'The decline and fall of English grammar'. At the time Rae expressed a dissenting view since the 'liberal' perspective was still in the ascendant; in the light of Kingman, though, his remarks now appear oddly prophetic.

Rae begins by making it explicit that you teach children grammar not just in order to improve their own linguistic performance (in passing, it should be said that we know of no evidence that grammar teaching has any such effect) but to make it clear to them that there are rules of conduct: people may not simply do as they please, either in language or in any other kind of social interaction. Rejecting grammar is one mark of a society which rejects rules, and the result is anarchy. As Rae comments:

> Grammar was a predictable victim of the self-indulgent sixties. It was associated with authority, tradition and elitism. Grammatical rules, like so many other rules at the time, were regarded as an intolerable infringement of personal freedom.

This argument is, of course, an absolute deformation of the critique of traditional prescriptive grammar put forward for instance by linguists. For a linguist, it is axiomatic that every speaker has a grammar, and there is little 'personal freedom' involved, at least in Rae's sense of breaking the rules at will. The anti-prescriptivists had no desire to abolish grammar *per se* (one might as well try to abolish gravity); they wanted only to break the connection between grammar and 'authority, tradition and elitism'.

If the connection has in fact survived, it is because for our culture 'authority, tradition and elitism' form the central meaning of grammar. It is only secondarily about language at all.

Rae obligingly makes this point crystal clear towards the end of his article, where he draws an explicit parallel between grammatical and other kinds of correctness.

> There is a further claim that can be made for the restoration of the teaching of correct English. Attention to the rules of grammar and care in the choice of words encourages punctiliousness in other matters. That is not just an intellectual conceit. The overthrow of grammar coincided with the acceptance of the equivalent of creative writing in social behaviour. As nice points of grammar were mockingly dismissed as pedantic and irrelevant, so was punctiliousness in such matters as honesty, responsibility, property, gratitude, apology and so on.

It appears here that grammar is to bear an immense symbolic weight, being associated with the values of hierarchy, order and rule-government in general. That is why it is both passionately advocated and passionately opposed. A return to traditional grammar marks a return to the associated social values.

It must, however, be said that the Kingman view of grammar is *not* unequivocally traditionalist. It is obviously significant that the report insists throughout on the euphemism 'knowledge about language' which distances it from traditional prescriptive models and placates those for whom 'grammar' would be anathema.

Because Kingman takes a moderate line on grammar – the rallying point for both traditionalists and progressives – it may well seem that the whole tenor of the report is moderate. But if we turn to the matter of what Kingman makes of 'English' we shall see that this impression is misleading.

KINGMAN AND THE QUESTION OF ENGLISH

We alluded above to the historical connection often made between the perceived state of the language and the identity of the nation. This connection is familiar in many contexts all over the world (language riots in Belgium and India; the systematic oppression of Catalan speakers under Franco; or conversely, the irredentist ambitions of Hitler in the Sudetenland). An authoritarian state frequently uses 'the national language' as a point of unity and social cohesion, and analogously, finds linguistic diversity threatening, a force to be contained or even eliminated.

The National Curriculum represents a move towards uniformity. Previously it was up to Local Education Authorities (LEAs) to determine their curricula, and in doing this they took account of local needs (e.g. the ethnic and socio-economic profile of their schools). As is well known, Britain is linguistically highly diverse, both in terms of languages spoken and of divergent varieties of English (related to region and to social class). A national curriculum must inevitably address this diversity on a greater scale than any one LEA was obliged to cope with. The tendency of Kingman was to take an authoritarian position by advocating cohesion around one variety of one language (Standard English, hereafter SE) while at the same time seeking to contain diversity by downgrading minority languages and non-standard varieties.

It is worthwhile discussing the manner in which Kingman has chosen to describe the linguistic diversity of this country. It eschews – and one imagines by conscious choice – any mention whatever of social divisions such as race and class. All linguistic variation is described as either 'historical' (i.e. the English language changes through time) or 'geographical' (i.e. different accents/dialects are used in different regions of the country). Such a model of variation is actually false. It omits both class and ethnic group variation. Each variety is seen as changing within itself over time and located in its own space, without contact with other varieties or languages (except for sometimes sharing a standard written form which can cross regional boundaries). Contact and shift (which in the view of many linguists are the fundamental sources of much language change) have no place in this account.

Synchronic diversity for Kingman is a matter of regional varieties with clear boundaries. Such dialects are acceptable and to be valued as long as they are easily 'comprehensible' (to whom is not specified) and so long as they remain within spheres where their use is 'appropriate'. For as the Kingman Report (ch. 2, para. 5) remarks,

> The dialect usages of family and immediate circle are sufficient to their purposes; but membership of the smaller group entails membership of the larger, and for the wider community – that of the nation and the world – the standard language will be indispensable.

The indispensability of SE has apparently nothing to do with its social prestige (since the fact that it is a *class* dialect, spoken by the elite in every region, cannot be stated within the Kingman framework of 'history' and 'geography') but merely relates to its communicational appropriateness as something that belongs to 'the nation' (not to mention the world) rather than to a region, a class or an ethnic group. We shall go on to explore how Kingman fits into a tradition that makes SE the symbol of nationhood and the mark of citizenship or 'belonging'.

CITIZENSHIP AND NATIONHOOD (1):
ENGLISH AND MINORITY LANGUAGES

The report has little to say directly about the position of those school pupils (in some localities up to 41 per cent, and in certain schools an overall majority of children) who are bilingual in English and another language. But Kingman's historical/geographical model of language variation has serious implications for the status of minority languages and their speakers. The covert function of the model is to strengthen and protect English at the expense of other languages; and this becomes overt in the Secretary of State's notes of 'Supplementary Guidance' (DES, 1988c) to the National Curriculum Working Group on English which took over where Kingman left off (see above). The notes enjoin readers to bear in mind 'the cardinal point that English should be the first language and medium of instruction for all pupils in England' (para. 13).

The use of the term *England* (not *Britain*) here is significant, since there is of course one minority language whose claims are respected by the government and in the national curriculum: Welsh in Wales. It is instructive to examine the case of Welsh in more detail, since contrasting attitudes to Welsh and, say, Greek or Gujerati help to clarify what assumptions are being made about language and nationhood.

Welsh was granted legal status in Wales by the Welsh Language Act of 1967 – interestingly enough, at the very time when the English language was becoming an educational issue in England following a period of immigration from the old Empire (now the 'new Commonwealth'). In England, the response to linguistic diversity was to set up structures for English language teaching, both for children and for adults. Documents of the time express the fear that the presence of pupils in English schools speaking languages other than English would be detrimental to the indigenous school population and lead to falling standards (cf. DES Circular 7/65; Commonwealth Advisory Committee, 1964).

The perceived need to 'protect' English speakers from the dangers of contact with other languages was also seen in the Welsh legislation. Welsh was granted 'equal validity' as a language alongside English in Wales. This was done to 'raise the status of Welsh' but it crucially did not threaten the position of English monolinguals in Wales either socially or economically, by requiring them to learn Welsh. Provision for bilinguals in both England and Wales was premised, in other words, on the need to affect the monolingual majority as little as possible.

The difference between the bilingual provision made possible in Wales and the compensatory English programmes favoured in England is nevertheless a significant one, and one that can be analysed precisely in terms of *territory*. The use of territorial criteria to define language provision and minority language rights is not peculiar to Kingman – indeed, it is not even acknowledged as such in Kingman – but it is crucial to our understanding of Kingman as an ideological text.

In 1967 Welsh gained equal validity only within the borders of Wales. Welsh speakers outside Wales had no claim for equal treatment. In other words, the whole discourse of language rights in the Welsh case is focused on territorial considerations, to wit, the existence of a region (historically, a nation) to which the Welsh language 'belongs'. It is a discourse of national boundaries rather than one of minority rights (as we can see very clearly from the fact that individuals travelling beyond the Welsh borders could not take their language rights with them).

The nationalistic 'land and language' argument articulates very comfortably with the right-wing ideas on the subject of English and the English literary heritage in England (e.g. Marenbon, 1987; Hillgate Group, 1987). If one allows that Welsh is the 'natural' language of Wales, it follows that English is the 'natural' tongue of England. But what is the effect of this stance on languages *without* a historic territory inside the British state? Clearly, the effect is to render such languages *alien*. If languages belong to geographical areas with unbroken continuity of use in those areas, then each has its own proper place within which speakers may have 'rights'. Punjabi in Birmingham becomes a historical accident and a territorial aberration, a temporary occupation of someone else's space. At best we can teach children to respect the languages their classmates bring to school, but the territorial model makes it clear that those languages do not 'belong' here in England. Within that model, it seems that resident bilingual communities must choose either to share in 'our' linguistic heritage or to remain 'alien' with their allegiances elsewhere.

So while multicultural education of an approved type may encourage children to show tolerance towards cultural and linguistic diversity, in the territorial model such diversity will remain exotic, transplanted rather than inherent, and will need to be contained as a possible threat to the strong ethnocentric values which inform most of the national curriculum. [It is important in this context to note that the SCAA (1994) proposals for English did not contain even one reference to the existence of bilingual children, other than Welsh-speaking bilinguals within Wales.]

If ethnocentrism was strong in Kingman, so was elitism. The presence of sizeable linguistic minorities in England is a relatively new phenomenon for the British education system, but the existence of socially conditioned variation in English itself has been a perennial issue. We can therefore examine Kingman's treatment of it by comparison with earlier pronouncements by educationalists and commissions of enquiry. Such a comparison will reveal once again that Kingman does represent a shift to an authoritarian 'national unity' perspective which recalls the late nineteenth and early twentieth centuries but goes against the more recent post-war 'liberal consensus'.

CITIZENSHIP AND NATIONHOOD (2): STANDARD ENGLISH

As we have noted already, the concept of 'Standard English' is very important in Kingman's vision of the English curriculum. We will therefore begin by looking at this concept and the problems it raises.

Standard is something of a weasel word. It has two related but rather different meanings. One of these is 'uniform, as in the idea of a standard measurement. It means ordinary, common to all, invariant, normal. But the second sense of the word is 'something to aspire to', as in the idea of 'high standards'. This means not ordinary but excellent, the best there is, not normal but *normative.*

Discussions of Standard English often exhibit a slippage between these two senses of 'standard'. Thus the normative is passed off as the merely normal; or in this specifically linguistic case, the language of a class is passed off as the common tongue of a whole people (in Kingman's terms, which exclude the concept of class, SE is the language of the nation rather than that of the family and immediate circle). On the one hand, discussions about the desirability of 'standard' trade on the associations of the term with excellence – 'the best that has been said and written in our language'. But if one asks '*whose* language exactly?', if one raises the question of social inequality and the arbitrary nature of the purported excellence, the same discussions can easily retreat into the notion of 'standard English' as a uniform practice which all English speakers have in common. In the striking image of Kingman (p. 14), 'standard English is a great social bank, on which we all draw and to which we all contribute'. What is not addressed is the issue of who put up the capital, who controls the means of linguistic exchange. We might well ask why it is that some people are forced to borrow at exorbitant rates of interest while their own currency lies valueless in a sock underneath the mattress!

Wittingly or unwittingly, Kingman's economic metaphor reveals its underlying assumptions about the purpose of education. Promoting SE is an intervention in a linguistic economy where some start off with more resources than others. It can be justified in the language of equality of opportunity but it carefully avoids any challenge to the practice of the currently privileged. Redistribution of wealth may be on the agenda but transformation of the economy and its currency is not.

Kingman assumes that SE is a 'national heritage' to which citizens have a right (and crucially also, an obligation). Like the territorial perspective discussed in the last section this is nothing new. The history of English teaching has always been about giving to the many what the few could take for granted. We should recall here that the elite who attended public schools and universities had until relatively recently little or no formal education in their own language and literature, because it was assumed to be something they already possessed by virtue of their rank: instead they followed a classics-based curriculum. To get English accepted as a teaching subject took a prolonged struggle. 'Knowledge about language' had its place in that debate too; it was used to beef up the academic credentials of English as a subject, making it more like classics and thus acceptable to the elite.

On the other hand, though, some of the strongest arguments for teaching English language and literature referred explicitly to the need to educate a wider social constituency – groups who could not be expected to cope with Greek and Latin, such as middle-class recruits to the imperial bureaucracy, women and, eventually, the working classes who were to benefit from mass education.

KINGMAN, ENGLISH AND EDUCATION

English was crucial in mass education, not only because it was easier than classics or because of the need for a literate work-force, though doubtless these were factors, but for overtly ideological reasons to do with national identity and social cohesion. This emerges clearly from a reading of relevant documents of the nineteenth and early twentieth centuries, the forerunners of Kingman. Educational policy-makers saw in English the potential for containing social conflict caused by endemic class division.

The linguistic historian Tony Crowley has made a detailed study of discourse about English, including educational policy on the subject, from 1840 (Crowley, 1989). He points out that during the nineteenth century a perception developed of the English language as the proudest possession of a great imperial nation. It may well seem surprising that he puts this development so late as the 1800s: current texts tend to focus on the sixteenth and seventeenth centuries as the 'Golden Age', the age of Shakespeare and the King James Bible. But in fact this represents a judgement made much later. The elite consensus until at least the eighteenth century was that English remained an inferior language, less eloquent than Latin and Greek, even than French and Italian. Shakespeare had not had the advantage even of a decent dictionary and grammar – a fault the great eighteenth-century codifiers, men like Swift, Johnson and Lowth, wanted to correct.

In the nineteenth century, however, the ideas of commentators on the language became infused with European romanticism, which held that a language expressed the genius of a people ('*Volksgeist*'). The success of England as an imperial nation, a world leader economically and politically, combined with romantic ideas about language to produce an overtly patriotic and triumphalist attitude to English. The language was not so much to be improved (as in Swift's time) as to be preserved in the manner of a great national monument. The Oxford English Dictionary, for example, was conceived in the mid-nineteenth century as a work which would reveal both the continuity and the greatness of the nation from Anglo-Saxon times. In his 1855 treatise *English Past and Present*, Dean Trench (a leading architect of the OED) expressed the hope that work of this kind would 'lead through a more intimate knowledge of English into a greater love of England'.

Crowley goes on to examine the use made of ideas like Trench's by educationalists after the setting up of a compulsory mass education programme in 1870. This period and the period immediately following the Great War were characterized by anxiety about the gulf between social classes. A lot of attention was given to the potential of mass education for bridging the class divide – especially mass education in the linguistic and literary heritage of the nation, which might form the basis for a common national culture. Given the prevalence and influence of the ideas about language and nation which had been circulating in the nineteenth century, it seemed obvious that a solid training in English would be an excellent foundation for a national culture. This was most vigorously advocated in politically explicit terms by the Newbolt Report of 1921 (see Crowley, 1989) and also in a polemical essay by one of the Newbolt Commissioners, George Sampson, published in the same year under the title *English for the English* (see Sampson, 1921).

Sampson, like many other people at the time, was deeply worried about the possibility of class warfare escalating as it recently had in Russia. He was clear about the role of education and culture in breaking down dangerous class divisions, and he also had a good understanding of the relation between class and language. 'In this country', he wrote, 'classes are sundered by difference in language – difference of speech is a symbol of class antagonism' (quoted in Crowley, 1989) The Newbolt Report wanted action to change that state of affairs. 'If the teaching of the language were properly provided for', it said, 'the difference between educated and uneducated speech, which at present causes so much prejudice and difficulty on both sides, would gradually disappear' (ibid.).

One very interesting feature of Newbolt's and Sampson's views generally is that they were very critical of the Public Schools. Their classics-based curriculum, as much as anything, blocked the possibility of a truly national, classless culture. Sampson believed that the public as well as the national elementary school systems must change.

> There is no class in this country that does not need a full education in English. Possibly a common basis of education might do much to mitigate the class antagonism that is dangerously keen at the moment and shows no sign of losing its edge . . . if we want that class antagonism to be mitigated we must abandon our system of class education and find some form of education common to the schools of all classes. A common school is, at present, quite impracticable . . . but . . . a common basis of

education is not. The one common basis of the common culture is the
common tongue.

(ibid.)

Newbolt recommended exactly this 'common basis of education' on precisely the ground that it would bring unity between classes sharing one
native language. Sampson was deeply committed to the total eradication of
non-standard varieties which he called 'language in a state of disease'. SE is
the key to culture and value, and it is something all classes can be taught to
share. The alternative, which Sampson conjures up in apocalyptic terms, is
of a society where people's primary loyalties are not to the nation but to
their class, and where the lower classes have no culture of any kind.
In *English for the English* Sampson warns where this will lead: 'Deny to
working class children any common share in the immaterial, and presently
they will grow into the men who demand with menaces a communism of
the material.'

THE COMMON CULTURE

We should not, of course, deny the obvious differences between Newbolt
and Kingman – the accommodation of Kingman to educational and
linguistic theories unknown in 1921 is clear enough. Nevertheless there are
parallels between the two documents. In both cases 'English' is advocated
as the cornerstone of a national curriculum whose objective is to produce a
'common culture' in the nation's children.

The late 1980s, like the 1920s was a time when there was renewed concern with social polarization. Many people in Britain today are still dusting
off the old 'two nations' rhetoric, and some are worried, as Sampson was in
his time, about the potential for serious unrest among the dispossessed of
the Thatcher era. In its underlying attitudes of nationalism, ethnocentrism,
an authoritarian impulse to unity in culture, Kingman is far more
like Newbolt than it is like the more recent Bullock and Swann reports
(DES, 1975, 1985) where the model of culture was being reworked towards
diversity and pluralism. As an answer to social conflict it offers a radically
different solution, an 'English culture' in which all, if they are to be
'English', or at least 'British', are to take part.

But the context for Kingman is a wholly different Britain from the
Britain of 1921; the rhetoric of that bygone age is singularly inappropriate
even if the nation's social problems appear to be similar. The economic self-
confidence, imperial majesty and political status of the nineteenth century
are gone: present day conservatives are struggling to put something in its
place (as a recent election slogan had it, 'Making Britain Great Again'). And
this is also part of the meaning of Kingman: nostalgia.

Raymond Williams (in Osmond, 1985) has discussed what he calls the 'visible weakening of England' as a nation state, and the increasing uncertainty over whether there is any definable 'English way of life'. As Williams comments: 'many of the things that happened over centuries to the Welsh are now happening, in decades, to the English'. In the same volume, Jones writes of the Welsh experience: 'I know of an experience equally agonising and more irreversible [than exile] . . . the experience of knowing, not that you are leaving your country, but that your country is leaving you.' Kingman may be about authoritarian control in a polarized nation-state, but it also contains another, less evident strand, which is a feeling of nostalgia and loss for a changed nation.

What this strand signals is a point of transition for the idea of 'Englishness' as a national identity. Because of the close connection between language and nationhood, grammar and tradition, policy documents on English are bound to reflect that transition. For the children in our schools, however, it is important that we should not look to the past, but to the future, face up to present realities, and conceptualize language (which is not the same thing as English) in the context of Britain's future.

REFERENCES

Commonwealth Advisory Committee (1964) *Second Report*, London: HMSO.
Crowley, T. (1989) *The Politics of Discourse 1840–1987*, London: Macmillan.
Department of Education and Science (DES) (1965) Circular 7/65, London: DES.
—— (1975) *A Language for Life* (the Bullock Report), London: HMSO.
—— (1985) *Education for All* (the Swann Report), London, HMSO.
—— (1988a) *Report of the Committee of Inquiry into the Teaching of the English Language* (the Kingman Report), London: HMSO.
—— (1988b) *English for Ages 5–11* (The report of the National Curriculum English Working Group), London: DES.
—— (1988c) *National Curriculum English Working Group: Terms of Reference and Notes of Supplementary Guidance*, London: DES.
Hillgate Group (1987) *The Reform of British Education*, London: Claridge.
Jenkins, S. (1988) 'Dr. Syntax to Wed Mrs. Grundy Shock', *The Sunday Times*, 20 November 1988.
Marenbon, J. (1987) *English Our English*, London: Centre for Policy Studies.
Osmond, J. (ed.) *The National Question Again: Welsh Political Identity in the 1980s*. Llandysul: Gomer.
Rae, J. (1982) 'The decline and fall of English grammar', *Observer*, 7 February 1982.
Sampson, G. (1921) *English for the English*, London: English Association.
Schools Curriculum and Assessment Authority (SCAA) (1994) *English in the National Curriculum: Draft Proposals*, London: SCAA.

Chapter 10

Young children's writing: from spoken to written genre

Frances Christie

The study I intend to report on here commenced as an investigation into the processes by which young children learn to write. The focus was upon 55 children who entered the preparatory year, aged five years, and I studied them intensively for a period of three years, up to the point at which they completed year two. In undertaking the study, . . . I sought to . . . examine where children's written genres come from. That is to say, my focus has always been upon the curriculum context – upon the teaching/learning episodes which teacher and children negotiate, and out of which, as it were, the children are ultimately caused to produce written texts.

The search for a means of talking about the curriculum context has proved an interesting one, because it has, in a sense, taken me away from considerations of writing. Much more than I had foreseen in undertaking the study initially, it has caused me to focus upon the nature of the spoken discourse of the classroom. Specifically, I have sought to identify some means by which I can describe and account for the relationship between the patterns of spoken discourse used in teacher/pupil interaction, and the patterns of written discourse produced by the children. Central to the methodological tools I have sought to develop to this end, is the notion of the 'curriculum genre'. Using this notion, I would now argue (i) that it is quite impossible to understand the nature of the written texts children produce without an understanding of the curriculum context in which they are generated, (ii) that in significant ways much early childhood curriculum practice seriously underestimates what young children can do, with unfortunate effects for their writing development, and (iii) more specifically, that where the 'content' of the learning activity around which writing develops is of a limited kind, so too are the written texts the children produce. Since the notion of 'genre' is so central to the argument to be developed, it will be necessary to offer some definition of the term as it is to be used here.

GENRE DEFINED

Both Hasan (1985) and Ventola (1984) have shown that even such relatively casual conversations as service encounters have an overall linguistic pattern or shape justifying us as seeing these as examples of genres: linguistically patterned ways of behaving for the achievement of certain socially determined goals. For my purposes, Martin's definition of genre (1984: 25) is most useful: 'a staged, goal oriented, purposeful activity in which speakers engage as members of our culture'.

The term 'curriculum genre' refers to any teaching/learning episode which may be said to be structured and staged in this sense. It will involve participation of teachers and students in some activity which seeks to establish for the children understandings and/or tasks of various kinds. To illustrate the point quickly, we may refer to the Morning News genre, the function of which we are told in educational discussion, is that children are given opportunity to 'learn to talk'. In the creation of a text which is representative of the Morning News genre, a morning news giver is nominated, that person comes to the front of the group of children, and a formal exchange of greetings takes place, after which the morning news giver offers some item(s) of news, involving the reconstruction of some aspect of personal experience. The teacher and other pupils may comment and/or ask questions during this phase and finally, the morning news giving is brought to a close, sometimes because the teacher says so, and sometimes because the child indicates he or she has finished.

Close analysis of the kinds of linguistic behaviours children are required to produce in order to be judged proficient in the Morning News genre, reveals that they need to offer a series of observations about personal experience. The mood choice for the morning news giver will thus be declarative (while that of the teacher, by contrast, is frequently interrogative, for she in particular may ask questions), and, somewhat surprisingly, no evaluative comment upon personal experience will normally be offered by the child. It seems that the function of offering evaluation is that of the teacher, a significant measure of the authority accorded her, even in a situation in which the child is supposed to be encouraged to talk (Christie, 1989). Thus is an aspect of the ideology of schooling – more specifically, of the kinds of values associated with the roles of teacher and children – realized in the linguistic choices made in the production of a classroom text.

Ideologies or values, not only to do with the roles of teacher and pupils, but also to do with the kinds of knowledge children will examine, are, as we shall shortly see, also important elements of the Writing Negotiation genre. They have important implications for the language used both by teacher and by children, and hence for the kinds of capacities in writing the children are enabled to develop. In fact, as I hope to demonstrate in the curriculum activity I shall be examining, there is a very intimate relationship between the limited nature of the content dealt with and the limited nature of the written genres the children produce. As I shall further suggest, the terms of the curriculum activity are such that the children are constrained to do no more than produce aspects of personal experience in talk, and, just as there is no significant mental challenge involved in such an undertaking, so too, there is little challenge to significant learning in the writing task undertaken.

The values to education of identifying and talking about educational practice in terms of 'curriculum genres', are several. Firstly, the notion enables us to concentrate upon just how it is that we structure, organize, and hence regulate teaching learning experiences in schools. Secondly, because it obliges us to think about language in behavioural terms, it can enable us to identify the kinds of linguistic behaviour children need to master in order to be successful in their learning. Thirdly, because it becomes apparent that the practice of patterning experience in language, and of creating genres, is a feature both of speech and of writing, we are enabled to focus directly upon the relationship of written genres to spoken ones: that is, we are able to trace the relationship of the patterns of the written genre to the patterns of spoken discourse in which the actual task of writing was negotiated.

I propose now to turn to one Writing Negotiation genre, generated when the children involved were in year two. . . .

A WRITING NEGOTIATION GENRE

The lesson it is proposed to discuss was one in a series which constituted a major unit of work, or 'theme' on Food. Typically, in curriculum practice in the junior school, learning activities in language arts, science and social science will be developed around such a theme. The unit of work on Food lasted eight weeks, and the particular lesson of concern here came towards the end of the unit, in about the sixth or seventh week. The lesson was undertaken early in the day, immediately after roll call and morning news in fact. Later in the day the children were to make sandwiches with their teacher and eat them at lunch time, and they had all brought in various ingredients before the day's activities commenced.

The content of the lesson was built around the teacher's reading of a children's book, *My Lunch!* (Bambrough, 1982) and, inspired by listening to this, the children were to write texts of their own, under the title, 'What happened to my lunch?' The book is one of a series of basal readers widely used in Australia, and like the volumes from most such series, it is reasonably pedestrian, in that its choice of language is both limited and somewhat stilted. Its 'story' (not in fact a true narrative structure) is developed partly through the text, and partly through the associated illustrations, and it concerns a boy who discovers he has lost his lunch at school. A dog is found to have taken the lunch and the teacher takes the boy to buy another lunch in a shop.

In terms of the overall schematic structure of the lesson, an examination of the total pattern of classroom discourse reveals four major elements: the task orientation, the task reorientation, the task specification, and the task. The pattern of teacher/pupil negotiation – the curriculum genre involved here – is a familiar enough one. A course is set by the teacher in the task orientation: in this phase, some initial perspectives are established, and some basic understandings of the task established; a task reorientation is intended to develop upon the initial perspectives and understandings. Thence, the task is specified, and in turn the children are deemed ready to undertake it.

... My own investigation into curriculum genres (Christie, 1986) leads me to argue that an examination of theme is a particularly pertinent way of penetrating and explaining the ways in which classroom discourse builds its meanings. ...

Technically, theme is 'the element (in the clause) which serves as the point of departure of the message; it is that with which the clause is concerned' (Halliday, 1985: 38). In English, though not necessarily in other languages, theme is what comes first in the clause. ... Structural themes have the function of linking clauses together ... for they include the various conjunctions, which are often used in association with conjunctive adjuncts, such as *then*. The following are ... taken from the teacher's opening discourse:

> you know we had a monster sandwich, *and then* we made up our own monster sandwiches ... *and* I want you to listen to it [i.e. the story] ... *because when* we finish reading this story ...

In general, whoever controls structural themes directs the course the discourse takes, determining in particular the kinds of patterns of reasoning encoded in those patterns. Overwhelmingly, it is the teacher in this, as in many curriculum genres, who controls the structural themes, and the children in fact produce very few. When we examine the nature of the structural themes produced, we find that most have the effect of building connections between events of an additive kind, so that a simple connection is created, of the sort requiring no more than very simple narration of a sequence of events. Furthermore, when we examine the elements of the discourse which the children do produce, we find that their contributions to the text are often so minimal as not to contain any thematic component at all.

However, where they do produce themes, these are always ... of a personal kind, to do with self, a classmate or a family member. Collectively, the effect of these patterns of ... themes ... in the text is to construct a discourse, and hence a pattern of reasoning, which involves the children in the simple construction of personal experience, where that involves recon-struction of actual happenings, or construction of imagined experience.

As a basis for significant school learning, I would argue that recourse to personal experience is essential. However, contrary to much early childhood practice, I would also argue that personal experience should not constitute the entire content examined in a lesson. Where that does happen, I suggest, little learning of a significant kind may be shown to have taken place.

I propose to illustrate and support my observations, with respect to theme and its significance in the way in which meanings are made in the curriculum genre under discussion, by examining . . . that element of the schematic structure I have labelled the task specification, which allows a very good examination of the respective roles and contributions of the teacher and children. The object, very clearly, is the reconstruction of personal experience. Note that in setting out the discourse, I have inserted a row of dots to indicate a point at which an element of the text, to do with disciplining a child, has been removed, on the grounds that it does not constitute part of the curriculum genre involved.

Task specification

T:	Now what I want you people to think about is something coming along and taking your lunch, or something happening to your lunch so that you couldn't eat it. Not a dog, that's in the story. Well, you can have a dog if you want, but it'ud be better if you think of something else.
	. . . .
	All right put your hand up if you've thought of something that could come and take your lunch, or something that could happen to your lunch.
T:	Have you ever had a day when you've had no lunch to eat? Jodie? (she nods) What happened Jodie, when you had no lunch to eat?
JODIE:	Mum didn't bring it up. She left it at home.
T:	Left your lunch at home on the bench, and her mum didn't bring it to school, and she had no lunch. And what happened?
JODIE:	Found no lunch.
T	And then what happened? Who had to ring up your mum and dad?
JODIE:	Mr H.
T:	And then what happened?
JODIE:	My mum brought my lunch.
T:	And who else brought your lunch?
JODIE:	Dad.
T:	She had no lunch to start with, because it was left at home,

and she thought her mum was going to bring it at lunch time, and when her mum didn't bring it, Mrs S. rang her mum, and she wasn't at home, so her dad brought her lunch and then her mum remembered she hadn't brought her lunch, and she brought lunch too, so she ended up with two lunches. She ate the lot.

JOSEPH: What did she have?

T: You had – I can't remember – you had a sausage role and donut.

JODIE: I had a very nice lunch. I had a sausage roll and a jam donut and a (indecipherable)

T: Mm so that was an extra special thing. Who else has ever had no lunch, and then something's happened that they've had a different lunch? Emily? What happened yesterday?

EMILY: My sister left hers on the dressing table.

T: And what happened when she found that she had no lunch? Was she happy? What was happening to her?

EMILY: She was crying.

T: She was crying and she came to me, and what did I say?

EMILY: She could have one from the canteen.

T: What else happened to you?

EMILY: The day I put the lunch in the school bag and brought the other school bag instead.

T: Mm and what happened that day? Emily had two school bags at home, and she put the lunch in one school bag, and took the other school bag to school. And when she looked in her bag, no lunch. And what happened that day?

EMILY: I got a lunch from the canteen.

T: You had a special lunch order.

Table 10.1 sets out in summary fashion the distribution of themes across the teacher discourse and the children's discourse in the text. . . .

Table 10.1 The distribution of structural themes in the task specification phase

Structural themes	
Teacher discourse	39
Pupil discourse	1

This analysis serves to demonstrate how completely the teacher dominates the text, in this, the phase in which teachers and pupils are to negotiate some sense of the task to be undertaken. In addition, such an analysis reveals very clearly the kinds of meanings constructed. Of the 39 structural themes produced by the teacher, 19 are instances of the conjunction *and*, in four places in association with the conjunctive adjunct *then*, and twice in association with the other conjunction *when*. In addition, *when* is used once alone, while *so* and *that* are both used twice. The pattern built up over a stretch of discourse of the kind examined, where there is such a large concentration of the additive conjunction *and*, as well as use of the conjunctive adjunct *then*, and use of the temporal conjunction *when*, is to construct a pattern of reasoning which is essentially anecdotal. That is to say, the requirement upon the children is that they build simple sequences of events drawn from personal experience. In the terms of the discourse which is essentially created by the teacher, the children are not enabled to do more than that.

. . . There is another sense in which theme in the contributions of both teacher and children is very similar: namely, the fact that they identify primarily class members or their relatives. Some examples include *mum, she, her dad*, and *my sister*. The 'content' of the lesson is very clearly personal experience. This latter observation causes me to return to an issue I alluded to earlier: namely, the ideologies concerning knowledge and teaching learning which appear to apply in the junior primary school. This will in turn cause me to take up, regrettably rather briefly, two of the texts written by the children, selected on the grounds that they are quite representative of those generally produced by the children in the class.

THE RELATIONSHIP OF THE WRITTEN GENRES TO THE CURRICULUM GENRE

As I indicated earlier, a great deal of early childhood curriculum practice appears to exploit and build upon the familiar personal experience of childhood, and this is in some senses defensible of course. Recourse to personal experience is probably for all of us a necessary first step or point of departure in undertaking new learning. What seems to make much early childhood education somewhat remarkable in this respect, however, is its tendency to view personal experience as a sufficient 'content' in itself for learning, about which children may both talk and write.

The trap in such a view, as I believe my analysis of the above curriculum text using theme in particular does demonstrate, is that it leads the children into patterns of reasoning and examination of experience of a most limited kind. It requires no more than the simplest construction of event of an anecdotal kind, both in talk and in writing. In the text I have examined, the language the teacher generates actually constrains the children, so that the discourse patterns she and they construct, and hence also the patterns of reasoning encoded in these, involve nothing of the speculation or enquiry which are ostensibly part of the purpose of education. Were such matters to be more centrally part of the classroom discourse, they would be apparent in several ways: in the use of ... themes whose collective effect was to construct more than a simple sequence of events; in the capacity of the children to control and use a greater number of the ... themes, so that they also exercised some share in the directions taken in the discourse; and finally, in the use of a much greater number of themes than in the text examined to do with matters other than the most immediate personal experience.

Let me conclude by citing two of the written texts produced in the lesson I have discussed, both of which, in the terminology Martin and Rothery (1980, 1981) have proposed, are examples of recounts, the first of which is somewhat more complete than the second.

Text 1

One day I forgot my lunch and Mrs S. hat [had] to ring my mum up to bring my lunch and I got a jam donut and two pese [pieces] of fru[i]t and a sosisg [sausage] roll and a drink. It was yummy. The end.

Text 2

One day I went [to] school and I remembered I forgot my lunch and I rang my mother she brot [brought] fich [fish] and chips.

Recounts – involving the simplest reconstruction of personal experience – are arguably the most commonly produced written genres in primary school education. The children in the particular study I undertook, and who included the writers of the two examples in Texts 1 and 2, wrote a very large number of texts using the same basic generic structure throughout years 1 and 2 of schooling. In short, they showed remarkably little advance in their developing control of written genres, though they did, admittedly, achieve some greater control of spelling and handwriting.

The children were, in fact, capable of doing considerably more in their writing development than such a finding may appear to reveal. Whenever a deliberate attempt was made to intervene, and to teach more explicitly for a control of other genres, they demonstrated a capacity to handle these. We must conclude, therefore, that the persistence of the recount in writing was a direct response to the demands of the curriculum genres in which they were generated, and which were a very frequent feature of the children's total curriculum experience over the first three years of schooling. In participating in such genres with their teachers, the children were enabled to do no more in the linguistic patterns they generated, both spoken and written, than to revisit and recreate aspects of personal experience. Yet personal experience – the theme of Food is itself a good example – does open up many possibilities for exploration of new experience and information, in ways more consistent, I would argue, with what an education is supposed to be about.

It is time for education – teacher education in particular – to look much more directly at the very intimate relationship between the curriculum context and genre and the written genres children produce. It is time, too, to re-examine some of the basic assumptions about what constitutes useful knowledge for the early years of schooling. Since knowledge, experience and information will be themselves encoded in the various linguistic patterns used, it should be clear that as we seek to change the nature of the knowledge examined, offering more genuine intellectual challenge to young children, we will also necessarily need to change the linguistic patterns, spoken and written, which are a part of early schooling.

REFERENCES

Bambrough, L. (1982) *My Lunch!*, Reading 360 Series, Melbourne: Longman Cheshire.

Christie, F. (1986) 'Learning to write: where do written texts come from?' A keynote paper at the Twelfth Australian Reading Association Annual Conference on Text and Context, held at the Sheraton Hotel, Perth, 2–5 July.

—— (1989) *Language Education*, Oxford: Oxford University Press.

Halliday, M. A. K. (1985) *An Introduction to Functional Grammar*, London: Edward Arnold.

Hasan, R. (1985) 'The structure of a text' in M. Haliday and R. Hasan (eds), *Language Context and Text: Aspects of Language in a Socio-semiotic Perspective*, Geelong, Victoria: Deakin University Press.

Martin, J. R. (1984) 'Language, register and genre', A reading in the Deakin University BEd *Children Writing Course, Course Reader*, Geelong, Victoria: Deakin University Press, pp. 21–30.

Martin, J. R. and Rothery, J. (1980, 1981) Writing Project Reports, Numbers 1 and 2, *Working Papers in Linguistics*, Linguistics Department: University of Sydney.

Ventola, Eija (1984)'Can I help you?: a systemic functional exploration of service encounter interaction', Unpublished PhD thesis, University of Sydney.

Chapter 11

Planning for writing across the curriculum

Beverly Derewianka

This paper describes an action research project involving a class of seven-year-olds at a country school in Australia. Their teacher, Fran Egan, had been introduced to Michael Halliday's functional grammar and was keen to try applying her new insights about language in her classroom.

Although Fran was delighted with the children's progress and attitude to writing in their 'whole language/process writing' classroom, many of the whole language activities had become isolated exercises – retellings, cloze passages, shared book, and so on – divorced from the 'real' language happening in other curriculum areas. How to get language out of 'the language block' and into the curriculum? How to promote purposeful inter-action between speaking, listening, reading and writing?

In her language programming, Fran widened her perspective from the individual activity to a whole thematic unit. The focus became *language for learning*, fostering an explicit consciousness in the children of how language functions in the learning process.

In particular, Fran was interested in Halliday's notion of register. Register is a way of describing how the *context* influences the language produced in a particular situation. In the classroom situation it is essentially the teacher who controls the context. The ways in which he or she constructs the class-room context can help promote the sort of language which contributes to learning. The following pages describe the ways in which Fran programmed to create certain contexts and how these contexts influenced the language of the classroom.

PLANNING THE CONTEXT

According to Halliday, there are three main variables which determine the register of any particular context – the field, the mode and the tenor. . . . Let's look at how each of these influenced Fran's programming.

THE FIELD

In basic terms, field refers to 'content'. The content of any learning is ultimately embodied in language. To learn content is to learn language. The
class had developed an avid interest in rocks and Fran decided to build on
this, taking 'Why We Study Rocks' as the theme of the unit. In a broad
sense then, the field which Fran was planning to develop was geology, and
in particular 'rocks'.

Fran acknowledged the children's existing knowledge of the field of
'rocks' and was concerned with extending the field in both planned
and unplanned directions. One of the functions of education is to help
children to explore and make sense of their world, and language is a
major resource in this endeavour as it is through language that we represent
our world. Language enables us to express the relationships we perceive
between phenomena in the environment. The children's understanding of
the field would be developed not only through the labelling or naming
of various rocks, but through the identification of relationships within the
field.

Fran therefore planned for opportunities for the children to develop and
use the language needed to observe, describe, define, compare, contrast,
group, classify, and generalize. The children's knowledge of the field then
would hopefully grow during the unit from their fairly random, everyday
'commonsense' knowledge about rocks to a more explicit, systematized,
integrated knowledge.

This might sound like a rather onerous, sobre undertaking for such
young children, but Fran didn't want to patronize them. She had high
expectations and so did they. They were eager to 'name their world' in ever-
increasing detail, to discover how it is organized and how it functions. And
to do that they needed the appropriate language tools.

THE MODE

Learning can take place through the oral mode or the written mode. Fran
was interested in the different roles these modes played in the learning
process.

We could look upon learning as a gradual 'distancing' process – from an
involvement in the detail of the here-and-now to stepping back, reflecting,
seeing the bigger picture, relating and consolidating and putting things in
perspective. And in fact Halliday talks of a variety of modes – each playing
a part in this distancing process. He plots these modes along a continuum,
ranging from the sort of language that accompanies action to the sort of
language employed in reflection. At the 'action' end of the continuum the
language tends to be oral – the sort of exploratory, interactive language used
when coming to grips with the world. Stepping back further, one might

reconstruct the action by telling someone what happened or writing a recount of it. Further towards the 'reflection' end of the continuum, we can exploit the 'frozen' nature of the written mode as it invites us to play around with the thoughts captured on paper – to share and refine them, to extend them, to make connections between them. At each step backwards, choices are being made to select significant aspects of the experience/subject matter and order them coherently.

ACTION ⟵——————————————————⟶ REFLECTION

e.g. language → commentary → reconstruction → construction
accompanying the action

Fran decided to use this mode continuum as the guiding principle in her programming. She would let the children explore the content first in the oral mode – interacting, sharing, bouncing off each other, with all the hesitations, unpredictability, backtracking, and approximations typical of spoken language. Then she would gradually move them along the continuum, shunting backwards and forwards as necessary, until they were able to reflect upon their experiences and understandings and pull them together in the written mode.

THE TENOR

Fran was aware however that the learning power of the various modes could only be fully utilized if the tenor in the classroom situation allowed for this to happen.

Tenor refers to the relationships between the participants and the roles that the participants engage in. The traditional classroom relationship between teacher and pupil is one in which the balance of power is very unequal, with the teacher in control of the knowledge and the patterns of classroom interaction. The sort of language which flows from such a relationship is typically long slabs of teacher monologue, punctuated by routines of pseudoquestions, programmed answers, evaluative comment by teacher, with the occasional regulatory outburst.

More conducive to learning might be the sort of language which reflects a more even balance of power – where children feel comfortable to contribute information, to hypothesize, to admit ignorance, to ask questions, to make suggestions, to give opinions, to initiate topics, to take responsibility. Fran planned therefore that, at appropriate stages during the unit, the children would enter into a variety of relationships – teacher/class, teacher/group, parent/child, child/child, child/group, child/class – each relationship enabling the child to interact and learn in a particular way.

Another closely related aspect of tenor which she took into account was the *roles* adopted by child and teacher. At times these were deliberately structured into the programme according to the learning activity at the

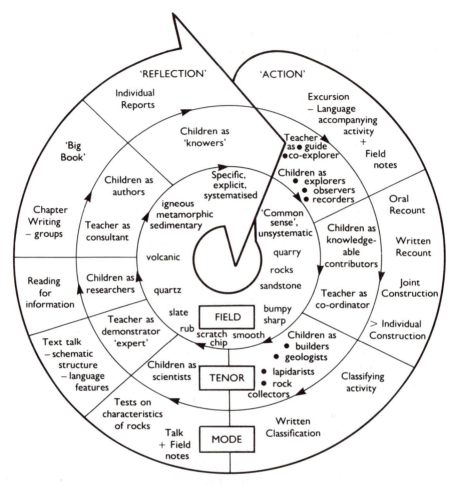

Figure 11.1 Diagrammatic description of a three-week unit of work

time. The teacher's role would range from 'knower' to 'co-learner', while the children became 'geologists', 'lapidarists', 'builders', 'researchers', 'authors', 'apprentices', 'experts', etc. They were expected to live the role, posing the sorts of questions and making the sorts of observations that such a role would demand. The adopting of these roles aimed at empowering the children, encouraging them to see themselves as responsible learners, apprentice members of the discipline, moving from a tentative grasp of the field towards a more definite, confident control.

The unit was designed not only to develop knowledge about rocks, but also to provide opportunities for the children to learn the sorts of roles necessary to become independent learners.

In summary, we can see learning language (and even learning itself) in terms of the mastery of a wide range of registers. Each of these registers is characterized by a particular mode, field, and tenor.

Figure 1 is an attempt at describing how a number of registers were developed over the three-week unit, starting at the 'action' end with physical engagement with rocks, employing a variety of modes as the children worked towards the 'reflection' end with the production of a written text – a jointly composed 'Big Book' drawing together what they had learnt about rocks. It represents the learning process as a spiral with no definite beginning or end.

PUTTING IT INTO PRACTICE

By now Fran had designed a programme which consciously structured the learning context in terms of mode, field and tenor:

- The mode would range from oral/active through to written/reflective as the unit progressed.
- The overall field involved an ever-increasing knowledge of 'rocks', deliberately introducing an awareness of how the field is constructed through comparing, contrasting, classifying, etc.
- The tenor would reflect the various roles and relationships engaged in by teacher, children (and parents).

Now Fran was curious to see whether this structuring of the context did in fact produce the sort of language which we would associate with learning.

In the following pages, we will trace through the stages of the unit as described in the spiral diagram, giving examples of the typical language produced at each stage.

LANGUAGE ACCOMPANYING ACTION

To initiate the children's formal study of rocks, an excursion into the surrounding countryside was organized, with a number of parents volunteering to drive the children around. To a certain extent the activity was planned – they would visit a variety of sites where different types of rocks could be observed, and it was suggested that the children note rocks in their natural state and rocks that had been used in construction. But otherwise the 'content' was determined by the children themselves, the open-ended nature of the activity allowing them to relate current knowledge to new information.

They first stopped at some old rock walls, previously just part of the landscape but now seen through new eyes. While they speculated on the origin of the rocks, parents recounted tales from local history about how the walls were constructed by Irish immigrants. Then on to a cutting where the freeway was slashing its way through a hillside. The children observed the layers of rock telling their stories of different geological eras. Nearby was a rock platform at the beach where they saw how the molten lava from nearby extinct volcanoes had solidified at the ocean's edge. Then around to the harbour with its pebbly shore and smooth rounded rocks. And finally the local quarry surrounded by stately walls of columnar basalt.

Along the way, the children had noted four sandstone churches, several stone walls, the rock fences in the paddocks, a few houses and a school made of basalt, the retaining walls of the harbour, the road surface, a couple of stone park benches, and a number of other rock constructions, including of course their own sandstone school building.

Mode

The language, captured on audiotape and video, was primarily oral: very much 'language accompanying activity' – the language of observing, exploring, coming to terms with the here-and-now. The written mode also played a minor role in its function of recording, capturing fleeting thoughts for later retrieval. The field-notes represented more than mere 'memory-joggers' however. They were early attempts at identifying significant details from the wealth of experiences surrounding the children. . . .

Tenor

The relationship between the adults and children in this context was more of an 'equal status' nature, allowing the children the freedom to make discoveries along with their teacher and parents. The children themselves were asking the questions, sharing information and giving instructions . . .

'Come and see this!'
'This one's got holes.'
'Look – sparks!'
'Why have they got that column shape?'
'It's sort of crumbly.'
'I know why it's smooth.'

They believed themselves to be apprentice geologists and their language reflected this role.

Field

Their command of the field at this stage was a mixture of everyday terminology ('moss rocks', gravel, orangey rocks, stones) and more specific terms (quartz, basalt, quarry, sandstone). In context, and in response to their questions, terms such as igneous, latite, columnar basalt, etc., were introduced.

RECOUNT

Mode

On their return to school, the class shared their experiences in the form of an oral recount. This was intended not only as a pooling of information, but as an initial 'distancing' from the action of the excursion – putting things in perspective, selecting significant aspects, ordering them in time.

This was followed immediately by a written recount of the day's outing in the form of a 'joint construction'. With the teacher acting as scribe using the overhead projector, the class, drawing on their shared experience, jointly composed the text. Within this functional context, questions arose regarding sequence, tense, singular/plural, spelling and punctuation. Most of these were initiated and worked through by the children themselves, though Fran explicitly guided them to a recognition of the typical features of the recount genre:

- an opening *orientation* (putting the reader in the picture – who took part? when? where?) followed by a series of *events* sequenced in time, finishing with a *reorientation*;
- the use of conjunctions of time to link up the events (first, firstly, then, next, then, then, next . . .);
- the use of location indicators (in the Jamberoo, Jerrara and Kiama areas, out of the school yard, at Jerrara, on the top of the fence;
- individual, named, known participants (Year Two, Nicole, we, Jamberoo school, the Little Blowhold, Kiama, the Quarry);
- action verbs in the past tense (we walked, we touched, they wiggled, we stopped, we travelled, we talked, we went, we finished).

Here is part of the 'joint construction' text:

Year 2 excursion to observe rocks

Year Two became interested in studying rocks when one of the class-members (Nicole) talked about a rock book she had read in Silent Sustained Reading. Year Two and their class teacher Miss Egan decided to go on an excursion in the Jamberoo, Jerrara and Kiama area.

As we walked out of the school yard we noticed the Jamberoo School Infants building is made out of sandstone. Our first stop was at Jerrara where we could observe rock fences. We observed lots of things here. Firstly we saw how the rocks were not stuck together properly. Then we touched them – they wiggled. Barbed wire was placed on the top of the fence. There was dried coloured moss on the rocks. The colours were green, grey, white and light orangey brown. There were different colours in the rocks.

Next we stopped at the new bridge work. The bridge was made out of cement. We saw mountains of rock that had been cut through. We saw little lines in the rock cutting. These were left by big building drills (Jackhammers). . . .

Tenor

Because they had all participated in the excursion, the children came to the writing task with something to say – the experience had been shared and each participant had something to contribute. The teacher therefore withdrew to the role of scribe, allowing the children to debate which points they felt were worthy of inclusion in an account of the outing. The teacher did not always play a passive role however. The scribe can in fact exercise a great deal of power, and when necessary the teacher used this power to guide the children towards a more effective text – reminding them of their audience, pointing out inconsistencies in tense, pronoun reference, helping with the overall structure, and so on.

Field

Generally the field of a recount is 'What went on' and tends to emphasize events. This recount however is not simply an itinerary of the excursion. It also records the observations made by the children. (This is reflected in the high incidence of verbs such as 'we noticed', 'we observed', 'we saw'.) We could represent the field of the recount by drawing up strings of related phenomena from the text (Table 11.1).

Table 11.1 Field of recount

Human participants	Locations	Rocks	Constructions
Year Two	Jamberoo	rocks	Jamberoo
Nicole	Jerrara	sandstone	PS Infants
Miss Egan . . .	Kiama	cement	School
	the school yard	mountains of rock	rock fences
	Jerrara	rock cutting . . .	bridge's
	the bridge . . .		foundations . . .

From the 'Rocks' string we can see that at this stage the children's knowledge about rocks is still expressed in everyday terms, with the occasional technical term creeping in . . . As yet there is not much evidence of the children attempting to bring order to the field, but this is understandable, as the purpose of a recount is simply to tell what happened.

CLASSIFICATION ACTIVITY

Mode

At this point we 'shunted' slightly backward along the mode continuum towards the 'action' end. The children had brought back their rock samples and were now going to classify them. The small-group discussion, while fairly reflective and orderly, nevertheless allowed the children to question, interject, change their minds, react to feedback. This oral give-and-take led to rather unsophisticated written classifications in diagrammatic form. So rocks were organized into two categories – 'beach rocks' and 'mountain rocks', for example. The ability to summarize in a precise, logical way is an important function of the written mode and was a significant step along the continuum.

Tenor

Roles were quite deliberately structured for this activity. The children were able to choose whether to be geologists, builders, lapidarists or rock-collectors according to their interest and knowledge. The children looked for the particular characteristics in the collection of rocks which would be of interest to their group:

- The geologists examined the features of each sample, noted the location where it was found and hypothesized as to its origins, justifying their decisions.
- The builders considered the different attributes of the rocks and classified them according to their possible uses.
- The lapidarists grouped their rocks with an eye to aesthetic qualities.
- The rock-collectors classified their samples according to idiosyncratic criteria – shape, colour, size, etc.

In each group the children took their roles very seriously, genuinely trying to tackle the problem from the specialist point of view.

The peer/peer relationships of the small groups permitted the children to interact as equals, without the 'expert' adult inhibiting their attempts. For example:

P1: I think this comes from down in the earth because it's all got kind of bits of dirt in it.
P2: I don't reckon this is glass. It doesn't feel like it.
P3: I know, cause it's been washed around.

Classifying activity

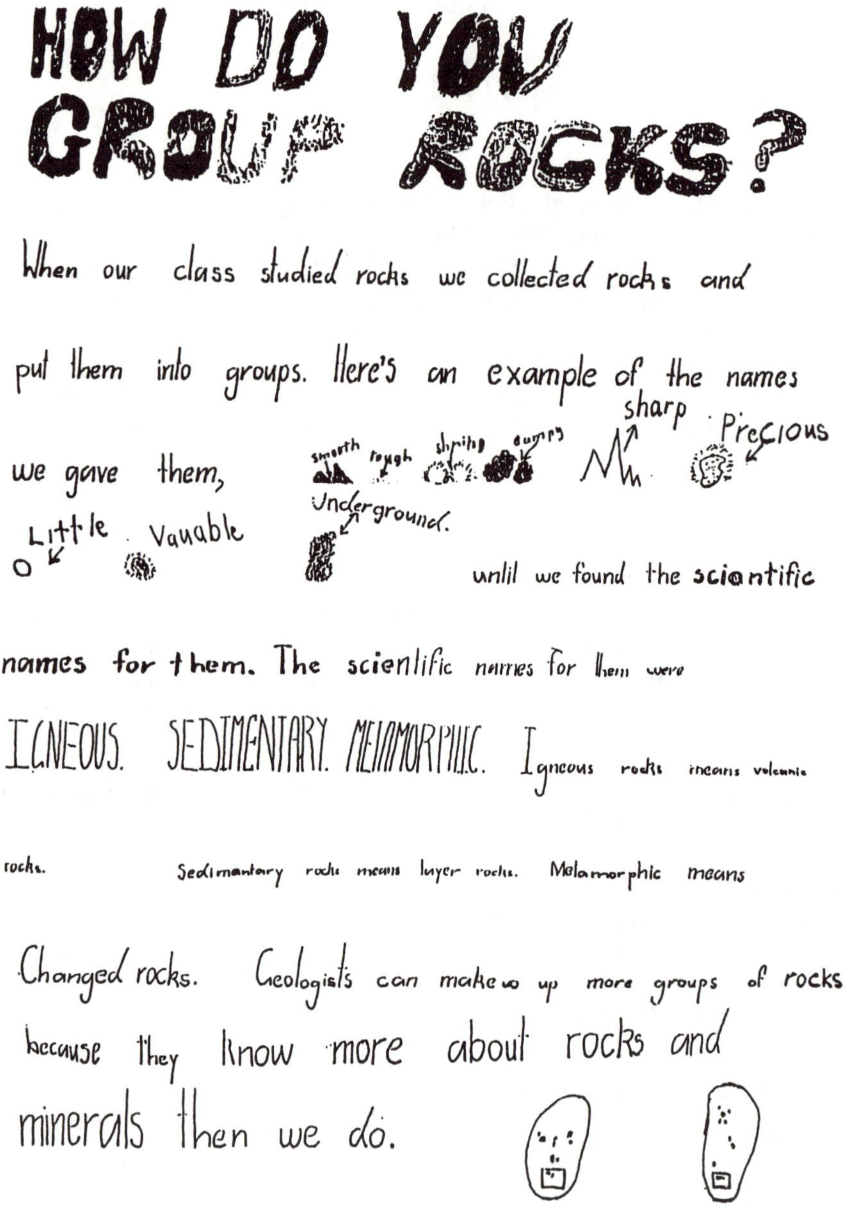

HOW DO YOU GROUP ROCKS?

When our class studied rocks we collected rocks and

put them into groups. Here's an example of the names

we gave them, smooth rough shining bumps sharp Precious

Little Vauable Underground.
o

                        until we found the **scientific**

names for them. The scienlific names for them were

IGNEOUS. SEDIMENTARY. METAMORPHIC. Igneous rocks means volcanic

rocks.   Sedimantary rocks means layer rocks.   Metamorphic means

Changed rocks.   Geologists can make up more groups of rocks

because they know more about rocks and

minerals then we do.

Figure 11.2 The children classified their rocks

P4: Geologists can tell what . . . they can tell what is what and which is which because they've got these special tools and stuff like that to open them up and see what they're like.

Field

The children made a valiant effort at the classifying activity . . . but whilst they learned a lot about the process of classifying, (i.e. going from the most general to increasingly specific classes, according to particular attributes) they were frustrated by the lack of a more detailed knowledge of rocks and their attributes. This awareness of their limited knowledge of the field is reflected in their later write up (see Figure 11.2).

EXPERIMENTING

Mode

Still towards the 'action' end of the continuum, the children carried out a variety of experiments on their rock samples in order to come to a more detailed understanding of the attributes of different types of rocks. The dominant mode was oral, although again the written mode played an ancillary role as the children dictated their observations to a group scribe. These notes were later shared with the whole class.

Tenor

In their role as 'scientists', they chipped and hammered and rubbed and scratched. Their language reflected a sense of responsibility for their own learning – an expectation that they would ask the sorts of questions and make the sorts of observations one would expect of a scientist . . .

'The crystal cr . . . smashed up in three goes.'
'That's why I'm experimenting with it.'
'I'm gonna experiment with this one.'
'You get a little bit on your finger and dab it onto the paper and it makes a sort of red colour.'

The small group resulted in a peer relationship which encouraged the children to participate on an equal footing. The following transcript shows children utilizing the oral mode to negotiate meanings about rocks, empowered by their roles as respected, knowledgeable equals:

Hammering test

    P1: What happened to it?
    P2: Nothing. It's a bit hard.
    P1: What is it?
    P2: Too hard to smash up.
    P1: What name of the stone? . . . Igneous . . . firestone.
    P2: No. It's too hard . . . too hard . . . too hard.
          (Spontaneously consult named rock collection)
    P1: Probably be that one.
    P2: Check with this.
         . . .
    P2: Check it out with this one.
    P1: That will be shale. It could be shale.

Field

The field was one of *doing* ('smashing', 'crushing', 'experimenting', 'squash-ing', 'watching') and of discovering *attributes* ('very sharp edges', 'a bit too hard', 'too hard to smash up', 'crushed', 'orangey'). The group was also keen to find out the names for the various rocks ('What's the name of the stone?' 'Igneous. Firestone.' 'Crystal.' 'Sandstone'.) They regularly compared their samples with those in a labelled rock collection ('That's slate. See how it's the same? . . . We know the name – we know the stone's name.')

By this stage the children had had plenty of opportunities to explore the subject of rocks in the oral mode – using familiar terminology but gradually acquiring more specific terms at the point of need. Every so often, they employed writing to preserve their observations. Now Fran started to exploit the power of the written mode to start ordering their experiences. All their understandings about rocks were to be brought together in the form of a 'Big Book'. The children decided which aspects they were particularly interested in and formed themselves into groups to produce a chapter on their chosen topic. We were now moving towards the reflective end of the mode continuum – going from the multitude of specific details to more generalized, orderly reflection.

TEXT TALK

Mode

The emphasis now shifted to written texts, although oral language still played an important interactive role. Fran chose a short expository text on rocks. Using the overhead projector, she guided the children to engage with the text by identifying and underlining various features (schematic struc-ture, major 'participants', the use of exemplification, etc., as well as layout aspects such as headings, illustrations, captions, glossary).

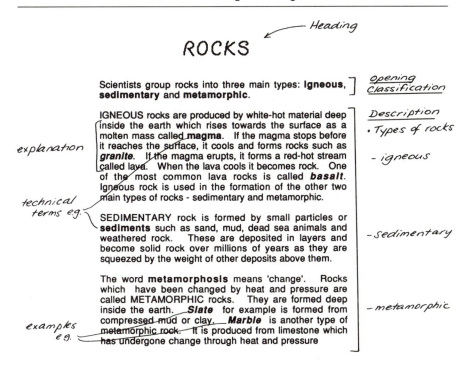

Figure 11.3 Identifying features of a written text

This demonstration was aimed at helping the children develop strategies for locating information in written texts. It also served as an explicit model for the children's own writing. (See Figure 11.3 for model text and indication of the sorts of features identified by Fran and the children.)

Tenor

In this activity, the teacher took on the role of 'expert', sharing her knowledge of text with the class. The children, however, were not passive recipients, but were invited to actively participate in an unthreatening, supportive environment.

Field

The written text presented the field in an organized manner – filling in gaps in the children's knowledge and drawing out relationships, in particular the class/subclass taxonomy [rocks were organized into 3 groups, metamorphic, sedimentary and igneous].

THE BIG BOOK

Mode

By now the class was well into 'the writing process'. The oral mode was still important as the groups pooled their knowledge and collaborated in researching and constructing their joint texts. But it was the written mode that took precedence as they sought information from books, jotted down their notes, organized their knowledge, drafted, redrafted, edited and finally published.

The children also worked on individual reports, summarizing what each one now knew about rocks.

Tenor

The children assumed the roles now of researchers and authors and were learning the skills to make them competent in these roles. Most of the interaction was at the peer level as they shared their information, asked each other questions, made suggestions and came to decisions. Because of the constant and explicit modelling by the teacher (e.g. text talks, joint constructions, public editing, shared book) the children were able to be independent and productive in their small groups. Before publication, the class was fortunate to be visited by a real-life editor of children's books, who took on the role of expert to answer their questions about what an editor does. They also had discussions with a group of Indonesian geologists visiting the area who were quite taken with the way the children rook seriously their role of 'apprentices' in the field.

Field

A perusal of the published 'Big Book' revealed a well-developed knowledge about the field of rocks. The children appeared to be quite comfortable with the three major classes of rocks and happily took to the terms 'igneous', 'sedimentary', 'metamorphic', defining them in their own words ('fire rock', 'a rock made up of lots of layers', 'two rocks pressured for a very long time'). They also became aware of an extensive variety of subclasses (quartz, crystals, gems, slate, shale, marble, latite, sandstone, pumice, coal, columnar basalt, blue metal, etc.). They had started to look at the composition of rocks and had an inkling about minerals. They had a good knowledge of the characteristics of various rock-types and the uses of different rocks. . . .

Best of all, they did not see the acquisition of such knowledge as 'difficult' or 'a bore', as evidenced by the fact that many weeks after the theme had finished, their enthusiasm had not diminished and they kept bringing samples to class and making collections at home.

A detailed analysis of the transcripts and written texts has since revealed that Fran's planning had in fact produced the kind of registers which we would associate with learning, the children engaging purposefully with a variety of modes from active through to reflective; experiencing a number of different roles within a supportive environment; and gaining an increasing control over the field in question.

Part III

Science: views of the domain and learning

Chapter 12

Introduction

Patricia Murphy

Current innovations in the science curriculum for primary schools reflect a long history of debate and controversy. A considerable body of research has been conducted in the field of science education with a specific focus on how children learn. Typically this has concentrated on children's difficulties in acquiring scientific conceptual understanding to explain phenomena in the physical world – the traditional objective of science education. This research has revealed the intimate relationship between children's knowledge structures and cognitive processing. Another significant outcome of the research was the attention focused on the nature of science learning which came to be seen as a process of initiation into the ways of seeing, thinking and acting practised by the scientific community. Central to this was the view of knowledge as a tool. In this view, what children need to learn are both the concepts of science and an understanding of how and when to use them. This type of learning is therefore dependent on understanding both the purposes and tasks that scientists engage in and the processes by which they come to know and see the world. This view of the nature of science learning opened up debate about the nature of science and the practices of scientists. At issue here were the implications of this perspective for what children should learn and how they should learn it.

These three interrelated strands in research and developments in science education are reflected in the selection of chapters for this part of the book. Taken together they invite the reader to consider the connections between changing views of learning and of the domain and developments in the curriculum in terms of what are considered valuable learning objectives and the practices advocated to achieve them.

The influence of constructivist views of learning in determining the science curriculum of the 1990s is the subject of Solomon's critical review. She details the developments in constructivist theories of teaching and learning and how these have impacted on the science curriculum. For Solomon the aim of science learning, to acquire scientific ways of explaining phenomena, constitutes a 'second way of knowing' distinct from children's life-world ways of thinking. The demands made on children encountering another 'system of knowing which is overarching, abstract and consistently applied', i.e. the domain of 'scientific knowing', whilst continuing to operate in the domain of the life world is, in her view, not well addressed by theories of personal constructivism. She argues that in consequence, some of the practices advocated by constructivists do not facilitate children's acquisition of scientific understanding but rather consolidate their everyday beliefs and explanations.

In chapter 14, Driver and her co-workers focus on the implications for curriculum planning and sequencing of research into young people's acquisition of domain-specific knowledge. The evidence from cross-age studies into the evolution of children's domain-specific reasoning reveals what Driver refers to as 'broadly similar conceptual trajectories in their acquisition of scientific knowledge'. The analysis of these suggests three dimensions along which children's reasoning progresses, dimensions that it is argued can be incorporated into curriculum planning in science. Driver is careful to point out that learning science involves more than learning science concepts. Hence, for example, the relationship between these conceptual trajectories and children's progression in procedural understanding is not addressed, nor indeed is the significance of domain-specific knowledge from other areas of the curriculum.

The focus on procedural understanding in the science curriculum is quite a recent one marked by much controversy. Gott and his co-workers have played a pivotal role in developing thinking in this area. Their more recent research is the focus of the next chapter. Like Driver, Gott and his co-workers have turned their attention to issues of progression. Gott questions what the aims of science education in the 1990s should be. He argues that the traditional emphasis in science education has been on understanding scientific concepts rather than on understanding scientific evidence. Yet the need to evaluate evidence is in his view central to being a scientifically competent or literate citizen. Hence, in his view, procedural understanding is an essential component of any description of the science curriculum.

The final chapter in Part III looks more closely at the practices that are advocated as a consequence of shifting views of learning and of the domain. Howe looks at the advocacy of peer interaction in the context of practical scientific activities and provides a useful review of recent research. She identifies some of the characteristics that are prerequisites for successful collaboration, in particular the need for individuals in groups to hold different preconceptions. This finding conflicts with common practice in primary schools where children are often grouped because of the similarity in their ideas. This is done with the intention of enabling children to develop a shared task and goal. Howe and her co-workers' findings also suggest that such activities rarely lead to immediate learning outcomes and that a significant time gap is needed before progression can be observed. This finding has clear implications for teacher assessment. Also of interest is the evidence that the type of task used significantly affects the potential for individual learning in group situations. The evidence from Howe's review provides a useful way of constructing links between the research of Driver and her co-workers into conceptual progression and Gott *et al.*'s findings concerning the nature and understanding of evidence: links which indicate potential future directions for practice in science education.

Chapter 13

Constructivism and quality in science education

Joan Solomon

EXPLAINING THE TITLE

This is an opportunity to look carefully at two entities – constructivism and education – which we are now well used to considering together, but might well seem to be worlds apart. On the one hand we have a complex philosophical approach to the conceptualization of the phenomenological world within the head of the observer; on the other stands a public project which has firm external goals of cognition involving all the paraphernalia of school classrooms, pupils and teachers. Indeed it is quite curious that the science education community has found itself welcoming into the very heart of its deliberations a way of thinking so fundamentally alien to its practice. As we shall see, it happened partly by chance, and partly by the unexpected transformation of a descriptive child-centred study into the bleakest of old-fashioned scepticism.

The inclusion of 'quality' in the title warns any reader that the argument has no intention of being caught in the morass of an indefinite 'science' made up from a loose amalgam of individual preconceptions. Our science will not have to be naively positivist or empirical, but it must be recognizably science. Its recognition, and those who recognize it, will be a central part of the evidence.

THE EMERGENCE OF PERSONAL CONSTRUCTIVISM

Most people know how constructivism, within science education, began. It started with the words of children. Some might date it back to Rosalind Driver's thesis of 1973, others to the early work of Piaget where he so delightfully described *The Child's Conception of the World* (1929). Possibly no one before him had listened properly to children as thinkers in their own right: he asked them why they thought the way they did, and the answers he received showed their different ways of interpreting observations of wind and sky, of sun, moon and trees.

But there was, inevitably, a difference between the intentions of Piaget and Driver in their approach to children's thinking. For Piaget the logician, the forms of their thinking were the deep structures of the mind, and he devoted his long life to their examination. For Driver the search was more empirical with children thinking 'like scientists', and yet each one differently. At this point a social historian might make much of the difference of approach which had developed over these fifty years from the era of Bertrand Russell's triumphs in *Principia Mathematica* perhaps, to that of relativism and post-modernism in the 1970s. (I include such references to ideas of the times as no more than a way of emphasizing differences.)

Driver (1983), in her opening chapter, describes a boy moving a spring balance which was weighing a stone, up to a higher level. He explained that as stones released from higher up fell faster, he had thought that gravity would be greater up there. I encountered a similarly eccentric but well thought out idea some two years ago. A middle-aged science teacher whom I was re-training to teach physics, warned me as she first entered the room that she would take advantage of the course to ask all the questions she had not dared to ask at school. Sure enough, as we were studying circuit electricity, she challenged me – 'Why should you add all the resistances in a circuit together?' She explained that just using the biggest one would be enough to calculate the current flowing since it would be responsible, she thought, for controlling the current, just as the worst of any series of traffic-jams determines the overall flow of road traffic.

Both these people, the boy and the science teacher, were sophisticated thinkers with conceptual schemata which they had developed for themselves in order to model natural phenomena. More than that, they were both able to articulate their theories and were willing to test them. (Both, I imagine, would be a delight to teach – I can vouch for the fact that the teacher certainly was. This is a point we shall return to later.)

It was evidence like this which fuelled the popularity of the 'personal construct theory' in the first phase of educational constructivism. The book of the theory had been written earlier by George Kelly (1955). He was a psychologist who studied patients locked away in the solitary world of the schizophrenic. Every person, Kelly said, construed the world differently, testing out their constructions against experience. Although others were to use his dictum 'Every man his own scientist', Kelly himself wrote of the fragmentation of an individual's constructs, calling it the 'problem of consistency' and commenting that a person may successively employ a variety of subsystems which are inferentially incompatible with each other. This does not read at all like the programme of science. He also wrote that no one was able completely to construe another's constructs, and that only to the extent that one can, is it possible to play a social role involving the other. This point went almost without mention in the initial enthusiasm of the science education community. In New Zealand where an enterprising group of gifted young researchers took up the idea of personal constructivism in the early 1980s, it was firmly applied. They too listened to children's ideas about science and, in the fashion of Driver's thinking rather than Piaget's, called what they heard 'Children's Science' (Gilbert *et al.* 1982).

PERSONAL AND RIGOROUS OR COMMON AND FLEXIBLE?

Meanwhile more evidence was accumulating which had, or should have had, worrying implications for a simple application of Personal Construct Theory. First of all there were a great number of children, at least within the same language group, who shared common schemata. In optics they believed that light travelled from the eye to the object, in electricity that current was used up by the light bulb, and in biology that plants fed on the soil. None of these ideas were very surprising. In every case there were common language usages which could explain how the children could have come to hold ideas like these, e.g. 'he threw a glance at her', 'we are using up too much electricity', and 'dig in fertilizer to feed the plant'. Cross-national studies (Ross and Sutton 1982; Duit and Talisayon 1984) confirmed that children's spontaneous constructions varied markedly from one language to another.

That conclusion did not, in itself, oppose the personal construct theory; it just dulled a little the rather grand picture of the lonely thinker tracing out a uniquely personal cognitive path. The next finding was that children did not apply their constructions consistently, as indeed Kelly had warned. They could hold two different ideas and apply the first at one time, and the other a few seconds later in a situation which was only marginally changed. Often they could hardly tell why they thought as they did, or why they changed their schema. When they did reply to questioning it was usually to answer that 'it all depends on the circumstances' (Solomon, 1984a).

It should have surprised no one that children thought like this. Language owes much of its poetic power to its capacity to have double, or ambiguous, meanings. In everyday thought and common maxims people do adapt their ways of reasoning using logic rarely, and rhetoric more often. Especially when they talk together, both adults and children change meanings and ways of talking because social conventions require it. These effects were antagonistic to personal construct theory only because its proponents had staked their faith on two rather shaky premises. The first was that children had constructed and tested out their own schemata against experience, whereas many seemed to have picked up ideas from language. The second premise was that children used their mini-theories just as scientists use their scientific concepts and theories. There was evidence, if it was looked for, that this was not true either. Scientists are a sub-group who have trained themselves to use concepts, language, and the communal construction of knowledge in a way which is often substantially different from everyday thinking. This point will be examined later in more detail.

It was fortunate for the early constructivists that about this time a resoundingly relativist book by Feyerabend was published which seemed to be saying that scientists did just the same as the children. If 'anything goes' for scientists, as Feyerabend (1975) asserted, it must have seemed that the constructivist premise that children's ways of thinking were 'scientific' could survive and flourish even if their ideas were not consistently applied. It was not difficult to find historical incidents where scientists did not at once relinquish their theories when some of the evidence seemed to go against them. Kuhn (1962) had explained this earlier in terms of dominant scientific paradigms, but educationalists could be forgiven for not reading deeply into a philosophical argument which was messy, and even ill-tempered. Few had the time, patience or scholarship to inquire whether a relativistic philosophy of science really was similar to what they had already named 'children's science'.

CONSTRUCTIVISM FOR TEACHING?

The next phase in the argument was about learning. All the early researchers reported that children's ideas were astonishingly resistant to teaching, or to the demonstrations of counter-instances. This was inconvenient for the image of the child as scientist, able and willing to drop any idea that did not match up to testing. While this did show a surface similarity to the Kuhnian notion of the dominant paradigm tending to colour everything which the holder sees, there was an important difference. Children do not expect their meanings and explanations to work in all situations, whereas scientists are made to feel uneasy with the 'anomalies' that they encounter, even if they do succeed in ignoring this for the time being when the remainder of the theoretical structure proves valuable.

The practical problem, which was far more serious for education than were the echoes of philosophical argument, was how pupils could be taught the 'correct' accepted scientific ideas in school – the pursuit of quality in science education.

For classical constructivists this was awkward. Even to admit that one theory could be more 'correct' than another took a lot of swallowing. Then they found how difficult it was to dislodge the very ideas which they had been at pains to explore. It was too much for most of them to simply ignore the ideas of the children and teach orthodox science with enough authority to overpower them. Even to suggest such a method was tantamount to saying that the research on children's ideas, interesting though it had been, really contained nothing of any pedagogic value. The image of children as scientists, coupled with a simplistic view of scientific history, could be taken to suggest that by discussing their 'wrong' ideas, pupils would soon come to see the 'right' ones for themselves, with a minimum of assistance. In the event most children were found to cling even harder to their spontaneous ideas once they had discussed them with their friends. This whole problem area was called 'conceptual change'. It still figures in most research programmes, and I do not wish to denigrate its obvious educational value for exploring new and better teaching strategies.

In order to explain these difficulties, constructivists used two new concepts. One of these was the 'empty vessel'. Children's minds, they said, were not like this. On the contrary they were full of their own ideas so that was why teaching new ones was hard. Secondly, children were, or should be, 'active learners' since they had to 'construct' what they learnt while they were being taught it. This item of constructivist orthodoxy is certainly not false; no one would imagine that children, or any one else, can possibly learn in the same fashion as a sheep is branded with a hot iron. Learning is difficult and the worse pupils are taught, the more work has to be put into the learning process. Poor quality lecturing, for example, requires very substantial follow-up in private study, whereas engaging in a progression of activities where the students learn and then try out the new ideas in a succession of stages makes for sound learning which will need little extra study for internalization.

Constructivism, to this way of thinking, is about what goes on inside the learner's head during learning. This process may well be effectively unknowable, but the emphasis is certainly helpful for teachers. The fact that children sometimes start the learning process with conflicting ideas and a variety of meanings makes the job of teaching all the more difficult.

Most traditional constructivists engaging in conceptual change programmes still begin by encouraging the children to discuss in depth what they believe about a particular phenomenon, even though it may well strengthen these beliefs. Their reasons for doing this may be ideological in a constructivist sense. Some have advanced another argument for not just ignoring or contradicting the original 'misconceptions'. They suggest that managed discussion of a crucial experiment could teach pupils about the scientific process at the same time as they are coming to understand accepted scientific theory. This part of the constructivist programme sounds promising and there is some evidence (Solomon *et al.*, 1992) that it produces good results in terms of understanding the nature of science. The CLIS project in Leeds has carried out complete constructivist programmes over a number of topics, but without emphasis on scientific method. We need to remind ourselves, astonishing as it may be, that no properly evaluated teaching research so far set up has supported constructivist assumptions about teaching.

TWO DOMAINS OF THINKING

Those who have taught secondary science, or conducted classroom research, often recognize the persistence of old ideas alongside new ones. Surprisingly, the two sets of ideas seem to be able to co-exist in the pupils' minds. Sometimes it is assumed that the new work is not properly understood, or that it is in the process of fading away under the dominance of older familiar ways of thinking. There is, however, a different way of interpreting this common phenomenon which makes interesting links with the learning of other bodies of knowledge.

According to the sociologists of knowledge, all of us learn a life-world way of thinking at our mother's knee. It is mobile, responsive, with a modest scale and small 'horizon of meaning' for the events it tries to explain (Schutz and Luckmann, 1973). Like many folk-sayings and proverbs, this life-world thinking is accepted as true in one situation and not in another, and may be shifted to match its meanings to those of the people we are speaking with. That makes it strongly interactive, and all the more comfortable for that. Encountering another system of knowing which is over-arching, abstract and consistently applied is very demanding and uncomfortable for most young pupils. It usually operates in a less familiar situation, such as a school. At other times outside the school, pupils need to continue to use the more familiar life-world way of thinking in order to fit in with families and friends. Hence it follows that those who attempt to learn the scientific way of explaining phenomena are effectively learning a second kind of knowing. This is not only difficult in itself, it presents difficulties of choice in memory retrieval. Which kind of explanation and meaning does the teacher expect when she asks about energy, plants or light? For many students it is the most familiar domain of thinking, the life-world, which is first to reach the tongue; but successful teachers know that appropriate cues can also trigger the scientific domain of thought. Its explanations have not been lost. This movement between the two knowledge domains can be shown to be easier for the more 'intellectually able' students (although such a statement is probably tautological). If the movement, or 'bringing' between domains is encouraged it certainly produces more durable learning (Solomon, 1984b, 1992a).

This theory of learning finds interesting parallels in the work of anthropologists like Pierre Bourdieu (1977), and linguists like Michael Halliday (1978). The former compared life-world maxims for behaviour (the habitus) with legal knowledge; the second compared everyday speech with literary language. Both found the same discontinuities and the same movement between the two domains of knowledge which had to be triggered by the recognition of appropriate cues. These findings are not strange to most people, although they are very remote from what an application of logic might lead us to suppose. Their value lies in showing what pronounced effects social conditions can have on knowing. It moves the argument away from strictly personal constructivism without eliminating the need to construe in order to learn. The social cues of everyday living can now be recognized as important features of the process of constructing knowledge.

SOCIAL CONSTRUCTIVISM AND INTER-SUBJECTIVITY

The enormous prestige of the Socratic dialogue has blinded many to the quite different subtleties of social talk and action. There is no room here to go into all the subtleties of what constitutes this everyday process; some, however, will be needed when we return to a discussion of the latest incarnation of personal constructivism.

Teaching, which is an act of persuasion, is a part of social constructivism, and in the context of education it is clearly the most important. However, it is neither the simplest nor the most common. It is complex and asymmetric because of the power structures which urge compliance with new ways of thinking in a way that everyday talk between friends does not. In both these arenas, however, there is a need for feed-back of some sort; by speech, eye contact or head nodding. Even when giving a lecture, one of the least social of all communication methods, good lecturers run their eyes round the room to find someone to provide the minimum of confirmatory feed-back. This is not so much to reassure themselves that someone is listening and agreeing, but to obtain confirmation of the communication process in which they themselves are taking part. The important point to notice is that the incentive for this search for social approval is that all communication is two-way and interactive. The speaker receives as much from the listener, in this sense, as the listener does from the speaker. Consensuality, or at least response, is the stuff of the social construction of knowledge. Without it we would be brain-washed and uncertain with all we think we know or attempt to communicate disintegrating like a telephone conversation down a line which has gone dead. In order to accomplish this interaction we change our meanings a little in order to try to make a match with those who respond. This flexible semantic behaviour of individuals talking together, which is so very much more than the sum of their separate opinions, is what constitutes 'inter-subjectivity'.

The best passage to illustrate this function of talk and response in the social construction of knowledge comes from a book written by teachers of English, about understanding children's talk.

> we all need to work through, sort, organise and evaluate the events of our daily lives ... we have to assimilate our experiences and build them into our continuing picture of the world; as social beings we need to legitimate the world picture we are continuously constructing ... and the responses we receive in the course of these conversations profoundly affect both the world picture we are creating and our view of ourselves.
>
> (Martin *et al.*, 1976)

The special social actions of science teachers, in addition to the others which all humans need in order to communicate with each other, are designed to socialize students into the domain of science knowledge. The pupils need to know not just what facts or theories are correct and what are not; they need to appreciate new ways of explaining, a new system of allocating meanings to words, and what it means to test out ideas. This is sometimes called the 'game' science is playing. For the two individuals described in the second section of this paper, the boy and the science teacher, the scientific method of constructing knowledge would not be altogether new. In their own way, each had already used something of the method for modelling gravity or electric current. However, the difficulty that many pupils have in understanding the logical connection between hypothesizing and testing, and between explaining and describing (Duveen *et al.*, in press), provides overwhelming empirical evidence that most children simply do not 'think like scientists'. Often their own thinking is quite opaque to them. Only when the teacher has succeeded in socializing them into this new and more logical way of thinking can they enter the domain of scientific knowing. Even then the older domain of the life-world is still open, beckoning them back to the amiable fluidity of everyday talk once the school door is shut.

RADICAL CONSTRUCTIVISM?

The sociological approach to learning, including the two-domain effect, indicates a way through one of the oldest of philosophical puzzles. It could be put like this –

> How can I know that another knows what I know, or observes what I observe, since observation must involve personal interpretation. Can either of us ever know if our internally constructed perceptions correspond to a 'real' phenomenon?

If all knowledge-making is private construction, this isolates observation, mental imagery, and all aspects of knowing, within the skull of the knower. There can be neither agreement with others nor 'truth to reality'. This was the central problem of Berkeley's solipsistic philosophy and also worried the pre-Socratics, Hume, Kant and Montaigne, to mention just a few. It was latent in Kelly's personal construct theory and has recently turned up again as 'radical constructivism'.

The chief proponent of this view within science education is von Glasersfeld, who describes it in this way:

> If experience is the sole contact a knowing individual can have with the world, then there is no way of comparing the outcomes of experience with the reality which is supposed to be the source of all the messages

which we receive. . . . So the paradox is that in order to find out if our understanding is 'true' we would have to know what we were trying to understand before understanding it.

(von Glasersfeld, 1983 my translation)

His views have been taken up by Laroche and Desautels (1992), who concluded that they present a new scenario in which the subject who seeks knowledge, the things which are to be known, and the processes of knowing them, stand in a new relationship to each other. Understanding does not exist on its own because it can only be constructed by someone experiencing something. (The parallel with Bishop Berkeley's dilemma about the existence of the 'tree in the quad', when God is not about to observe it, is almost complete!) But I would suggest that their conclusions, although not formally wrong, are misleading in three ways.

Firstly, the scenario is not new, as Laroche and Desautels point out. Secondly, there is new work on this ancient problem which has not so much solved it, as shown it to be of less importance. Indeed one of the triumphs of Wittgenstein, and later of Taylor (1985) and Rorty (1989), has been to show not that the problem exists, but that there are excellent grounds for *ignoring* it. Wittgenstein, for example, said simply that 'My life shews that I know or am certain that there is a chair over there, or a door, and so on' (quoted in Grayling 1988: 96). Rorty (1989) claims that the culture of a liberal society should aim at curing us of the purely metaphysical need for certainty and adds

> To sum up, the moral I want to draw is that this charge [of being relativist] should not be answered but ignored. We should learn to brush aside such questions as 'How do you know that . . .?'
>
> (Rorty, 1989: 54)

Thirdly, the presentation is misleading because it is asocial. Personal knowing is notoriously precarious and subject to brain-washing, unless socially reinforced. Rorty (ibid.) writes that we call something 'fantasy' rather than 'philosophy' simply on the grounds that it does not 'catch on with other people'. Similarly, the sociologists of knowledge maintain that our common ways of communicating are sophisticated efforts not so much to describe things as they 'really' are but to share meanings through the operation of empathic intersubjectivity. Von Glasersfeld's argument (1989) that to understand what someone says means to have built up a conceptual structure in which 'the receiver hearing nothing which contravenes his expectations', will not do. Understanding manifests itself through interchange and a skilful dynamic during which meanings are chosen from a repertoire of language tools into which the speaker/hearers have been socialized. That is the meaning of intersubjectivity both in the domain of science and in that of the life-world.

The radical constructivist's dilemma can simply be considered as part of the human condition like exchanging gossip, sharing the observation of a strange cloud formation, or describing what happened on the way to the forum. Observing phenomena and communicating what we have observed becomes not a philosophical impasse but a familiar social situation. This argument is not a simple-minded rejection of difficult philosophical problems but an understanding of them illuminated by twentieth-century insights in sociology. Most importantly it helps us to explain the success of two exploits which sceptical philosophy seemed to threaten – the scientific community's construction of its common knowledge archive, and pupils' learning of school science.

THE SOCIAL WORLD OF SCIENCE

What do practising scientists do in the face of this old problem about the reality of the phenomena that they are attempting to explore and explain? This is no place to go deeply into the current epistemology of science, but we can begin with two statements with which few scientists would disagree.

1. *Scientific knowledge is not certain.* Theories come and go in the course of history, and with them whole ways of looking at the world. Almost every scientist, however set in (his?) ways, knows at heart that the scientific knowledge in use today may be superseded tomorrow. It is provisionally constructed knowledge, not the certain verdict of nature.

2. *Scientists are no different from other mortals.* They need frequent reassurance through sharing their meanings, problems, and new ideas, with other who have the same interests. Doing this within science is doubly valuable. Isaac Newton is famous for saying something like 'If I have seen further than other men it is because I have stood on the shoulders of giants.' Knowledge-making in science is essentially a social endeavour, so consensus and communication are of the greatest importance.

In recognizing that objective truth is a chimera, science tries to use institutionalized intersubjectivity in its place. Of course it is not difficult to catch out scientists pontificating in public as though they are completely sure that all the knowledge contents of science are objectively true. Just as philosophers continue to debate the problems of reality in a post-Wittgensteinian age, so scientists can and do behave either like positivists insisting on the methodological truth of what they do, or like realists who take the existence of quarks, gravitons or punctuated evolution as indubitable starting points for problem-solving. In both these cases it is easy to see the psychological advantages to scientists of taking up such positions during working hours, even if they revert to more philosophically sound reflections on the nature of science after dinner.

In the second half of this century the epistemology of science has drawn heavily upon the sociology of knowledge. Kuhn (1962) wrote of the paradigms of science which allowed a school of scientists to share meanings and communicate with each other. Ziman (1968) emphasized the methods of communication of scientists which led to their virtual consensus on the knowledge to be incorporated into the community archive – until ousted sometime in the future by a new consensus. Merton (1973) wrote in more detail about the self-regulating norms espoused, if not adopted, by working scientists about how knowledge is to be collected (see also Ziman, 1978 on *Reliable Knowledge*). References to these well-known authors are enough to see that there is an acceptance of constructivism within science. Awareness of this process on the most basic level is what has led the community to formulate rules and procedures to guide them through, for example, the careful refereeing of papers for publication and the accessibility of research data.

SCIENCE EDUCATION AFTER CONSTRUCTIVISM

This chapter has explored constructivism in science education from several perspectives. It has not led to a simple conclusion, although it has exposed some ideas which are either over-blown, or unhelpful. At the core of the theory still lies the child's thinking and learning about phenomena of the natural world which are clearly central to good quality science teaching.

New ideas, or critiques of those already existing, can be surprisingly damaging in education because there is a worrying lack of *gravitas* in the ideas and practice of science education. Just as primary schools suffer as one fashion in teaching children how to read takes over from another, so in science education we have seen swings of the pendulum going, as pendula do, far beyond the equilibrium position first on one side and then on the other. In practical work, for example, there was a time when the excellent idea of giving students an occasional open-ended problem to explore, turned into an ideology of disengaging all practical work from the learning of concepts and theories. Now that has changed and suddenly no new practical work can begin without students rehearsing what they have learnt and using it to identify variables – as though this is the essence of all that is worthwhile in all experimental science.

The same mistake could easily be made again in respect of constructivism. The question is how much of what has passed for constructivism in science education over the last decade should be retained, and what part of it we could release without loss. We need to persuade and help children to recognize a new way of thinking about the world in the terms of scientific concepts and theories. This is a long job which is made especially difficult if conflicting ideas are already entrenched in their minds.

1 Knowledge of the common misconceptions of children is valuable to teachers who then know what sort of problems students are likely to face, and which persuasive demonstrations might best be used.
2 If the ideas are embodied in everyday language they may live on along- side the scientific knowledge learnt at school. Appropriate cuing will be needed for retrieving scientific ideas and concepts.
3 Learning new or alternative explanations is a difficult process which needs the active collaboration of the learner.
4 Social reinforcement of life-world misconceptions can be the unfortunate outcome of small group discussions about them.

This last point is not widely understood by personal constructivists but is the inevitable result of social exchange. Talk between friends is a search for consensus with meanings which can shift to suit the circumstances. The hardening of common misconceptions is a frequent finding by classroom teachers, and is documented in the research literature.

I would like to add more conclusions from research which may be useful to . . . teachers. Both have arisen in the recent classroom research on children's understanding of what scientists do. Both relate to construc- tivism.

5 Having tutored expectations about what will occur in their experiments [and investigations] and watching what happens in the light of these ideas, is an aid to the students' construction of understanding, as well as mirroring what scientists do.
6 Teachers can make changing ideas more acceptable to students if they show that the process of change has happened to scientists in the past.

The first of these (number 5 above) suggests that students can be helped to use experiments for the process of conceptual construction. I have written before (Solomon 1980) that conceptual understanding is an essential pre- requisite to carrying out an experiment in a valuable way, and not an outcome of its result. Children use their mental constructions as well as their language, hands, and [equipment] for doing practical work. Concepts and models are tools for investigating. This implies that expectations can be confirmed or gently tuned by experimental outcomes far more easily than they can be refuted. That alone suggests that teaching about concepts should either proceed or go hand in hand with [practical] work. Our recent research showed that many children hold a serendipitous view of experiment – that 'anything may happen'. This may be due to a cartoon image of sci- entists, or to a common meaning of 'experiment' in everyday language, and is entirely unhelpful to the construction of new knowledge.

The sixth and last suggestion for improving science teaching has to do with what I would like to call 'social modelling'. It also arose in our action research on the Nature of Science. At the time when this began, we were commissioned to use case-study methodology to explore how stories from the history of science could be used in science teaching. The results of this work showed that if the emergence of a new concept in science, like Galileo's 'discovery' of mountains on the moon, or Jenner's invention of vaccination against smallpox, was embedded in a story about the scientist in question it was far better recalled by the student. Understanding the science seemed to have been achieved through the medium of the scientist, by the almost empathic modelling of how he must have thought, felt and acted.

. . . Social modelling is much more familiar to most students. They are quite used to 'modelling' people – their parents or friends in the first place – in order to suggest what they might do in a particular situation. Research shows that non-scientific adults also use social modelling when they try to understand the conflicting advice that scientists sometimes give (Wynne, 1989; Solomon, 1992b). This is a process which uses social psychology rather than scientific theory. When it is deliberately harnessed to the school learning of science it can be surprisingly useful and efficacious as a point of entry.

Science teaching is a craft in which knowledge of children and how they learn is far more central than is philosophy. This chapter was written in the hope that it would prove valuable to explore the arguments about constructivism – just so long as we return, in the end, to the thinking and learning of our important pupils.

REFERENCES

Bourdieu, P. (1977) *Outline of a Theory of Practice*, Cambridge: Cambridge University Press.

Driver, R. (1973) 'Representation of conceptual frameworks in young adolescent science students', PhD Thesis at University of Illinois.

—— (1983) *The Pupil as Scientist?*, Milton Keynes: Open University Press.

Duveen, J. Scott, L. and Solomon, J. (in press) 'Pupils understanding of science: description of experiments or a passion to explain', *School Science Review*.

Duit, R. and Talisayon, V. (1981) *Comprehension of the Energy Concept: Philippine and German Experience*, paper presented at the Conference on Energy Education, Providence RI.

Feyerabend, P. (1975) *Against Method*, London: Verso.

Gilbert, J., Osborne, R. and Fensham, P. (1982) 'Children's science and its consequences for teaching', *Science Education* 66(4): 623–33.

Glasersfeld, E., von (1983) 'L'apprentissage en tant qu'activite constructive', in J. Bergeron and N. Herscovics (eds) *Actes de la cinquieme rencontre annuelle PME-NA*, Montreal. 288–304.

—— (1989) 'Cognition, construction of knowledge and teaching', *Synthese* 121–40.

Grayling, A. (1988) *Wittgenstein*, Oxford: Oxford University Press.

Halliday, M. (1978) *Language as Social Semiotic*, London: Edward Arnold.

Kelly, G. (1955) *The Psychology of Personal Constructs*, New York: Norton.

Kuhn, T. (1962) *The Structure of Scientific Revolutions*, Chicago: University of Chicago Press.

Laroche, M. and Desautels, J. (1992) *Autour de L'idee de Science*, Sainte-Foy: Presse de L'Universite Laval.

Martin, N., Williams, P., Wilding, J., Hemmings, S. and Medway, P. (1976) *Understanding Children Talking*, Harmondsworth: Penguin.

Merton, R. (1973) *The Sociology of Science*, Chicago: University of Chicago Press.

Piaget, J. (1929) *The Child's Conception of the World*, London: Routledge & Kegan Paul.

Rorty, R. (1989) *Contingency, Irony, and Solidarity*, Cambridge: Cambridge University Press.

Ross, K. and Sutton, C. (1982) 'Concept profile and the cultural context', *European Journal of Science Education* 4(3).

Schutz, A. and Luckman, T. (1973) *Structures of the Life World*, London: Heinemann.

Solomon, J. (1980) *Teaching Children in the Laboratory*, London: Croom Helm.

—— (1984a) 'Prompts, cues and discriminaton: the utilisation of two separate knowledge systems', *Eur J Sci Educ* (6): 277–84.

—— (1984b) 'Messy, contradictory and obstinately persistent: a study of children's out of school ideas about energy', *School Science Review* 65 (231): 225–9.

—— (1986) 'Children's explanations', *Oxford Review of Education* (12): 41–51.

—— (1992a) *Getting to Know about Energy*, Lewes: Falmer Press.

—— (1992b) 'The classroom discussion of science-based social issues presented on television: knowledge, attitudes and values', *Int. J. Sci Educ* 14(4): 431–44.

Taylor, C. (1985) *Human Agency and Language*, Cambridge: Cambridge University Press.

Vygotsky, V. S. (1979) in M. Cole, F. John-Steiner, S. Scribner and E. Souberman (eds) *Mind in Society*, Cambridge MA: Harvard University Press.

Wynne, B. (1989) 'The sheep farmers and the scientists'. Paper given at the 'Public Understanding of Science' Conference, SPSG: University of Lancaster.

Ziman, J. (1968) *Public Knowledge, The Social Dimension of Science* Cambridge: Cambridge University Press.

—— (1978) *Reliable Knowledge*, Cambridge: Cambridge University Press.

Chapter 14

Young people's understanding of science concepts

Rosalind Driver, John Leach, Philip Scott and Colin Wood-Robinson

This chapter addresses the issue of how our current understanding of the way young people acquire domain-specific knowledge in the sciences can inform the planning and sequencing of science curricula. By taking this focus, it is not intended to convey the view that the development of scientific concepts is the only, or even necessarily a primary, goal of science education. It is our view that, where conceptual understanding is seen as an appropriate goal of the curriculum, instructional courses may benefit from planning which draws on knowledge of the way in which understanding of science concepts evolves.

A wide range of factors is usually taken into account when decisions are made about curriculum content in school science courses, whether at a local or at a national level. Such factors can include social and cultural aims, employment needs, as well as considerations of the nature of the science subject matter to be taught. A central argument of this chapter is that, if courses are to relate appropriately to learners, curriculum decisions may need also to take account of what is known about the processes of knowledge acquisition in science. Furthermore, it is suggested that cross-age research data on students' domain-specific reasoning in science, undertaken over the last two decades, provides an important information base on which decisions about such developmentally organized curricula can be made.

The idea of taking account of theories of learning in planning courses is not new. In the 1960s, a developmental view based on Piaget's operational stages was influential in the design of a number of science curricula. The Science Curriculum Improvement Study (SCIS) in the United States, the Australian Science Education Project (ASEP) and Science 5–13 in the UK are all examples of the influence of Piaget's developmental theory on curriculum design. The general approach taken in these projects was to use stage theory as a basis for matching the logical demands of a particular science topic to the level of intellectual capability of the learner. A significant problem for this developmental approach to curriculum design has emerged from a number of studies (e.g. Donaldson, 1978) which suggest that children may perform at different operational levels in different contexts and that this variation in performance may be due to the extent of the child's familiarity with the domain in question.

A further approach to sequencing, reinforced by the attention that Bruner (1963) drew to the notion of the structure of subjects, has been to base curriculum design on an analysis of the hierarchy of concepts within a domain. The implementation of this approach, reflected in the work of Gagne (1970), influenced the American project, Science: a Process Approach (SAPA) and, to a lesser extent, the Schools Council Integrated Science Project (SCISP) in the UK. These approaches to curriculum sequencing, which are based on the logical structure of the subject, also have their limitations in that they take no account of the learner's existing knowledge structures, and how new ideas might be interpreted by learners in terms of that existing knowledge. The logical organization of the science domain is acknowledged, but not the structure of the child's knowledge.

There are clearly limitations to each of these approaches to curriculum sequencing, whether in terms of a reliance upon context-independent measures of intellectual capability or neglect of learners' existing knowledge structures. It is our belief that research on children's conceptions in science, in particular cross-sectional studies of students' reasoning in specific conceptual domains, has implications for curriculum planning.

Research on children's conceptions in science

Since the post-Sputnik science curriculum development projects, there has been a major international research programme into children's conceptions in science. There are now substantial bibliographies with over 1,000 references to studies of children's conceptions in science (Pfundt and Duit, 1990; Carmichael *et al.*, 1990); books of edited papers relating to aspects of young people's ways of interpreting natural phenomena (Driver *et al.*, 1985; Black and Lucas, 1993; Glynn *et al.*, 1991) and collected works on the teaching implications of this field of work (Fensham *et al.*, 1994). Some studies in the field have tended to focus on documenting student misconceptions in subject matter areas; the educational implications being that instruction needs to counter the misconceptions and replace them by the scientific view. Evidence from cross-age studies of students' conceptions in science supports a more complex and dynamic view of the evolution of students' conceptual understanding over the school years. It is this body of research which we believe has implications for curriculum planning and sequencing.

In a paper written a decade ago, Finley identified an important research question for science educators when he commented: 'What is needed are studies that identify the commonalities and variations of students' prior knowledge in the most frequently taught content domains' (1985: 704). He argued further that 'If all students share approximately the same knowledge of a subject, then developing effective curriculum and instruction that accounts for students' prior knowledge is simplified' (p. 697). Nearly ten years later, it is interesting to review the research that has been undertaken and to comment on the extent to which Finley's question has been addressed.

CROSS-AGE STUDIES OF STUDENTS' CONCEPTIONS IN SCIENCE

Over the last ten years, a number of cross-age studies have been conducted within the Children's Learning in Science Research Group at the University of Leeds. These studies have documented the conceptions of young people, aged between 5 and 16 years, in a range of science domains. The domains that have been studied include the structure of matter (Holding, 1987), the physical properties of air (Brook *et al.*, 1989) and ecology (Leach *et al.*, 1994). Since subsequent sections of this paper will be drawing on findings from these studies, a brief description of each is provided here. The studies investigated trends in young people's conceptions about specific classes of phenomena through interviews and written surveys with samples of students drawn from primary and secondary schools. Typically, students were presented with a range of phenomena or situations which they were asked to explain. Since they can only provide such explanations in terms of the conceptions they have available to them, inferences were made about students' underlying conceptions from an analysis of the explanations given, both within and across the range of presented situations. By conception we mean the conceptual entities used as basic descriptive categories (e.g. weight, temperature, living thing) and the relationships posited between these entities (e.g. hot air rises). Conceptions are thus propositional in form and can be judged as true or false in relation to experience.

The structure of matter (Holding, 1987)

This study investigated the ideas of young people about the structure of matter using dissolution as a problem context. A representative sample of 588 school students (aged 7, 9, 11, 14 and 16 years) was involved in the study. Students were interviewed individually on a series of practical tasks designed to probe their understanding of the process of dissolution, the changes that were involved and their representation of the process in terms of an underlying model of matter. In one of the tasks, students were shown a pair of scales with a glass of water and an egg cup of sugar on each side. The scales could be seen to balance. The problem set each student was to predict what would happen to the scales if the sugar from the egg cup on one side was added to the water and the egg cup returned to the scale pan. They were asked whether the side of the scales where the sugar was added

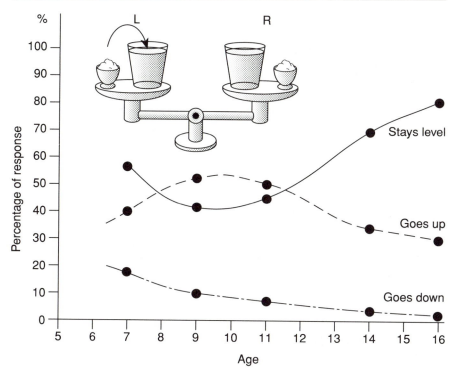

Figure 14.1 Prevalence of students' responses about the weight of sugar on dissolving (N=588)

Source: Holding 1987

to the water would go up, go down or remain level, giving their reason. Figure 14.1 indicates the prevalence of the three different responses at different ages.

The interesting feature of the results is not simply the prediction that the students gave, but the reasoning behind that prediction. The youngest students tended to suggest that the scales stay level; they used conservation reasoning, arguing that the sugar is still there, only now it is in the water. Around age 9, a change in reasoning could be identified. Students started to speculate about the existence of particles of sugar and initially this conflicted with their conservation reasoning. The most common prediction at this age was that the side with the sugar in the water will go up; arguments for this included 'the sugar is breaking up into little bits and the little bits are so small that they weigh hardly anything', or 'the sugar breaks up into little bits and these lose weight because they are floating in the water'. The key feature of their reasoning was the notion of 'little bits that you cannot see'. Students were thus beginning to construct notions of matter as particulate. (These early notions, however, are far from the chemist's conceptions of atoms or molecules – they are essentially macroscopic matter broken down.) The older students continued to reason in terms of the sugar breaking into little bits, or particles of sugar, but more tended to appreciate that the weight of the parts add up to the whole, and so they predicted that the weight will remain the same. From this and other tasks in this study, it appeared that reasoning about particles of matter tends to emerge in children's explanations at around ages 9–11. Reasoning in terms of such particles however, initially interfered with students' reasoning about other features of the system, such as whether or not the mass of sugar is conserved.

The physical properties of air (Brook *et al.*, 1989)

This study investigated the ideas of a representative sample of 100 school students (aged 5, 8, 12 and 16 years) about a number of physical properties of air, including whether or not it exists, that it occupies space, that bodies of air weigh something and can exert a pressure. Overall, students

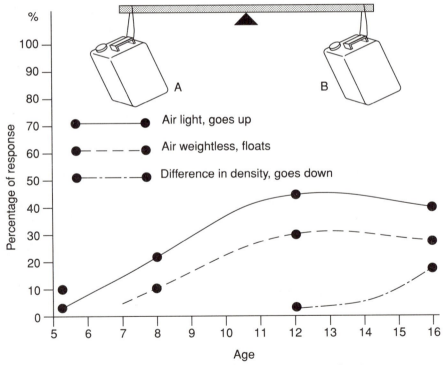

Figure 14.2 Prevalence of students' responses about the weight of air (N=100)
Source: Brook *et al.* 1989

were interviewed on seven tasks relating to the physical properties of air. The notion that air as a substance exists and occupies space was not used by 5 year olds. At this age 'air' is identified only when it is moving as a 'wind', 'breeze' or 'draught'. By age 8, however, students were predicting that water will not enter an inverted glass when it is lowered into a bowl of water, because of the air already in it. Air as a substance existing in space appears to emerge in children's reasoning around ages 7–10.

In one of the tasks in this study, students were asked to predict what would happen to a balance beam, initially in equilibrium, with sealed plastic containers on each end, when more air was pumped into one of the containers. The prevalence of responses at the different ages is given in Figure 14.2.

The younger students had difficulties formulating a clear response to this task. This is not perhaps surprising if they have no stable notion of air as a substance. After age 8, students made a range of predictions. Nearly half predicted that adding air makes the container go up because air is weightless – it just floats around. The scientific prediction that the air in the container is more dense than the air outside the container and therefore the side with the additional air will go down, increased in prevalence over the secondary years and was made by about a fifth of the 16 year olds.

The property of weightlessness or even of negative weight ascribed to air by children, has been reported in studies undertaken in other countries, (e.g. Stavy, 1990; Carey, 1992). There are many common phenomena which support this aspect of children's reasoning, such as bubbles of air or gases rising through water, and smoke rising from a chimney or from the ends of cigarettes. Experience with water play indicates to children that objects containing more air are more buoyant and harder to push beneath the surface of water. The point that emerges from this study is that while children from the age of 8 accept that air (and other gases) exist and can occupy space, and although air is seen as some kind of material substance, weight (or mass) is not seen as an essential feature of material substances. Older students begin to accept that air, as a substance, has weight. This shift reflects a deep change in students' reasoning about matter which involves a change in the ontological status of what constitutes material substance. As Carey (1992) points out, the association of mass/weight as an essential characteristic of matter was only being introduced by Newton's time. Prior to Newton, the concept of inertial mass was not formulated and the notion of an object having weight was not taken as a necessary condition for considering an object or substance as being material in nature.

The notion of air as weightless or as having negative weight, is an example of what we refer to as an intermediate conception in the evolution of students' reasoning. Another such example occurred in response to a range of tasks involving pressure differences. Students were asked to explain

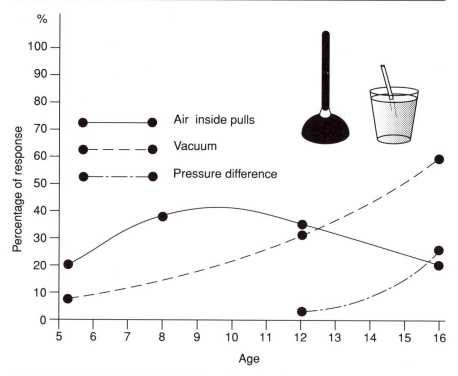

Figure 14.3 Prevalence of students' explanations for pressure difference phenomena (N=100)

Source: Brook *et al.* 1989

what happens when a person drinks juice through a straw, how a sink plunger 'sticks' to a surface, and how a liquid is taken into a syringe. Similar types of responses were identified for each task, though the prevalence varies from task to task.

The most common conception among the two younger age groups was that there is 'air' inside the device which pulls or sucks (Figure 14.3).

In these responses in which the air inside the device is seen to pull or suck, the air used in students' reasoning can be interpreted as a necessary medium through which some otherwise unexplainable action-at-a-distance takes place. This parallels reasoning about action-at-a-distance which has been identified in other contexts. For example, children predict that a force of a magnet only acts through 'air'; when asked whether a magnet will act on the Moon, many children said 'no, because there is no air on the Moon' (Bar, 1989). A more prevalent idea in the old age groups, and one which is dominant up to age 16, involves the notion of a vacuum which 'sucks' or 'pulls'. An explanation in terms of differences in pressure of the air inside and outside the device is used progressively during the secondary years, but by only a minority of students.

Again, in this task, intermediate conceptions have been identified. The first notion is that of air inside the device causing the effect. This is in keeping with the view of air as 'wind' or 'breeze', a view of 'active air' that makes things happen. The notion of a vacuum which emerges at a later age is also conceptualized as an active agent. It is however, a more sophisticated notion in that a vacuum is seen by students to be a region where there is no air. Students, therefore, need to have a stable conception of air as a material substance which can occupy space to envision a region where this invisible substance does not exist. An explanation involving an analysis of the system in terms of bodies of air at different pressures was given by a minority of the older students, even though this would have been taught in science lessons. In this example, there is evidence of young people's conceptions of air being characterized by a number of intermediate notions based on distinctly different presuppositions about the nature of material substances.

Students' reasoning about ecology (Leach *et al.*, in press)[1]

This study investigated the ideas of school students aged 5 to 16 years about a number of aspects of the interdependence of living things, including cycling of matter and energy. A range of interview and written tasks was devised to probe these aspects. About 450 students, across the age range 8/9 to 15/16, responded to written tasks and a smaller number were interviewed across the age range. Students aged 4–6 were also interviewed on the same tasks. One aspect focused on was the process of decay and the cycling of matter. In one of the tasks, students were presented with a photograph of a rotting apple on the ground below an apple tree and they were asked to say what happens when the apple rots. A number of the youngest children in the study appeared quite unfamiliar with the phenomenon of decay. For the remainder, rotting was seen as 'rotting away' – a dead organism rots and leaves no material products. This lack of conservation of matter was also noted in students' reasoning about other biological processes such as growth. Students in the upper primary and lower secondary years typically talked about rotting things giving 'fertility' to the soil. Air or gases were not generally included in their explanations of chemical processes involving living things. The most sophisticated view, held by a minority of the oldest students, involved an appreciation of conservation of matter in decay and the role of decomposers in returning matter into the environment. In this example, we see that the evolution of more sophisticated conceptions of decay required students to consider living material as behaving by the same laws as other material substances and to make connections with a larger range of other relevant knowledge.

A further task presented students with a picture of a range of organisms in a rural habitat, together with the feeding relationships between them. Students were asked to explain what would happen to the populations of each of the other organisms if one of the species were removed. This was asked for species at different trophic levels. Many of the students below the age of 7 years used anthropomorphic reasoning in the context of animals. Younger students tended to reason in terms of the fate of individual organisms, rather than at the population level. They also predicted more limited changes. Whereas the majority of students from about age 8/9, correctly predicted changes in the populations of organisms through three trophic levels when the primary consumer was removed from the ecosystem, this was not the case when they considered what would happen if a top predator were removed. In this case, the majority of students below the age of 10 years, and a significant minority of the older students, argued that the removal of the top predator would result in no change to the populations of the other organisms.

Although characterizations of change in students' conceptualizations in biological domains tend to be more complex than in physical science domains, two features are worthy of a brief note. The first has already been alluded to and concerns the distinction seen by young people between living material and other material substances. The conservation of matter as applying to living systems is appreciated much later than for non-living systems. The second concerns the nature of what constitutes explanation for students in biological systems which is different from explanation in physical science domains. Anthropomorphic reasoning continues to feature in students' explanations of biological systems at older ages.

Summary of cross-age studies

A number of cross-age studies of young people's conceptual developments in specific domains have been reported in the literature over recent years as shown in Table 14.1.

Such studies characterize children's conceptions within a particular domain and report variations in prevalence of these conceptions at different ages. Typically, a limited number of common conceptions used by young people are identified and changes in the overall prevalence of particular conceptions with age are reported. The studies that have been reported vary in the extent to which they cover a particular domain and in the depth of analysis they provide of students' reasoning. Some studies present only descriptive accounts of students' responses, whereas others (e.g. Carey, 1985; Vosniadou and Brewer, 1992) interpret changes in students' responses in terms of changes in underlying features.

Findings from such cross-age studies, including those described earlier in this paper, support the view that young people's conceptions about natural

Table 14.1 Cross-age studies of students' conceptions within specific science domains

Domain	Authors
Biological	
Photosynthesis	Stavy *et al.*, 1987
Inheritance	Karbo *et al.*, 1980
	Engel-Clough & Wood-Robinson, 1985
Homeostasis	Westbrook and Marek, 1992
Human circulatory system	Aranudin and Mintzes, 1985
Ecology	Leach *et al.*, 1994
Chemical	
Material kind	Dickinson, 1987
Evaporation	Beveridge, 1985
Change of state	Stavy, 1990
	Osborne and Cosgrove, 1983
	Bar and Travis, 1991
Particulate theory	Novick and Nussbaum, 1981
Diffusion	Westbrook and Marek, 1991
Dissolving	Holding, 1987
	Abraham *et al.*, 1994
Physical	
Density	Smith, Carey and Wiser, 1985
Physical properties of air and gases	Brook *et al.*, 1989
	Benson *et al.*, 1993
	Séré, 1982
Earth and gravity	Nussbaum, 1979
	Mali and Howe, 1979
	Vosniadou and Brewer, 1992
Light	Andersson and Kärrquist, 1983
	Osborne *et al.*, 1993
Light and sound	Boyes and Stanisstreet, 1991
Force and motion	Twigger *et al.*, 1994
	Bliss *et al.*, 1988
Energy	Trumper, 1993

phenomena are not idiosyncratic. In the domains that have been more systematically studied, such as mechanics, light and sight, matter, biological inheritance, plant nutrition and ecology, similar forms of reasoning are reported in different studies.

Cross-age studies and individual learning

While cross-age studies can provide information which can be useful in curriculum planning, they do not enable claims to be made about the ways individual students' reasoning evolves. To do this would require longitudinal designs in which the reasoning of individual students is followed over a period of time. Without the evidence of such studies, care needs to be taken in making inferences about the sequences that individual learners pass through in their scientific reasoning. Longitudinal studies, which track the evolving conceptions of individual students over extended periods of time (Novak and Musonda, 1991; Scott, 1991; Engel-Clough *et al.*, 1987), can provide detailed information about learning routes and enable features of students' developing knowledge to be characterized, but do not necessarily provide information about what prompts change and how it occurs. In order to obtain information of this kind, it is necessary to study students' learning in science as a consequence of specific interventions. Examples of such intervention studies would include work by Brown and Clement (1992) on the use of bridging analogies in promoting conceptual change, and Nussbaum and Novick (1982) on the use of cognitive conflict.

CONCEPTUAL TRAJECTORIES IN STUDENTS' DOMAIN-SPECIFIC REASONING

Results from cross-age studies, including those described in the previous section of this paper, can be interpreted from an evolutionary perspective on knowledge acquisition. From this perspective, learning within a particular domain can be characterized in terms of progress through a sequence of conceptualizations which portray significant steps in the way knowledge within the given domain is represented. This sequence of conceptualizations we call a conceptual trajectory. While the notion of a conceptual trajectory does not describe a pathway in the reasoning of any individual student, it does, however, indicate in broad terms the nature of the changes in reasoning which may be demonstrated by students in particular curricular settings. In developing an understanding of the properties of air and gases, for example, it appears that the conceptual trajectory starts with notions of air as insubstantial and existing only as 'wind' or 'breeze'. The first important change is the development of the notion of air or gas as a material substance. This is followed by an appreciation that the property of weight or mass is characteristic of all material substances and hence applies to bodies of gas as well as to solids and liquids.

Such sequences in the evolution of students' conceptions have been postulated in other domains. Students' evolving representations in the domain of light and sight (Guesne, 1985; Andersson and Kärrquist, 1983; Boyes and Stanisstreet, 1991) indicate that young children tend not to represent light as existing in space. This is followed by children using the notion of a 'bath of light' which illuminates objects and enables them to be seen. The notion that light travels from a source rather than just existing in space, is a further development and finally the notion that non-luminous objects can be seen because light is scattered off them and enters the eye involves an additional and critical step in the conceptual trajectory.

Cross-cultural studies have also been undertaken to investigate whether there are similarities in the conceptual trajectories of students from different countries. Mali and Howe (1979) replicated Nussbaum's (1979) study on the Earth in space in Nepal and identified a similar pattern in students' representations. In a more recent study in the same domain, Vosniadou and Brewer (1992) conducted a very detailed investigation comparing the evolving conceptions of school students in Greece and the United States of America. They noted that there were some differences among younger children from Greece and the USA in the notions about the Earth in space (such as interpretations of day and night), which they attributed to exposure to a different culture (for example Greek children made reference to Greek mythology). However, there was similarity in the intermediate notions identified. In a biological domain, Karbo *et al.* (1980) working in Canada, Engel Clough and Wood-Robinson (1985) in the UK, and Ramorogo and Wood-Robinson (1994) in Botswana have documented similar intermediate notions concerning inheritance, albeit with different frequencies, in three countries.

The origins and nature of students' domain-specific reasoning

The evidence outlined here about the commonality in students' reasoning about natural phenomena raises interesting questions with regard to the nature and origins of those ideas. These theoretical questions have been addressed by a number of researchers.

Vosniadou and Brewer, in interpreting their findings about children's knowledge acquisition in astronomy, use the term 'assimilatory concepts' to describe the misconceptions which they have identified in children's thinking in this field. They explain assimilatory concepts as being 'attempts on the part of children to reconcile their presuppositions (that the ground is flat and unsupported things fall) with the information they receive from the adult culture that the Earth is a sphere' (1992: 578); they further argue that children's presuppositions or initial concepts represent inferences or hypotheses about the observed world constructed by individuals on the basis of their everyday experience, and that these concepts change as children are exposed to the dominant theories held by adults within a given culture. In some cases, this change involves replacing the initial concept (that the Earth is flat) with the accepted cultural view (that the Earth is spherical) and the outcome may be an assimilatory conception (e.g. that the Earth is round like a plate) which can be seen as resulting from the child's attempt to assimilate the cultural view into their initial concepts.

Vosniadou and Brewer focus principally upon the situation where the accepted cultural view is taken to be the science perspective, introduced to children through formal instruction. Westbrook and Marek (1991, 1992) have also investigated the effect of instruction on children's initial conceptions and report a prevalence of misconceptions, resulting from instruction, which increases with age. They follow a similar line of argument to Vosniadou and Brewer in suggesting that in these cases the taught scientific explanation conflicts with the students' initial conceptions and, in an attempt to assimilate the scientific explanation, a misconception arises as students construct a hybrid interpretation. In some cases such misconceptions induced in teaching one topic, have resulted in problems in other topics, where misconceptions developed earlier have been imported.

Whilst these studies focus upon the outcomes of socialization into the scientific view, we would argue that intermediate conceptions are also generated and reinforced through socialization into the representations of phenomena prevalent in everyday language and culture (see Driver *et al.*, 1994). In the cross-age study on air reported earlier (Brook *et al.*, 1989), it was noted that the idea of 'sucking' predominated in students' explanations over the scientific pressure difference explanation. It is certainly the case that notions of sucking are likely to be supported by everyday discourse to a greater extent than the scientific view and it is this model that is therefore sustained and reinforced. Brook *et al.* (1989) report that students up to age 16 may base their explanations of simple air phenomena on the notion of a *vacuum* sucking. Here the scientific notion of 'vacuum' has simply been added to the stable, socialized view of sucking. The entities appearing in the explanation have been revised but the basis of the explanation remains the same. Common-sense ways of conceptualizing natural phenomena are often supported by everyday experience and language such as 'wood burns down', 'air is weightless and floats about', 'you have to keep pushing to keep things moving', and 'heat rises'. In all these examples, the common-sense conceptions are functional for reasoning in everyday situations insofar as they enable people to make reasonable predictions and to act effectively.

These perspectives on the developments of scientific reasoning have much in common with the views of Vygotsky (1978). Vygotsky made a distinction between what he called 'spontaneous concepts' on the one hand and 'scientific concepts' on the other. He saw spontaneous concepts as deriving inductively from experience and relating to perceptual or functional properties of events as experienced by the child. In this respect, spontaneous concepts are seen to be similar to Vosniadou and Brewer's 'presuppositions' or 'initial concepts'. Vygotsky did, however, introduce a cautionary note about the extent to which we are *ever* able to learn through individual experience:

From the very first days of the child's development, his activities acquire a meaning of their own in a system of social behaviour and, being directed towards a definite purpose, are refracted through the prism of the child's environment. The path from child to object passes through another person. The complete human structure is the product of a developmental process deeply rooted in the links between individual and social history.

(Vygotsky, 1978: 30)

Human beings can and do learn from experience but that experience, particularly after the development of language, is located in a social context which will mediate any learning that takes place. Vygotsky saw scientific concepts as having meanings through their relationships with one another and being transmitted through the culture and social institutions of society rather than evolving 'naturally' in the course of development of individual learners. Furthermore, he recognized that learning scientific concepts, like learning a second language, is mediated through the word meanings for children's spontaneous concepts. Internalization of new concepts by the learner is thus consequent upon a process of transformation of meaning in which understanding of new concepts is mediated through students' spontaneously acquired concepts. Although Vygotsky himself did not develop this work to any extent, tracing the complex interweaving of spontaneous concepts with culturally transmitted scientific models during the years of schooling may be what is being portrayed in the cross-sectional studies reported here.

GENERAL FEATURES IN THE EVOLUTION OF STUDENTS' SCIENTIFIC REASONING

Underlying the evolutionary perspective of knowledge acquisition in science portrayed in the previous section is a recognition of discontinuities in learning. New knowledge is the result not only of the broadening in use of existing conceptions or the addition of new notions. It also involves the reorganization of conceptual schemes themselves. For example, changing from a 'vacuum sucks' notion to a pressure difference explanation for the way a syringe works involves both reorganization of concepts (the notion of vacuum has to be interpreted in the new theory as empty space rather than active agent) and the construction of new conceptual entities (such as atmospheric pressure). It would be oversimplifying the picture to say that one conception replaces an earlier one. Students (and adults) may maintain a range of ways of representing the world and continue to use them in contextually appropriate ways.

Furthermore, from cross-age studies of the evolution of students' domain-specific reasoning, it appears that students may follow broadly similar conceptual trajectories in their acquisition of scientific knowledge. This is not to say that there is a universal natural developmental sequence in the ways in which students' science conceptions evolve. The point that is being made is that from the evidence available, it appears that the commonalities which do exist are enough to warrant using them to inform educational curricular decisions within specific scientific knowledge domains. Unlike the general framework that was provided for curriculum planning by the Piagetian stage theory, the research on the evolution of students' domain-specific knowledge does not, as yet, lead to a general theory to underpin curriculum planning. The picture is a complex one, with curriculum planning needing to draw on specific research findings domain by domain.

While for curriculum planning purposes it may be necessary to chart the evolution in students' conceptualization for each individual science domain, there are a number of general features of students' reasoning which emerge from the cross-age studies. Here we identify three dimensions along which students' reasoning progresses: the evolution of new ontological entities, the development of reasoning strategies and changes in epistemological commitments.

The construction of new ontological entities

The range of objects that children take to exist in the world, i.e. their ontologies, extends and changes as children's reasoning evolves. Direct experience has an important influence on young children's conceptions about physical phenomena. To the young child air is thus perceived as wind which can be detected by its effects, whilst older children begin to develop a belief in the existence of air or gas as unseen entities. Such entities are then taken for granted by students as existing in the world and are used in explaining new phenomena. At a later stage still they may conceptualize air in terms of particles and so a broadening of their ontology occurs. As described earlier in studies of children's conceptions about light (Guesne, 1985; Andersson and Kärrquist, 1983), it has been found that young children when asked 'where is there light in this room?' will identify light as the source (the sun, the light bulb) or the effect (the sunny patch on the wall). They do not have a concept of light existing in space. Later, children will identify something existing between the source and the effect, a bath of light which has to be there if you are to see things. Light as an invisible entity which exists in space becomes part of the student's ontology. A subsequent step in the representation is to appreciate that this entity, light, travels outwards from a source, thus extending the features of light that are taken as real.

A similar development can be seen with children's notions of matter. Young children do not view matter as being necessarily conserved. When a fire burns, matter burns away, when a puddle of water evaporates, the water disappears. The view that material substances in the world do not just appear or disappear, but that the matter itself is conserved in these transformations, constitutes a major change in students' ontology. This is a particularly significant point in relation to living material. As has been suggested earlier, there is a dominant view among school children that living material is different in kind from other material substances. It is capable of growth when it is alive. When an organism dies, it then rots away. This vitalist ontology interferes with students' learning about a range of biological processes (for example in appreciating the process of photosynthesis whereby simple chemical substances such as carbon dioxide and water combine to form some of the materials of which green plants are constituted).

A significant problem for the effective communication of science is that entities that exist in the world of the scientist or the science teacher (gene, chromosome, electric field, atom, molecule, ion, gamma radiation, etc.) may have no corresponding existence in the world of the learner. The task of the science educator is literally to bring to life these entities, to make them real and meaningful for the learner.

Changes in students' reasoning strategies

Not only do young people of different ages have different ontological entities in their worlds but they tend to reason about them in different ways. Younger children tend to provide explanations for phenomena in terms of the properties of objects themselves rather than in terms of relationships. So, for example, an object falls because it has weight rather than because of an interaction between the object and the Earth. Likewise, colour is seen to be a fixed property of an object (Anderson and Smith, 1986).

There is a dominant tendency for school students to provide explanations which reflect a linear causal chain of reasoning. This form of reasoning which has an underlying explanatory structure of an agent causing an effect as a linear sequence in time, has been identified as being characteristic of common-sense reasoning in science. Students explain, for example, that when the plunger of a syringe is pulled out, this creates a vacuum. The vacuum then draws liquid into the syringe. A similar linear form of reasoning was identified in the study of students' ecological concepts outlined earlier. In considering a simple food web involving grass, rabbits, mice, foxes and hawks, students would predict population changes in terms of a linear sequence concerning which species eats which other species. But this linear sequence was seen as operating in one direction only. Thus the removal of an organism from a lower trophic level, such as the grass or the rabbits, was seen as affecting the population size of organisms from higher trophic levels which would have less to eat, whereas the removal of the hawk, from the highest trophic level, was not seen by the majority of students to affect the population of the other species at lower levels.

This form of reasoning has been identified by other researchers. In a paper entitled 'The experiential gestalt of causation', Andersson (1986) identifies linear causality as characterizing common-sense reasoning about a range of physical phenomena. Rosier and Viennot (1990) identified a similar feature in reasoning about physics problems among undergraduate physics students. Such spontaneous reasoning, in which explanations are represented as a sequence of causes and effects, differs radically from explanations used in science. In many cases, scientific explanations are based on models, which may, for example, be mathematical models (as in Newtonian mechanics), or analogue models (as in the kinetic molecular theory of gases), or relation models (as in the representation of populations of organisms in a food web). Explanations in these cases are in terms of the relationships between entities in the model, which map onto the event or phenomenon under consideration. The underlying structure of the form of explanation involving modelling, which is implicit in the science that is taught, may therefore not fit with students' expectations of what constitutes an explanation.

Changes in epistemological commitments

In addition to changes in the substance of students' conceptions with age, there is also evidence that students' views of the nature and status of scientific knowledge, i.e. their epistemological commitments, evolve. A number of studies have examined the ways in which children relate observations and explanations (e.g. Carey *et al.*, 1989; Kuhn, 1989; Larochelle and Desautels, 1991; Aikenhead, 1987; Driver *et al.*, 1993).

In a recent study,[2] Driver *et al.* (1993) identify three representations of the nature of scientific enquiry and the nature and status of scientific knowledge used by students in the 9 to 16 age range in a variety of contexts. In the first of these, knowledge claims are seen as absolute and unproblematic and theories are not differentiated from the phenomena that they explain. The issue of warranting knowledge claims is not, therefore recognized. Investigations are seen as involving either direct observation or simple interventions in phenomena 'to see what happens'. Such representations were common amongst 9 year olds in certain contexts, but far less common at ages 12 and 16. Carey *et al.* (1989) and Kuhn (1989) have also claimed that children below the age of 9 often do not separate theory from evidence.

The most common representation of science at all ages, described by Driver *et al.* (1993), portrays knowledge claims as emerging from observable data in an unproblematic way. The possibility of different interpretations of phenomena is acknowledged (i.e. explanations and phenomenon are distinguished). Explanations, however, are viewed as being either 'true' or 'false' and judgements are made through a simple empirical process. The nature of this empirical process involves testing whether particular variables influence a phenomenon, and tests tend to be interpreted in a simple causal way, i.e. changes in an independent variable causing changes in a dependent variable. Although explanations and phenomena are distinguished, there is no sense of theoretical entities (which might consist of a number of inter-linking parts as in a theoretical model) being posited to provide a coherent system of explanation. Similar views of the warranting of knowledge claims have been reported by Larochelle and Desautels (1991) and Aikenhead (1987).

A more sophisticated representation of science is identified amongst a small number of 16-year-olds in a limited range of contexts by Driver *et al.* (1993), where knowledge claims are portrayed as conjectural rather than absolute, and the possibility of multiple explanations is acknowledged. Causal and descriptive explanations of phenomena are differentiated explicitly: knowing what happens is not the same as knowing what causes it to happen. Theoretical entities and models are posited and referred to in giving coherent explanations. Theories are seen as being evaluated using empirical evidence, and this process is recognized as inherently problematic. This representation was used by students across a range of contexts, illustrating a commitment to generalizability and consistency of scientific theories.

Samarapungavan (1991) draws a distinction between the ability of children to appreciate particular epistemological features of theories, such as empirical and logical consistency, parsimony, and *ad hoc* modifications, and the type of explanations that they construct given free choice. In a study using a theory choice design, she reports that the majority of 6-year-olds are able to differentiate theories which are empirically, and logically consistent from those which are not, theories which are parsimonious from those which are not, and explanations involving *ad hoc* modifications of theory from those which do not. The proportion of older students constructing explanations following these norms is accounted for in terms of changing epistemological commitments amongst older students, rather than the development of particular reasoning skills.

IMPLICATIONS FOR CURRICULUM PLANNING AND SEQUENCING

Although there are a number of general features which can be identified in the ways students' conceptions evolve with age, it is the studies of conceptual progression within specific conceptual domains which can be particularly informative to curriculum developers. It has been argued in the literature that research on students' conceptions in science has been characterized by its variety and that for the research to be useful in teaching, some order and theoretical underpinning is necessary. We would argue that the field has now developed to a point where there is evidence to support a view that there are common conceptual trajectories in the ways in which students' scientific understanding evolves within specific domains, and that this information is important to take into account in planning and sequencing the curriculum.

While we would not postulate a 'natural' development in children's conceptions of physical phenomena (environmental and cultural influences may clearly vary), evidence does suggest that there are strong commonalities in the trajectories of the reasoning of young people. Results from surveys can thus enable the likelihood of particular ideas being used within a group of students of different ages to be anticipated.

Before commenting further on the implications of these studies for curriculum development, it is important to make three points so as to avoid misinterpretations of work reported here.

First, as was stated in the introduction, we would not wish to claim that conceptual development is the only consideration that needs to be taken into account in curriculum planning. Our second caveat, as also already stated, is that the studies reported here should not be seen as describing pathways in the development of thinking of individual students. They are not longitudinal studies and no claims can therefore be made about the pathways in thinking that individual students follow. The final caveat is that reports on the prevalence of certain ideas at different ages do not give information on the process or the dynamics of change. A different theoretical basis is needed to inform teaching from that required to guide curriculum planning and sequencing. Bearing these points in mind, we now consider a number of implications of the results of cross-age studies for such planning and sequencing.

Sequencing of the curriculum

We view science teaching as involving mediation between the public scientific knowledge agreed within the scientific community, and the informal knowledge developed and used by school students in their everyday lives. Research on the evolution of students' conceptions reported in this paper can provide information about the informal knowledge likely to characterize the reasoning of students at given ages in a range of domains, and as such is of value in planning how to sequence the introduction of scientific knowledge to students. The following example is offered as an illustration of how the research evidence presented earlier can inform curriculum sequencing relating to matter cycling in ecological contexts.

Scientific explanations of matter cycling in ecosystems are complex, drawing upon notions about cellular processes, such as photosynthesis, respiration and excretion, as well as the processes of exchange with the environment associated with each of these. Explanations also draw on notions of decay, as well as detailed models of the relationships between populations in communities. The structure of the subject matter thus suggests that a curricular sequence for teaching about matter cycling will require the cellular processes, decay and the relationships between organisms to be introduced at some level prior to full explanations of matter cycling.

However, it is apparent from research that students face challenges in understanding these component processes. In the case of the process of decay, for example, research evidence (see Leach *et al.*, 1994) suggests that many students between the ages of 5 and 7 are unfamiliar with some of the phenomena relating to the decay process. From the age of 7, however, a number do refer to decay as enriching the soil in some way. An appropriate early step in a curriculum aiming for understanding of matter cycling therefore involves ensuring familiarity of students with appropriate phenomena involving decay. Following this, an appreciation of the conservation of matter is then an essential pre-requisite to understanding matter cycling.

Many students below the age of 7 do not appear to conserve matter in their explanations of processes such as decay and growth, assuming that matter can appear and disappear. Studies suggest that students accept matter conservation involving the solid and the liquid state before they develop a stable notion of gas-as-matter. There is also evidence that the processes of photosynthesis and respiration are poorly understood by many students, even up to the age of 16 after relevant teaching (see, for example, the review by Wood-Robinson, 1991). This is possibly due to difficulties on the part of students in conceptualizing solid matter being formed from gases, and being oxidized to gases. For this reason, it is likely that early teaching about matter cycling will be better understood initially in contexts which do not involve gases. For example, in the decay process, the cycling of matter via the soil is likely to be grasped more readily than the cycling of matter via the atmosphere. Teaching about chemical and exchange processes in matter cycling which involve gases, such as those concerned with respiration and photosynthesis, is likely to require many students to construct a new ontological entity of gas-as-matter – a challenge even for older students.

A further aim for subsequent teaching involves developing an epistemological commitment towards generalizability. For example, many students up to the age of 16 appear to view living matter, and matter in the gaseous state, as different in kind from 'typical' solid matter in non-living systems. Understanding of matter cycling involves an appreciation that the behaviour of all matter is governed by the same laws.

In addition to the implications which prior conceptions have for learning within specific domains such as ecology, are the broader consequences they may have for curriculum sequencing across a number of domains. For example, early teaching about processes such as burning, rusting, respiration and photosynthesis requires students to appreciate that the reactions involve chemical combination with a component of air. In the case of burning and rusting, this results in an increase in the weight of the substance formed. For students who tend to consider that air or gases are weightless or have negative weight, making sense of the evidence from such experiments on weighing substances before and after burning is problematic. Opportunities to construct the idea of gases as substantive will thus be an important prior topic.

Age placement of topics

A further important aspect of curriculum planning concerns the use of information from research about the ages at which it is appropriate for certain ideas to be introduced. For example, it has been suggested earlier that students tend to develop particulate views of matter between the ages of 10 and 12 years. There is therefore probably little to be gained educationally from the investment of effort required to introduce such notions at much earlier ages. It may be more efficient to use the teaching time available to focus on the development of other notions. This does not mean that spontaneous use by students of particulate ideas should be discouraged before this age, but rather that instructional focus will not be given to them. It is worth emphasizing that cross-sectional data on children's prior conceptions cannot be taken as an indicator of the *limits* of possible achievement, given appropriate study. Rather, the information can be used to anticipate the difficulties that learners may face in coming to understand particular scientific concepts, and to inform judgements about the most effective sequence for introducing such concepts to learners.

Teaching time required for different topics

The patterns of change in the prevalence of certain ideas gives an indication of the amount of time that can be required for students to adopt and use new concepts with confidence. (In the case of some of the central concepts in science this time period can be months and years rather than days.) This gives a realistic indication of the pace at which some basic scientific notions develop. We would argue that there are concepts which are central to students' scientific understanding in a wide range of topics and in such cases giving an appropriate amount of teaching time to them is educationally worthwhile. We would suggest that the conservation of mass and the particular theory of matter are examples of such topics. Furthermore, these topics are applicable to contexts in all areas of science and as such need to be revisited frequently during a student's school career, each time giving opportunities to reconceptualize the related phenomena in more sophisticated and general ways. Attention to students' conceptual development thus supports a 'spiral curriculum' and careful analysis of curriculum sequences is needed to check that appropriate opportunities are given for important conceptions to be established. (For a discussion of the issue of sequencing in the context of physics in the UK National Curriculum, see Black, 1993.)

There are particular problems for curriculum planning in areas where studies show clearly that despite careful teaching, students tend to maintain their prior conceptions. Newtonian mechanics and current electricity are both such topics. We suspect that in such cases students' everyday experiences tend to reinforce their prior conceptions. Any change in this situation will require extended curriculum time and carefully researched instruction to address the problem issues. If curriculum time is a constraint, then this raises questions about priorities for the best use of the available time.

Epistemological commitments

There tends to be little explicit attention given to epistemological issues in school science courses, yet it is clear that at all ages particular epistemological perspectives (such as the nature of theory and its relationship to evidence) implicitly underpin much of the teaching and learning. Knowledge of the development of young people's epistemologies of science could therefore be important in addressing such issues in teaching (Driver *et al.*, 1993).

FINAL COMMENTS

In this chapter we have argued that research on students' domain-specific reasoning in science is now at a point where it can usefully be drawn upon to inform curriculum planning across the primary and secondary age range. Within many specific domains in science, characteristic conceptual trajectories in students' reasoning can be identified. It is suggested here that knowledge of these trajectories can be drawn on in planning and sequencing the curriculum so that instructional materials can interact with and address the conceptions that students are likely to have at different points in their schooling. In doing this, it is important to consider not simply the surface features of students' conceptions but to take account of the underlying assumptions on which students' reasoning is based.

Underlying the domain-specific changes in students' conceptions, three strands have been identified in the evolution of students' reasoning in science. These relate to changes in students' ontologies within specific domains, changes in reasoning strategies and changes in epistemological commitments.

In identifying these three strands, we explicitly draw attention to the fact that learning science involves more than learning science concepts. Learning science also involves coming to appreciate a new epistemological domain, complete with its own accepted patterns of reasoning. This epistomological domain and associated patterns of reasoning provide the framework within which new conceptual entities must be manipulated. As such, we would argue that research evidence on all three strands in students' reasoning can usefully be drawn upon in curriculum planning and in the design of science teaching. Cross-age studies on students' representations of epistemological issues and patterns of reasoning provide an important complementary perspective to concept-based studies.

NOTES

1 The project 'Conceptual Progression in Science' was commissioned and funded by the National Curriculum Council. The research is reported in full in *Progression in Conceptual Understanding in Pupils from Age 5 to Age 16: Cycles of Matter, Flows of Energy, and Interdependency and Classification of Organisms in Ecosystems*, by John Leach, Rosalind Driver, Philip Scott and Colin Wood-Robinson, Children's Learning in Science Research Group, Centre for Studies in Science and Mathematics Education, The University of Leeds, 1992.
2 The research project 'Progression in children's ideas about the nature of science from age 9 to age 16' involving John Leach, Rosalind Driver, Philip Scott (University of Leeds), and Robin Millar (University of York), was funded by the Economic and Social Research Council.

REFERENCES

Abraham, M., Williamson, V. and Westbrook, S. (1994) 'A cross-age study of the understanding of five chemistry concepts', *Journal of Research in Science Teaching*, 31, (2): 147–65.

Aikenhead, G.S. (1987) 'High school graduates' beliefs about science-technology-society III: characteristics and limitations of scientific knowledge', *Science Education*, 71 (4): 459–87.

Anderson, C.W. and Smith, E.L. (1986) *Children's Conceptions of Light and Color: Understanding the Role of Unseen Rays*, (Research series No 166), Michigan: Institute for Research on Teaching, Michigan State University.

Andersson, B. (1986) 'The experiential gestalt of causation – A common core to pupils' preconceptions in science', *European Journal of Science Education*, 8 (2): 155–72.

Andersson, B. and Kärrquist, C. (1983) 'How Swedish pupils, aged 12–15 years, understand light and its properties', *European Journal of Science Education*, 5 (4): 387–402.

Aranudin, M. and Mintzes, J. (1985) 'Students' alternative conceptions of the human circulatory system: A cross-age study', *Science Education*, 19 (5): 721–33.

Bar, V. (1989) Personal communication.

Bar, V. and Travis, A.S. (1991) 'Children's views concerning phase changes', *Journal of Research in Science Teaching*, 28 (4): 363–82.

Benson, D., Wittrock, M. and Baur, M. (1993) 'Students' preconceptions of the nature of gases', *Journal of Research in Science Teaching*, 30 (6): 587–97.

Beveridge, M. (1985) 'The development of young children's understanding of the process of evaporation', *British Journal Educational Psychology*, 55: 84–90.

Black, P.J. (1993) 'Progression in physics in the National curriculum', *Physics Education*, 28: 351–55.

Black, P.J. and Lucas, A.M. (1993) *Children's Informal Ideas in Science*, London: Routledge.

Bliss, J., Morrison, I. and Ogborn, J. (1988) 'A longitudinal study of dynamics concepts', *International Journal of Science Education*, 10 (1): 99–110.

Boyes, E. and Stanisstreet, M. (1991) 'Development of pupils' ideas about seeing and hearing – the path of light and sound', *Research in Science and Technological Education*, 9 (2): 223–44.

Brook, A., Driver, R. and Hind, D. (1989) *Progression in Science: the Development of Pupils' Understanding of Physical Characteristics of Air Across the Age Range 5–16 years*, Leeds: Children's Learning in Science Project, CSSME, University of Leeds.

Brown, D. and Clement, J. (1992) 'Classroom teaching experiments in mechanics', in R. Duit *et al.*, *Research in Physics Learning: Theoretical Issues and Empirical Studies*, Kiel: IPN.

Bruner, J.S. (1963) *The Process of Education*, New York: Random House.

Carey, S. (1985) *Conceptual Change in Childhood*, Cambridge MA: MIT Press.

—— (1992) 'The origin and evolution of everyday concepts', in R.N. Giere (ed.), *Cognitive Models of Science*, Minnesota Studies in the Philosophy of Science, Minnesota: University of Minnesota Press.

Carey, S. *et al.* (1989) 'An experiment is when you try it and see if it works', *International Journal of Science Education*, 11 (5): 514–29.

Carmichael, P., Driver, R., Holding, B., Phillips, I., Twigger, D. and Watts, M. (1990) *Research on Students' Conceptions in Science: A Bibliography*, Leeds: Children's Learning in Science Group, CSSME, University of Leeds.

Dickinson, D. (1987) 'The development of a concept of material kind', *Science Education*, 71 (4): 615–28.

Donaldson, M. (1978) *Children's Minds*, London: Fontana/Collins.

Driver, R., Asoko, H., Leach J., Mortimer, E. and Scott, P. (1994) 'Constructing scientific knowledge in the classroom', *Educational Researcher*, 23 (7): 5–12.

Driver, R., Guesne, E. and Tiberghien, A. (1985) *Children's Ideas in Science*, Milton Keynes: Open University Press.

Driver, R., Leach, J. Millar, R. and Scott, P. (1993) *Students' Understanding of the Nature of Science: Working Papers 1–11*, Leeds: Children's Learning in Science Research Group, CSSME, University of Leeds and University of York Science Education Group.

Edwards, D. and Mercer, N. (1987) *Common Knowledge*, London: Methuen.

Engel-Clough, E. and Wood-Robinson, C. (1985) 'Children's understanding in inheritance', *Journal of Biological Education*, 19: 304–10.

Engel-Clough, E., Driver, R. and Wood-Robinson, C. (1987) 'How do children's scientific ideas change over time?',*School Science Review*, 69 (247): 255–67.

Fensham, P., Gunstone, R. and White, R. (eds) (1994) *The Content of Science: A Constructivist Approach to its Teaching and Learning*, Lewes: Falmer Press.

Finley, F. (1985) 'Variations in prior knowledge', *Science Education*, 69 (5): 697–705.

Gagne, R.M. (1970) *The Conditions of Learning* (Second Edition), New York: Holt, Rinehart & Winston.

Glynn, S., Yeaney, R. and Britton, B. (1991) *The Psychology of Learning Science*, USA: Lawrence Erlbaum Associates.

Guesne, E. (1985) 'Light', in R. Driver, E. Guesne and A. Tiberghien *Children's Ideas in Science*, Milton Keynes: Open University Press.

Holding, B. (1987) 'Investigation of schoolchildren's understanding of the process of dissolving with special reference to the conservation of matter and the development of atomic ideas'. Unpublished PhD thesis, University of Leeds.

Karbo, D.B., Hobbs, E.D. and Erickson, G.L. (1980) 'Children's beliefs about inherited characteristics', *Journal of Biological Education*, 14: 137–46.

Kuhn, D. (1989) 'Children and Adults as Intuitive Scientists', *Psychological Review*, 96 (4): 679–89.

Larochelle, M. and Desautels, J. (1991) ' "Of course, its just obvious": adolescents' ideas of scientific knowledge', *International Journal of Science Education*, 13 (4): 373–89.

Leach, J., Driver, R., Scott, P. and Wood-Robinson, C. (1994) 'Children's ideas about ecology (1), (2) and (3), *International Journal of Science Education*, (in press).

Mali, G.B. and Howe, A. (1979) 'Development of earth and gravity concepts among Nepali children', *Science Education*, 63 (5): 685–91.

Novak, J.D. and Musonda, D. (1991) 'A twelve-year longitudinal study of science concept learning', *American Educational Research Journal*, 28 (1): 117–53.

Novick, S. and Nussbaum, J. (1981) 'Pupils understanding of the particulate nature of matter: A cross-age study', *Science Education*, 65 (2): 187–96.

Nussbaum, J. (1979) 'Children's conceptions of the earth as a cosmic body: A cross-age study', *Science Education*, 63 (1): 83–93.

Nussbaum, J. and Novick, S. (1982) 'Alternative frameworks, conceptual conflict and accomodation: towards a principled teaching strategy', *Instructional Science*, 11: 183–200.

Osborne, J.F., Black, P. and Smith, M. (1993) 'Young children's (7–11) ideas about light and their development', *International Journal of Science Education*, 15 (1): 83–93.

Osborne, R.J. and Cosgrove, M.M. (1983) 'Children's conceptions of the changes of state of water', *Journal of Research in Science Teaching*, 20: 825–38.

Pfundt, H. and Duit, R. (1990) *Bibliography. Students' Alternative Frameworks and Science Education*, Kiel: IPN.

Ramorogo, G.J. and Wood-Robinson, C. (1994) 'Botswana children's understanding of biological inheritance', *Journal of Biological Education*.

Rosier, S. and Viennot, L. (1990) 'Students' reasoning in thermodynamics', in Ljinse *et al.* (eds) *Relating macroscopic phenomena to microscopic particles. Proceedings of a Seminar*, Utrecht, CD-ß Press.

Samarapungavan, A. (1991) 'Children's metajudgements in theory choice tasks: scientific rationality in childhood'. Paper presented to the American Educational Research Association, Chicago.

Scott, P.H. (1991) 'Pathways in learning science: A case study of the development of one student's ideas relating to the structure of matter', in R. Duit, F. Goldberg and H. Niedderer (eds) *Research in Physics Learning: Theoretical Issues and Empirical Studies*, Kiel: Schmidt & Klannig.

Séré, M. (1982) 'A study of some frameworks in the field of mechanics used by children (aged 11 to 13) in the interpretation of air pressure', *European Journal of Science Education*, 4 (3): 299–309.

Smith, C., Carey, S., and Wiser, M. (1985) 'On differentiation: A case study of the development of the concepts of size, weight and density', *Cognition*, 21: 177–237.

Stavy, R. (1990) 'Children's conception of changes in the state of matter: from liquid (or solid) to gas', *Journal of Research in Science Teaching*, 27 (3): 247–66.

Stavy, R., Eisen. Y. and Yaakobi, D. (1987) 'How students aged 13–15 understand photosynthesis', *International Journal of Science Education*, 9 (1): 105–15.

Trumper, R. (1993) 'Children's energy concepts: a cross-age study', *International Journal of Science Education*, 15 (2): 139–48.

Twigger, D. *et al.* (1994) 'The conceptions of force and motion of students aged between 10 and 15 years: an interview study designed to guide instruction', *International Journal of Science Education*, 16 (2): 215–29.

Vosniadou, S. and Brewer, W.F. (1992) 'Mental models of the earth: A study of conceptual change in childhood', *Cognitive Psychology*, 24: 535–85.

Vygotsky, L.S. (1978) *Mind in Society: The Development of Higher Psychological Processes*, Cambridge, MA: Harvard University Press.

Westbrook, S.L. and Marek, E.A. (1991) 'A cross-age study of student understanding of the concept of diffusion', *Journal of Research in Science Teaching*, 28 (8): 649–60.

Westbrook, S.L. and Marek, E.A. (1992) 'A cross-age study of student understanding of the concept of homeostasis', *Journal of Research in Science Teaching*, 29 (1): 51–61.

Wood-Robinson, C. (1991) 'Young people's ideas about plants', *Studies in Science Education*, 19: 119–35.

Chapter 15

Progression in investigative work in science

Richard Gott, Sandra Duggan, Robin Millar and Fred Lubben

This chapter considers progression in procedural understanding in the context of investigative work in science. It looks at the rationale for the inclusion of procedural understanding as a substantive element of a curriculum and details its possible 'content'. An example, drawn from an extensive research base, is used to illustrate the problems pupils have with one element of procedural understanding and suggests that the search for progression in the science curriculum has some way to go.

INTRODUCTION

Historically, the development of investigative work in science in the UK has come to the point where many schools are adopting it with some enthusiasm and, reports from the inspectorate suggest, with a degree of success (Office for Standards in Education, 1993). Investigative work in this context is to do with practical work in which pupils encounter relatively open-ended tasks for which they have to devise their own solutions. Investigations are, of course, a statutory commitment within the UK National Curriculum, but it is one thing to prescribe an innovation and quite another to effect a real change in delivery. Fullan (1991), in discussing educational change, points to the loose relationship between *initiation* and *implementation.* In investigative work, what is still missing is a coherent rationale both for the place of investigations within the curriculum, and for progression within them.

Progression in a curriculum relies on there being a number of factors in place:

- there must be an agreed set of endpoints,
- there must be an agreed content, described in sufficient detail for it to be usable by teachers, and
- the sequencing of the material must be identified against an appropriate level of detail.

In the UK National Curriculum, none of these conditions is met. The same is true of the Australian system which has recently introduced a strand in the science curriculum, 'Working Scientifically', which mirrors to a great extent its counterpart in the UK. It is important, then, that we tackle the problem of progression from its root: we need a more complete justification for investigative work, and thereby an agreed endpoint and content. We will sketch out such a justification here. We will then suggest a possible 'content', defined as a set of skills and understandings, and illustrate one possible element of progression within that content from the research evidence of the Procedural and Conceptual Knowledge in Science or 'PACKS' project.

SCIENCE AND SOCIETY

Science education must accomplish two major aims in the context of its role in the wider society:

- it must so educate the populace in general that it can contribute to the democratic process with a degree of confidence and
- it must give pupils the necessary knowledge and skills to enter the workforce.

What does an informed public need to know about science to become involved in decision making at all levels of society? It may be best to illustrate this with a simple example, one that has been the focus of attention for a number of years in the UK. The Sellafield complex in Cumbria, which is intended to reprocess radioactive waste, has been the cause of much concern amongst residents in the area as to whether or not it is the cause of clusters of leukaemia. The informed citizen may well have some idea of what radiation is, but to many it is an undifferentiated term somehow concerned with atomic bombs and reactors. The notion that the radiation comes from material which is itself deposited through rainfall or via leaching into surface water is one which causes confusion. There is also the point that radioactive materials, such as plutonium, are of themselves chemically toxic. But having said all that, the public is well aware that radioactivity is dangerous even if they are not certain as to its precise origins or the mechanisms by which it may be transmitted.

But there is another side to the argument concerned with the evidence which is used by various pressure groups both for and against the contention that radiation from Sellafield is causing the clusters of leukaemia. We would argue that an informed public needs to be able to look critically at that evidence. There is a need to be aware that the data are capable of different interpretations and to understand that the proponents of the various positions should be able to demonstrate that their evidence is valid and reliable. These are key issues which school science should endeavour to teach.

The work in the UK on the public understanding of science has tended to concentrate on the understanding of scientific concepts rather than on the understanding of evidence (see, for example, Layton *et al.*, 1993). The Royal Society, in discussing the public understanding of science, wrote:

> the individual needs to know some of the factual background and to be able *to assess the quality of the evidence* being presented. Greater familiarity with the nature and the findings of science will also help the individual to resist pseudo-scientific information. An enhanced ability to sift the plausible from the implausible should be one of the benefits from better public understanding of science.
>
> (authors' emphases)

At present, professional scientists are seen by the public as the only arbiters of what is 'truth' in the matter. That need not be the case, and indeed should not be. There are too many cases of scientists making bad and/or subjective judgements for science to be left to scientists alone. An informed public needs to be able to enter the debate and evaluate evidence, particularly when judgements are made in matters affecting their lives. We would argue that, to date, science education has failed to make pupils aware of and familiar with the ideas surrounding the collection, validation and interpretation of 'objective' evidence.

Science and employment

Turning now to the requirements of the workforce in science-related employment, in a liberal education where the aim is to provide a broad science education which will be of value to all citizens, these requirements cannot be seen to dominate the curriculum, but they are an important factor which must be taken into account, for self-evident reasons. Industry cites the need for 'transferable skills'. But what are they? A recent report from a task group (the Council of Science and Technology Institutes, 1993) set up by industry and the Department of Employment in the UK gives a picture which can help to define these skills.

The authors of the report developed a framework to describe what scientists, technologists and mathematicians do. They defined the key purpose as being:

> To explore, establish, apply, manage and administer safe and ethical practices and procedures of science, technology and mathematics to generate new knowledge, and to exploit this knowledge to serve the economy, the environment and society.

To achieve this purpose three 'skills' or abilities were identified:

1   A central core of skills concerned with the doing of science;

2 Communication skills;
3 Management skills.

The first of these, the central core of skills, or 'transferable skills', are common to a wide range of occupations where science is used. These transferable skills (perhaps better defined as 'common skills' since the evidence of their transferability is not clear-cut) are defined in more detail as the ability to:

• Generate own ideas, hypotheses and theoretical models and/or utilize those postulated by others;
• Design investigations, experiments, trials, texts, simulations and operations;
• Conduct investigations, experiments, trials, tests and operations;
• Evaluate data and results from the processes and outcomes of investigations, experiments, trials, tests and operations.

This is not to argue, of course, that such occupations do not require conceptual understanding in the appropriate discipline(s). But what the above does point to is that notions surrounding evidence, such as the testing of ideas and the evaluation of data, are thought to be important both for the public understanding of science and for the requirements of employment in occupations where science (as well as maths and technology) are a significant part of the job. These headings will not be unfamiliar to those who recall the work in the mid-1960s of the American Association for the Advancement of Science (1967) where similar statements were arrived at which led to the introduction of so-called 'process science'.

However, the process science movement of the '60s and '70s failed to make a significant impact. We wish to argue here that this is largely because the aims, laudable through they were, were prescribed in insufficient detail for them to be incorporated unambiguously into a curriculum. Neither was there any agreement that the 'processes' might be anything other than a means to the traditional conceptual end; a teaching approach rather than a putative content. It is this failure of recognition of the content of investigative work in its own right that has plagued its development in the UK science curriculum, since without it there are no agreed endpoints, and therefore no agreed and logical progression.

THE ROLE OF EVIDENCE IN PHYSICS AND ENGINEERING

Whichever of these views we adopt, what is certainly true is that data, set in the wider notion of evidence, are a central issue in science. It is, also, an unproblematic statement since science and engineering without evidence is clearly a nonsense. But evidence, and data, have different roles in different branches of science.

To the research physicist, evidence is collected to challenge a theoretical position or to provide the basis on which a tentative hypothesis can be inspected. The key element here is the theory, or hypothesis, because physics is about underlying patterns and their mathematical descriptions.

To the engineer, however, the theories play a more subservient role. To take a simple example, the bending of a concrete beam follows a Hooke's law type pattern. But the value of the 'spring constant' is a very unreliable number, depending on aggregate size and setting time and conditions. So the data are much more idiosyncratic to the particular problem. Theory can help, but empirical evidence and modelling are now central. Here the reliability and validity of the data determine the safety of the structure. Whether or not it agrees with theoretical or modelled predictions is of secondary importance and is only helpful to future designers in setting parameters within which they can begin their design.

In technology, data are the guide to the next step in improving the design of a machine or process. Patterns, whether theoretical or empirical, are less important than ensuring that the finished article is optimized for its purpose.

A CONTENT DESCRIPTION FOR THE SCIENCE CURRICULUM

A simple model to locate the content of the science curriculum will help in the search both for a justification and an associated content description (Figure 15.1).

Conceptual understanding refers to the understanding of the ideas in science which are based on facts and which are sometimes referred to as 'substantive' or 'declarative' concepts. Examples are energy, the laws of motion, heredity, solubility, photosynthesis and so on. Procedural understanding is the understanding of a set of ideas which is complementary to conceptual understanding but related to the 'knowing how' of science. It is concerned with the understanding needed to put science into practice and can be regarded as *the thinking behind the doing*. Procedural understanding requires the use of 'skills' which here refer to activities such as the use of measuring instruments and the construction of tables and graphs, which are necessary but not sufficient in themselves to the carrying out of most practical work. For example, in measurement in a plant growth study, procedural understanding does not refer to the measuring itself, but to the decisions that have to be made about what to measure, how often and over what time period. It also includes the understanding of the notion of the fair test as well as the nature of a line graph, how it differs from a bar chart or how it illustrates patterns between variables.

An analogy may be useful here. The facts, skills and understandings can be envisaged as information or patterns in the brain's memory bank. When

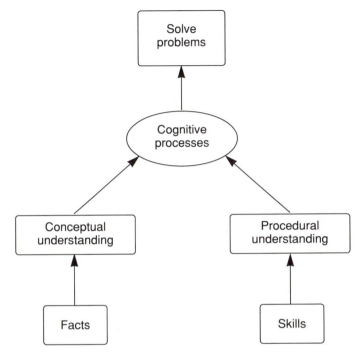

Figure 15.1 A model for science

Source: Gott and Duggan 1994

faced with a problem of any sort, in the sense of some new experience which requires resolution, the brain can be imagined to scan its data banks for facts or previous experiences that may help with the new problem. In the above example, those 'hard disk stores' will contain ideas about speed, measurement of distance and time, skill routines about using instruments, notions of a fair test and how it relates to the validity of any resulting data and so on. The central processing unit will then examine the problem and look on the hard disk for help; this may be in the form of particular ideas, or past experiences in similar circumstances. These will be pulled into the working memory. Then they must be 'processed', via a series of thought patterns that we label for example, hypothesizing, or predicting, into a solution consonant with, and evaluated against, the demands of the original problem.

The elements of science we identified in the introduction, the understandings that underpin both the requirements for democratic decision making and the 'common skills' sought by industry, can be seen to lie in the 'procedural understanding' area of the model. The question now is to produce an (embryonic) content description. Some of the elements are in

Table 15.1 Concepts of evidence

Reliability and Validity	
Concepts of evidence	*Definition*
Associated with design	
Variable identification	Understanding the idea of a variable and identifying the relevant variable to change (the independent variable) and to measure or assess if qualitative (the dependent variable).
Fair test	Understanding the structure of the fair test in terms of controlling the necessary variables and the importance that the control of variables has in relation to the validity of any resulting evidence.
Sample size	Understanding the significance of an appropriate sample size to allow, for instance, for biological variation.
Variable types	Understanding the distinction between categoric, discrete, continuous and derived variables and how they link to different graph types. For example, a categoric independent variable such as type of surface, cannot be displayed sensibly in a line graph. The behaviour of a continuous variable on the other hand is best shown in a line graph.
Associated with measurement	
Relative scale	Understanding the need to choose sensible values for quantities so that resulting measurements of the dependent variable will be meaningful. For instance, a large quantity of chemical in a small quantity of water causing saturation, will lead to difficulty in differentiating the dissolving times of different chemicals.
Range and interval	Understanding the need to select a sensible range of values of the variables within the task so that the resulting line graph consists of values which are spread sufficiently widely and reasonably spaced out so that the 'whole' pattern can be seen. A suitable number of readings is therefore also subsumed in this concept.
Choice of instrument	Understanding the relationship between the choice of instrument and the required range, interval and accuracy.
Repeatability	Understanding that the inherent variability in any physical measurement requires a consideration of the need for repeats, if necessary, to give reliable data.
Accuracy	Understanding the appropriate degree of accuracy that is required to provide reliable data which will allow a meaningful interpretation.
Associated with data handling	
Tables	Understanding that tables are more than ways of presenting data after it has been collected. They can be used as ways of organizing the design and subsequent data collection and analysis in advance of the whole experiment.
Graph types	Understanding that there is a close link between graphical representations and the type of variable they are to represent.
Patterns	Understanding that patterns represent the behaviour of variables which can be uncovered from the patterns in tables and graphs.
Multivariate data	Understanding the nature of multivariate data and how particular variables within those data can be held constant to discover the effect of one variable on another.

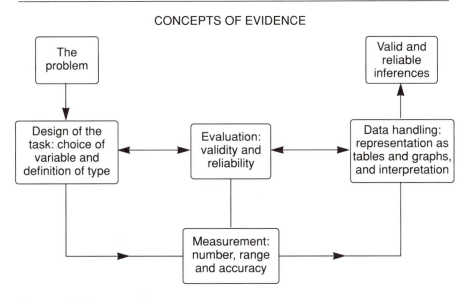

Figure 15.2 Concepts of evidence in an investigation

Source: Based on Duggan *et al.* 1994

place in curricula, notably the skills of scientific working and the notion of a 'fair test'. But there are considerable gaps. We have suggested elsewhere (Duggan and Gott, 1994; Gott and Duggan, 1994; Duggan *et al.*, 1994) that these gaps should be occupied by 'concepts of evidence', a term chosen in order to distinguish these understandings from the manipulative connotations of scientific 'skills'. They are outlined in Table 15.1

The overarching notions of validity and reliability address the question: is the evidence '*believable*' and does it reflect the problem that is to be solved? Only when this has been established can we go on to draw valid conclusions or offer alternative interpretations. This we can represent in the model in Figure 15.2 in which concepts of evidence and skills are brought to bear on the problem in an iterative way, but one in which the iterations are guided by notions of the validity and reliability of the resulting evidence.

In terms of the title of this paper, the point we wish to make here is that progression relies on a definition of what is to be taught in order that it can be structured. The research suggests that procedural understanding as defined here is largely a 'black hole' in current science schemes. We tentatively suggest that this lack of a content description in schemes of work is bound to lead to an incoherent experience for pupils and a reversion by teachers, particularly at the secondary level, to the more familiar concept-focused curriculum. They will tend, then, to see investigative work as the well-trodden, and not necessarily efficient, means to conceptual understanding rather than, as we would argue, involving a knowledge base of its own with its own content and teaching techniques. It would not be surprising, if that is the case, for pupils to fail to make any coherent linkages in their procedural understanding and to fall back on a set of apparently acceptable rituals.

Having established at least the bones of an argument which defines the procedural endpoint and outlines a possible content description, we must turn to evidence as to how that content might be structured and sequenced. Here we meet a fundamental problem. Since the 'content' has not been defined tightly, it has not been taught in any coherent fashion. Various of our skills and concepts of evidence are included in current science schemes, but as disembodied items rather than elements of a sequential structure. So if we look for evidence on pupil performance, we cannot say that it will give us a basis for curriculum sequencing. That performance may be a consequence of some skills or concepts of evidence being taught and others not, rather than a reflection of their inherently progressive 'difficulty'. But we must start somewhere.

PROCEDURAL UNDERSTANDING – SOME RESEARCH EVIDENCE

Evidence concerning pupils' performance on investigations has been accumulating over a number of years, beginning in the early 1980s with the work of the Assessment of Performance Unit, and continuing more recently with research under contract to the National Curriculum Council in the UK in the context of the UK National Curriculum (Foulds *et al.*, 1992). Investigations have been defined within the UK curriculum as being open-ended practical tasks in which the pupils are required to develop their own strategy for a solution (see Table 15.2 for some examples). Progression has been largely defined by the complexity of the task in terms of the number and type of variables.

One of the key findings of the previous research referred to above was the extent to which performance on investigations depends on the interaction between conceptual and procedural understanding. The PACKS project was designed to investigate this interaction in the context of a number of investigations set in different concept areas and with samples of pupils in the 9 to 14 age range. This paper will deal with one small but indicative example of this interaction. A fuller account of the PACKS project can be found in Millar *et al.* (1994).

In the Forces II task (see Table 15.2), pupils would, we hope, treat the height of the ramp (or the angle) and the force as continuous variables. We might further hope that they would draw a line graph to show the pattern in the data. This is an example of the linking of a number of skills and concepts of evidence into a strand of ideas that guides the investigation.

Table 15.2 The investigations used in the PACKS project

Task	Description	Materials
Shrimps	Find out whether shrimps prefer light or dark conditions, or to be near the top or bottom of the water.	Tank of shrimps, containers of various shapes, pipettes, water, black polythene.
Cool drink	Find out how the thickness of the padding material affects how well a cool bag (for keeping a cool drink cold) works.	Beakers, measuring cylinders, supply of ice-cold water, thermometer, stopclock, supply of bubble wrap, fleece and foam sheet.
Buggy	Find out how the speed of a battery-powered buggy depends on the diameter of the wheels and the weight of the buggy.	Battery-powered buggy, sets of wheels of 3 sizes, 100g masses, stopclock, metre rule, screwdriver (to change wheels).
Dissolving I	Find out how quickly four different sugars dissolve in cold tap water and put them in order from the one which dissolves quickest to the one which dissolves slowest.	Small pots of four different sugars, stopclocks, scales, spatulas, spoons, graduated and ungraduated beakers, tap water.
Dissolving II	Find out how the temperature of the water affects the time sugar takes to dissolve.	Small pots of sugar, stopclocks, scales, spatulas, spoons, graduated and ungraduated beakers, thermometers, water (previously boiled and tap water available).
Forces I	Find out how the type of surface affects the amount of pull needed to drag a brick along.	Half bricks into which hooks have been fitted, planks with a rough and a smooth side, a piece of corrugated card and a piece of carpet to fit on the plank, forcemeters, metre rules.
Forces II	Find out how the height of a slope affects the amount of pull needed to move a brick uphill.	Half bricks into which hooks have been fitted, planks, forcemeters, metre rules.

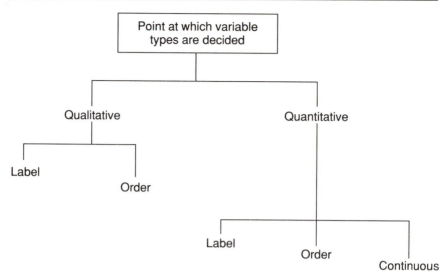

Figure 15.3 A classification of variable identification and subsequent data handling

Source: Millar *et al.* 1994

It conjoins ideas about the nature and type of the variables, the range, number and accuracy of the measurements, the recognition and description of the pattern in the results and the controlling principles of reliability and validity to produce credible evidence. As we see from the data that follow, a variety of ways of treating the variables have been identified in the case study records.

Through a detailed case by case analysis of interview and observation records, pupils were placed in one of three groups: 'label', 'order' and 'continuous'. The descriptors were defined as follows:

Label   children treat any datum, quantitative or qualitative as if it were merely a label such as 'red' or 'large'.

Order   children put their data into an ordered list, for instance, but show no understanding that continuous data must be placed on an interval rather than an ordinal scale.

Continuous   children treat the data in the scientifically correct manner, making the necessary links to produce a valid and reliable pattern from which to draw their conclusions.

The various alternative ways of identifying variables are outlined in Figure 15.3, and Table 15.3 shows how groups of children at various ages operationalized variables. We see a progression with age towards identifying variables as ordered or continuous. But, in secondary school, it seems as

Table 15.3 The classification of performance in the Forces II task at three ages (figures represent number of groups)

		Year 4 (9 year olds)	Year 6 (11 year olds)	Year 9 (14 year olds)
Qualitative	Label	1	—	—
	Order	6	2	—
Quantitative	Label	3	1	—
	Order	5	4	10
	Continuous	1	10	5

if pupils regress in that many groups treated the data as an ordered set rather than as continuous. The sample size is relatively small, however, and caution must be exercised in making any generalizations. We suggest, however, that the introduction of more formal science may have resulted in pupils adopting a ritual approach to graphs in science to the extent that they draw a graph and then stop, failing to interpret it or to draw a generalized conclusion. We make a further tentative suggestion, based on preliminary analyses of data on their level of conceptual understanding in the area covered by the investigative task, that if pupils understand the nature of any continuous variable *and* have an understanding of the *particular* variable in the task (force in this case) and how it 'behaves' in relation to the height of the ramp, then they will operate in the 'scientific' manner which we ultimately expect (Figure 15.4). Whether or not this association is real, and, if it is, whether it is causal or contingent, is under investigation.

Figure 15.4 Possible progression in children's understanding of the identification of variables

So our search for progression has some of its elements in place. The example quoted above suggests that a progression from seeing data as merely labels, through to associating them with the physical situation is one possible strand. We are beginning the task of defining other strands. But until teachers are operating a scheme of work which incorporates procedural understanding and its associated content explicitly, the search for progression can only be tentative and provisional.

ACKNOWLEDGEMENT

The research reported here was funded by Grant No. X208 25 2008 from the UK Economic and Social Research Council as part of their research programme on 'Innovation and Change in Education: the Quality of Teaching and Learning'.

REFERENCES

American Association for the Advancement of Science (1967) *Science – A Process Approach*, Washington D.C.: Ginn & Co.

Council of Science and Technology Institutes (1993) *Mapping the Science, Technology and Mathematics Domain*, London: Council of Science and Technology Institutes.

Duggan, S. and Gott, R. (1994) 'The place of investigations in practical work in the UK National Curriculum for Science', *International Journal of Science Education.*

Duggan, S., Gott, R., Millar R. and Lubben, F. (1994) 'Evidence in Science Education', in M. Huges (ed.) *Teaching and Learning in Changing Times*, Oxford: Blackwells.

Foulds, K., Gott, R. and Feasey, R. (1992) *Investigative Work in Science*, University of Durham.

Fullan, M.G. (1991) *The New Meaning of Educational Change*, London: Cassell.

Gott, R. and Duggan, S. (1994) *Investigative Work in the Science Curriculum*, Milton Keynes: Open University Press.

Layton, D., Jenkins, E., Macgill, S. and Davey, A. (1993) *Inarticulate Science? Perspectives on the Public Understanding of Science and some Implications for Science Education*, E. Yorkshire, Studies in Education Ltd.

Millar, R., Lubben, F., Gott, R. and Duggan, S. (1994) 'Investigating in the school science laboratory: conceptual and procedural knowledge and their influence on performance', *Research Papers in Education* 9 (2): 207–49.

Office for Standards in Education (1993) *Science Key Stages 1, 2, 3 and 4. Fourth Year, 1992–93*, London: HMSO.

The Royal Society (1985) *The Public Understanding of Science*, London: The Royal Society.

Chapter 16

Learning about physics through peer interaction

Christine Howe

Educators could currently be forgiven for feeling very confused about the relevance of peer interaction to teaching and learning in physics. On the one hand, recent pronouncements aimed at education in general might seem to undermine peer interaction as the proper concern of teachers. On the other hand, developments relating to physics itself could be construed as giving peer interaction an unprecedented boost. A clear example is the 'National Curriculum for Science' which makes 'talking in groups' statutory for numerous school activities in England and Wales. A similar emphasis appears in the Scottish 'Environmental Studies 5 to 14', a programme which includes physics, amongst other subjects. In addition, physics teaching is being increasingly supported by expensive artefacts, whose cost necessitates shared (and hence collaborative) usage. The most obvious instance is computer-based work. Computers are becoming commonplace in physics for the simulation of effects, for the control of experiments, and (perhaps unfortunately) for the drilling of 'facts', and their usage is very largely with pupils working in groups. As just one of many illustrations, a recent survey by Erica McAteer and Ayal Demissie of Strathclyde University revealed that 93 per cent of computer use in Glasgow schools involves two or more pupils working together.

Given undeniable contradictions at the level of policy, educators might be expected to turn for clarification to the research community. Unfortunately, here too, there are a number of competing positions. Within the research community, particular attention has been paid to situations where pupils have strong preconceptions about the topic being studied. It is generally accepted that such preconceptions have to be eased very gently towards science wisdom. A head-on assault is seen as counterproductive. Taking this for granted, some researchers believe that gradual change is achievable if pupils are presented with tasks which oblige them first to make predictions based on their preconceptions, second to test the predictions against empirical data, and third to re-examine the preconceptions in the light of the results. Such researchers often acknowledge that peer interaction over the formulation of predictions can provide a natural context for making preconceptions explicit, and hence ensuring that pre-conceptions are the basis for predictions. However, they would worry about the implications when the peers differ over their preconceptions, for here predictions about outcome would also be likely to differ. This means that the predictions which pupils test would have to be negotiated between then or be imposed by some dominant individuals. In neither case would they reflect the preconceptions of all the pupils, and in some cases they may be compromises reflecting the preconceptions of none. Thus, when precon-ceptions differ, many pupils would be precluded from testing the conse-quences of their own ideas, and this runs counter to the whole spirit in which the tasks were conceived.

Expressed more generally, researchers who emphasize the testing of personal conceptions would hypothesize that there will be value in peer interaction so long as preconceptions are similar. If preconceptions are different, the usefulness of interaction in drawing preconceptions out would be more than countered by the drawbacks of testing negotiated predictions. On first hearing, this hypothesis sounds only too convincing. However, it turns out to be diametrically opposed to some major traditions in child psychology. For example, followers of the Swiss psychologist Piaget em-phasize the resolution of internally experienced conflicts as the trigger of growth. The process of negotiation when preconceptions differ should often find pupils starting with one set of ideas, and then committing themselves, albeit temporarily, to a contrasting set as they agree their predictions. This, as Piaget's followers have acknowledged, should be a fertile source of internally experienced conflict. Moreover, no such conflict should be antic-ipated when preconceptions are similar, leading to the hypothesis that there will be value in peer interaction so long as preconceptions differ. Similarly, followers of Vygotsky, Piaget's Russian (and increasingly acclaimed) con-temporary, see development as the gradual piecing together of partial truths. During negotiation when preconceptions differ, pupils must inevitably appraise and hone down a range of ideas, leading potentially to a pool of partial truths. It is hard to see how an equivalent pool could emerge when preconceptions are similar.

Faced with competing theories about an educationally important topic, it seems crucial to obtain empirical data, and that has been a major concern of my recent research. This research began with three studies with primary school children. The children worked in groups of four on tasks which obliged them to predict, test and re-examine. In some groups, the children had similar preconceptions and in others they had different, and the focus was the amount of learning in each type of group. The next stage was two studies which attempted first to replicate the results with older subjects and second to examine directly the relation between learning and on-task nego-tiation. I intend to outline all five studies briefly, showing how they yield a ꞏ i̯ ꞏy consistent picture as regards different and similar groups. Having done so, I want to look more carefully at the conditions in which the results were obtained, referring briefly both to some further features of the studies and also to some additional and recently completed work. With extensive data from a range of studies, I hope that this chapter will constitute a fairly authoritative statement about peer interaction and learning in physics.

PEER INTERACTION IN PRIMARY SCHOOL PHYSICS

The first three studies were conducted jointly by myself, Cathy Rodgers and Andy Tolmie. Two of the studies were concerned with floating and sinking, one looking at pupils' appreciation of the role of object density and the other at their appreciation of the role of fluid density. The third study was concerned with motion down an inclined plane. All three began with individual pre-tests to assess preconceptions. In each study, these were administered to over one hundred eight- to twelve-year-old pupils. For example, the object density pre-test started with the presentation of a tank of water and eight small objects, including a metal key, an ebony cylinder and a glass bottle. The pupils were asked whether each object would float or sink in the tank, and why they thought this. Next, descriptions were given of eight 'real-world' scenarios, such as the floating of boats and the sinking of anchors, and the pupils were asked why the scenarios turned out as they did. Real-world scenarios also featured in the motion down an incline pre-test, but the main focus was apparatus which allowed manipulation of the angle and friction of slopes and the starting position and weight of toy vehicles. Pupils were asked to predict the distance that the vehicles would travel from the foot of a slope under different combinations of the four factors, and to explain their proposals.

In all three studies, the pupils' responses were noted as they were given, and used as the basis for subsequent grouping into foursomes. For the two floating and sinking studies, the following groups were formed:

1 DD groups – the pupils in a group had differing preconceptions and some pupils were more advanced in their science knowledge than others;
2 DS groups – the pupils in a group had differing preconceptions, but they were all roughly equivalent in their science knowledge;
3 SS groups – the pupils in a group had similar preconceptions.

For the motion down an incline study, the groups were as follows:

1 LowDD – the pupils in a group had differing preconceptions, with some very low in science knowledge and some only moderate;
2 HighDD – the pupils in a group had differing preconceptions, with some moderate in science knowledge and some reasonably high;

3 LowSS – the pupils in a group had similar preconceptions, either all low or all moderate;

4 HighSS – the pupils in a group had similar preconceptions, either all moderate or all high.

The group tasks were administered by researchers who were kept in ignorance about the type of group that individual pupils were assigned to. The group tasks had two main stages, the first involving each pupil making private predictions. The predictions related to events which were similar to those in the pre-test. The pupils made their predictions by ticking on cards in response to the researchers' questions. The second stage involved the pupils working through books which invited them to compare their private predictions one by one, come to an agreement where these differed, test the agreed predictions using relevant apparatus, and agree an interpretation of what transpired. The researchers stayed with the groups while they considered the first few predictions, checking that the book reading was manageable and that the pupils discussed predictions and test results as fully as possible. No feedback was given on the validity of the ideas that the pupils expressed. After this preliminary monitoring, the pupils were left on their own, although a video recorder was kept running throughout.

In each of the studies, there was a post-test to all group participants a few weeks after the task. This post-test was equivalent in structure to the pre-test, although it contained a few novel items. To look at learning, pre- and post-test responses were scored for approximation to received science knowledge, and pre-test scores subtracted from post-test as measures of change. Comparison of the change scores between the differing and similar groups gave strong support to the second of the two hypotheses outlined above: peer interaction has value so long as preconceptions differ. In the two floating and sinking studies, both the DD and DS pupils progressed significantly from pre- to post-test. The amount of change was similar in the DD and DS conditions, and the more advanced pupils in the DD groups progressed as much as the less advanced. The SS pupils, by contrast, did not make any gains from pre- to post-test. In the motion down an incline study, the SS pupils showed limited progress. However, the LowDD pupils made significantly more progress than the LowSS pupils. Only the HighDD pupils were an exception to the overall trend, failing to differ from the HighSS pupils in pre- to post-test change.

PEER INTERACTION WITH COMPUTER-BASED TASKS

With only one inconsistent result across the three studies, the picture with primary-aged pupils seemed reasonably clear, and thus the next stage of the research addressed an older age group. The two studies that comprised this stage were conducted by myself in collaboration with Tony Anderson, Terry Mayes, Andy Tolmie and Mhairi MacKenzie. The topic area of one study was the paths that objects follow during freefall through space, and was conducted with twelve- to fifteen-year-old pupils. The topic area of the other was judgements of relative speed when distance/time information is available, and was carried out with undergraduate students of Arts, Science and Social Science.

As with the primary school studies, these studies began with a pre-test to over one hundred individuals. However, in the case of the freefall study, the pre-test was a paper-and-pencil instrument that was administered in a classroom setting. The pupils were first asked to draw the paths that, in their view, the objects would follow under different combinations of pre-fall path, pre-fall velocity and object weight. They were next invited to answer questions about the forces that would be operating at the moment of fall. In the case of the relative speed study, the pre-test was, like the primary school pre-tests, administered in one-to-one interviews. However, this pre-test, unlike any others, used computer displays. These displays depicted the horizontal motion of two trains, and the students were told that there was one point at which the speeds of trains were identical. Their task was to identify the point by clicking on the screen. With some displays, the trains started simultaneously; in others, they started sequentially. With some displays, both trains moved from left to right; in others, one train moved from right to left. Finally, with some displays, the judgements were to be made from the students' perspective; in others, they were to be made from the perspective of a third moving train. The thrust of the interviews was the factors that the students considered in making judgements, particularly their recourse to a 'Help' facility which included distance/time data.

The pre-test responses were used to formulate groups for the next phase of the studies. This phase was working through group tasks which had the same structure as the primary school ones, namely private decisions, joint decisions, empirical tests, and joint interpretations. The tasks were also like the primary school ones in that they were introduced by researchers who monitored the first few items and then left the participants on their own, interaction being videotaped. However, there were two points of contrast with the primary school work. The first was that the tasks in both studies were computer-presented. Thus, in the freefall study, the pupils inputted their ideas about the paths by clicking on a screen. They then witnessed simulations of the objects' motion which left traces for comparison with the input. In the relative speed study, pupils inputted their judgements and then received a message telling them if they were right or wrong. The second point of contrast with the primary schoolwork was that in both studies, pairs were used rather than foursomes. There is evidence that pairs are the typical (and perhaps optimal) group for computer-based work. The pairs were formed to include differing and similar combinations, the contrast in both studies being DD versus SS. Gender composition was also carefully controlled.

Post-tests along the lines of the pre-tests were administered to group participants a few weeks after the tasks, with both pre- and post-tests being scored for the extent of science knowledge. Although the SS participants learned, progress was once more superior in the DD groups. Thus, the main finding was a replication of the results already obtained with the younger age group. Replication was not, however, the only aim, for as mentioned earlier, there was also an interest in the relation between learning and on-task dialogue. What emerged when this was considered was an intriguing interaction with gender. For the female–female groups in the freefall study, learning was a function of the sheer volume of relevant ideas. For the male–male groups in the freefall study and both the male–male and the female–female groups in the relative speed study, learning depended on the extent to which ideas were co-ordinated while working on the task. It has seemed to my research associates that Piaget could make more sense of the former finding, and Vygotsky more sense of the second!

SOME CONCLUSIONS AND SOME PROVISOS

Summing up, we now have evidence with five topics and with the eight to undergraduate age group that there is value in peer interaction so long as preconceptions differ. This is not simply an important conclusion in the present political context. It should also be reassuring to those concerned with teaching. Through running the studies, I have become aware that at any given age, pupils vary enormously in the notions they hold. Thus, any teacher grouping pupils at random would be almost guaranteed to achieve differing groups, meaning that the achievement of such groups in ordinary educational contexts would require neither time nor expertise. Similar groups would be the problem ones! However, while this is both true and encouraging, I do not wish to imply that success with our tasks is complete plain sailing. On the contrary, I want to conclude with two provisos that should be considered by anyone wishing to employ the tasks for educational purposes.

The first proviso is that it is not necessarily realistic to look for instant success. One point that I have not previously mentioned is that in all five studies, we used the video recordings to score the participants' performance while working on the tasks. Scoring was on the same basis as for pre- and post-test performance. The scores showed that it was rare for on-task performance to be better than the pre-test performance. Indeed, in the motion down an incline study, on-task performance was markedly worse! Another additional point is that in the motion down an incline study, we administered immediate post-tests as well as the delayed ones that have been outlined already. Although there was clear progress from the pre-tests to the delayed post-tests, immediate post-test scores were equal to pre-test scores. Even more telling, however, is a very recent study, conducted by myself, Andy Tolmie, Karen Greer and Mhairi MacKenzie. This study was also with primary school children and once more used floating and sinking as its topic. The study had post-tests at four and eleven weeks after the group tasks. There was marked improvement between four and eleven weeks, without, as far as I can tell, any additional teaching.

Although this new study bears on the issue of post-group change, its main function was to clarify more precisely the role of task structure. It will be remembered that all our tasks had a predict/test/interpret format, but of course within that format a number of options could be followed. For example, the items could be presented for prediction in an unordered fashion, which is what we did in our studies. However, they could also be presented with systematically varying factors, allowing for approximation to a critical test. Thus, in a study of floating and sinking, we could have a wooden block followed by a metal block of equal size and weight, then a wooden block followed by another wooden block of equal size but different weight. Equally, the instructions regarding interpretation could be open-ended, as with the 'Try to work out why things turned out the way they did' that featured in our studies. However, they could also give hints, with the hints potentially varying in the degree of specificity. Thus, there could be a general suggestion to think up an all-encompassing rule, for example 'Write down the best thing to look for to decide if something will float or sink' and/or 'Write down the things that do not matter when deciding if something will float or sink'. Alternatively, there could be a specific instruction to choose the best rule from a list, for example 'Choose one of the following rules: What an object is made of doesn't matter to floating and sinking/The most important thing for floating and sinking is what an object is made of.'

Recognizing the existence of options such as these, the most recent work has been directed at ascertaining whether they make any difference. To date, we have completed two studies, the new study on floating and sinking and a parallel study on heating and cooling. Both studies were conducted with eight- to twelve-year-old children and, apart from the tweaking necessary to explore the options, followed the methods of our initial research. What these studies show is that task structure makes a great deal of difference. Perhaps counter-intuitively, it is not helpful to give children a list of rules from which to choose. We have a suspicion that when children choose from a list, they get the impression that they have solved the task. Thus, they are less inclined to engage in the post-group thought which, as we have just seen, may be crucial. Critical testing is also unhelpful, at least in isolation, because it restricts the scope of the dialogue. However, when critical testing is accompanied by hints that an encompassing rule should be chosen, the outcome is excellent, better even than in our original work. Thus, the second proviso is that to achieve success with group work in physics, the structure of the task needs to be carefully monitored. Our most recent studies give some guidance as to the optimum structure, but a lot remains unknown. Exploring this issue is clearly a crucial avenue for future research. Our existing data are surely sufficient to say that peer interaction can be valuable in physics. The question that researchers should now be addressing is how to make that value as great as possible.

BIBLIOGRAPHY

For further information about the research that is summarized in this chapter, please see:

Howe, C.J., Rodgers, C. and Tolmie, A. (1990) 'Physics in the primary school: peer interaction and the understanding of floating and sinking', *European Journal of Psychology of Education*, 4: 459–75.
Howe, C.J., Tolmie, A. and Anderson, A. (1991) 'Information technology and group work in physics', *Journal of Computer Assisted Learning*, 7: 133–43.
Howe, C.J., Tolmie, A., Anderson, A. and Mackenzie, M. (1992) 'Conceptual knowledge in physics: the role of group interaction in computer-supported teaching', *Learning and Instruction*, 2: 161–83.
Howe, C.J., Tolmie, A. and Rodgers, C. (1992) 'The acquisition of conceptual knowledge in science by primary school children: group interaction and the understanding of motion down an incline', *British Journal of Developmental Psychology*, 10: 113–30.
Tolmie, A., Howe, C., Mackenzie, M. and Greer, K. (1993) 'Task design as an influence on dialogue and learning: primary school group work with object flotation', *Social Development*, 2: 183–201.

Part IV

Mathematics:
teaching strategies,
perspectives on numeracy

Chapter 17

Introduction

Michelle Selinger

The mathematics curriculum, like the science curriculum, has been significantly influenced by the adoption of constructivist views of learning. The selection of texts in this area examines the history of constructivism in mathematics and how this has influenced the definition of the domain in terms of what is taught and how it is taught. These influences are considered in approaches to the learning and teaching of numeracy and the introduction of investigative learning in the maths curriculum. Thus parallels exist with the previous part in terms of the value placed on conceptual achievement over and above procedural understanding. However, what is meant by conceptual and procedural understanding varies between the two domains. The focus in this part shifts to look at implications for teaching of a constructivist perspective and highlights some of the limitations in current understanding when research ideas are translated into practice.

Askew, Bliss and Macrae (Chapter 18) also conducted research from a social constructivist viewpoint. They examine the metaphor of scaffolding which explicitly acknowledges the role of the teacher in the learning process, and its relationship to Vygotsky's notion of zone of proximal development. They outline from the research what might be described as evidence of scaffolding in mathematics and science lessons in primary classrooms. They found little evidence of scaffolding. A problem in their view is that current conceptions of the term do not translate well in practice in classrooms. Askew *et al.* argue that scaffolding is concerned with what pupils can achieve on their own yet this form of learning is rare in classrooms. In addition scaffolding is predicated on the roles of the adult or peer teacher and the learner becoming equal, again a situation hard to imagine in today's classrooms. Perhaps of more significance is that scaffolding as it is conceived fails to take account of tasks and contexts and their consequences for learners achieving autonomy.

The context in which Cobb, Wood and Yackel describe mathematics teaching in Chapter 20 is within a framework of teaching and learning about number. What does it mean to teach number? What sense do we expect children to make of tasks that require them to use their number skills? The notion of number sense is defined in Chapter 19 where McIntosh, Reys and Reys state clearly what they believe a facility with number ought to be. They stress that within their definition of number sense there is not only the ability to perform routine algorithms, but also the development of a 'feel' for number in which one can select and apply relevant skills appropriately in a range of contexts. This view of number sense sets a rationale for learning about number in school through investigation, and emphasizes the importance of talk and informal recording in this process.

Mathematical discussion between pupils and between pupils and teachers depends very much on the way teachers encourage communication and how they set up mathematical discussions with their classroom. In the last chapter, Love and Mason examine in some detail the different forms of telling (expounding, explaining and conjecturing) and asking (focusing, rehearsing and enquiring) and look at their purpose in mathematics teaching and learning. They also explore how the notion of scaffolding can be implemented through teachers' interactions with their pupils.

Chapter 18

Scaffolding in mathematics, science and technology

Mike Askew, Joan Bliss and Sheila Macrae

INTRODUCTION

Understanding the relationship between the role of the individual learner and the social context in which learning takes place is not a trivial task. A constructivism derived either from Piagetian or Kellyan perspectives has been adopted in much of mathematics or science education as the 'catch-all' rationale for teaching and learning. While this has focused attention on the active role of the pupil, many current constructivist approaches do not sufficiently take into account notions of interaction and the place of 'others' in supporting learning; the model of the learner is predominantly one of an explorer discovering knowledge in isolation.

In reconciling the individual and the social, the metaphor of 'scaffolding' learners is gaining popularity. In contrast with other metaphors, for example 'facilitating' learning, scaffolding explicitly acknowledges the role of the teacher in the learning process. The overtones of the physical building-site scaffolding carry a sense of teaching as an intentional, supportive activity. Given the prevalence of the language of construction in the literature on learning, scaffolding seems an almost 'natural' way to describe teaching. But beyond acknowledging the intentionality of teaching, does describing a teacher's activity in terms of scaffolding, provide new insights into the nature of teaching and learning? Further, does the metaphor carry prescriptive advice? Just as builders have to learn to scaffold buildings, can teachers learn to scaffold pupils?

We have been exploring what scaffolding might actually look like in primary classrooms in the contexts of mathematics, science and design and technology,[1] and discuss here some of the issues that have arisen out of this work. The following case study provides a background against which to discuss some of the features that scaffolding might entail.

JENNY

One of us, visiting a class of 7-year-olds, joined Jenny who was putting into order six cards, going up in tens from 100 to 150. Jenny could explain that the numbers were getting 'ten bigger' and predict that 160 would be next. Moving away, I asked Jenny if she would write down the numbers and carry on the pattern as far as she could. Bringing her paper to me, Jenny had written the numbers as far as 190, and said she did not know what came next. She knew that the last number was one hundred and ninety, and when asked what came after ninety, knew it was one hundred. I asked what she thought might come after one hundred and ninety (emphasizing the one hundred) and she correctly predicted two hundred, which she could write. She was now confident that the next number would be two hundred and ten but wrote 20010. I praised this as sensible and directed her attention to 100, 110 and 200, drawing the parallel between 100 and 200, and asked how else she thought two hundred and ten might be written. Jenny wrote 210 and deduced that the next would be 220. I left her with the request that she try to continue the pattern to 350.

When Jenny next found me she had successfully completed her list to 350 and could read back various numbers. I asked if she could write 560. Her first response to this was 500 + 60 = and after explaining that I had meant as a single number, she responded with 50060. Again I acknowledged the sense in this but directed her attention to 350 and asked if she could write three hundred and sixty. She did this correctly, then four hundred and sixty and was happy to change her answer to 560. She succeeded with a couple of other random numbers and I was happy to leave it at that.

A little later, Jenny arrived to show me 1010 on her paper and tell me that she knew how to read it: ten hundred and ten. After praising her for this generalization, we talked about other ways of 'reading' 1010 and tried reading some other numbers in both Jenny's way and in the conventional way.

SCAFFOLDING

The work of Vygotsky is increasingly being drawn upon because of his attempt to bring together the individual and the social. Vygotsky is generally regarded as one of the first major theorists to recognize the importance of the social context in learning, but he did more than this. For Vygotsky, learning did not simply take place in a social context, rather social interaction was the basis of learning.

> Every function in the child's cultural development appears twice: first on the social level, and later, on the individual level; first *between* people (*interpsychological*), and then *inside* the child (*intrapsychological*).
>
> (Vygotsky, 1978: 57; original emphasis)

To understand Vygotsky's explanation of the transfer from the inter-psychological to the intrapsychological, it is necessary to examine his theory of the relationship between development and learning. Vygotsky saw intellectual or cultural development (as opposed to physical development) as following on from learning, in contrast with the popularly held view of learning being determined by the child's developmental level. He stressed the importance of distinguishing a child's actual developmental level from their potential developmental level, the difference between these being the child's 'zone of proximal development':

> the distance between the actual development as determined by indepen-dent problem solving and level of potential development as determined through problem solving under adult guidance or in collaboration with more capable peers.

> (Vygotsky, 1978: 86)

Jenny appeared to be operating within her zone of proximal development. She could do a certain amount of the task independently but needed adult intervention to extend what she could do.

Although Vygotsky provided theoretical arguments about adults and children working together in the zone of proximal development, there is little empirical evidence of what this might look like in practice and the practical implications for teaching are difficult to detect. It has been left to later authors to develop frameworks for teaching based on Vygotsky's theory (see for example Cole, 1985 and Tharp and Gallimore, 1988). The work of Bruner is particularly pertinent here.

Bruner (1985), discussing some earlier work (Wood et al., 1976), argues that Vygotsky's theory implies that through scaffolding the learning task, the tutor or peers make it possible for the learner 'to internalise knowledge and convert it into a tool for conscious control' (p. 24). In this process adults serve as 'a vicarious form of consciousness until such a time as the learner is able to master his own action through his own consciousness and con-trol'. The example of Jenny illustrates this vicarious consciousness. The adult had the overview of what successful completion of the task would involve and had to monitor the success or failure of Jenny's responses until she was able to do this herself.

Bruner suggests that there are three aspects of the learning experiences that need to be examined – props, processes and procedures. Each of these has a parallel aspect in education – curriculum, learning and teaching respectively. Props are those cultural tools that enable children to work within their zone of proximal development, i.e. to operate at a level beyond that of their current development. Processes are those aspects of the learner that make them receptive to such learning approaches. Procedures refer to the strategies of the teacher or more competent peer in supporting the learner. Scaffolding is one such procedure.

In working with a learner in the zone of proximal development, Bruner considers there to be three 'inevitabilities' or procedures. The first is the need to model the task and demonstrate to the learner that what they are invited to engage with is not only interesting but possible. The aim of this stage is, in Bruner's terms, to encourage the child to 'venture into the zone'. The means of accomplishing this are not clear, but Bruner suggests that it is necessary to reduce the consequence of error, possibly eliminating it altogether. The particular task which Bruner refers to, and which is fully discussed in the Wood *et al.* paper, is the construction of a wooden pyramid by fitting together a number of interlocking pieces. By fitting pairs of pieces together herself, the tutor modelled a part of the task.

Scaffolding, Bruner's second type of procedure, follows and involves 'reducing the number of degrees of freedom that the child must manage in the task' (1985: 29). For example, if the child was unable to identify pairs of blocks that fitted together in the pyramid building task, the tutor might reduce the degrees of freedom by presenting the child with two of the blocks that would fit. Only if a strategy such as this failed to enable the child to succeed would Bruner's third type of procedure be used: actually telling the child what to do.

It is worth noting that, as Maybin *et al.* (1992) point out, the metaphor of scaffolding originally arose from work in child psychology and only subsequently came to be adopted in education. Bruner himself suggests that there are links between the pyramid task study and teaching in general, arguing that '[w]e were exactly in the position of most schools that set out to teach a subject without the advice or consent of the pupils involved and without the task having any contextualization in the children's lives' (1985: 29). However if the idea of scaffolding is to transfer to school settings, Bruner's work must also be examined for the ways in which it is unlike the position in school. The most obvious differences from classroom activities are the highly structured practical nature of the task and that the tuition described took place in a one-to-one situation. Building a pyramid is very different from, say, learning fractions: while practical embodiments of fractions may be found, the teaching goal is a change in understanding of an abstract concept rather than the development of a practical skill. These points are taken up further below.

Following the work of Wood *et al*, early research into scaffolding looked at areas of informal, out-of-school learning, focusing on problems which, through their concrete and repetitive nature, are not dissimilar to the pyramid task, for example, weaving a piece of cloth, making a basket, or putting away shopping (Rogoff and Gardner, 1984). The general idea behind the studies was to observe the manner in which the adult introduced the child to information regarding cultural tools and practices and how the adult gradually transferred responsibility to the child for management of joint problem-solving activities. In such circumstances, although teaching strategies were employed, they appeared to be not necessarily deliberate or consciously considered by the adult. Teaching was intuitive.

Greenfield (1984) contrasts such successful out-of-school learning, which seems to use the scaffolding principle frequently, with school learning where, she argues, trial and error seem to be more prevalent. She questions whether or not school learning could be more successful

> by greater use of the principle of scaffolding, thus putting more emphasis on cooperative success in the early stages of learning and less emphasis on independent discovery through a process of trial and error.
>
> (1984: 137)

The suggestion that scaffolding does not occur in school implies that teachers act differently in classroom from the way they do in their everyday lives. If adults in informal learning appear to use scaffolding strategies spontaneously, it is not likely that teachers, as adults and often with children of their own, also employ intuitive scaffolding strategies in classrooms? Edwards and Mercer (1987) in their study of primary classrooms state:

> All the teachers in our sample appear to operate with something like the scaffolding and handover principle as an implicit part of their teaching method, though none of them talked of it in the interview.
>
> (1987: 88)

Our expectation was that in many classrooms we would observe forms of subtle, intuitive scaffolding taking place. We set out to try to understand further the deployment of scaffolding strategies in primary classrooms, beginning by identifying and categorizing the scaffolding strategies that we expected teachers would already be using. In the event, despite detailed observation and analysis of some 105 lessons, there was little evidence to support the hypothesis of teachers being intuitive scaffolders. In our opinion, this was not the fault of the teachers – they had been selected on the basis of being regarded as good practitioners – and the lessons observed were typical of what might be expected in any sound primary school. Rather, the experience has raised issues and questions about the nature of scaffolding and its usefulness, in particular:

- To what extent does the model of scaffolding in everyday settings transfer to school settings?
- To what extent does the model of scaffolding of everyday knowledge transfer to school knowledge?

EVERYDAY SETTINGS AND SCHOOL SETTINGS

One of the most obvious differences between the out-of-school contexts studied and classrooms is the adult–child ratio. Most primary teachers have to deal with approximately thirty pupils, whereas the situations described in the literature involve one novice with one expert. The high child–adult ratio of classrooms raises the question of the extent to which teachers can establish what the pupils can do on their own; their level of 'independent problem solving'. In our experience, Jenny's story is unusual in the manner in which she reveals an aspect of independent problem solving. The problem of reading 1010 was not only solved by Jenny but also posed by her.

Given the constraints and dynamics of class teaching, pupils' levels of independent problem solving usually have to be judged, if at all, on the basis of problems posed by the teacher. There are at least two difficulties that this presents. First, it is well established that pupils' performance in problem solving is affected by the presentation and context of the problems (Foxman *et al.*, 1991; Murphy, 1991). Second, our research confirms what others have found before (Bennett *et al.*, 1984; Francis, 1988), namely that teachers' judgements of pupils' level of attainment are made on the basis of limited information. If scaffolding builds on what pupils can do on their own, then the extent to which a measure of independent problem solving can be achieved in classrooms needs careful consideration.

It is interesting to note that one application of the use of scaffolding in the school context where the construct does seem to be helpful is in the area of reading recovery (Clay and Cazden, 1990). But reading recovery is notable precisely because of its lack of resemblance to 'normal' school activities; an intensive period of one-to-one instruction.

A further difficulty in the application of scaffolding to school contexts lies in adult–child relationships. The out-of-school contexts studied emphasize the joint accomplishment of tasks, the learner being given responsibility for what he or she can do, the adult completing the rest. As the child's skill and learning progresses, so the adult relinquishes appropriately the scaffolding. In other words, the roles of the adult and the learners change, with their roles becoming very similar – the learners becoming equals with the teacher and being able to do autonomously what they could previously only achieve with collaborative help.

However, the constant accretion of skills and understanding that characterizes school learning dramatically alters the dynamics between teacher and learner. They can never be true partners in an activity, and as soon as one part of the curriculum is learnt, another follows. Thus the nature of scaffolding is possibly different from that of the informal learning context. Teachers may well withdraw the scaffolding in one context but might need to reinstate it when pupils are tackling a similar problem in a different context; or there could be partial withdrawal at one level with the introduction of scaffolding at a new more advanced level. What this might look like in practice is far from clear.

EVERYDAY KNOWLEDGE AND SCHOOL KNOWLEDGE

The type of problem-solving carried out in some out-of-school situations is very different from that in school. Out-of-school problem-solving, as examined in the scaffolding literature, is more likely to have a heavy element of procedural learning to it: the making of some artifact or the accomplishment of a practical activity. There are at least two advantages to this. First, such experiences provide feedback for both the adult and learner. The adult can actually see the extent to which the learner is succeeding, and the learner, from the outset, has an understanding of what the task entails. Secondly, this everyday, routine characterization means that skills can be practised and repeated until mastered.

It is interesting to note that those instances where authors have suggested that scaffolding, or something like it, is employed in classrooms have a large element of the procedural: for example, making a clay pot or setting up a pendulum (Edwards and Mercer, 1987), learning the algorithm for long multiplication (Newman *et al.*, 1989). But school learning also lays emphasis on the conceptual. In mathematics and science the role of problem solving is not only to be able to solve similar problems but to manage contextually different ones. Helping children come to an understanding of fractions is very different from weaving a basket. The extent to which scaffolding is domain-specific in its applicability to school knowledge is open to further investigation.

We return to Bruner's point of the importance of the teacher modelling a task to engage the learner's interest. This may be easily accomplished when the task is a practical one, but in the school situation the role of the tasks may be somewhat different. The task may not be easily modelled, it may not have a practical outcome to provide a 'hook', the task may be a means to an end, rather than an end in itself. The end results of practical activities can be demonstrated to pupils so that they can gain a sense of what they need to accomplish. But how do pupils gain a sense of what, say, conservation of energy is about before they have learnt about it?

Scaffolding does draw attention to the importance of teachers' subject knowledge. In Jenny's case the adult was the one with access to and understanding of the socially accepted knowledge, the conventions of reading and writing mathematics. Jenny's deduction that 1010 could be read as ten hundred and ten is perfectly reasonable, and there is nothing intrinsic in our number system which means that should not be the accepted convention (as indeed it is with dates). Jenny could not discover nor invent for herself the alternative reading of one thousand and ten, someone more knowledgeable had to introduce her to it. If teachers are to scaffold successfully they must be secure in their own knowledge of the subject.

DESCRIPTION OR ORIENTATION?

While scaffolding may be useful as a descriptive, *post-hoc*, metaphor for producing accounts of some teaching/learning situations, we must be careful not to over-extend it to the point where it becomes meaningless. From the perspective of an observer, looking at lessons for evidence of scaffolding is not unproblematic. As Mason, (1991) points out, one person's scaffold is another's cued elicitation. From the perspective of the practitioner, how useful is the metaphor for teachers themselves in helping them understand the dynamics of the classroom? Jenny's story was presented as an example of successful scaffolding. But another child, Jon, working on the same task, was not prepared to go any further than putting the cards in order. Whatever the reason, he was not prepared to enter into a joint activity in the same way that Jenny was, despite an attempt to interact with him in a similar fashion. If scaffolding is a 'hit-or-miss' affair, and interactions can only be labelled as involving scaffolding after the event, then what is gained in our understanding of the nature of teaching?

If scaffolding is problematic as a descriptive metaphor, then its value as a prescriptive metaphor guiding practice must be even more dubious. Without an awareness of the work of Vygotsky that ultimately lies behind the metaphor, it is potentially open to misinterpretation. Scaffolding on the building site is an unresponsive activity, the scaffolding erected and the building put up according to a predetermined plan. Scaffolding in the classroom must be much more dynamic, and ways must be found for teacher and pupils to work jointly on activities. Beyond acknowledging the role of the teacher our research has made us question whether, at best, scaffolding is difficult to implement, and at worst, impossible because of the interacting demands/influences of:

- the social context and dynamics of classrooms
- teachers' subject knowledge
- the nature of school knowledge

Perhaps the best way to regard scaffolding is as some form of general orientating metaphor, alerting the teacher to watch out for the extent to which pupils can succeed at tasks on their own, suppressing the desire to step in and help too soon yet being prepared to work alongside the pupil when a genuine need arises. Teaching after all is an art, not a science and it certainly is not a construction industry.

NOTE

1 Development of a taxonomy of primary teachers' scaffolding strategies in three contexts', Economic and Social Research Council, Award R000 23 3265.

REFERENCES

Bennett, N., Desforges, C., Cockburn, A. and Wilkinson, B. (1984) *The Quality of Pupil Learning Experiences*, London: Lawrence Erlbaum.

Bruner, J. (1985) 'Vygotsky: a historical and conceptual perspective', in J. V. Wertsch (ed.), *Culture, Communication and Cognition: Vygotskian Perspectives*, Cambridge: Cambridge University Press: 21–34.

Clay, M. M. and Cazden, C. B. (1990) 'A Vygotskian interpretation of Reading Recovery', in L. C. Moll (ed.), *Vygotsky and Education: Instructional Implications and Applications of Sociohistorical Psychology*, Cambridge: Cambridge University Press: 206–22.

Cole, M. (1985) 'The zone of proximal development: where culture and cognition create each other', in J. V. Wertsch (ed.), *Culture, Communication and Cognition: Vygotskian Perspectives*, Cambridge: Cambridge University Press: 146–61.

Edwards, D. and Mercer, N. (1987) *Common Knowledge: The Development of Understanding in the Classroom*, London: Methuen.

Foxman, D., Ruddock, G., McCallum, I. and Schagen, I. (1991) *APU Mathematics Monitoring (Phase 2)*, London: School Examination and Assessment Council.

Francis, H. (1988) 'Individual approaches to learning', *Educational and Child Psychology*, 5(3): 39–48.

Greenfield, P. M. (1984) 'A theory of the teaching in the learning activities of everyday life', in B. Rogoff and J. Lave (eds), *Everyday Cognition*, Cambridge, MA: Harvard Universith Press: 117–38.

Mason, J. (1991) 'Speaking *to* teaching and speaking *about* teaching: the role of metaphor and metonymy', in H. G. Steiner (ed.), *Proceedings of Theory of Mathematics Education*, University of Leiden, Bielefeld: 340–7.

Maybin, J., Mercer, N. and Stierer, B. (1992), '"Scaffolding" learning in the classroom', in K. Norman (ed.), *Thinking Voices: The Work of the National Oracy Project*, London: Hodder & Stoughton: 186–95.

Murphy, P. F. (1991) 'Assessment and gender', *Cambridge Journal of Education*, 21(2): 203–14.

Newman, D., Griffin, P. and Cole, M. (1989) *The Construction Zone: Working for Cognitive Change in School*, Cambridge: Cambridge University Press.

Rogoff, B. and Gardner, W. (1984) 'Adult guidance of cognitive development', in B. Rogoff and J. Lave (eds), *Everyday Cognition*, Cambridge, MA: Harvard University Press: 95–117.

Tharp, R. and Gallimore, R. (1988) *Rousing Minds to Life: Teaching, Learning and Schooling in Social Context*, Cambridge: Cambridge University Press.

Vygotsky, L. S. (1978) *Mind in Society*, Cambridge, MA: Harvard University Press.

Wood, D. J., Bruner, J. S. and Ross, G. (1976) 'The role of tutoring in problem solving', *Journal of Child Psychology and Psychiatry*, 17: 89–100.

Chapter 19

A proposed framework for examining basic number sense

Alistair McIntosh, Barbara J. Reys and Robert E. Reys

A boy in a classroom was being observed by a visitor. After writing the problem 37 + 25 in vertical form, and drawing a horizontal line, he recorded the answer of 62. 'Fine,' said the visitor, 'tell me how you did that'.

'All right' answered the boy hesitantly, 'but don't tell my teacher. I said 37 and 20 is 57 and 5 makes 62'.

'That's a very good way,' commented the visitor. 'Why can't I tell your teacher?'

'Because I wouldn't get a mark then. I can't understand the way she tells us to do it on paper, so I do it this way in my head and then write down the answer and I get a mark'.

A clerk was serving in a newsagent's shop in England. A customer wanted to purchase two identical diaries, each originally costing 2.50 pounds, but now, in February, marked 'half marked price'. The customer picked up the two diaries and took them to the counter. 'How much please?' asked the customer.

The clerk picked up the first diary and a pencil, wrote the original price, divided by two using the standard written algorithm for long division, and obtained the new price 1.25 pounds. She then picked up the second identical diary, wrote the original price, used the standard written algorithm again, and obtained the new price 1.25 pounds. She then wrote 1.25, underneath it wrote 1.25, added them correctly using the standard written algorithm, turned to the customer and, without a shadow of a smile, said 'That will be two pounds fifty, please'.

The boy could not follow the formal written algorithm but understood enough about numbers to invent his own efficient mental method. The clerk showed impeccable performance in the formal written algorithm and yet revealed an alarming lack of awareness of fundamental arithmetic relationships.

One might say that the boy, but not the clerk, exhibited number sense.

A LITTLE HISTORY

The word 'numeracy' was coined in 1959 (Crowther, 1959) to describe quite a high degree of ability to cope with current mathematical demands on the community. However, its meaning, because of its association with 'literacy', became debased to mean only an ability to cope with the basic mathematical demands of everyday life. As these demands were not closely reexamined, it again, to most, implied the same range of skills as did arithmetic. In *Innumeracy: mathematical illiteracy and its consequences*, Paulos (1988) highlights the reality and dangers of a growing population of people who view mathematics as a mystifying subject beyond their ability to grasp. It is somewhat ironic that many people still view mathematics as facts, rules and formulas in a time when mathematics as a sense-making process is more highly valued for a numerate society.

Indeed, a review of present computational needs of adults reveals that relatively little use is made of formal written computation. Calculators are not only inexpensive, but also a universally available and highly reliable means of calculation. In addition, there is general acceptance of both mental computation and estimation as efficient processes for calculating. These facts have led to a need to examine the role and nature of computation in elementary school mathematics and to consider the increased roles both of choosing a computation strategy and of reflecting on both the process and the result of employing the strategy.

Over the past few years the phrase which has gained wide acceptance as embracing the essence of these changes is 'number sense'. The origin of this phrase is not clear, although it is clear that it springs largely from a desire to replace the word 'numeracy' by one which does not have its abstract ring or its association with a conservative and sterile view of mathematical needs. The Cockcroft Report (Cockcroft, 1982) used the phrase 'at-homeness with numbers' to describe one aspect of the desirable attributes of a numerate adult. The *Curriculum and evaluation standards for school mathematics* (NCTM, 1989) in the United States and the *National statement on mathematics for Australian schools* (AEC, 1991) both describe the development of 'number sense' as a major essential outcome of school mathematics.

The phrase is an excellent one – simple and appealing – but its meaning is as open to different interpretations as was numeracy. In this discussion 'number sense' will be used to refer to the basic number sense which is required by all adults regardless of their occupation and whose acquisition by all students should be a major goal of compulsory education. This paper attempts to clarify the term by first presenting a brief description of number sense and by then elaborating on this description by presenting a framework for thinking about number sense.

WHAT IS NUMBER SENSE?

Number sense refers to a person's general understanding of number and operations along with the ability and inclination to use this understanding in flexible ways to make mathematical judgements and to develop useful strategies for handling numbers and operations. It reflects an inclination and an ability to use numbers and quantitative methods as a means of communicating, processing and interpreting information. It results in an expectation that numbers are useful and that mathematics has a certain regularity.

Number sense exhibits itself in various ways as the learner engages in mathematical thinking. In particular, it is an important underlying theme as the learner chooses, develops and uses computational methods, including written computation, mental computation, calculators and estimation. Number sense plays a role in the use of each of these methods to varying degrees. The invention and application of an invented algorithm calls upon facets of number sense such as decomposition/recomposition and understanding of number properties. As learned paper/pencil algorithms and calculator algorithms are used, number sense is important as answers are reflected upon.

The acquisition of number sense is a gradual, evolutionary process, beginning long before formal schooling begins. The young boy in the opening paragraph serves as a reminder that number sense is often evident at an early age as children think about numbers and try to make sense of them. Although evidence of number sense can be demonstrated early, growing older does not necessarily ensure either the development or utilization of even the most primitive notions of number sense, as demonstrated by the actions of the clerk described earlier. Indeed, although many young children exhibit creative and sometimes efficient strategies for operating with numbers, attention to formal algorithms may, in fact, deter use of informal methods. Ironically, as students' technical knowledge of mathematics is expanding, their range of strategies may be narrowing. The learned methods (traditional paper/pencil algorithms) become the methods most cherished for some students as they can be executed without having to think. For example, the reaction of a student when asked if a calculation seems reasonable is often to recalculate (generally using the same method as for the initial calculation) rather than to reflect on the result in light of the context and numbers involved. . . .

There is evidence that the context in which mathematical problems are encountered influences thinking. Silver (in press) documents this position and argues persuasively for the need to provide students with rich situated activities which not only promote problem solving but stimulate different components of number sense as well. Clearly, number sense is, at times, triggered by the context in which the mathematics evolves. For example, while a student may be comfortable in school with a sum of 514 produced by applying a learned algorithm to the computation of 26 + 38, the same student in a store may demand a reexamination if asked to pay $5.14 for two items priced at 26c and 38c.

Number sense is highly personalized and is related to what ideas about number have been established and also on how those ideas were established. Students highly skilled at paper/pencil computations (often the gauge by which success in mathematics is measured) may or may not be developing number sense. For example, when a sixth grader reports that 2/5 + 3/7 = 5/12 or a second grader says that 40 − 36 = 16, these students are attempting to apply a learned algorithm but are not reflecting number sense. In fact, much of the recent attention to developing number sense is a reaction to over-emphasis on computational procedures which are algorithmic and devoid of the number sense being characterized here.

The level of number sense necessary for children and adults today may be greater than in the past. For example, today both students and adults encounter a greater range of numbers (e.g. government budgets in the trillions of dollars, athletic events timed to the thousandth of a second), in more varied contexts (e.g. graphs, surveys), utilizing new tools (e.g. computers and calculators) than was the case a generation ago. Indeed, in a technological age it might be said that the possession of number sense is one major attribute which distinguishes human beings from computers. There is every reason to believe that the 21st century will introduce additional reasons for an increased focus on developing and maintaining number sense.

A FRAMEWORK FOR BASIC NUMBER SENSE

. . . The framework suggested in Figure 19.1 is an attempt to articulate a structure which clarifies, organizes, and interrelates some of the generally agreed upon components of basic number sense, many of which have been conjectured by different people over many years. . . . It is likely that the whole of number sense is greater than its parts. Nevertheless, the proposed framework is an attempt to identify key components and to organize these key components according to common themes. A careful review of the framework together with systematic research efforts on number sense will likely reveal additions and deletions, or a reorganization of the proposed framework. Such reviews are welcome and necessary to establish dialogue for further refinement and development of a framework.

Figure 19.1 differentiates three areas where number sense plays a key role, namely number concepts, operations with number, and applications of number and operation. Figure 19.2 illustrates interconnections among the major components. These interconnections suggest a monitoring process which links number sense with metacognition. A person with good

Defintion of Number Sense: A propensity for and an ability to use numbers and quantitative methods as a means of communicating, processing and interpretating information. It results in an expectation that numbers are useful and that mathematics has a certain regularity (makes sense).

1. Knowledge of and facility with NUMBERS	1.1 Sense of orderliness of numbers	1.1.1 Place value
		1.1.2 Relationship between number types
		1.13 Ordering numbers within and among number types
	1.2 Multiple representations for numbers	1.2.1 Graphical/symbolic
		1.2.2 Equivalent numerical forms (including decomposition/recomposition)
		1.2.3 Comparison to benchmarks
	1.3 Sense of relative and absolute magnitude of numbers	1.3.1 Comparing to physical referent
		1.3.2 Comparing to mathematical referent
	1.4 System of benchmarks	1.4.1 Mathematical
		1.4.2 Personal
2. Knowledge of facility with OPERATIONS	2.1 Understanding the effect of operations	2.1.1 Operating on whole numbers
		2.1.2 Operating on fractions/decimals
	2.2 Understanding mathematical properties	2.2.1 Commutativity
		2.2.2 Associativity
		2.2.3 Distributivity
		2.2.4 Identities
		2.2.5 Inverses
	2.3 Understanding the relationship between operations	2.3.1 Addition/Multiplication
		2.3.2 Subtraction/Division
		2.3.3 Addition/Subtraction
		2.3.4 Multiplication/Division
3. Applying knowledge of and facility with numbers and operations to COMPUTATIONAL SETTINGS	3.1 Understanding the relationship between problem context and the necessary computation	3.1.1 Recognize data as exact or approximate
		3.1.2 Awareness that solutions may be exact or approximate
	3.2 Awareness that multiple strategies exist	3.2.1 Ability to create and/or invent strategies
		3.2.2 Ability to apply different strategies
		3.2.3 Ability to select an efficient strategy
	3.3 Inclination to utilize an efficient representation and/or method	3.3.1 Facility with various methods (mental, calculator, paper/pencil)
		3.3.2 Facility choosing efficient number(s)
	3.4 Inclination to review data and result for sensibility	3.4.1 Recognize reasonableness of data
		3.4.2 Recognize reasonableness of calculation

Figure 19.1 Framework for considering number sense

number sense is thinking about and reflecting on the numbers, operations and results being produced. This reflective thinking will at one time or another involve any of the framework components shown in Figure 19.1.

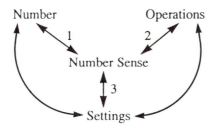

Figure 19.2 Interconnections of major components of number sense

In order to clarify the components in Figure 19.1, each of them will be briefly discussed. Specific questions or examples that might provide insight into each particular component of number sense will also be illustrated. The numbers in brackets refer to those in Figure 19.1.

Knowledge of and facility with numbers (1)

For many years educators have argued that meaningful understanding of the Hindu-Arabic number system, including an appreciation of its structure and regularity, is fundamental (Brownell, 1935; Hiebert, 1984). Various methods have been advocated to help children develop conceptual under-standing of number, including the use of manipulatives and/or models, the use of number lines, a study of various number bases, and units of instruction targeted at 'place value'. While these methods are undoubtedly important, the number sense framework proposed here is organized not by instructional 'topics', but by a collection of 'understandings' a learner is likely to exhibit/utilize. For the area of number, these include: a sense of orderliness of number; multiple representations for numbers; a sense of relative and absolute magnitude of numbers; and a system of benchmarks.

Sense of orderliness of number (1.1)

Number sense implies an understanding of how the Hindu-Arabic number system is organized and how this organization aids in reviewing and con-sidering numbers. The system of place value, including its application to whole and decimal numbers, is an important component of this area. Understanding rational numbers, including how they are represented, is also included in this component. An understanding of the number system helps the learner mentally organize, compare, and order numbers encountered in a mathematical environment. For example, a young child learning to count beyond 20 comes to appreciate the patterns identified both orally and in written form inherent in the number system. Once identified, these patterns provide a powerful source of support for extending the counting sequence. In the same way, a fifth grader explores decimal numbers by counting (with the aid of a calculator) from zero to 10 by tenths (or from zero to one by hundredths). As with the young student, the counting sequence (in particular, the calculator display) provides a powerful tool for helping the student recognize, identify and repeat patterns that emerge. Another example makes use of a number line to help a sixth-grade student understand relationships between decimal numbers:

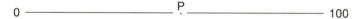

Ask the student to name the number marked at point P. Now change the endpoint of the number line from 100 to 10 and ask the same question. Next change the endpoint from 10 to 1 and finally from 1 to 0.1, after each change asking for the number represented by P. As number sense develops, students detect patterns and regularities between P and the various endpoints. As understanding of the orderliness and regularity of the number system develops, students begin to use this knowledge. For example, a middle-grade student exhibiting a sense of orderliness would respond 'yes' to the question, 'Are there any numbers between 2/5 and 3/5?' and be able to give several appropriate examples.

Multiple representations for numbers (1.2)

Numbers appear in different contexts and may be expressed in a variety of symbolic and/or graphical representations. Number sense includes the recognition that numbers take many forms and can be thought about and manipulated in many ways to benefit a particular purpose. For example, recognizing that $2 + 2 + 2 + 2$ is the same as 4×2 is a useful conceptual connection between addition and multiplication. Recognizing 30 cents as being a quarter plus a nickel or 3 dimes, or recognizing 30 minutes as 1/2 an hour, would also be useful in certain situations. At a later grade, number sense would be reflected by recognizing different symbolizations, such as $3/4 = 6/8$ or $3/4 = 0.75$ or $3/4 = 75\%$. The knowledge that numbers can be represented in many different ways, together with the recognition that some representations are more useful than others in certain problem-solving situations is both valuable and essential for developing mathematical power.

Decomposition/recomposition involves expressing a number in an equivalent form as a result of recognizing how this new equivalent form facilitates operating on the recomposed numbers. Suppose, for example, a person is checking out of a market and has a bill for $8.53. The person could pay with a $10 bill and get $1.47 change. Another person might pay the check with a $10 bill and three pennies. The change would be $1.50. In each case, the total amount paid is the same. However, in the latter example the person wanted to avoid carrying extra coins and recomposed the amount of payment to $10.03 to keep the change received more manageable. Decomposing $8.53 into $8.50 + $0.03 provided the rationale which led the buyer to pay with what appears to be an odd amount, yet results in dealing with fewer coins. For a younger student, decomposition/recomposition often manifests itself as the learner 'invents' ways to solve arithmetic problems. For example, a first grader might recognize that one could add 25 and 27 by decomposing 27 (thinking about it as 25 +2), then recomposing the new problem, 25 + 25 + 2, adding the 25s to make 50 then adding 2 to produce the sum of 52. This student manifests some important intuitive understanding about number and addition in both the invented procedure and in the ability to carry out the procedure.

Another component of number sense in this area, 'comparing to benchmarks', refers to the use of common 'anchors' in our number system which are often helpful in making judgements. For example, when considering the fraction 5/8, one could think about it graphically (as part of a circle or on a number line) or in an equivalent fraction or decimal form. An equally important representation is the sense that 5/8 is 'a bit more than 1/2' or 'between 1/2 and 3/4'. Here, one-half serves as an anchor (or benchmark) to represent and/or compare other numbers.

Sense of relative and absolute magnitude of numbers (1.3)

The ability to recognize the relative value of a number or quantity in relation to another number and the ability to sense the general size (or magnitude) of a given number or amount is a behaviour that develops with mathematical maturation and experience. For example, what notion does a third grader have about the size of 1,000? Asking students questions, such as, 'How long does it take to count to 1,000?' or 'Have you lived more or less than 1,000 days?' provides them an opportunity to think about 1,000 in a personal context, thus helping them better understand the size of 1,000 in a variety of contexts.

System of benchmarks (1.4)

Just as a compass provides a valuable tool for navigation, numerical benchmarks provide essential mental referents for thinking about numbers. Numerical benchmarks are generally powers of 20, multiples of powers of 10, or midpoints such as 1/2 or 50%, although any value for which the learner has a confident understanding can serve in this capacity. Benchmarks are often used to judge the size of an answer or to round a number so that it is easier to mentally process. Examples include recognizing that the sum of two 2-digit numbers is less than 200, that 0.98 is close to 1, or that 4/9 is slightly less than one-half. In each case, benchmarks are numerical values devoid of context, which have evolved from experience and/or instruction.

Benchmarks may also evolve from personal attributes or encounters. For example, a person weighing 50 kg may use this information in estimating the weight of another person. Similarly, a child who attends a baseball game where the attendance is 50,000 may at a later time use this as a referent for judging the size of other crowds. The variety and complexity of the benchmarks in making decisions about numbers and numerical contexts is a valuable indication of number sense.

Knowledge of and facility with operations (2)

Much of present-day school mathematics is dedicated to helping students understand operations, including how they are performed. For example, in elementary school a conceptual foundation for the operations of addition, subtraction, multiplication and division is provided, together with the development of specific skills necessary to perform each operation by a paper/pencil procedure. Over the course of schooling, the operands change from whole numbers to fractions, decimals and integers in elementary school to polynomials and matrices in secondary school. Although some old models are utilized (e.g. 'joining together' for addition) some new models are also introduced (e.g. a number line is utilized to facilitate the development of subtraction of integers). . . .

Key components of an ability to understand and use operations are: an understanding of the effect of operations, an awareness of mathematical properties of operations, and an awareness of the relationship between operations. In the near future it is likely that the emphasis traditionally placed on paper/pencil computation will be dramatically, if not completely, eliminated as calculators emerge as the common computational tool. However, the emphasis given to each of the components of number sense described in this section should not diminish. In fact, it is likely that more attention will (and should) be given to these understandings as they are at least as important to a calculator user as to a paper/pencil computer.

Understanding the effect of operations (2.1)

Fully conceptualizing an operation implies understanding the effect of the operation on various numbers including whole and rational numbers. Models are often used to help students understand the action of the operation. For example, modelling multiplication as repeated addition provides a concrete way of helping children think about multiplication as well as to carry it out. It is important that various models for multiplication be explored so that students see both the power of a model as well as its limits. For example, thinking of multiplication as repeated addition may lead to incorrect generalizations (e.g. 'multiplication always makes things bigger'). A variety of models such as a number line or an array model are helpful as children see multiplication in a variety of contexts and models.

Investigating the change in answer as the size of operands varies in an operation contributes to number sense. For example, what happens when two numbers less than 1 are multiplied? How can this situation be modelled? What does the general model imply? What happens if one of the factors is less than 1 and the other is greater than 1? Reflecting on the interactions between the operations and numbers stimulates high-level thinking and further enhances number sense.

Understanding mathematical properties (2.2)

Mathematical properties, including commutativity, associativity and distributivity, have long been included in school mathematics programmes. Unfortunately they are often thought of as formal rules, and often viewed as a statement of the obvious. For example, the statement $3 \times 4 = 4 \times 3$ is often perceived as trivial and of little practical importance. In fact, many young students memorize 5×2 and 2×5 as two unrelated facts, failing to take advantage of commutativity in learning the multiplication fact. Much later, when multiplying matrices in secondary school, students learn that if A and B are matrices, $A \times B$ is not necessarily equal to $B \times A$, and their concept of a commutative operation takes on greater significance.

Number sense often manifests itself as students, both young and old, intuitively apply arithmetic properties in inventing procedures for computing. For example, when multiplying 36×4 mentally, a student might think of 4×35 and 4×1, or $140 + 4$ or 144. This solution applied commutativity, as it changed the order of the factors to 4×36, and it also used the distributive property in recomposing 4×36 as $(4 \times 35) + (4 \times 1)$. This student might also recognize and use other equivalent forms such as $(4 \times 40) - (4 \times 4)$ or $(30 \times 4) + (6 \times 4)$, and these multiple solutions would be further evidence of number sense. The main intent here is to illustrate the value of linking practical applications to the development and understanding of fundamental mathematical properties. Students with good number sense have typically made these connections and are comfortable in applying the properties in a variety of different situations.

Understanding the relationship between operations (2.3)

Connections between operations provide more ways to think about and solve problems. For example, as a student considers this question: 'How many wheels are on 8 tricycles?' they may think about and apply a counting procedure (count by ones each wheel), they may apply repeated addition (adding the number of wheels on each tricycle: 3 + 3 + 3 + 3 + 3 + 3 + 3 + 3), they may add by grouping (make 4 groups of 2 tricycles each: 6 + 6 + 6 + 6) or apply multiplication (8×3 or 4×6). Each of these solutions reflects a slightly different way of thinking about the problem as well as differing degrees of attention to efficiency.

The inverse relationship between operations is another valuable connection in that it provides the learner yet another way of thinking about a problem. For example, when asked to decide the quotient of $480 \div 8$, a person might view this as $8 \times ? = 480$ rather than as a division problem. This does not mean the person is unable to perform the division, but rather that the person knows the inverse relationship exists between division and multiplication and is comfortable in using the relationship to conceptualize and solve the problem. . . .

Applying knowledge of and facility with numbers and operations to computational settings (3)

Solving real-world problems which require reasoning with numbers and/or applying operations to numbers involves making a variety of decisions including: deciding what type of answer is appropriate (exact or approximate), deciding what computational tool is efficient and/or accessible (calculator, mental computation, etc.), choosing a strategy, applying the strategy, reviewing the data and result for reasonableness, and perhaps repeating the cycle utilizing an alternative strategy. This process involves several different types of decisions. First, it involves understanding the relationship between the problem context and the necessary computation. Second it requires an awareness of a range of possible strategies for performing computation and an inclination to choose an efficient strategy. Finally, it includes an instinct to reflectively review the answer, and to check it both for indications of correctness and for its relevance to the original problem context.

Understanding the relationship between problem context and the necessary computation (3.1)

The problem context provides clues not only for appropriate operation(s), but also for the numbers to be used in these operations and whether an exact or an approximate solution is appropriate. Consider for example, the following information:

Skip spent $2.88 for apples, $2.38 for bananas and $3.76 for oranges.

Many different questions could be raised regarding this situation, and how these numbers are treated depends on the question asked. For example, if the question is 'How much did Skip spend for this fruit?' the prices need to be totalled to produce an exact answer, and any one of several different computational methods (mental computation, written computation or calculator) could be applied. On the other hand, suppose the question is, 'Could Skip pay for this fruit with $10?' In this case, estimation can be used to decide rather quickly and confidently that $10 is enough to make the purchase.

Awareness that multiple strategies exist (3.2)

Number sense involves recognizing that different solution strategies often exist for a given problem. When an initial strategy appears to be unproductive, formulating and applying an alternative strategy is an appropriate response. This tendency to pursue a problem by exploring it in different ways often allows comparisons of different methods before making a final judgement or pursuing yet another vantage point. This metacognitive reflection is sometimes difficult to identify because it often occurs quickly and sometimes without conscious thought. Here, the emphasis is on the general awareness that different strategies exist rather than the metacognitive process of choosing, executing, and reviewing the various outcomes.

Inclination to utilize an efficient representation and/or method (3.3)

Awareness that some strategies and/or computational tools are more efficient at times than others is also an indicator of number sense. For example, a competent second grader asked to add 8 + 7 would likely dismiss the strategy of counting on by ones, choosing rather to mentally recompose the problem (as 7 + 7 + 1, based on knowledge that two sevens equals 14, or as 8 + 2 + 5, using the knowledge that 8 + 2 = 10).

A corollary of this element is that the child or adult with little number sense often uses a more difficult method of calculation. The reasons for this vary, but often result from habits established from long practice of a particular method of calculation, a lack of confidence in alternative methods of calculation, and/or lack of knowledge of such alternatives.

Inclination to review data and result (3.4)

When a solution is produced, people with number sense examine their answer in the light of the original problem (considering the numbers included as well as the questions asked) to determine if their answer 'makes sense'. This reflection is generally done quickly, naturally, and becomes an integral part of the problem-solving process. This metacognitive review of the problem context might involve a reflection of the strategies that might have been used as well as an evaluation of the particular strategy selected, and finally a check to determine if the answer produced was sensible.

Students often omit this checking precisely because the result (indeed the problem itself) is not important to them. A striking example of this is given by an unmotivated group of secondary students. To stimulate interest their teacher asked what they would like to do. They replied that they would like to build a boat. 'Fine', said the teacher. 'Go away and calculate how much wood you need to build a boat'. The group reappeared shortly with a list of dimensions. 'Right', said the teacher, 'I'll go and get the wood'. It was only then that the students realized the teacher was serious. This was not just an artificial exercise: they were actually going to build a boat. They immediately asked for the list of dimensions; it was two whole days before they returned with thoroughly tested and checked calculations.

WHERE TO FROM HERE?

Number sense is a topic of great interest in school mathematics. It is also nebulous and difficult to describe, although it is recognizable in action. Continued productive discussion of number sense (by researchers, teachers and curriculum developers) must at some stage be based on a definition, characterization, or model which portrays number sense in a clear yet comprehensive manner. The more clearly number sense is understood, the more likely there will be progress made in research, as well as in curriculum development and instruction.

In this chapter, we have presented a model for characterizing basic number sense. We are aware of some imperfections (for example, is the third component of our framework the same as problem solving? If so, are number sense and problem solving different?) and some areas of overlap (in particular, 'benchmarks' appear in both the first and second components of the framework). We do not hold any illusions that this framework will or should be accepted as a definitive model. We do, however, feel that it provides a useful starting point and welcome continued dialogue.

ACKNOWLEDGEMENTS

The authors thank Edith Cowan University and the University of Missouri for internal support of work which led to the development of this chapter. In addition, the National Science Foundation provided support under Grant INT 9000203 for progress on this work. The opinions and framework proposed are those of the authors and should not be attributed to the National Science Foundation. We also thank Rita Barger, Hickman Mills High School, Terry Crites, Northern Arizona University, Linda Lembke, Central Methodist College, Richard Shumway, The

Ohio State University, Judith Sowder, San Diego State University and Ruthi Sturdevant, Lincoln University for reviewing, and offering comments and suggestions to earlier drafts of this chapter.

REFERENCES

Australian Education Council (1991) *A National Statement on Mathematics for Australian Schools*, Carlton, Vic: Curriculum Corporation.

Brownell, W. (1935) 'Psychological considerations in the learning and teaching of arithmetic', in *The Teaching of Arithmetic*, Reston, VA: NCTM.

Cockroft, W.H. (1982) *Mathematics Counts*, London: HMSO.

Crowther (1959) *A Report of the Central Advisory Council for Education*, Department of Education and Science, London: HMSO.

Hiebert, J.(1984) 'Children's mathematical learning: The struggle to link form and understanding', *Elementary School Journal*, 84: 497–513.

National Council of Teachers of Mathematics (1989) *Curriculum and Evaluation Standards for School Mathematics*, Reston, VA: NCTM.

Paulos, J.A. (1988) *Innumeracy: Mathematical Illiteracy and its Consequences*, New York: Hill & Wang.

Silver, E.A. (in press) 'Teaching estimation and mental computation as situated mathematical processes', in R. Reys and N. Mohda (eds), *Computational Alternatives for the 21st Century: Cross Cultural Perspectives from Japan and the United States*, Reston, VA: NCTM.

Chapter 20

Learning through problem-solving: a constructivist approach to second grade mathematics

Paul Cobb, Terry Wood, and Erna Yackel

. . . Constructivism as an epistemology is, for us, a general way of interpreting and making sense of a variety of phenomena. It constitutes a framework within which to address situations of complexity, uniqueness, and uncertainty that Schon (1985) calls 'messes', and to transform them into potentially solvable problems. Thus, like any epistemology, constructivism influences both the questions posed and the criteria for what counts as an adequate solution. Its value to mathematics education will, in the long run, depend on whether this way of sense making, of problem posing and solving, contributes to the improvement of mathematics teaching and learning in typical classrooms with characteristic teachers. If it eventually fails to do so, then it will become irrelevant to mathematics educators.

OVERVIEW OF THE PROJECT

Rationale for instructional activities

. . . It should be clear that, for the constructivist, substantive mathematical learning is a problem-solving process (Cobb, 1986; Confrey, 1987; Thompson, 1985; von Glasersfeld, 1983). In this context, substantive learning refers to cognitive restructuring as opposed to accretion or tuning (Rumelhart and Norman, 1981). Consequently, our primary focus, as we developed, implemented, and refined instructional activities, was on that aspect of cognitive development that is both the most significant and the most difficult to explain and influence.

At the risk of over-simplification, an immediate implication of constructivism is that mathematics, including the so-called basics such as arithmetical computation, should be taught through problem-solving. This does not mean that the instructional activities necessarily emphasize what are traditionally considered to be problems – stereotypical textbook word problems. In fact, the general notion that problems can be given ready-made to students is highly questionable. Instead, teaching through problem-solving acknowledges that problems arise for students as they attempt to achieve *their* goals in the classroom. The approach respects that students are the best judges of what they find problematic and encourages them to construct solutions that they find acceptable given their current ways of knowing. The situations that children find problematic take a variety of forms and can include resolving obstacles or contradictions that arise when they use their current concepts and procedures, accounting for a surprising outcome (particularly when two alternative procedures lead to the same result), verbalizing their mathematical thinking, explaining or justifying a solution, resolving conflicting points of view, and constructing a consensual domain in which to talk about mathematics with others. As these examples make clear, genuine mathematical problems can arise from classroom social interactions as well as from solo attempts to complete the instructional activities.

In general, the instructional activities, classroom organization, and flow of the lessons were designed to facilitate the occurrence of mathematical problems that the children could attempt to resolve in conducive settings. . . .

Classroom organization

The instructional activities are of two general types: teacher-directed whole class activities and small group activities. To the extent that any lesson can be considered typical (Erickson, 1986), the teacher might first spend at most five minutes introducing the small group activities to the children. Her rationale for doing so is to clarify the intent of the activities. She might, for example, ask the children what they think a particular symbol means or ask them how they interpret the first activity. In doing so, she does not attempt to steer the children towards an official solution method but instead tries to ensure that the children's understanding of what they are to do is compatible with the activity as intended by its developers. Any suggested interpretation or solution, however immature, is acceptable provided it indicates the child has made the appropriate suppositions.

Once the teacher is satisfied that conventions used to present the instructional activities have been established, she tells them to start work. One child hands out an activity sheet to each group of two or, occasionally, three children. As the children work in groups for perhaps 25 minutes, one notices that the teacher spends the entire time moving from one group to the next, observing and frequently interacting with them as they engage in mathematical activity. In this setting she is free of managerial concerns and can focus attention on children's thinking and interactions. Because the children are encouraged to take responsibility for their own learning and behaviour in the classroom, she is rarely interrupted by a child from another group asking for help or for permission to, say, use particular manipulative materials. Further, the teacher does not feel the need to monitor the children's conduct – she is comfortable giving her attention entirely to the group she is currently observing.

The noise level is somewhat higher than most classrooms because the children are talking about the activities with their partners. However, the teacher does not have to remind the children to lower their voices because the noise level always stays within reasonable bounds and she has learned that their talking is generally about mathematics and is not distracting to others. One soon notices the purposeful way that children move around the classroom on their own initiative. Some go to a table to take one of the available manipulatives that they have decided is needed. Others get additional activity sheets or perhaps a piece of scrap paper. It soon becomes apparent that some groups have completed four or five activity sheets while others might complete just one, and then only with the teacher's assistance. This disparity in the number of activities completed seems, for the most part, to be inconsequential to both the teacher and the children. Finally, the teacher tells the children when there is only one minute of work time remaining. Most of the children begin to put away the manipulatives and prepare for the discussion of their solutions.

The teacher starts the discussion by asking the children to explain how they solved the first activity. Typically, there is no shortage of volunteers. When called upon, children spontaneously come to the front of the class to give their explanations, often accompanied by their partner. If a child gives only an answer, the teacher asks for an explanation of the solution process. Sometimes she asks follow-up questions to clarify the explanation or to help the child reconstruct and verbalize a solution. Occasionally, a child will become aware of a problem with his or her solution while explaining it to the class. Because of the accepting classroom atmosphere, the child does not become embarrassed or defensive but might simply say, 'I messed up' and sit down. In the course of the dialogue, other children spontaneously explain why they now disagree with their own solutions or why they thought their partner was wrong but now think he or she is right. It is immediately apparent that the teacher accepts all answers and solutions in a completely nonevaluative way. If, as frequently happens, children propose two or more conflicting answers, she will frame this as a problem for the children and ask them how they think the conflict can be resolved. Children volunteer to justify particular answers and, almost invariably, the class arrives at a consensus. On the rare occasions when they fail to do so, the teacher writes the activity statement on a chalk board so that the children can think about it during the following few days. Although the discussion might continue for 15 to 20 minutes, the time is sufficient to consider only a small proportion of the activities completed by some groups – the children have much to say about their mathematics. Eventually, the teacher terminates the discussion due to time constraints. She collects the children's activity sheets and might glance through them before making them ready for distribution to parents. However, she does not grade their work or in any way indicate whether or not their answers are correct.

In the remaining ten minutes or so of the hour-long lesson, the teacher introduces a whole class activity and poses one or more questions to the children. She is again nonevaluative when the children offer their solutions and, as before, attempts to orchestrate a discussion among the children.

Development process

We . . . developed samples of a wide range of possible instructional activities in the year preceding the experiment, but the specific activities used in the classroom were developed, modified, and, in some cases, abandoned while the experiment was in progress. To aid this process, two video-cameras were used to record each mathematics lesson for the school year. Initial analyses of both whole class dialogues and small group problem solving interactions focused on the quality of the children's mathematical activity and learning as they tackled specific instructional activities. These analyses, together with the classroom teacher's observations, guided the development of instructional activities and, on occasion, changes in class-room organization for subsequent lessons. Thus the processes of developing materials, conducting a formative assessment, and developing an initial explanation of classroom life were one and the same.

Research emphases

Before describing our research emphases, it is perhaps well to state categoric-ally that our intent has not been, is not, and cannot possibly be to prove that constructivism is right or even the way that all researchers should frame the problems of mathematics education. It is simply a way of knowing which, we believe, might open up potentially fruitful avenues of investiga-tion. Further, we have tried to be consciously aware of the danger of forcing our observations into the conceptual boxes provided by constructivism as we understood it at the beginning of the project. As a consequence, we have had to revise and relinquish some basic assumptions that initially seemed beyond question. Thus, part of the research agenda requires that we become increasingly aware of and probe some of the weaknesses of constructivism. This, in our view, is the soundest way of contributing to the vigour of this or any paradigm.

The issues of current interest include the children's construction of increasingly abstract arithmetical objects, their emotional/moral develop-ment, the teacher's learning in the classroom, and the changing nature of the children's beliefs about the activity of doing mathematics, their role as students, and the teacher's role. There is, however, one overriding problem that touches each of these issues. Constructivism, at least as it has been applied to mathematics education, has focused almost exclusively on the processes by which individual students actively construct their own mathematical realities. Much progress has been made on this front in recent years. However, far less attention has been given to the interpersonal or social aspects of mathematics learning and teaching. Given the emphasis of the evolving subjective realities of individuals, how (to state the question in observer language) does mathematics as cultural knowledge become 'interwoven' with individual children's cognitive achievements (Saxe, Guberman, and Gearhart, 1985)? In other words, how is it that the teacher and the children manage to achieve at least temporary states of intersubjectivity when they talk about mathematics? More simply still, how do children learn in such instructional situations? In our view, these are critical questions for constructivism. We will be unable to talk about the specifics of instruction in a theoretically grounded way unless we place analyses of learning within the context of classroom social interactions. Brophy and other adherents of the process-product approach are clearly trapped on one side of the chasm that currently separates research on learning from research on teaching. Constructivists are in danger of becoming trapped on the opposite side of the same divide.

As a first step in coming to grips with the problem of learning in social settings, we are currently analysing the evolving regularities or patterns identified in both whole class and small group interactions. These patterns are, for the most part, outside the conscious awareness of both the teacher and the children and are repeatedly reconstructed in the course of interactions (Voigt, 1985) . . . Although the teacher and children do not have a 'blueprint' of the interaction patterns, each knows how to act appropriately in particular situations. The patterns reveal the largely implicit social norms negotiated by the teacher and children, the norms that constitute the social reality within which they teach and learn mathematics. Following Voigt (1985), we are analysing the patterns and associated norms in terms of both the implicit, taken-for-granted obligations that the teacher and children accept in particular situations and the expectations they have for each other. The investigation of how they mutually construct the social reality of the classroom will therefore elucidate their beliefs about their own and each other's roles and will document how they created a 'problem-solving atmosphere' (Silver, 1985).

At the same time, we are interested in how the evolving network of obligations and expectations influences individual children's construction of mathematical knowledge. The relevance of this question is apparent when one observes with Balacheff (1986) that 'most of the time, the pupil does not act as a *theoretican* but as a *practical man*. His job is to give a solution to the problem the teacher has given him, a solution that will be acceptable with respect to the classroom situation' (p. 12). Thus, the social norms constrain what is problematic for children and what might count as an acceptable solution. However, it is while the children attempt to complete the mathematical activities in groups and discuss their solutions in the whole class setting that the social norms are renegotiated. This leads us to the contention that neither the cognitions of individuals nor the mutual constructed network of obligations and expectations are primary; we find it impossible to give an adequate explanation of one without considering the other.

On the other hand, the social norms and consensually sanctioned mathematical knowledge are created, regenerated, and modified by the coordinated actions of the teacher and children as individuals. The norms and consensually sanctioned knowledge do not exist independently of these actions (except in the mind of the analyst). On the other hand, each individual's understanding of the norms and knowledge constrains his or her activity in the classroom. The norms (and consensually constructed mathematics knowledge) constrain the activity that creates the norms. Conversely, individuals' activity creates the norms that constrain that activity.

In this formulation, the individual and the social are interdependent, in that one does not exist without the other. We thus acknowledge that social context is an integral aspect of an individual's cognitions without reifying mathematics as a ready-made body of cultural knowledge that is somehow internalized from without by individuals. Neither the physical and mathematical, or the social realities of the observer are taken as solid, immutable bedrock upon which to anchor an analysis of learning and teaching.

EXAMPLES FROM THE CLASSROOM

We present out current, admittedly fragmentary understanding of classroom life in the following sections. At the same time, the protocols and narratives of specific episodes that support the analysis exemplify the kinds of interactions that typified the activities of learning and teaching mathematics in the classroom.

Whole class interactions

The teacher's overall intention as she led whole class discussions was to encourage the children to verbalize their solution attempts. Such dialogues give rise to learning opportunities for the children as they attempt to reconstruct their solutions, understand alternative points of view, resolve conflicts between incompatible solution methods, and so forth. The teacher also had learning opportunities in that she had to decentre and 'see' things from the children's perspectives when she helped them to say what they wanted to say. However, the teacher's expectation that the children should verbalize how they had actually interpreted and attempted to solve the instructional activities did not fit with the expectations the children had developed on the basis of their prior experiences of class discussions in school. During both first grade and second grade with the exception of mathematics, such dialogues were typically initiated with the intention of steering or funnelling (Voigt, 1985) the children towards an officially sanctioned interpretation or solution (Wood, Cobb, and Yackel, 1988). As a consequence, class discussions in subject matter areas other than mathematics were situations in which the children felt obliged to try and infer what the teacher had in mind rather than to articulate their own understandings. The project teacher therefore had to exert her authority in order to help the children reconceptualize both their own and her role during mathematics instruction. In effect, she had to actively teach the children that she had different expectations for them when they did mathematics. To this end, she *initiated* the mutual construction of expectations and obligations in the classroom. In doing so, she simultaneously had to accept certain obligations for her own actions. If she expected the children to honestly express their current understandings of mathematics, then she was obliged to accept their explanations rather than to evaluate them with respect to an officially sanctioned solution method. Thus, the teacher had obligations to the children, just as they did to her. This evolving, interlocking network of obligations and expectations was beyond the conscious awareness of both the teacher and the children, but nevertheless was mutually constituted. The teacher and the children initially negotiated obligations and expectations at the beginning of the school year, which subsequently made possible the smooth functioning of the classroom for the remainder of the school year. Once established, this mutually constructed network of obligations constrained classroom social interactions in the course of which the children constructed mathematical meanings as they attempted to achieve their goals (Blumer, 1969). Thus the patterns of discourse served, not to transmit knowledge (Mehan, 1979; Voigt, 1985), but to provide opportunities for children to articulate and reflect on their mathematical activities.

The teacher's and students' mutual construction of social as well as mathematical realities is reflected in the dual structure of classroom dialogues. In one conversation, they talked about mathematics whereas in the other they talked about talking about mathematics. As these two conversations were conducted at distinct logical levels (Bateson, 1973), one in effect setting the framework for the other, seemingly contradictory statements such as 'the teacher exerted her authority to enable the children to express their viewpoints' make sense. As in a traditional classroom, the teacher was very much an authority in the classroom who attempts to realize an agenda. The difference resides in the way that she translated her authority into action (Bishop, 1985).

In the following episode that occurred during the first day of school, the discussion centres on word problems that are shown on an overhead projector.

T:	Take a look at this problem. The clown is first in line. Which animal is fourth? Peter.
PETER:	The tiger.
T:	How did you decide the tiger? . . . Would you show us how you got the fourth?
PETER:	(Goes to the screen at the front of the room.) I saw the clown and then . . (He counts the animals.) Oh, the dog [is fourth]. (Hesitates) Well, I couldn't see from my seat. (He looks down at the floor.)
T:	OK. What did you come up with?
PETER:	I didn't see it. (He goes back to his seat quickly.)

The teacher realized that in making Peter obliged to explain his solution, she put him in the position of having to admit that his answer was wrong in front of the entire class. Peter's response to the situation was to offer an excuse for his error, 'I couldn't see it . . .' Peter's concern with social comparison became manifest by his construal of the situation as warranting embarrassment (Armon-Jones, 1986). This construal confounded the teacher's intention that the children should feel free to publicly express their own solutions to problems. For her purposes, it was vital that children feel no shame or embarrassment when they present erroneous solutions in front of others. Crucially, the teacher immediately initiated a second conversation by talking about talking about mathematics as she suggested an alternative construal of the situation.

T:	That's okay Peter. It's all right. Boys and girls even if your answer is not correct, I am *most* interested in having you think. That's the important part. We are not always going to get answers right, but we want to try.

The teacher was directive in her comments. She expressed her expectations by telling the children how she as an authority interpreted the situation. She emphasized that Peter's attempts to solve the problem were appropriate in every way, and simultaneously expressed to the other children her belief that what is important in this class is thinking about mathematics, not just getting right answers. She then terminated this conversation and returned to the first.

T:	All right, did anybody else come up with a different way to do the problem?

In this episode, the project teacher practiced what Schon (1985) called 'knowledge-in-action'. She did not follow a set of prescribed rules as she conducted this and other dialogues. Instead, as a practitioner, she made sense of a problematic situation by reframing the situation.

The example makes clear that constructivist teaching does not mean that 'anything goes' or that the teacher gives up her authority and abrogates her wider societal obligations. Because mathematical meaning is inherently dependent on the construction of consensual domains, the activities of teaching and learning must necessarily be guided by obligations that are created and regenerated through social interaction. Critically, the teacher attempted to achieve her agenda by initiating and actively guiding the mutual construction of obligations and expectations in the classroom. In doing so, she attempted to invite actions that she considered appropriate while hindering others. These invitations and her overall agenda reflected her beliefs that mathematical learning is a problem-solving activity and that children's understandings should be respected. As a consequence of the teacher's interventions, the realized dialogue patterns contrast sharply with those of a typical classroom (Mehan, 1979; Stake and Easley, 1978; Voigt, 1985). The teacher exercised her authority in different ways in each of the two conversations that intertwined in the dialogues. When she and the children talked about talking about mathematics, the teacher typically initiated and attempted to control the conversation. However, when they talked about mathematics, she limited her role to that of orchestrating the conversation. The following episode taken from a dialogue that occurred later in the year again illustrates her authoritarian role with respect to the classroom social norms.

> T: Now another thing I noticed was happening and it is something I *don't* like and I *don't* want to hear . . . and it's these two words. (She writes 'That's Easy' on the board and draws a circle around the phrase.) These words are no-no's starting today. What are these two words Mark?
>
> MARK: That's easy.
>
> T: . . . I've had kids come up to me and say, 'Oh, that's easy!' Maybe I look at it and say, 'I don't think that's very easy'. How do you think that's going to make me feel?

It is evident as she listened to several children's suggestions that she was looking for a specific answer. Finally she stated, 'You are not saying the word I am looking for.' She continued to fish for a specific interpretation of the situation without success, and ultimately directly told the children.

> T: . . . it hurts my feelings when someone says. 'Oh that's easy!' (She points to the words on the board.) When I am struggling and trying so hard, it makes me feel kind of dumb or stupid. Because I am thinking, gosh, if it's so easy, why am I having so much trouble with it?

Once she had explicitly told the children the officially sanctioned interpretation of the situation, she terminated the social conversation and turned to talking about mathematics.

T: That's easy is a real put down. It's like if I think it's easy, then you must not be very smart, because it is not easy for you . . . OK. The first activity is balances.

The teacher's highly directive intervention is consistent with her agenda for the classroom. By outlawing actions that might make others feel stupid, the teacher nurtured the sense of trust that was essential if the children were to talk publicly about their mathematics. She demonstrated that if the children accepted the obligations of expressing their mathematical understandings then she, as an authority, was obliged to protect them. Her efforts bore fruit in that even the most conceptually immature child seemed to feel that his thinking was valued and respected, and as a consequence continued to participate actively in whole class discussion throughout the year.

When a conflict existed between the two conversations, the teacher always gave priority to the social (Stake and Easley, 1978). She was right to do so in that the norms established in the course of the social dialogue made possible the conversations in which children felt free to take the initiative as they talked about mathematics. The teacher was then able to adopt a nonauthoritarian, nonevaluative role when the children explained their solutions. For the most part, she orchestrated their contributions to the class discussions. The manner in which the children felt free to take the initiative is illustrated in the following episode which occurred near the end of the school year. The instructional activities for the previous two days provided a setting in which to discuss the meanings of fraction symbols such as 1/4, 1/2, 1/6, etc. The discussion prior to this episode was about the meaning of 7/8ths. The episode begins when John, who had previously stated that he had a problem he had been thinking about, came to the front of the room where the teacher, the overhead projector, and the screen were located.

JOHN: But um . . . what about if it was one and one? What would that be?

T: Like this? (She writes 1/1). Good question. Or what if you had this over this? (She writes 4/4 and 6/6.) What does that mean?

JOHN   (Starts talking to the teacher while tracing two circles on the screen with his hand.) Put a circle down.

T: O.K. Put a circle down (she draws a circle on the overhead, then looks at John).

JOHN: Um like . . . what I'm thinking is one and one. (He points to 1/1.) How could you make like . . .? (He looks at the teacher.)

The teacher's response at this point deviated distinctly from typical patterns of classroom interaction in that she did not offer John an official explanation but instead she continued the turn-taking dialogue by asking him a question that placed him under the obligation of thinking through a solution.

> T: How could you show one and one, one over one?
> JOHN: (Looks at the teacher and says nothing.)
> ANN: (Interjects) Just fill it all in.
> MARK: Yeah! That's one piece.
> T: OK. If we remember what a fraction tells us, John . . .
> JOHN: (Interrupts the teacher excitedly.) But it's the whole thing (he gestures with his hands, indicating a larger item), not just one piece (holds up one finger).
> T: So, how many can we fill in?
> JOHN: The whole thing!

The conversations in which children discussed mathematics on *their* terms gave rise to problematic situations for them which constituted opportunities for reflection and the construction of mathematical knowledge. These interactions were characterized by a genuine commitment to communicate. All the participants came to assume that any contribution to the dialogue made sense to the speaker (Rommetveit, 1985). Participation in the discussions therefore involved a genuine attempt to exchange points of view and encouraged the children to distance themselves from on-going activity (Sigel, 1981).

The manner in which the patterns of interactions evolved during the school year exemplifies the development of what Silver (1985) called a 'problem-solving atmosphere.' The teacher's priority was to establish a non-evaluative, cooperative setting in which children could publicly verbalize and reflect on their mathematical ideas without risk of social comparison or public embarrassment.

The obligations and expectations mutually constructed during whole class discussions also provided a framework for the children's activity as they worked in small groups, in that they were expected to solve problems in a cooperative manner and to respect each other's efforts. However, the children still had to negotiate obligations and expectations in the small group setting that would constitute a productive working relationship.

Small group interactions

The children attempted to complete instructional activities in groups of two, or occasionally three, prior to the whole class discussions. From the beginning of the year the teacher used her authority to emphasize two major responsibilities for each small group, namely that they cooperate to complete the activities and that they reach a consensus. Ideally, consensus is attained when the children develop a mutually acceptable method of solution. In a more limited sense, consensus is reached when the children agree on a common answer, albeit via different methods of solution. Thus, the children had two distinct types of problem to solve. The first concerned the mathematical problems that arose as they attempted to complete the instructional activities, whereas the second was that of negotiating a viable relationship that would make it possible jointly to solve their mathematical problems.

As with the whole class setting, the teacher was very explicit about what she expected of the children as they worked to solve both types of problem. For example, she attempted to place the children under the obligation of persisting and thinking their problems through for themselves rather than trying to complete as many activities as possible. Thus, she assured the children 'it's OK to complete one problem or five problems. If you don't get one finished, don't worry'. The children not only demonstrated by both word and deed that they understood and accepted the teacher's expectations (gaining personal satisfaction by solving difficult problems, persistence, and task-involvement came to characterize small group work), but felt free to extend and further emphasize them. This is illustrated by the following dialogue which occurred in the whole class setting at the beginning of a mathematics lesson. This episode occurred on the first day following two weeks of winter holiday.

LOIS: How many problems are there?
TEACHER: There are eight. So the most you can do is eight. Some of them are very hard though, so you may only get two done. Is that OK if you only get two done?
STUDENTS: (in unison): Yeah.
TEACHER: You bet it is . . . if you only get one done because it was so hard and you worked so hard on it that it was the only one you got, that's OK too.
ADAM: If you get none done, but you're still working on it, it's OK too.

By contrasting her expectations with the typical classroom obligation of completing a prescribed number of tasks, the teacher attempted to place the children under the obligation of persisting to resolve what they found problematic. Adam's elaboration provides clear evidence that children understood the teacher's expectations and accepted the consequences. Even the most extreme case, completing none, was acceptable provided the children met the obligation of striving to solve their problems.

The above discussion illustrates that the teacher was very much an authority when she told the children what she expected of them as they tried to solve their mathematical problems. She was even more explicit about what she expected socially, as is illustrated in the following continuation of the episode. Here, the teacher reminded the children of their social obligations as they worked in small groups.

TEACHER: Any questions before we get started? OK. You're going to
cooperate. You're going to work with your partner. And if
you figure out the answer and your partner is looking at you
like, 'How in the world did you get that answer?' it's going
to be up to you and your partner to work it out and understand it together. *Then* you can get another [problem] card,
but not until then.

In this directive the teacher attempted to place the children under a dual
obligation. They were expected to work cooperatively and, at a minimum,
to develop solutions that produced the same result. Ideally, they should also
develop mutually acceptable methods of solution. The two obligations are
at very different levels of complexity. At the basic level, children must negotiate a way to work with each other and must share materials including the
activity pages (each small group received only one copy.) Cooperation at
this level includes listening to and attempting to understand each other's
comments and, more generally facilitating rather than hindering each
other's mathematical activity. The second level of cooperation, working
together to construct a mutually acceptable solution, is much more
complex. It requires that students communicate about mathematics,
verbally or otherwise.

The social problem of cooperating at the basic level always has priority
in the sense that it makes the construction of mutually acceptable solutions possible. The teacher played an important role in facilitating
cooperation at this level (Wood and Yackel, 1988). As the teacher observed
small group activity, she was able to identify those groups which were
having difficulty at this basic level. Comments such as, 'if you put the
paper here in the middle then both of you can see it' and 'Listen to
what your partner is saying' exemplify the interventions the teacher
made to encourage cooperation. If children were unable to resolve the
problem of achieving basic cooperation over several weeks, even with the
teacher's intervention, they were assigned new partners. In the few cases
where basic cooperation was not achieved, there were underlying reasons
for failure such as extremely immature social communication skills, high
ego-involvement, or large discrepancies in mathematical conceptual
level. As the year progressed, the children's social development alleviated
the difficulties of establishing cooperative relationships in the small group
setting. By the end of the year, instances of failure to cooperate at the basic
level were isolated and were typically resolved by the children themselves
within the group.

The problem of cooperating at the level of developing a mutually
acceptable solution is much more demanding. Nevertheless such cooperation became the norm in the classroom. At this level of cooperation, the
children have to appreciate what each finds problematic and coordinate

their mathematical problem-solving activities. Such interactions naturally give rise to opportunities for reflection and cognitive reorganization. As an illustration, extracts of a dialogue between two children as they solved a sequence of multiplication tasks are presented. The children had just successfully completed the task 5 × 4 = ? (The children's use of the term 'sets' in talking about multiplication is a result of the teacher's use of the term when she first introduced '×' as the mathematical symbol for multiplication.)

   10 × 4 = ?

JOHN: It's five more sets [of 4]. Look. Five more sets than 20.
ANDY: Oh! 20 plus 20 is 40. So its gotta be 40. No?
JOHN: Yeah!
ANDY: No. 4, 8, 12, 16, 20, 24, 28 (keeps track on his fingers).
JOHN: 40.
ANDY: 40.
JOHN: Yeah, I know . . . Cause ten fours make 40.
ANDY: Like five fours make 20.
JOHN: Four sets of ten makes 40. Just turn it around.
ANDY: Five sets of fours make 20 and so five more than that.
JOHN: Yeah, just turn it around. Just turn it around.
ANDY: 5 times 4 is 20, so 20 more than that makes 40.
JOHN: Just switch them round.

Notice that Andy constructed his solution by elaborating John's initial comment that 'It's 5 more sets [of four]'. However, in his final explanation John developed an alternative solution method. Andy's initial statement that 40 is the answer was followed by John's exclamation 'Yeah!' John's subsequent verbalizations suggest that once he heard '20 plus 20 is 40' he reconceptualized the problem as four tens, rather than as 20 and 5 more fours, and then successfully justified that conceptualization. This inference is supported by the frequency and enthusiasm with which he repeated 'Just turn it [or switch them] around.' Thus, even though each child eventually conceptualized the problem differently their initial verbalizations were instrumental in the development of the other's solution. This illustrates an extremely productive level of cooperation in which each partner facilitated the conceptual activity of the other.

   9 × 4 = ?

JOHN: Just take away 4 from that [10 × 4].
ANDY: 36
JOHN: (pause) Yeah!

In this brief dialogue we see a different form of cooperation. One partner, John, suggested a solution process and the other, Andy, carried it out. The pause before John's final agreement indicates that he verified Andy's answer. In the following dialogue the children agreed on an answer but constructed different methods of solution.

8 × 4 = ?

JOHN: Look! Look! Just take away 4 from that [9 × 4] to get that [8 × 4]. See! Just take away 4 from there [9 × 4].
ANDY: Just take 8 away from that [10 × 4].
JOHN: No. Take away 4 from there [9 × 4].
ANDY: Take 8 away from that [10 × 4]. That makes 32.
OBSERVER: Did you do it the same way as Andy?
JOHN: Yeah, but I used that one [9 × 4]. Take away 4. It makes 32.

John's final comment makes it evident that he was consciously aware of the similarities and differences between his and Andy's methods. Although they constructed different methods, each was satisfied that his was viable. This was sufficient to meet the obligation of reaching consensus. As the dialogue continued, the children encountered a situation where they disagreed on the answer.

8 × 5 = ?

ANDY: Five more than that [8 × 4] is 37.
JOHN: Eight sets of 4. Eight sets of 5.
ANDY: No. 9, 39, I think.
(Both children pause to reflect for a few moments.)
JOHN: (very excitedly) It's 40.
ANDY: It is?
JOHN: Yeah, its 40! Yeah, look!
ANDY: No, it's 39.
JOHN: 5, 10, 15, 20, 25, 30, 35, 40, 45, oops. Take away that last one. It's 40.
ANDY: 5, 10, 15, 20, 25, 30, 35, 40, 45.
JOHN: Huh?
ANDY: Wait. 40. Yeah, 40.

On this task, Andy first attempted to modify his previously successful method of solution and found eight fours plus five. Apparently John's remark, 'Eight sets of 4. Eights sets of 5', led Andy to reflect on this activity. His next answer, 39, indicates that he modified his initial conceptualization. Andy then challenged John's answer of 40, and John was obliged to justify his solution. Andy immediately adopted John's method but his conceptualization of it is open to question as he simply repeated exactly what John had said, including the error of going up to 45. But John's 'Huh?' prompted further reflection and they finally agreed on the answer. In this instance the problem of achieving a consensus provided the basis for their mathematical activity.

The final task in this excerpt is $7 \times 5 = ?$ The dialogue is very brief.

ANDY: Seven sets of 5.
JOHN: Oh, it's just 5 lower than that. It's . . .
ANDY AND JOHN (simultaneously)   35.
JOHN: We both said it at the same time.

John appeared amused and pleased that they said the answer simultaneously, as though that were the height of cooperation.

The above excerpts illustrate that the coordination of mathematical activity can take a variety of forms. Notice that nowhere in the dialogue did either partner make explicit reference to their obligation to cooperate. (Typically such comments are made only when cooperation breaks down.) Yet it is apparent that in every instance they persisted until each had constructed a viable method that produced a common answer. The smooth flow of their discussions indicates that they had mutually constructed a viable network of obligations and expectations. For example, each knew when it was appropriate to explain or to justify a solution without being explicitly asked to do so. The two children's mathematical discussions, which are characteristic of this level of cooperation, gave rise to a variety of learning opportunities that are unique to the small group instructional strategy.

The level of cooperation illustrated by John and Andy was made possible by their ability to make sense of each other's mathematical activity. Cases where a child, for one reason or another, is unable to make sense of his or her partner's mathematical activity make it impossible for such cooperation to occur. This in turn makes it more difficult for the children to cooperate at the basic social level. In the episode presented below the method used by one partner was incomprehensible to the other. Consequently, cooperation at the level of developing a mutually acceptable problem solution was impossible. Each worked independently to complete the instructional activities because they were unable to talk to each other about their mathematics. What dialogue there was, necessarily focused on whether or not they had the same answer and on the more basic level of cooperation. In this episode the partners were working on a multiplication activity. One child was using an (incorrect) algorithm to solve the problems. Her partner, unable to make sense of her approach, chose to solve the problems by drawing circles of tally marks and then counting. As a consequence, it took him longer to generate an answer to each task.

$5 \times ? = 35.$

ADAM: Will you wait for me? Five times something equals 35. I already know the answer to that. Five times five, I think. Let me check it again. (At this point Adam draws five circles of five.) Seven.

$4 \times 7 = ?$

ADAM: Four times seven equals something. Let me draw these here. You can go ahead. (He draws four groups of seven.) Oh, one more and then I'll be caught up.

ANN: (Writes 22 as her answer on the activity page.) Do you agree?

ADAM: Hold on. You're going ahead.

ANN: I hate waiting for you.

ADAM: I got 28 on that one but hold on.

Adam checks the answer 28 again and they agreed to give that as the answer.

Notice in the above dialogue that the children did not discuss their mathematics. At best, they could compare answers and share the activity page and any other materials they had. As a consequence, they continually had to resolve the social problem of synchronizing their independent activities. Adam, for example, continued to insist that Ann should wait for him and that they should at least work on the same activity. Ann reluctantly obliged; she too understood that they were expected to work cooperatively and to agree on answers. Despite their different mathematical understandings, they attempted to maintain a basic level of social cooperation. To do so, they had to continually negotiate cooperation at this level verbally. This dialogue contrasts sharply with that between John and Andy, who cooperated fully but made no verbal reference to it.

In the project classroom the social relationships the children negotiated were influenced by, but not determined by, their level of conceptual understanding of mathematics. For example, partners who were at approximately the same conceptual levels could readily make sense of each other's mathematical thinking. Thus, cooperation at the level of developing mutually acceptable problem solutions was facilitated. John and Andy exemplify this type of relationship. Partners at widely different conceptual levels could cooperate only if the more advanced partner operated far below his or her capabilities and discussed mathematics at the level of the less advanced partner, or if partners agreed to work independently on the instructional activities and compare answers. Although the first option presents opportunities for the more advanced child to serve as a tutor and can give rise to learning opportunities, in general it denies that child opportunities for conceptual advancement. In the project, classroom partners who evidenced such a relationship were reassigned.

Some children who were at very different conceptual levels did develop very productive working relationships. For example, in one pair the child who was less advanced conceptually was very task-involved and continually requested assistance from his partner. It was common for these children to work individually on the mathematics tasks and then compare their answers. Dialogue in this group, as in the Adam/Ann episode presented earlier, frequently focused on negotiating a basic level of cooperation.

The previous discussion and examples illustrate that the social interactions between partners influence their mathematical activity and give rise to learning opportunities. The interactions are in turn influenced by their conceptual understanding and by the network of obligations and expectations mutually constructed both within the group and in the wider whole class setting. Our observations in the project classroom indicate that, as early as second grade, children are remarkably successful at working together to complete instructional activities. In doing so, they solve not only their mathematics problems but also the problem of how to work together.

CONCLUSIONS

The teaching experiment was reasonably successful in that we were able to satisfy the school district administrators' expectations while allowing the children to solve their mathematical problems in ways that were acceptable to them. It also became apparent that the children's abilities to establish productive social relationships and to verbalize their own thinking improved dramatically as the year progressed. However, most observers seemed to attribute the greatest significance to the emotional tone of the classroom. In general, the children were enthusiastic, persistent, did not become frustrated, and experienced joy when they solved a personally challenging problem. We have, for example, been unable to identify a single instance when a child evidenced frustration while problem-solving during the second semester of the school year. Further, the children's persistence was such that we found it necessary to allocate three consecutive one-hour class periods to general problem-solving whenever these instructional activities were used. The children requested additional time because they wanted to continue working on an activity they had been unable to complete during an entire class period.

We have tried to make the point that the teacher was very much an authority in the project classroom, albeit a benevolent one. Her success in placing the children under certain obligations while readily accepting compatible obligations for herself was crucial to her effectiveness. As a constructivist teacher, she did not merely refrain from carrying out certain activities characteristic of traditional teachers and relinquish her authority. Rather, she expressed that authority in action by initiating the mutual construction of certain obligations and expectations. In doing so, she influenced the children's beliefs about both the nature of the activity of doing mathematics and their own and the teacher's roles in the classroom. Above all else, the obligations and expectations that were established constituted a trusting relationship. The teacher trusted the children to resolve their problems and they trusted her to respect their efforts. This trust is, in our opinion, the most important feature of constructivist teaching.

REFERENCES

Armon-Jones, C. (1986) 'The thesis of constructionism', in R. Harré (ed.), *The Social Construction of Emotions*, Oxford: Blackwell.

Balacheff, N. (1986) 'Cognitive versus situational analysis of problem-solving behavior', *For the Learning of Mathematics*, 6 (3): 10–12.

Bateson, G. (1973) *Steps To An Ecology Of Mind*, London: Paladin.

Bishop, A. (1985) 'The social construction of meaning – a significant development for mathematics education?', *For The Learning of Mathematics*, 5 (1): 24–8.

Blumer, H. (1969) *Symbolic Interactionism*, Englewood Cliffs, NJ: Prentice-Hall.

Cobb, P. (1986) 'Concrete can be abstract: a case study?, *Educational Studies in Mathematics*, 17: 37–48.

Confrey, J. (1987) 'The current state of constructivist thought in mathematics education'. Paper presented at the annual meeting of the International Group for the Psychology of Mathematics Education, July, Montreal.

Erickson, F. (1986) 'Qualitative methods in research on teaching', in M.C. Wittrock (ed.), *The Handbook of Research on Teaching*, 3rd edition, NY: Macmillan.

Mehan, H. (1979) *Learning Lessons: Social Organization in the Classroom*, Cambridge, MA: Harvard University Press.

Rommetveit, R. (1985) 'Language acquisition as increasing linguistic structuring of experience and symbolic behavior control', in J.V. Wertsch (ed.), *Culture, Communication, and Cognition*, Cambridge: Cambridge University Press.

Rumelhart, D.E. and Norman, D.A. (1981) 'Analogical processes in learning', in J.R. Anderson (ed.), *Cognitive Skills and Their Acquisition*, Hillsdale, NJ: Erlbaum.

Saxe, G.B., Guberman, S.R. and Gearhart, M. (1985) 'The social context of early number learning'. Paper presented at the annual meeting of the American Educational Research Association, April, Chicago.

Schon, D. (1985) *The Design Studio: An Exploration of Its Traditions and Potentials*, London: RIBA Publications.

Sigel, I.E. (1981) 'Social experience in the development of representational thought: distancing theory', in I.E. Sigel, D.M. Brodzinsky, and R.M. Golinkoff (eds), *New Directions in Piagetian Theory and Practice*, Hillsdale, NJ: Lawrence Erlbaum Associates.

Silver, E.A. (1985) 'Research on teaching mathematical problem solving: some under-represented themes and needed directions', in E.A. Silver (ed.), *Teaching and Learning Mathematical Problem solving: Multiple Research Perspectives*, Hillsdale, NJ: Lawrence Erlbaum.

Stake, R.E. and Easley, J. (1978) *Case Studies in Science Education* (vol. 2), Urbana, IL: University of Illinois Center for Instructional Research and Curriculum Evaluation.

Thompson, P. (1985) 'Experience, problem solving, and learning mathematics: considerations in developing mathematics curricula', in E.A. Silver (ed.), *Teaching and Learning Mathematical Problem Solving: Multiple Research Perspectives*, Hillsdale, NJ: Erlbaum.

Voigt, J. (1985) 'Patterns and routines in classroom interaction', *Recherches en Didactique des Mathematiques*, 6: 69–118.

von Glasersfeld, E. (1983) 'Learning as a constructive activity', in J.C. Bergeron and N. Herscovics (eds), *Proceedings of the Fifth Annual Meeting of the North American Chapter of the International Group for the Psychology of Mathematics Education*, Montreal: PME-NA.

Wood, T., Cobb, P. and Yackel, E. (1988) 'The influence of change in teacher's beliefs about mathematics instruction on reading instruction'. Annual meeting of the American Education Research Association, July, New Orleans.

Wood, T. and Yackel, E. (1988) 'Teacher's role in the development of collaborative dialogue within small group interactions'. Paper presented to the Sixth International Congress on Mathematical Education, July, Budapest.

Chapter 21

Telling and asking

Eric Love and John Mason

INTRODUCTION

Every act by a teacher in a mathematics classroom is a manifestation not only of their perception of mathematics but also of their perception of what is involved in teaching (and by implication also in learning) mathematics. How a teacher behaves in the classroom in a mathematical situation, and the habitual interactions which take place, speak volumes to pupils about mathematics and about the possibilities in it for them.

The totality of pupil–teacher interactions is a vast and complex domain. This chapter concentrates on just a few aspects of verbal interactions. It looks at three modes of verbal interaction, suggesting frames for probing behind some of the prevalent slogans about telling, about asking and about mathematical discussion. . . .

Teacher intentions when speaking may be multiple. What is said can arise from local, detailed concern about the mathematical ideas, from larger concerns about the conduct of the lesson, and from global concerns about the nature of education and the discipline of mathematics.

Since the first person to speak after silence has fallen is usually the teacher, teaching usually begins with the teacher and so the next two sections start from teacher-talk and look at ways of interacting which involve the teacher *telling* pupils things, then at ways in which teachers try to initiate pupils' participation, through *asking questions,* and then at pupils *discussing* among themselves and interacting with a teacher who intervenes in order to help or stimulate the activity.

TELLING

Most verbal interactions involve people asking and telling. In the midst of asking and telling, it is hard not to assume that the audience is experiencing the same thoughts as the speaker. Yet asking people questions and telling them things are problematic enterprises at the best of times, whether in the classroom or outside it.

- in asking questions, it is tempting to assume that the responder has taken the question to heart and that the reply represents what the responder thinks;
- in telling people things, it is tempting to assume that they then know what they have been told.

But just because it is easy to make inappropriate assumptions, it does not follow that asking or telling people is necessarily ineffective. When people are able to hear what is said, telling can be very helpful – just as when a seed is sown in prepared ground. When people are engaged and interested, asking can indeed be stimulating – just as when a seed germinates and begins again the cycle of growth.

As a mode of interacting with pupils, *telling* received a particularly bad press in the 1980s. Emphasis on investigation, group work and pupil experience led to a dislike of and reaction against exposition, probably as a reaction against memories of sitting in lessons being told things endlessly by a succession of teachers. But there are many circumstances in which it is not only proper and effective, but essential to tell people things.

People can be told things in more than one way. Indeed, Ainley (1987) suggests that not only assertions but also questions do their share of telling people things: things about the speaker's interests and concerns and things about how the subsequent lesson is likely to develop. People tell each other things all the time, often very effectively, though very often the significant communication is not the literal meaning of the words, but the exchange of attention – what Eric Berne (1966) called 'stroking'. Examples of stroking include the ritualized exchanges such as 'Good morning', 'How are you?' and 'Thank you' which serve to lubricate the cogs of personal interactions. Absence of such stroking exchanges makes other 'more important' communication difficult.

There are social settings in which telling is a response to an implicit or explicit request:

To find out the bus or train times or when a TV programme is going to be broadcast: information is wanted, not a series of questions or deflections.

To find out what someone else thinks about a topic: having them ask a series of questions is not what is wanted.

In school contexts, where the teacher is expected to help the pupil to learn, it is not so clear whether telling or not telling is likely to be more effective. In the midst of a complicated calculation when the answer to 'seven eights' is needed, but momentarily forgotten, the answer is what is wanted, not an invitation to work it out. But is that the most fruitful thing to do for the pupil? There are of course no rules. Any principles, such as: *Never tell them something they can work out for themselves*, or: *Treat them as adults. If they ask a direct question, given them the answer,* over-stress one aspect at the expense of another.

A common feature of social situations in which telling is desirable is that someone wants to know something. Unfortunately this is not always the situation in classrooms. Pupils do not always want to know things. Sometimes they just want to cope. They want to get by. However, it may be possible to stimulate interest, to engage pupils in activity, to generate surprise or contradiction, so that the wish to know begins to form and pupils begin to take some of the initiative.

The Cockcroft report (DES, 1982) suggested a need for balance among exposition and other forms of interaction in classrooms but, for a long time afterwards, HMI continued to report that it was difficult to find a classroom in which exposition did not play a major part. Emphasis was therefore placed by the mathematics education community on small-group and individualized work. Continued emphasis on mixed-ability teaching in secondary schools reinforced interest in individualized learning schemes and so resulted in even less emphasis on exposition. There grew up in mathematics education circles a suggestion that exposition was to be avoided, that pupils should instead be given every opportunity to explore, construct and make sense for themselves. For some reason, the idea of pupils making sense for themselves is often seen as incompatible with telling them things. We shall argue that they are in fact entirely compatible. The point about telling people things is to choose carefully what to tell and when to tell it.

It is natural to want to tell people things and natural to want to be told things as well. Since it is impossible in one lifetime to discover everything for yourself, people try to learn from others. There are two awkwardnesses about telling: one is choosing to tell people things that they are just about to find out for themselves anyway and so disrupting productive thought or deflating them by taking away the pleasure of discovery. The other is assuming that the hearers know what they have been told.

If it is not sensible to assume that people know what they have been told, why tell them at all? Yet denying telling is just as unbalanced as relying upon it for the main form of interaction with pupils. To refuse to tell on the grounds that it does not help (because 'they still don't know') contradicts the belief that telling is liable to deflate or disrupt. If telling is indeed so ineffective, then it would not be possible to disrupt or deflate by telling!

Learning is a much more complex process than a simple cause and effect relationship between what the teacher says and what the pupils learn. It makes sense to tell people things when they are in a state to be able to hear, to relate to, to make connections with, and to assimilate what is being said and yet not able to work it out quickly for themselves. If people are not in a state to hear what is being said, then they are unlikely to make much of it. For example, the pupil who remarked to his mother:

> Mr P. is being very silly at the moment. He's doing all sorts of complicated things to add fractions together, when all he needs to do is add the tops and add the bottoms.

may not be in a position to hear the teacher's algorithm. Neither is the pupil who is confident about using a ruler, but always starts from the '1' mark 'because you always start counting from one'.

For telling to be successful, there usually has to be something problematic, something uncertain, paradoxical or striking in order for the ground to be adequately prepared. Interest has to be aroused and awareness sharpened in order for someone to be in a position to be told something effectively. What is said has then to relate to pupils' experience and to call upon their confidence in order to push at the boundaries of their current understanding.

Three forms of telling

The following classification of forms of telling into *expounding, explaining* and *conjecturing* is intended to be sufficiently compact not to be unwieldy, yet sufficiently discerning in order to inform practice.

Expounding

> We use the terms *expounding* and *exposition* to refer to speaking from one's own vivid images, from being in contact with mathematical ideas, like a tour guide pointing out sights of interest on either side, and providing insightful observations.

Exposition typically introduces new words or terms, new ways of thinking, new ideas. When a teacher is expounding effectively, she is exposing, or 'putting out in plain view', thoughts and ideas which have been worked on and clarified over a period of time. She is laying out the territory, indicating that a map exists, even though pupils are not expected to 'take it all in'. Aspects of a heritage of intellectual development are presented for consideration. She enters her rich world of experience and speaks vividly from there. The audience (literally, the 'hearers') are drawn into that world, as with a good story-teller.

Exposition involves pupils being in the presence of someone working and thinking mathematically, someone who is in touch with important mathematical ideas. An expositor can make the ordinary seem strange and exciting and can stimulate interest to know more or to resolve some unexpected uncertainty or surprise. Pupils do not learn how to do something from exposition, how to perform some technique just from being told or shown, but they can be inspired, stimulated and challenged. They can see that there is something surprising to be accounted for or sorted out, something unexpected to accommodate to their current intuitions.

Exposition can be a precursor to exploration. The exposition provides a vague sense or overview, a map of the territory and pupils can find out from particular examples what a certain technique or idea is about in detail. The teacher may feel, as do authors of texts and schemes, that it is necessary to demonstrate to pupils how a particular technique is carried out. But that demonstration is merely a starting point for the pupils to reconstruct and assimilate for themselves.

For example, having collected together a mass of data on height, and wrist, hand, arm and foot lengths, pupils may want to know whether one measurement can be predicted from another. A plot of wrist size against arm length (for example) is a standard technique in such circumstances, but pupils are unlikely to think of it without considerable prior experience. Telling pupils about such a technique may be helpful, including demonstrating its use (preferably using a computer programme), but pupils then have to get down and use the programme themselves, make their plots and contemplate and interpret the resulting graph. They need to do this in several situations, so that their attention moves from the data and associated questions, to data handling as a technique. Thus, exposition can set the scene for personal exploration and reconstruction of ideas encountered fleetingly.

Exposition is sometimes seen as reinforcing both dependency on the teacher and the authority of that teacher. Being an authority, that is, being experienced or even expert in something is no bad thing either. Disaffection with exposition has to do with its being the sole mode of classroom interaction and with expertise turning into excessive control, leading to dependency. The teacher/expositor, knowing more about the topic, controls pupils' access to the ideas and techniques. Some degree of control is both needed and wanted if people are to learn. But the aim is to reduce the dependency on the teacher or expert as judge of correctness and source of ideas while still using them to challenge and stimulate. To achieve this, it is necessary to exploit interactions in which pupils explore and express themselves, whether through discussing, writing notes, drawing pictures and diagrams, making films, using computer programmes or specifying calculator sequences.

Engaging in exposition is good for pupils as well as for teachers. Being stimulated to organize one's thoughts, to make real contact with the ideas in order to speak coherently about them to others plays a vital role in learning to express oneself on paper – something that pupils have to do ultimately to pass examinations.

Explaining

The term *explaining* can be used to describe interactions with pupils in which the teacher tries to enter the pupils' world, tries to see things their way, to make 'plain' what the pupil is thinking and how that differs from what the teacher is thinking.

The words *explain* and *expound* are often used interchangeably. One reason is that to *explain* can mean both 'to make clear', and 'to justify' (to explain why, to explain oneself). But the two terms can also be used to distinguish distinct forms of telling which sometimes merge in classrooms, with unintended and unhelpful results.

An explanation uses words and ideas already familiar to the pupil: it operates in the pupil's world. Whereas exposition typically introduces new ideas, explanation juxtaposes words already understood with terms whose meaning is uncertain or unclear, in order to help the pupil to be more certain as to their use and meaning.

When people 'explain how' to do something, it usually amounts to a demonstration: 'do this, then this, then this', which is actually much more like exposition, because pupils are invited to enter the demonstrator's world and do things 'that way'. The teacher outlines the steps, slowly and methodically, and the pupil is expected to copy. To explain something in the sense of justifying, of 'explaining why', it is necessary to root what is said in the audience's experience and this is the essence of explanation.

To explain something effectively to a pupil, it is essential to listen and, when speaking, to attend carefully to facial expressions and other body language. Effective explanation usually comes in short bursts. A long 'explanation' almost necessarily turns into exposition, because the speaker naturally slides into his own world, hoping that the pupil will follow. Once the explanation required comes to mind and the words start flowing fluently, it is very difficult to remain in the pupil's world.

One role of exposition is to inspire through generating surprise. To be effective in explaining, it is helpful to be able to experience the world of the pupil to recapture the state of surprise and wonder – even in topics which are very familiar. Any of the following mathematical facts can simply be asserted from a base of complete familiarity and a sense of 'it's obvious', yet each is an important part of the mathematics curriculum precisely because of the surprise it generated originally and its general applications in many different places. In each case the familiar can be experienced as strange:

It does not matter what order you count things in (provided you don't make a mistake) because you always get the same answer. *How amazing that independence of order is and it certainly doesn't hold when you are taking things away.*

The number after one thousand and ninety-nine is one thousand one hundred. *How powerful is the naming system, how mysteriously the numbers all receive not just one, but a variety of different names (6 also has the names 4 + 2, 30/5, √36, . . .).*

The sum of any two even numbers is also even. *Amazing in its generality, since it covers such a vast range of cases.*

Explanation, like exposition, plays an important part in being taught mathematics. If explanations do not come from somewhere, from the teacher or from each other, pupils may abandon hope altogether. Getting pupils to express things to each other is just one of the ways in which pupils can work at refining and honing what they understand and, in the process of explaining to someone else, learn. For this sort of activity to be successful, an appropriate classroom atmosphere, based on conjecturing, is essential.

Conjecturing

A *conjecture* is an assertion which may be true, but which may need modification or even rejection in the light of further thought or evidence.

A *conjecturing* atmosphere is one in which everything said is taken as a conjecture; in which pupils seek to express their thinking when they are unsure, and to listen carefully to each other when they are sure about the topic to hand.

Conjectures are usually expressions of patterns and regularities which a person perceives, expressed in words, pictures, symbols, or some other form. They cover a range of certainties from unsupported beliefs, through possibilities that seem intuitively correct, to assertions which the speaker believes can be justified by evidence and argument. Conjectures are most frequently intuitions which are changing into assertions.

Conjectures are a form of telling, in that offering a conjecture is a way of telling yourself, or someone else, what is currently believed to be the case, but in a way which suggests being open to considering modifications. In a conjecturing atmosphere, there is no need to tell someone that their answer is wrong. They may however be encouraged to reconsider their conjecture, to modify or amend it, and suggestions along these lines may be made by others. In a conjecturing atmosphere pupils are encouraged not to take assertions as facts, but to investigate matters for themselves.

There is a big difference between being told something and being told something which must subsequently be checked out against experience. The first type of telling brooks no argument, no questioning. The second is consistent with how mathematicians of all ages go about exploring with and in mathematics; as patterns are contemplated and examples catalogued, they form conjectures about what might be the case. Then further examples are examined in order to try to check that conjecture. Examples are sought which might disprove the conjecture or which might show why the idea will always work.

Conjectures are modified: they change and develop. They are part of what one tells oneself while exploring mathematically, yet they are often so fleeting and transitory that within moments it is hard to recall what it was that set a certain train of thought in motion. It is useful therefore to acknowledge utterances as conjectures and to note them down in a public place for later consideration. Working publicly this way reinforces the value in pupils doing the same thing when working individually or in small groups. Making a note of conjectures as they arise is worth while, because when a line of exploration is exhausted, there may be no other access to what prompted that direction apart from returning to the conjectures from which it originated. Writing conjectures down also helps if progress slows down or stops altogether because it is possible to go back and see recent thoughts and perhaps make some changes or set off in a new direction. And if work is abandoned for a few minutes or days or years, it is much easier to come back to a conjecture than to rough notes. Furthermore, when time runs out, it is good mathematical practice to stop work with the current conjectures stated as clearly as possible, with a few notes about why the conjecture seemed reasonable. Not all questions that pupils consider can be resolved, but if they learn to suspend judgement, without looking for immediate resolutions, they will be better prepared to develop their thinking in the future.

Summary

Expounding is often frowned upon, yet in its highest form it can have a 'telling' effect. The audience may not be able to act differently but they may be more attuned to some possible ways of thinking or inspired to find out more. Pupils expound their ideas to each other and tell the teacher what they think are important facets of learning. To communicate a mathematical idea, it is essential to make mathematical contact, to summon up relevant and vivid mental images, to recall useful technical words and ideas that are related and to bring to mind the variety of different contexts in which the ideas occur to gain access to a world of experience connected with that topic.

Explaining involves entering the world of the listeners, making the thinking plain to them and to oneself, and offering additional and alternative versions to consider. Explanation often turns into exposition and one value in distinguishing between them as modes of telling is so that a transition is detectable while it is occurring, allowing a decision about which is likely to be the more effective mode to be made.

Exposition and explanation are both useful for setting up conditions in which exploration is appropriate, so that pupils have direction and purpose to their investigations.

Conjecturing involves externalizing thoughts which are in the process of being refined and made precise. It means being open to assistance in modifying and altering one's ideas. When a conjecturing atmosphere is established, pupils respond to exposition not as assertions to be 'learned' but as a stimulus to check out the ideas for themselves, to make sense for themselves through exploration and through explaining to each other.

ASKING

In a classroom, a teacher asks 'What did I just ask you?' It may sound and look like a question, but is it? It could be:

- a genuine enquiry – the questioner having forgotten;
- exerting control by effectively asserting that the person was not listening;
- designed to focus attention on some mathematical process or idea;
- an indication of teacher frustration;
- a subtle working in the zone of proximal development.

As with telling, the words alone do not enable a definitive analysis. A clue to the intention may be given by the amount of time before the teacher's next intervention. There seems little point in asking a reflective question if time is not given for pondering, considering and conjecturing. By holding silence, by not fidgeting or allowing one's own thoughts to wander off to something else, pupil attention can be focused on the content of the question rather than just its form.

Instead of analysing what other people said, it may be more profitable to catch oneself in the act of asking a question and observing your intentions and experience 'from the inside'. Often the intention in asking a question emerges only in reaction to the response from the person questioned: a question is asked of pupils, pupils respond and the subsequent reaction highlights the original intention. For example:

> The teacher notices a pattern of bricks in a wall. It occurs to her to ask pupils, 'What do you notice about the wall?'

One pupil replies with talk about colours, another about the height, another about its age. The teacher's reaction 'What about the pattern?' or 'How many bricks do you think there are?' reveals the existence of a particular and definite focus.

> A pupil is measuring with a ruler, but using the '1' mark as the starting-point. The teacher asks, 'What must you do when using a ruler?' and the pupil replies, 'Keep it still.'

The teacher's reaction will reveal to both teacher and pupil what sort of a question was being asked.

> In a primary classroom, pupils are playing a domino-type game with logiblocks in which each new block added to the sequence has to match the last block in exactly two attributes. The teacher sees a pupil add an inappropriate block to the chain and asks, 'What are you matching for?'

Pupils offer things like 'Colour', 'Colour and shape', 'It looks right' and the teacher's reaction reveals both to them and to the other pupils the original intentions of the questions.

In each case, the actual response summons up a reaction and it is that reaction which is most informative about the original intention in asking the question.

It is a particular feature of adult–children interactions that adults will ask questions which would not be acceptable in a gathering of adults. Mehan (1986) has built an entire article around the apparently innocuous question, 'What time is it Denise?' so the reply, 'It's 2:30, Miss' is likely to get the response 'Thank you' at a railway station and 'Well done!' in an infant classroom. Many adults are exercised about adult–pupil questions, especially in the classroom, but pupils exhibit less concern and confusion about the difference between in- and out-of-school questioning than do researchers. Pupils seem to accept that they should be asked questions in school as part of the social practice of school.

Three aspects of asking

Researchers have delineated dozens of different forms of questions. We propose three aspects of asking questions as a suitable number to provide a sufficiently informative framework for making further investigations without being submerged in too many subtle distinctions. Each form or mode takes into account not just the words uttered, but the intentions of the teacher, which in turn may only be revealed when a pupil responds and the teacher then reacts to that response.

Focusing

In the midst of a lesson, the teacher 'sees' something happening. For example:

- a pupil has generated a sequence of numbers such as 1, 4, 9, . . . but does not seem to see the pattern of square numbers which leaps off the page at the teacher;
- pupils are lost in details of measuring and cannot seem to see what calculations they need to do, yet to the teacher it is entirely obvious what they should do;

. . . [In the] situation, above . . . the teacher sees a pattern in the number sequence but the pupil does not seem to. After each question the pupil offers little or no response, so another question is asked:

Can you see a pattern?

What is the same about this and this and this? (The teacher points to the individual terms).

What connections are there between this and this and this? (The teacher again points to the terms).

(Writing down the differences 3, 5, 7 . . .) Do you recognize this sequence of numbers?

Will these numbers keep going up in odd numbers? Will you always get square numbers?

Heinrich Bauersfeld (1993) calls this sort of questioning sequence the *funnel effect*. Each time a pupil responds hesitantly, or not at all, the teacher feels drawn to be more precise, to ask something which the pupil will surely be able to answer.

John Holt (1964) describes an incident in which he eventually realized that the pupil had a strategy of saying almost nothing until Holt had refined and simplified the question until there was no risk in answering. Such situations arise when the questioner has a sharp sense of what they want the pupil to know/see/say, and it is all too easy to be sucked down the funnel by some form of 'guess what's in my mind' questioning. Familiarity plays a role in funnelling, for a pattern of routine questions, asked without much real thought, can create a sterile atmosphere which forces the teacher into more and more specific questions until teacher and/or pupil actually start thinking.

Funnelling in itself in neither good nor bad: rather its value depends on what teacher and pupil think is happening. If the teacher believes himself to be genuinely enquiring, or if the pupils wait for the questions to become more detailed and precise without working at the more diffuse and imprecise ones, then the interaction is likely to be a waste of time. If, on the other hand, the pupil is working hard at trying to relate ideas so that the funnelling helps focus attention in some unexpected or unfamiliar way, then the interaction could be fruitful.

The value of the term *funnelling* lies in the way it can come to mind in the midst of an interaction and so draw the teacher's attention out of the interaction details, and on to the nature of the interaction, thus providing a moment of choice: to continue down the funnel or to seek an alternative route or direction. A term such as funnelling is much more useful for observing one's own behaviour than it is for analysing other people's behaviour . . .

Although of increasing specificity, funnelling questions all have the same intention, namely to get the pupil to see what the teacher sees. Their purpose is to focus attention. If in the midst of interacting with pupils the teacher becomes aware of funnelling, of being driven by 'guess what's in my mind', there is an opportunity to pause, and to choose to continue or to back off or to indicate more directly to pupils the point of focus.

Focusing questions often arise in interactions to which Vygotsky's (1978) notion of the *zone of proximal development* applies. For example, when pupils are working on a challenging task, the teacher may support their efforts by keeping track of the major goals, so that pupils can attend to the details. The following questions:

What was the question?

What are you trying to do now?

Does that calculation seem to be giving the sort of answer you expect?

are all of this type, intended to pull pupils out of the details and to focus their attention on some global aspect. A teacher might use them to find out what the pupil is doing, so that the question helps both teacher and pupil to refocus. Such questions also serve to illustrate the way an internal mathematical-monitor might work. In the midst of a calculation, experts may find themselves asking 'Is this the right calculation?' Their internal monitors are relatively well developed. By way of contrast, a novice may be so deeply embedded in the calculation that he keeps on struggling, getting deeper and deeper into a mire, without any internal monitor to make him pause and step back from what he is doing to get an overall picture. Vygotsky was convinced that the only way such a monitor will develop is through social interactions with others whose monitors are active.

Focusing is a two-way activity. Teachers as experts are likely to be aware of connections, details and processes which the pupils do not see, but pupils are often aware of other features of questions and tasks, and it behoves a teacher to be sensitive to pupils' focus of attention and to try to enter that focus some of the time, as in the explanatory mode of the previous section.

Rehearsing

It is a common and natural part of teaching to ask questions which test pupils' knowledge, memory or awareness. For example:

What do we call a six-sided shape?

What do you have to remember when using a protractor?

How do you round a number to one decimal place?

Here the teacher certainly knows the answer, but is trying to get the pupils to *rehearse* the answers for themselves. In *Maths Talk* (Mathematical Association, 1987) this is described as *checking up* and contrasted with *exploratory* questioning. It may be enough that pupils rehearse the words in their heads, though usually teachers like someone to give an answer so that everyone gets confirmation. Unfortunately this often has the effect that only the person answering pays much attention to the answer! At the beginning of a lesson, it is easy to want to 'just rehearse some of the ideas from last time' and to get caught up in a sequence of laconic, even sullen, responses from pupils. A large proportion of teacher questions are of the 'going over old ground' type. Rehearsal of terms and techniques is one good way to internalize ideas, to begin to employ them to express thoughts rather than simply to repeat memorized phrases. But rehearsal need not always be initiated by questions.

For example, the teacher can weave a story about animals or people based on ideas on a collection of cards with mathematical terms and objects on them. Pupils can then make up their own story or even tell a collective story. In primary classrooms, such stories are likely to be about animals, with the teacher providing structural elements such as teddy bears of different sizes, wiggly worms of different lengths, and other stuffed animals, which need to be measured for clothes and food requirements as in squirrels checking their supply of nuts (and so needing to count them) and so on (Mathematical Association, 1987). . . .

Ainley (1987) points out that asking questions to which one already knows the answer is a cultural phenomenon associated with the European idea of school teaching. Aboriginal children in Australia come from a culture in which it is considered ill mannered to ask a direct question, so to ask a question to which one already knows the answer is thought to be bizarre! Constant questioning and extending the limits of knowledge of younger people may be typical of middle-class interaction patterns, rather than endemic to society as a whole.

And yet it is hard to imagine not asking questions which stimulate pupils to rehearse, to reconstruct what they know, in the sense of Dewey. Where pupils perceive questions as testing rather than as opportunities for rehearsing, for 'explaining to themselves' but out loud in the presence of others, they may be confined by tensions and concerns about getting things right rather than being open to opportunities to get things not quite right and then to modify and correct them. Rehearsing need not be a burden but, in parallel with the bad press which exposition has received, getting pupils to exercise new techniques or ideas on examples is sometimes thought to be incompatible with an investigative approach to mathematics. In order to be able to reconstruct ideas from their own experience, pupils need opportunities to rehearse those ideas, to try to explain things to others. They also need to automate techniques and this can be done both on routine exercises and through explorations which call upon those techniques. For example, board games which involve pupils in counting serve to exercise counting while attention is focused on the game; trying to find a quadratic expression with given roots or whose roots have a given sum and product serves to exercise factoring while attention is directed toward a larger goal.

The widespread popularity of Trivial Pursuit, Mastermind and similar quizzes, attests to the challenge that some people get from a series of testing questions. It is an opportunity for them to rehearse what they know, in public, so it must be possible to set up similar conditions in classrooms. But testing can gain the upper hand and start to drive teaching, so that the teacher and then the pupils focus on what will be in the test, not on encountering the subject matter.

Enquiring

A third form of questioning is called by some, the 'true' or 'genuine' question where information is genuinely sought. For example:

> What were you thinking of when you wrote that down? (Referring to something in a piece of pupil work.)

> How did you get that?

> Can you put something on the paper lid so that you can remember how many beans are in it?

However, genuineness depends as much on the teacher's intention as it does on the words used. Most of the examples above can be interpreted as focusing or as rehearsal or as some form of classroom control, rather than as genuine enquiry. For example, if a teacher asks a pupil:

> What do you see in the picture?

The intention could be a genuine enquiry, meaning:

> I am interested in what you see and I cannot know unless you tell me.

When the teacher is seeking information the question-situation can be labelled as *enquiring*. To stimulate pupils to enquire, it is at least useful, if not essential, to provide a model of enquiring. Simulating interest is not enough because pupils will soon see through any pretence. Although it is not always easy to remain in a state of genuine enquiry about the mathematical content of some pupil's work, it is possible to be genuinely interested in how pupils are thinking, in how they express themselves, in what they see in their heads. Teachers who are evidently interested in their pupils are more likely to generate and support an enquiring attitude in them.

The trouble with using questions to enquire is that even a question such as 'What do you see in the picture?' could be intended to, or interpreted as an attempt to focus attention without being directive:

I have something in mind that I see. Do you see it too?

or even to test:

You are supposed to be attuned to seeing what I am seeing. Are you?

As with other forms of questioning, it is the follow-up reactions which signal both to teacher and pupil what sort of an interaction is intended.

The adjective 'genuine' is unfortunate because in a classroom questions are part of a power structure in which the teacher's aim is to evaluate the pupil's understanding so as to be of further assistance and also because it implies that other forms of question are fake, misleading or in some way of lesser value. Some people use the term 'genuine' as a value judgment, implying that all questions should or could be 'genuine'. A question is not rendered fake or 'ungenuine' simply because it is deployed for rehearsal or focusing purposes. All three forms of questioning have their place in classroom practice. A particular form of questioning is problematic only if teacher and pupils are unclear or at odds about what sort of questioning is taking place. If pupils are in the habit of interpreting all teacher questions as *testing*, then work has to be done to show them that there are indeed other opportunities being offered, other types of questioning.

Summary

It has been suggested that teacher–pupil interactions involve a variety of forms of telling and asking. A pedagogy based solely on exposition ('This is what it's about'), example ('This is how you do it') and exercises ('Now you practise it') is no more and no less deadening than a pedagogy based solely on exploration ('Here's an activity to get started on') and writing up ('Write about what you did and what you found out'). As with telling people things, asking questions is only problematic when questioner or questioned misconstrues what the intentions of the questioner are; when it is assumed that questions asked become genuine questions, which evoke a considered response rather than simply a reaction. When pupils interpret all questions as testing, as seeking a correct answer, they are likely to focus on getting or giving the correct answer and this will inhibit the establishment of a conjecturing atmosphere.

It is natural for reactions to what pupils say to become habitual and automatic but this reduces the opportunities to respond freshly and to see what pupils are really thinking. Labelling pupils by their reactions can produce habitual responses in them.

REFERENCES

Ainley, J. (1987) 'Telling questions', *Mathematics Teaching*, 118: 24–6.

Bauersfeld, H. (1993) 'Theoretical perspectives on interaction in the mathematics classroom', in R. Biehler, R. Scholz, R. Straßher and B. Winkelman (eds) *Didacties of Mathematics as a Scientific Discipline*, Dordrecht: Kluwer.

Department of Education and Science (DES) (1982) *Mathematics Counts*, London: HMSO (the Cockcroft Report).

Holt, J. (1964) *How Children Fail*, Harmondsworth: Penguin.

Mathematical Association (1987) *Maths Talk*, Mathematical Association/Stanley Thorne.

Mehan, H. (1986) ' "What time is it Denise?": asking known information questions in classroom discourse', in M. Hammersley (ed.) *Case Studies in Classroom Research*, Milton Keynes: Open University Press.

Vygotsky, L.S. (1978) *Mind in Society: The Development of Higher Psychological Processes*, Cambridge, MA: Harvard University Press.

Part V

Approaches to knowledge in the future curriculum?

Chapter 22

Introduction

Patricia Murphy

What of the future for the subject-based curriculum? There remains much concern about balance in the school curriculum, what it means and how to achieve it. Time allocation via timetables can, as Thomas (Chapter 2) notes, be the 'single means of prescribing and analysing the curriculum'. Such an approach can lead to subjects being viewed in isolation to the detriment of children's learning. Yet timetables can be organized in numerous ways depending on how learning is seen to occur. Underlying the current emphasis on subjects in the primary curriculum is a belief that 'children learn best when use is made of separate subject teaching' (Pascall, 1993). However, such beliefs have not been justified by evidence nor indeed is 'best' ever specified. HMI publications (Aspects of Primary Education), on the other hand, have demonstrated that topic work or integrated work can be powerful vehicles for children's learning. However, such an approach has been brought into disrepute and blame apportioned to teachers and teacher educators. This has led to a concern about teachers' subject knowledge which resulted, in the UK, in a series of funded INSET programmes aimed at teaching teachers about subjects. What is absent from the debate about the primary curriculum and its implementation is any examination of what *kind of knowledge* should be aimed for in primary education. This understanding is essential before decisions can be made about how best to achieve it. Statements of learning objectives which begin 'understands that . . .' 'knows about . . .' say nothing about what understanding and knowing mean.

The final part of the book looks at this. One of the key messages that emerges from the texts is the importance of the tasks which are selected to achieve successful learning. The kinds of tasks that foster successful learning can be located in numerous forms of curriculum organization. However, the need to ensure that learning crosses the boundary between school and community suggests that using a variety of approaches in a flexible way is most appropriate. Yet this will only enable progress for teachers and children if the choice of tasks and their purposes, the ways of working in classrooms and the types of interventions teachers provide do match genuine learning objectives. To ensure this, teachers need to be able to analyse task demands and relate these to genuine learning outcomes rather than abstract entities of the kind found in most curricula guidance. The argument for curricula guidance of this kind is often premised on the need for continuity and progression in the curriculum. Yet, as earlier chapters show, continuity and progression rely much more on understanding the detail of progression in children's learning along dimensions of subject curricula.

In the first chapter of this part, Glaser provides an analysis of highly competent performance in domains. He argues that this is needed to better understand how to foster the progress of young people. He suggests that the key to experts' competence lies in the highly integrated structures of their knowledge. Glaser concludes from examining experts' performance in alien domains that general problem-solving skills are not applied in a decontextualized way but rather as a means of accessing both conceptual and procedural domain-specific knowledge. He argues that attempts to teach thinking skills or strategic knowledge in the abstract may well fail as a consequence. Glaser's analysis is particularly valuable as it is applied to both literacy practices and mathematical problem-solving.

Nisbet, in the next chapter, provides a rationale for teaching thinking. He describes the way individuals build 'frameworks of interpretation, modes of understanding and strategies of problem-solving through experience' which can be enhanced with appropriate teaching. He goes on to provide a thorough review of the field, noting the consensus that has emerged about the theories of learning that lie behind it. However, he also notes the absence of consensus about how best to teach thinking. He identifies two distinct approaches. The first focuses on teaching the skills and strategies of thinking in isolation, the second he refers to as the 'infusion approach'. In this approach, thinking is considered to be domain-specific in accordance with Glaser's view. Consequently, thinking and problem-solving are not taught in isolation from the domain, as it is recognized that specific domains of knowledge have characteristic models of thinking associated with them. For Nisbet the curriculum of the future has to pay attention to the teaching of thinking, and current trends suggest that an infusion approach to teaching is the most appropriate.

The final chapter by Brown *et al.* has prompted widespread comment both positive and negative. This is not unusual in ground-breaking research. The authors themselves state that their theory of learning is in its infancy. However, its influence is abundantly clear in many of the texts in this book. The chapter provides a view of what constitute domain knowledge and learning which as yet have not impacted on the school curriculum. The authors argue persuasively that if children are to acquire the conceptual tools of subject domains rather than inert knowledge they need to understand the culture of the domain and its practices. To achieve this, learners need to participate in *authentic* activities, i.e. activities which reflect the ordinary practices of the culture. This follows because learning, in the authors' view, is situated. Thus the activity in which knowledge is learned is an integral part of that knowledge. On the basis of this, the authors propose an approach to teaching and learning of cognitive apprenticeship, and argue for a new epistemology to inform curriculum development which begins with 'activity and perception that is embedded in the world'.

REFERENCE

Pascall, D. (1993) 'The curriculum's essential core', *Independent* 21 January: 15.

Chapter 23

Expert knowledge and the processes of thinking

Robert Glaser

Highly competent performance is intrinsically fascinating, regardless of whether we witness it in memory experts, quiz kids, Olympic players, medical diagnosticians, chess masters, or mathematicians and biophysicists. In the past 15 years or so, describing competence and the processes that underlie it has become a significant endeavour in the study of human cognition. The tactic in these studies has been to explore the well-established performances that proficient people display, which have developed over time, and the components and properties of knowledge and skill that characterize highly competent performance. The results of this work define objectives for human attainment – goals for learning that can inform teaching practices at all levels. Expertise is proficiency taken to its highest level, and understanding of the experts' hard-won knowledge and skill can be used to foster the novices' progress and, perhaps, to expand the proficiencies of experts themselves.

The seeds for work on expertise were sown in the widely cited Newell and Simon (1972) book, *Human problem solving*. Newell and Simon described the observations of Adrian de Groot, a famous Dutch chess master who compared chess masters' and novice chess players' accounts of their thinking as they confronted various chess problems (de Groot, 1965, 1966). De Groot's findings anticipated key ideas in our current understanding of the nature of expertise. Although de Groot was unsuccessful in attempting to distinguish stronger from weaker players' performances using various assessments of memory or facility with the general problem-solving heuristics, he succeeded in identifying a critical difference by asking them, after 5 second's viewing, to recall and reproduce the positions of chess pieces that would occur in a game. Experts reproduced the board layouts perfectly, but this ability was less apparent in weaker players. Pure memory capacity was not involved, for strong and weak players alike had trouble remembering randomly arranged layouts of chess pieces; rather, perceptual abilities and knowledge organization clearly were characteristic of highly competent players. Strong players automatically viewed particular configurations of pieces as laden with meaning: a given configuration suggested possible moves and helped the player anticipate the consequences of those moves.

The perceptual aspects of problem solving in chess seem to be crucial. Research that has followed up on de Groot's work has shown that chess masters recognize clusters of related pieces as familiar constellations and they store each cluster in memory as a single symbol or pattern. Less skilled players have to describe the board as a larger number of simpler patterns – hence, they cannot hold in memory all of the information required to reproduce a layout. When the same number of pieces is arranged in a scrambled pattern on the board, few of the resulting configurations are familiar even to grandmasters. They then need more symbols to describe the position than they can hold simultaneously in short-term memory – hence, their recall is as poor as weaker players'. Chess masters, thus, do not show greater memory capacity for chess pieces in general, but only for the board's instantiations of chess principles as they crop up in a game. The quantities of patterns demanded by their expertise are of a high order of magnitude. In the many years required to attain chess mastery, a player might be expected to acquire a 'vocabulary' of subpatterns comparable in extent to the verbal knowledge required to read English (Chase and Simon, 1973).

The study of expert/novice differences in other domains has deepened our appreciation of the significance of the experts' perceptions of patterns. This perceptiveness, we can now suggest, is one of the critical manifestations of experts' highly organized, integrated structures of knowledge. In electronics, for example, skilled technicians reconstructing symbolic drawings of circuit diagrams do so according to the functional nature of the elements in the circuit, such as amplifiers, rectifiers, and filters. Novice technicians, however, reconstruct the diagrams on the basis of the spatial proximity of the elements (Egan and Schwartz, 1979).

Expert radiologists' readings of x-rays show that the expert first builds a mental representation of possible abnormalities and that this representation guides the diagnosis and must satisfy tests of applicability before it is allowed to control viewing and interpretation. The expert works efficiently to reach a stage where an appropriate general model or schema guides the diagnosis. Less-expert interns do not confirm the applicability of the patterns they invoke, and an incomplete model may be triggered and control their efforts (Lesgold et al., 1988).

Like the chess results, such evidence shows that the expert in a domain takes in and uses information in *chunks* – in organizations and integrations of knowledge, or meaningful patterns – extremely rapidly. Whether the domain is chess configurations, functional interpretations of circuit diagrams, or representations of anatomical abnormalities in x-rays, the central underlying properties or meaningful deep structure of the situation is key to experts' perceptions, whereas the surface features and structural properties (such as proximity and literal descriptive aspects) organize the less-than-expert individual's perceptions.

This aspect of expertise has been investigated in studies of scientific problem solving. In experiments where novices and experts were asked to classify a set of elementary physics mechanics problems in terms of the requirements for solutions, the two groups tackled the task on entirely different bases. The novices used surface features to group rotation problems, inclined plane problems, or spring problems in their classifications. In contrast, the experts grouped problems that had little surface resemblance; they saw as similar problems that involved the principle of conservation of energy or Newton's second law. The experts were able to tie the surface features of problems to deeper principles, and inducing these principles was predictive of fast, efficient, and accurate methods of solution (Chi *et al.*, 1982).

Another observable difference between expert and novice problem solvers' performances is their pause-times for retrieving successive equations. Experts appear to invoke sets of equations; eliciting one equation activates rapid retrieval of related equations. Novices do not exhibit such chunking in setting up equations. It appears that, for experts, physics equations are stored in functional configurations, so that accessing one procedure leads to another (Larkin, 1979).

The results of research to date have made it clear that experts' knowledge structures play a critical role in their performances. Experts, as the studies mentioned indicate, have a great deal of domain-specific information, and this information is highly organized and conceptually integrated. This organized knowledge appears to account for the experts' capacities for rapid pattern recognition and categorization.

Co-ordinate with these abilities, experts in science and mathematics often make use of qualitative reasoning to approach a problem that will require quantitative solution. Expert physicists, for example, appear to exercise a form of *physical intuition* (Simon and Simon, 1978) prior to their retrieval of equations – that is, before they even consider calculations or specific solution procedures. In contrast, novices rush into quantitative manipulations and plug in formulas (Larkin *et al.*, 1980; McDermott and Larkin, 1978). This initial qualitative phase of problem solving is key in the investigation of expert performance.

One aspect of such qualitative analysis is the representation of a problem in terms of a *runnable mental model*. This model specifies the main causal connections of the components of a situation and, like other aspects of problem representation, has a formative influence on performance. For example, in a statics problem involving a ladder leaning against a wall, the mental model would probably include the ladder, the floor, the wall, and the points of contact, as well as gravity and the forces operating at points of contact. Once this kind of representation has been constructed in memory and the expert has a feel for the situation, the equations of equilibrium can be constructed readily (Simon and Simon, 1978).

Research on algebra students' initial representations of problems is revealing here. In confronting pseudo word-problems (i.e., problems about physically unrealizable situations), a few highly proficient students immediately perceived the incongruity in the problems (Paige and Simon, 1966). The rest proceeded to invoke equations before realizing that the solutions would be meaningless (e.g., a negative quantity would be obtained for the length of an object). The good solvers apparently constructed a representation that provided a basis for inferences about problem features and their relations that were not available from the problem statement. This model gave them a basis for questioning the problem content and monitoring applicability of solution procedures.

SIX GENERALIZATIONS

In general, then, experts' highly integrated structures of knowledge lie behind many salient features of their performances. Current understanding of expertise now allows a set of generalizations about its nature. The implications and impact of experts' knowledge are far reaching in shaping their thinking, as these generalizations indicate.

1. *Experts' proficiency is very specific.* The precision of experts' performances derives from the specialized knowledge that drives their reasoning. Specificity of performance is evidenced by the disruption of proficiency in instances where random or meaningless patterns or poorly structured problems are presented. Under these conditions, experts lose their rapid perceptual and representational ability and resort to general problem-solving strategies. It may be, however, that certain task domains are more generalizable than others, so that adults who are experts in applied mathematics or aesthetic design, or younger students who have learned measurement and quantitative concepts, have transferable forms of expertise. Nevertheless, competence in one domain is no guarantee of effectiveness in others.

2. *Experts perceive large, meaningful patterns.* These patterns guide experts' thinking in everyday working activities. Pattern recognition occurs so rapidly that it appears to take on the character of intuition. In contrast, the patterns that novices recognize are smaller, less articulated, more literal and surface-oriented, and far less related to abstracted principles. Like other aspects of experts' performance, this extraordinary representational ability depends on the organization of knowledge existing in memory.

3. *Experts' problem solving entails selective search of memory or use of general problem-solving tactics.* Whereas novices display a good deal of search and processing of a general nature, experts' fast-access pattern recognition

and representational capability facilitate approaches to problems that reduce the roles of these processes. Even where it can be assumed that experts and novices have similar cognitive capacities, the experts' performances have an efficiency that derives primarily from their knowledge being structured for retrieval, pattern recognition, and inferencing.

4. *Experts' knowledge is high procedural and goal-oriented.* In experts' highly structured knowledge base, concepts are bound to procedures and the rules and conditions for their application. This functional knowledge is closely tied to knowledge of the goal structure of a problem. Experts and novices may be equally competent at recalling small specific (multiple-choice type) items of domain-related information, but high-knowledge individuals far more readily relate these items of information in cause-and-effect sequences that link the goals and subgoals needed for problem solution.

5. *Experts' knowledge enables them to use self-regulatory processes with great skill.* Experts proficiently monitor their own problem-solving activities; they have the ability to step back, so to speak, at appropriate points, and observe their solution processes and the outcomes of their performances. Their self-awareness is also shown in their allocation of attention and their sensitivity to information feedback as they work. Use of self-regulatory processes sometimes slows experts as they initially encode a difficult problem, although they are faster problem solvers overall. Here, novices' reliance on surface features allows them speed initially.

6. *Experts' proficiency can be routinized or adaptive.* Competence is influenced by the task demands and by the conditions for work; thus, experts' attained proficiencies can be context-bound. Under some conditions, maybe most, their performances become routinized as well as efficient and accurate. Under others, experts develop the capability for *opportunistic planning,* which is manifested by their revising problem representations readily and accessing multiple possible interpretations of a situation. The conditions and demands of education and of work can foster combinations of highly competent routine and adaptive expertise.

A NOTE ON EXPERT PERFORMANCES IN UNFAMILIAR TERRITORY

The picture of expertise presented thus far does not take into account the competence (or perhaps the lack of competence) that experts demonstrate when they work at the frontiers of knowledge – when the problems they confront are from unfamiliar domains or are not well structured, so that patterns and solution procedures cannot readily be perceived.

Working such problems – which can be called *ill-structured problems* or *problems of discovery* – requires: (a) the resolution of open constraints; (b) decisions about imposing parameter values that are entailed in the problem presentation or conceptualization; (c) a search for analogies; and

(d) most importantly, pursuit of equivalents to the powerful principles that underlie solutions for well-structured or familiar problems. In these novel situations, the definition of subproblems for which patterns can be seen that enable particular approaches is a key step. The solver must invent an organization that synthesizes potential understandings – that is, the solver must come up with some representation or model as a basis for proceeding (Simon, 1973; Voss and Post, 1988).

What is of interest here is that, somewhat like novices, experts bring *general* problem-solving processes to bear. They do decompose an ill-structured problem into a better structured set of subproblems, but with greater facility than a novice would. They also are able to select parameter values for open constraints that lead to a possible meaningful solution by supplying testable candidate problem representations. In general, where problems do not yield to straightforward approaches, experts can usefully resort to analogies with systems they understand well and search for matches and mismatches. They may attempt to impose some model of the workings of another phenomenon on the problem at hand to try to understand how the model would behave in the new context. They may pose extreme-case arguments or construct simpler problems of a similar sort and bring those solutions to the original problem.

This use of general heuristics does not take on significance as a substitute for domain knowledge. On the contrary, general heuristics serve mostly in the attempt to gain access to domain knowledge that can be used for problem solution. In a sense, the use of general heuristics reflects the attempt to move ill-structured problems of discovery into the familiar domain where extant knowledge can be brought into play. Rather than using general heuristics in a decontextualized way – as free-floating interrogators of a situation – the expert uses them to make contact with available knowledge and the solution processes it might afford. The abstract use of general heuristics in courses on thinking skills or reasoning may not be successful for this reason.

EXPERTISE AND WRITING SKILL

As an illustration of how the properties of expertise interact, the domain of writing competence is interesting. An increasing amount of analysis is being undertaken on the nature of novice and expert writing. Writing is a skill that we must rely on in much of our schooling and working lives. It is a basic skill of educated people, yet involves, it seems, a neverending process of acquiring competence. Writing can be viewed as a form of domain-specific problem solving; through structuring and expressing our ideas in written texts, we think and learn to think in our fields. For these reasons, it is an apt arena in which to examine the interdependence of the various aspects of expert performance. Consider then the specificity, integrated knowledge, problem representation, task monitoring, and goal orientation of experts' performances in writing.

Specificity

Writing, in a fundamental way, requires linguistic knowledge, that is, a strong vocabulary; a good grasp of grammar and syntax; and an awareness of rhythm, voice, and figures of speech. The student, the poet, the playwright, and the novelist all develop this knowledge, more or less, as does the academician or scientist writing about research. The domain specificity of writing expertise is now widely acknowledged by teachers and educators. In an illuminating analysis of the import of this for education, David Bartholomae observed that:

> Every time a student sits down to write for us, he has to invent the university for the occasion – invent the university or a branch of it, that is, like history or anthropology, or economics, or biology. He has to learn to speak our language, to speak as we do, to try on the peculiar ways of knowing, selecting, evaluating, reporting, concluding, and arguing that define the discourse of our community. . . . [a student must learn] to work within fields where the rules governing the presentation of an example or the development of an argument are both distinct and (often), even to a professional, mysterious.
>
> (Bartholomae, 1985: 4)

Bartholomae pointed out that, while in introductory writing courses, students are concerned with university discourse in its most generalized form. Expertise in writing, in the longer term, requires students to locate themselves in disciplinary forms of discourse that are not immediate accessible. Those who can write reasonably coherent expositions in one domain, say, political science, may be incoherent when faced with crafting an essay in sociology or philosophy. This is not unlike the loss manifested by experts when they are required to operate outside of their disciplines.

Integrated knowledge

Writing expertise requires substantial declarative and procedural knowledge. Students who are novice writers in a domain are not necessarily inept thinkers; they are rather insufficiently familiar not only with information about specialized topics but also with the specific conventions or techniques of expository discourse – the procedures for describing and arguing for an interpretation or for presenting claims and counterclaims. The patterns of reasoning that we expect in academic writing are not inherent in our thinking; they are conventional, learnable forms of argumentation and rhetoric.

For example, student writers must learn to support the generalizations on which their reasoning hinges. As novices, they may not be aware that they must explicate how examples and illustrations support generalizations. Proficient writing requires sophisticated forms of this sensitivity to grounding generalizations, interpretations, and claims. Writing knowledge also includes responsiveness to the intended audience; proficient writers shape their prose differently for specialists or for informed generalists. These forms of writing knowledge are rather specific to the task and comprise the integrated knowledge that underlies proficiency.

Representation

In writing, the initial representation of the task is highly influential (Flower et al., 1986). The individual's perceptions of the aims of a piece of writing largely determine the nature of subsequent revision, and revision, of course, is where the real work goes on. Perspectives on the task can be of a local and shallow nature or of a global and more meaningful nature. Consequently, inexperienced and experienced writers make different kinds of changes in the course of revision. Novices typically focus on the conventions and rules of writing, but more advanced students make many changes, including a significant number that affect the text's meaning. Here, again, surface as opposed to deeper problem representations characterize novices' performances: Novice writers work on surface features, using word and punctuation deletion and addition as important strategies, experienced writers conceptualize the task as a wholistic enterprise that may require elaborating the treatment of a point, insuring the effectiveness of argument structure, and estimating the utility of shifts in voice as well as checking grammar and punctuation.

As noted, expert/novice studies in various domains have shown that experts arrive at solutions quickly in problem-solving tasks, although they often appear to spend more time in the initial process of problem representation than novices. Studies of revision suggest that novice writers do not approach this task as a time-consuming, recursive one. They made little use of their drafts, making most of their changes as they produce the text; they hardly reread their papers before they begin a new version. Experts spend a significant portion of their time rereading their drafts in the attempt to develop more complete representation of the problems that must be attacked, and thus this aspect of revision is one to which instruction should attend (Bridwell, 1980; Flower et al., 1986).

Representation of the problems to be attacked in revision can be accomplished in two ways. First, there is a monitoring and evaluation process that builds up a representation that carries with it information and strategies for solving the problem. Second, there is a more immediate categorization or pattern recognition process that occurs quickly. In the first kind of representation (Flower *et al.*, 1986) experienced writers monitor their progress; they observe the features of their draft, search the possible writing strategies in their repertoires, and focus on an appropriate goal, for example, decide whether to work at the level of the whole text or at a more syntactic proofreading level. A representation of the task is generated from this interplay between the analysis of text features and the student's store of knowledge about revision strategies and currently attainable goals.

The second kind of representation requires rapid categorization of a particular task to be accomplished. Like experts in other areas, the good writer must learn to recognize a wide array of patterns. Recognition of a familiar pattern brings forth the strategies and goals applicable to it, just as board patterns do for chess masters and x-ray patterns do for expert radiologists. Proficient writers, because of their stores of knowledge, employ problem classifications that go beyond superficial features to the deeper structure of text meaning and presentation. As noted, this rapid categorization of situations takes on the character of intuitive performance.

Task monitoring and goal orientation

In carrying out revision, experts show a significant sensitivity to task demands and to features of prose; they match their performances to the goals entailed in their representation of the task. Sometimes, a subgoal at a particular level is chosen because a more complex or complete goal is not attainable at the moment. This may be done to simplify the task at hand, to get on with it, so that more complex goals can be eventually attained. At other times, the demands of a task are such that proficient writers see no reason for working at a complex level when a goal requiring less level of effort will suffice, and their technique is adjusted accordingly. Inexperienced writers are less facile in generating goals suitable to a portion of a task or in adjusting to the task required. Their subgoal analysis is superficial, with the result that changes appropriate to the text are never addressed. Thus, analysis of subgoals of revision should be a significant focus of instruction.

Writing competence, like other forms of expertise, probably ranges along a continuum from routine or conventional expertise to adaptive expertise. Routine experts are outstanding in terms of speed, accuracy, and automaticity of performance; they construct mental models convenient and efficient for performing their tasks, but they may lack adaptability when faced with new kinds of problems. Repeated application of a procedure, with little variation, can lead to routine expertise. Adaptive expertise requires variation and is encouraged by playful situations and educational settings and experiences where understanding and transfer are valued along with efficient performance (Hatano and Inagaki, 1986).

IMPLICATIONS FOR TEACHING AND RESEARCH

What do the accruing findings on expertise generally suggest for teaching and designing experiences for students that will enable them to attain high levels of competence in the various domains of knowledge? Four points seem essential: the nature of practice, the development of self-monitoring and of principled performance, and the social context of learning.

The nature of practice

Obviously, proficiency is a matter of experience and practice requiring highly motivated learners who spend long hours and do the hard work necessary. But there is more to practice than motivation. Practice, as it comes about in the usual course of training, is not necessarily very efficient. On the basis of our knowledge of the specific aspects of competence and expertise, we are now able to find ways to compress or shortcut experience, or at least to present experience in more systematic fashion so that its impact is optimized. These findings suggest that practice should focus on situations where there are complex patterns to be perceived, and where recognition of these patterns implies particular moves and procedures for solution. An organized sequence of increasingly complex forms of pattern recognition tasks, associated with their procedural meaning, might be developed in sequences of instruction. For example, such experiences have been designed for technical training, including components of the job of air traffic control (Schneider, 1985), for geometry (Anderson *et al.*, 1985), and for electronic trouble shooting (Lesgold *et al.*, 1988).

A consideration in designing practice is its resulting in automaticity for some components of competence, that is, in the ability to perform certain actions with little conscious thought. If practice produces this automaticity, then an individual has greater memory processing capability available to engage in parts of the task that require conscious thought, such as re-representing a problem or self-monitoring performance. Automatic processes are very apparent in competent performers; skilled readers can decode words with little conscious thought and, as a result, have greater cognitive space left over for interpreting the meaning of a text. The point here is that practice must continue until certain aspects of behaviour become effortless when carried on as part of a larger exercise. Situations that assess students' progress toward some proficient performance, therefore, must not test component skills separately because, although performed adequately when tested by themselves, taken in combination, some components might interfere with other aspects of the larger task (Glaser, 1981).

The value of practice can be increased, if we see it as something to be carefully designed. Much learning in elementary physics is thought to take place as students practice by solving the problems at the end of textbook chapters. These are usually done as homework assignments that may later be illustrated on the blackboard in the classroom. But, the opportunity for sustained, guided practice – practice in which the student sees the principles that relate groups of problems and links them to the procedures required for those problems – is rarely afforded. To optimize teaching, we need to design practice in which learners are encouraged to search for the important connections between principles and procedures (Chi *et al.*, 1989).

Self-monitoring

Because self-monitoring – the ability to observe and, if necessary, reshape one's performance – is a hallmark of expertise, this skill should be emphasized in instruction. The work of Alan Schoenfeld (1985) has opened up new ideas for teaching self-monitoring heuristics in the context of learning mathematical problem solving. Heuristics are taught in a contextualized way that makes contact with the students' mathematics knowledge base. One aspect of Schoenfeld's work involves the teaching and demonstration of control or management strategies that make explicit such processes as generating alternative courses of action, evaluating which course can be carried out and whether it can be managed in the time available, and assessing progress. The students learn to monitor and direct their activity by asking such questions as: What am I doing now? Am I making progress? What else could I be doing instead? Through demonstrations and practice, students focus on critical decisions and actions at strategic levels as well as on the rote specifics of the solution.

Furthermore, Schoenfeld has directly confronted the issue of imparting an appropriate belief system about the interpretive nature of mathematical problem solving. During the process of learning mathematics, students begin to realize that searches often come to dead ends; exploration of possible heuristics and different paths does not guarantee solution. He challenges his students to find difficult problems for him to solve, so they can observe his own struggles and floundering, which legitimate students' floundering as well. Students begin to realize that mathematics requires neither merely recognizing principles, nor merely applying procedures, but, rather, a creative interpretive process of exploration and reasoning. Student adoption of this view seems especially helpful when problem representations are not readily constructed, and revisions of equations and procedures are needed so that adequate solutions can be carried out.

Principled performance

Education also must emphasize that the most salient and ubiquitous hallmark of expertise – whether in chess, writing, science, or mathematics – is principled performance. Performance takes place not only with well-learned procedural knowledge, but also in a space for thought – in the context of a model, a theory, or a principle that guides performance through constraints and structures for inference, and allows competent individuals to avoid disconnected trial and error (Greeno and Simon, 1988). This permits understanding of one's performance, the swift and graceful recovery from error, and the seizing of opportunities for more elegant and precise solution and discovery. Expertise then becomes more than a matter of sheer efficiency and, as it is acquired, knowledge becomes an object for questioning and learning from experience and, thereby, is reorganized to enable new thought and action. An essential aim of instruction and the design of curriculum materials should be to enable the student to acquire structured knowledge along with procedural skill. Too often the fragmented bits of information supplied by textbook and teaching presentations do not encourage students to construct organized knowledge usable for thinking and principled performance.

The social context of learning

A fourth aspect of cognition that should be emphasized as central to change in educational practice turns us away from internal cognition alone to the influence of the situation in which learning occurs. Cognitive activity in school and outside is inseparable from a cultural milieu. The acquisition of competent performance takes place in an interpersonal system in which participation and guidance from others influences the understanding of new situations and the management of problem solving that leads to learning. Certain theories of human development have emphasized the social genesis of learning (Vygotsky, 1978). Conceptual development involves internalizing cognitive activities experienced in social settings, and many studies have pointed out the motivational variables involved in shared responsibility for thinking that enhance learning in group settings (Brown and Campione, in press; Brown and Palincsar, 1989).

From a cognitive perspective, a group can serve several roles. First, it extends the locus of self-monitoring activity by providing triggers for cognitive dissatisfaction outside the individual. An audience monitors individual thinking, opinions, and beliefs, and can elicit explanations that clarify points of difficulty. Moreover, the learner's exposure to alternative points of view challenges his or her initial understanding. In addition, with the help of advanced peers or a teacher who provide supportive scaffolding, the collaborative group maintains a mature version of a target task. By sharing it, a complex task is made more manageable, yet is not oversimplified. Each learner contributes what he or she can and gains from the contributions of those more expert. In this context, to use Vygotsky's term, a zone of proximal development is created where learners perform within their range of competence while being assisted in realizing their potential levels of higher performance.

A most salient aspect in a social context for learning is the elevation of thinking to an overt, observable status. As students participate in group roles, various problem-solving procedures, strategies of reasoning, and techniques for accomplishing goals become apparent. This reality is to be compared with classroom learning where thinking may be rarely an observable enterprise and opportunities for its shaping through external influences are limited. Thus, school instruction might well consider how teaching practice can make apparent the forms of student's thinking, in ways that can be observed, transmitted, discussed, reflected on, and moved toward more competent performance and dispositions for reasoning.

In conclusion, it should be emphasized that, for the most part, investigations of the nature of expertise have emphasized the characteristics of the performance system and not the learning and developmental processes through which performance is attained. Research must now turn to the study of conditions for learning. Undoubtedly, the significant contributions of the methods and the results produced by the analysis of complex human competence will contribute to this work. Investigation of learning processes in a pursuit of well-specified principles for instruction are accelerating (Glaser and Bassok, 1989). Significant studies are under way of instructional programs that facilitate the transition from declarative to more proceduralized functional knowledge (Anderson *et al.*, 1984; Lewis *et al.*, 1988), the use of self-regulatory processes that foster learning and understanding (Brown and Palincsar, 1989; Collins *et al.*, 1989), and the processes of knowledge interrogation that contribute to the development of the structured knowledge that enables expert problem-solving (Clancey, 1986; White and Frederiksen, 1986). With the expansion of experimental programmes that are grounded in well-articulated instructional principles, both theoretical and applied work on learning will gain in precision and effectiveness. With studies of expertise as the groundwork, a science of learning can make the path to proficiency one that is well marked and can be more readily followed than ever before.

ACKNOWLEDGEMENT

Preparation of this article was sponsored in part by the national Center for Student Learning at the Learning Research and Development Center of the University of Pittsburgh. The national Center for Student Learning is funded by the Office of Educational Research and Improvement of the U.S. Department of Education.

REFERENCES

Anderson, J. R., Boyle, C. F. and Yost, G. (1985) 'The geometry tutor', *Proceedings of the International Joint Conference in Artificial Intelligence*, Los Angeles.

Anderson, J. R., Farrell, R. and Sauers, R. (1984) 'Learning to program in LISP', *Cognitive Science*, 8: 87–129.

Bartholomae, D. (1985) 'Inventing the University', in M. Rose (ed.), *When a Writer Can't Write: Studies in Writer's Block and Other Composing–Process Problems*, New York: Guildford Press.

Bridwell, L. S. (1980) 'Revising strategies in twelfth grade students' transactional writing', *Research in the Teaching of English*, 14: 197–222.

Brown, A. and Campione, J. (in press) 'Communities of learning and thinking, or a context by any other name', *Human Development*.

Brown, A. L. and Palincsar, A. (1989) 'Guided, cooperative learning and individual knowledge acquisition', in L. B. Resnick (ed.), *Knowing and Learning: Essays in Honor of Robert Glaser*, Hillsdale, NJ: Lawrence Erlbaum Associates.

Chase, W. G. and Simon, H. A. (1973) 'Perception in chess', *Cognitive Psychology*, 4: 55–81.

Chi, M. T. H., Bassok, M., Lewis, M. W., Reimann, P. and Glaser, R. (1989) 'Self-explanations: how students study and use examples in learning to solve problems', *Cognitive Science*, 13: 145–82.

Chi, M. T. H., Glaser, R. and Rees, E. (1982) 'Expertise in problem solving', in R. J. Sternberg (ed.), *Advances in the Psychology of Human Intelligence*, Hillsdale, NJ: Lawrence Erlbaum Associates.

Clancey, W. J. (1986) 'From Guidon to Neomycin and Hercules in twenty short lessons: ONR final report 1979–1985', *AI Magazine*, 7: 40–60.

Collins, A., Brown, J. S. and Newman, S. E. (1989) 'Cognitive apprenticeship: teaching the crafts of reading, writing and mathematics', in L. B. Resnick (ed.), *Knowing, Learning, and Instruction: Essays in Honor of Robert Glaser*, Hillsdale, N.J.: Lawrence Erlbaum Associates.

de Groot, A. (1965) *Thought and Choice in Chess*, The Hague: Mouton.

—— (1966) 'Perception and memory versus thought: some old ideas and recent findings', in B. Kleinmuntz (ed.), *Problem Solving*, New York: Wiley.

Egan, D. and Schwartz, B. (1979) 'Chunking in recall of symbolic drawings', *Memory and Cognition*, 7: 149–58.

Flower, L., Hayes, J. R., Carey, L., Schriver, K. and Stratman, J. (1986) 'Detection, diagnosis, and the strategies of revision', *College Composition and Communications*, 37: 16–55.

Glaser, R. (1981) 'The future of testing: a research agenda for cognitive psychology and psychometrics', *American Psychologist*, 36: 923–36.

Glaser, R. and Bassok, M. (1989) 'Learning theory and the study of instruction', *Annual Review of Psychology*, 40: 631–66.

Greeno, J. G. and Simon, H. A. (1988) 'Problem solving and reasoning', in R. C. Atkinson, R. Hermstein, G. Lindzey and R.D. Luce (eds), *Stevens' Handbook of Experimental Psychology*, New York: Wiley.

Hatano, G. and Inagaki, K. (in press) 'Sharing cognition through collective comprehension activity', in L. B. Resnick (ed.), *Socially Shared Cognition*, New York: W. H. Freeman.

Larkin, J. H. (1979) 'Processing information for effective problem solving', *Engineering Education*, 70: 285–88.

Larkin, J., McDermott, J., Simon, D. P., and Simon, H. A. (1980) 'Models of competence in solving physics problems', *Cognitive Science*, 4: 317–45.

Lesgold, A., Rubinson, H., Feltovich, P., Glaser, R., Klopfer, D. and Wang, Y. (1988) 'Expertise in a complex skill: diagnosing x-ray pictures', in M. T. H. Chi, R. Glaser, and M. Farr (eds), *The Nature of Expertise*, Hillsdale, NJ: Lawrence Erlbaum Associates.

Lewis, M. W., Milson, R. and Anderson, J. R. (1988) 'Designing an intelligent authoring system for high school mathematics ICAI: the teacher apprentice project', in G. Kearsley (ed.), *Artificial Intelligence and Instruction: Applications and Methods*, New York: Addison-Wesley.

McDermott, J. and Larkin, J.H. (1978) 'Re-representing textbook physics problems', in *Proceedings of the 2nd National Conference of the Canadian Society for Computational Studies of Intelligence*, Toronto: University of Toronto Press.

Newell, A. and Simon, H. A. (1972) *Human Problem Solving*, Englewood Cliffs, NJ: Prentice-Hall.

Paige, J. M. and Simon, H. A. (1966) 'Cognitive processes in solving algebra work problems', in B. Kleinmuntz (ed.), *Problem Solving*, New York: Wiley.

Schneider, W. (1985) 'Training high performance skills: fallacies and guidelines', *Human Factors*, 27: 285–300.

Schoenfield, A. H. (1985) *Mathematical Problem Solving*, New York: Academic Press.

Simon, D. P. and Simon, H. A. (1978) 'Individual differences in solving physics problems', in R. Siegler (ed.), *Children's Thinking: What Develops?*, Hillsdale, NJ: Lawrence Erlbaum Associates.

Simon, H.A. (1973) 'The structure of ill-structured problems', *Artificial Intelligence*, 4: 181–201.

Voss, J. F. and Post, T. A. (1988) 'On the solving of ill-structured problems', in M. T. H. Chi, R. Glaser and M. Farr (eds), *The Nature of Expertise*, Hillsdale, NJ: Lawrence Erlbaum Associates.

Vygotsky, L. S. (1978) *Mind in Society: The Development of Higher Psychological Processes*, Cambridge, MA: Harvard University Press.

White, B. Y. and Frederiksen, J. R. (1986) *Progressions of Quantitative Models as a Foundation for Intelligent Learning Environments* (Tech. Rep. No. 6277), Cambridge, MA: Bolt, Beranek & Newman.

Chapter 24

The thinking curriculum

John Nisbet

The argument of this chapter is that the concept of 'the thinking curriculum' is winning long-overdue recognition in education. A 'thinking curriculum' is one which involves learners actively in thinking, which abhors 'inert ideas' (Whitehead, 1932) and which aims to foster transferable thinking skills:

> Culture is activity of thought, and receptiveness to beauty and humane feeling. Scraps of information have nothing to do with it. A merely well-informed man is the most useless bore on God's earth . . . In training a child to activity of thought, above all things we must beware of what I will call 'inert ideas' – that is to say, ideas that are merely received into the mind without being utilised, or tested, or thrown into fresh combinations . . . Education with inert ideas is not only useless: it is, above all things, harmful . . . Let us now ask how in our system of education we are to guard against this mental dry rot.
>
> (1932: 1–2)

Can we teach thinking? Should thinking play an important part in school learning? Most teachers (and possibly most psychologists) would be hesitant about the first of these questions, but would give a confident 'yes' to the second. In higher education, the recent MacFarlane Report (1992) has reminded us all of the importance of 'deep learning', learning which involves a construction of meaning and understanding and the transformation of knowledge, and the limitations of 'surface learning' which aims at memorizing and the reproduction of knowledge (Entwistle, Appendix A in the MacFarlane Report, 1992). In primary education, 'rote learning' has been a term of criticism ever since the end of Payment by Results in 1890; and the progressive education movement throughout the 20th Century has encouraged pupils' active involvement in learning. The secondary school examination system since at least the 1920s has striven (with questionable success) to develop modes of assessment which would test understanding and defeat the strategy of learning by heart; and the current drive for 'flexible learning' emphasizes a problem-solving approach and pupils taking more responsibility for their own learning (Employment Department, 1992; Tomlinson and Kilner, 1992).

But the notion that we can teach people to think still encounters cautious scepticism. Partly this is because of vagueness on how it might be done. The scepticism is also a residue of the discrediting of the concept of 'transfer of training' – the belief dominating educational provision in the 19th and early 20th centuries – that the study of mathematics, philosophy and the classical languages of Latin and Greek provided a 'training of the mind', which would prepare people for higher posts in the Civil Service and enable them to rule India and other outposts of empire. Another main reason for scepticism about teaching thinking is the powerfully resistant concept of 'intelligence' as an inborn quality of mind which determines our capacity for learning and thinking. On this theory (hopefully outmoded now), educational achievement was the product of intelligence and motivation: if pupils failed to learn, they were urged to 'try harder' and if this failed they were judged to be of low intelligence and were shunted on to a less demanding educational track.

The teaching of techniques of study, learning to learn, has won general acceptance nowadays. Virtually all secondary schools, and some primary schools, include guidance on study methods in their curriculum. However, study methods are often limited to strategies for coping with the demands of the system, preparing to pass examinations, or aids to memorizing, or sound advice on organizing one's learning. Few would claim that this is teaching thinking. Teaching thinking implies more generalizable or trans-ferable skills and procedures. While the value of these is undeniable, there remains some doubt as to whether these can be taught and, if so, how.

THE CASE FOR TEACHING THINKING

The argument for teaching thinking can be expressed briefly as follows. Thinking is a process which we all have to learn. We build up our own personal frameworks of interpretation, modes of understanding and strategies of problem solving, through experience. A rich culture like ours offers many of these frameworks ready-made, in language, mathematics and science, for example; but each of us has to make these frameworks our own. Even apparently simple activities like perception and reading involve a search for meaning. There are skills and strategies in thinking which we build from experience; the mastery of these skills need not be left to chance – they are too important for that. Some people are quicker than others at acquiring these thinking skills; but (as with study skills) appropriate teaching can help all of us to improve our competence. As a result, there has been an explosion of interest worldwide in the teaching of thinking. This takes the form either of specific programmes which provide practice in selected strategies (over 100 are currently on the market in the USA), or of restructured curricula and methods which are designed to promote and practise thinking and reasoning within the traditional curriculum subjects. The changing social and economic demands of our modern way of life oblige our educational systems to aim at broader competences than the traditional 'basics'. While such things as memorizing and calculating are still important capacities, a new range of cognitive skills is called for to meet the demands of this changing context.

A REVIEW OF THE FIELD

It is difficult to establish an originator or a date for the emergence of what has become a worldwide movement. Selecting only four of the pioneers, we can illustrate the diversity of the field from the start. Edward De Bono founded his Cognitive Research Trust (CoRT) in 1969, for creative and lateral thinking, but it was in 1976 that his book, *Teaching Thinking*, was published (one of 41 books which he has published on the topic, in 26 languages). Reuven Feuerstein, in Israel, is another of the earliest workers in the field: his first concern was with remedying cognitive deficiencies in slow learners, which led to his Instrumental Enrichment Program (Feuerstein *et al.*, 1980). Matthew Lipman was a founder of the 'Philosophy for Children' movement: his first book, *Harry Stottlemeier's Discovery*, was published in 1974. In 1977, Robert Sternberg published his 'componential analysis' of human abilities, intelligence, information processing and analogical reasoning, which was the basis of his Componential Training Program.

By the mid-1980s, American development in the field far outstripped work elsewhere. Excellent research reviews by Presseisen (1986, 1987), Resnick (1987) and Nickerson (1988) are still topical. *Teaching Thinking Skills: Theory and Practice*, edited by Baron and Sternberg (1987), and the ASCD (Association for Supervision and Curriculum Development) book, *Dimensions of Thinking* (Marzano *et al.*, 1988) are major texts. Lipman's work is developed in the journal, *Thinking*, which is published quarterly. Richard Paul, at the Center for Critical Thinking and Moral Critique at Sonoma State University, California, has developed the concept of critical thinking, the theme of an annual conference which attracts a large international participation; his series of three *Critical Thinking Handbooks* (Paul *et al.*, 1989) contains extensive examples of classroom workshop exercises.

In Europe, the Organization for Economic Co-operation and Development (OECD) held an international conference in Paris in 1989 on 'Learning to think: thinking to learn' (Maclure and Davies, 1991) which attracted delegates from 22 countries. One of the most vigorous research communities is in The Netherlands (see, for example, Boekhaerts, 1988; Simons, 1989); and in Belgium, at the Centre for Instructional Psychology at the University of Leuven, De Corte (1990) has put his work on LOGO and arithmetic into the wider framework of 'powerful learning environments for the acquisition of problem-solving skills' (p. 12). In France, the traditional curriculum of language and philosophy is seen by many as an effective route to teaching thinking; but the Ministry of Education also sponsored a training agency, Initiative et Formation, to implement the ideas of De La Garanderie (see Maclure and Davies, 1991: 127–36). (See also Barth, 1987; Caillot and Dumas-Carre, 1989.) In Germany, Mandl at Tubingen, Klauer at Aachen and Schneider at Munich and their colleagues have published significant contributions (see, for example, Pressley et al., 1989, on the analysis of 'the good strategy user'). Sweden is the country from which some of the most important theoretical contributions have come: for example, Marton and colleagues at Gothenburg developed the concepts of 'deep' and 'surface' learning which have been widely adopted (Marton and Saljo, 1976; Marton et al., 1984). In Finland, the FACE Project (the Formal Aims of Cognitive Education) aims to adapt teaching to encourage students in analysis of their thinking (Voutilainen, 1991). In Greece, Demetriou and Efkleides (1987) have developed a theory which they call 'experiential structuralism'; in Portugal, Project Dianoia at the University of Lisbon aims to promote thinking skills and metacognitive awareness in classroom lessons (their published bibliography lists 728 references – Valente et al., 1989); and in Spain, the University of Barcelona has run international conferences on 'Enseñar a pensar a traves del curriculum escolar' (Monoreo, 1991).

Australia also has its contributors to this field: White and Gunstone (1992) at Monash; Rose (1985) at the Australian Council for Educational Research; Ramsden (1988) at Melbourne; and Lawson (1984) and Langrehr (1990) at Adelaide – to mention only a few.

Research and development work in Britain is also extensive – too much to be adequately summarized here. A comprehensive review is to be found in Coles and Robinson (1991). Special mention should perhaps be made of the CASE project (Cognitive Acceleration through Science Education: Adey et al., 1989); Blagg's Somerset Thinking Course, based on Feuerstein's approach; and the Thinking Skills Network run by Robert Fisher at the West London Institute, which publishes a quarterly bulletin of news about conferences, courses and recent publications. One of the best books on the subject is Fisher's (1990) *Teaching Children to Think*. Philosophy in Schools is also promoted by several networks in Britain – even for very young children, using picture books (Murris, 1992).

For further details on this rather formidable list, the reader is referred to McGuinness and Nisbet (1991) for a review focusing on psychological developments; Coles and Nisbet (1990) for a more general review; and a short *Spotlight* (Nisbet, 1990) designed as an introduction to the topic for busy teachers and available free from the Scottish Council for Research in Education in Edinburgh.

In addition, mention should be made of the growing use of computers in schools, for problem-solving, simulations and information processing and retrieval, which has created new opportunities for teaching thinking. Also, professional training courses in management, business studies, medicine and law are increasingly concerned with problem-solving and decision-making processes and critical thinking, using case studies, simulations and a problem-oriented approach.

THE UNDERLYING COGNITIVE THEORY

Psychological theories are reviewed in other papers in this issue of the journal (*Educational Psychology*, Vol. 13, 1993). The advocates of teaching thinking rely primarily on a constructivist interpretation. The Piagetian view of cognitive development is that it proceeds through the formation of schemata, or 'mental representations', which serve as a guide to action and which continually develop and change throughout life as we interact with our environment. On this view, understanding is a construct, built up from experience which may be incidental, or guided through language or culture, or deliberately developed in specifically designed learning situations.

> One common but mostly unexamined way of talking about knowledge is as a *thing* which we receive – an abstract kind of thing, certainly, but having the thing-like property of being able to be handed over . . . [This] carries the implication, no less powerful for going often unnoticed, that the knower is passive and that knowledge comes to us ready-made. . . . Most of the knowledge that matters to us . . . is not developed in a passive way. We come to know through processes of active interpretation and integration. We ask questions . . . We have strategies of many kinds for finding out. We struggle – and it can be a long, hard struggle – to make sense.
>
> (Donaldson, 1992: 19)

In the struggle for meaning and sense, learners create their own knowledge. They structure it: they interpret experience by fitting it into a structure which makes sense or has meaning. Thus, learning is a personal construction of knowledge. We do not learn merely from being told: we learn from action and interaction – interaction with the material to be learned, with the teacher, with our peers and with ourselves. We go 'beyond the information given' (Bruner, 1974).

> Learning is not something that happens *to* students; it is something that happens *by* students.
>
> (Zimmerman and Schunk, 1989: 22)

Blagg (1991: 1–8) gives a concise summary of a wider range of cognitive theories which have contributed to the 'teaching thinking' movement.

These include the work of Vygotsky and Feuerstein, the 'cognitive behaviour modification' approach of Meichenbaum and Goodman, Sternberg's information-processing model and Flavell's concept 'metacognition', the conscious awareness of our own mental processes. Other contributory developments are: the interventionist programmes in educational disadvantage; the success of 'access' courses for adults returning to education, which have demonstrated that the 'pool of talent' is greater than was once believed; the teaching of study skills in schools; and the rapid growth of artificial intelligence.

METHODS

Though there may be some consensus on underlying theory, there is no clear agreement on how to teach thinking in school or college. The main distinction is between those who advocate thinking as a separate programme in the syllabus and those who favour infusion of thinking through all the conventional subjects of the curriculum. The 'thinking programme' adopts a 'skill approach': analyse the process of thinking into skills and strategies, and provide training and practice in the hope that these will prove transferable. 'Infusion' represents the 'thinking curriculum' in which the methods of teaching promote thinking by means of a 'problem-solving approach' with an emphasis on application and integration of knowledge.

If the teacher opts for a separate course on thinking, she must make a choice between programmes which are 'content-free' and those which give practice in procedures for dealing with practical problems. For example, the materials in Feuerstein's *Instrumental Enrichment* (Feuerstein *et al.*, 1980) have abstract headings derived from psychological analysis – patterns, comparisons, orientation, analytic perception and so on. In contrast, De Bono's CoRT materials (1976) practise a range of procedures – Consider All Factors, Plus Minus Interest, First Important Priorities, Other Points of View, etc. – as practical strategies for tackling problems as they arise. Other examples in this category are Bransford's IDEAL algorithm (Bransford and Stein, 1984) – Identify the Problem, Define, Explore, Act, and Look at Effects; and the formidable list in *Dimensions of Thinking* (Marzano *et al.*, 1988) which identifies eight 'thinking processes' (e.g. concept formation, principle formation, comprehending) and 21 'core thinking skills' (e.g. focusing skills, information-gathering skills, remembering skills).

The infusion method is familiar to most teachers, especially in science, mathematics and technology, where problem solving and practical work have a well-established place. The problem approach is used also in history, social studies, law, medicine and management. An older generation will associate it with the Nuffield programmes of the 1960s in English schools; but it is the basis of 'flexible learning', currently advocated for schools and further education (Employment Department, 1992) and in higher education (MacFarlane Report, 1992). Flexible learning involves a shift from formal, whole-class didactic teaching towards individual or group management of learning, giving learners more responsibility for their own learning within a framework of support, using problems extensively in investigations and collaborative team work. A different interpretation of 'infusion' appears in language and literature, in which thinking is essentially verbal and is, therefore, taught through the analysis and mastery of language. Literature deepens the quality of our thinking by letting us experience other people's response to human problems, in the novel, drama and poetry. In schools, the teaching of writing – drafting and revising, with word processors or in co-operative learning – can make explicit the process of communicating thought.

Thinking is infused into the curriculum in these ways without having to add a new 'subject' to an already overloaded syllabus. There are other approaches which cut across this rather arbitrary categorization between separate courses and infusion. Paul *et al.* (1989) favour a style of Socratic dialogue which they call 'dialectical teaching', but their critical thinking exercises are set in practical contexts which fit the school pattern. In Lipman's 'Philosophy for children' (1982), discussion is the prime method: special materials and procedures are recommended, but, again, the context is practical, with emphasis on creating 'a climate of inquiry' in the classroom. Others select particular aspects of change as crucial: a change in the teacher's role, or the fostering of metacognitive aware-ness, which can be encouraged by modelling (the teacher thinking aloud in tackling a task, as in computer protocol analysis), or a change in the examination system towards profiling and portfolios of records of work.

The growth of information technology and the use of computers have opened up a new approach to the teaching of thinking. At a simple level, there are many computer games on the market which involve strategies of thinking and if these strategies are brought out in metacognitive monitor-ing, through discussion of strategies (which children often do sponta-neously) then there is a potential here for stimulating thinking. Simulation is another powerful device, especially effective because computers allow individual working, active involvement and instant feedback; and they do this in a way which seems to tap an underused source of energy in many young learners. Beyond this, we can look ahead to people doing their own programming. Papert's LOGO, for example, was designed as a computer language for easy programming: the author's aim was 'to contribute to mental processes not only instrumentally but in more essential conceptual ways' (Papert, 1980: 4). Specialisms like artificial intelligence, intelligent tutoring, hermeneutics and hypertext open up a new dimension to this topic and may soon transform our access to thinking and knowledge, in the same way as television has transformed our leisure.

ISSUES AND TRENDS IN RESEARCH

Implicit in the infusion approach is the assumption that thinking tends to be 'domain-specific': that there are characteristic modes of thinking which are associated with specific domains of knowledge, rather than a general thinking capacity (reminiscent of former theories of intelligence) which can be turned like a searchlight on any problem. This leads into the interesting debate on the nature of thinking and knowledge – well covered in the American literature (see Ennis, 1962, 1989; McPeck, 1981; Siegel, 1988), but a theme beyond the scope of this chapter. More simply, it is the issue of process versus content: can we teach process independently of content? 'Thinking is always thinking about something,' McPeck (1981) argued: we cannot dispense with factual knowledge which is crucially important for many fields of human activity. If we over-emphasize the teaching of process, we shall encounter a justified criticism from a society in which precise, immediately accessible factual knowledge is demanded in many fields of activity. What we must avoid is Whitehead's (1932) 'inert ideas': to use his old-fashioned, but powerful, terms, we need to turn 'facts into faculty'. Clearly what is needed is a proper balance, in the form of De Corte's (1990) 'powerful learning environments', which are characterized by a good balance between discovery learning and personal exploration, on the one hand, and systematic instruction and guidance, on the other.

Another issue is the optimum age at which to teach thinking – in early childhood, in primary school, as self-awareness develops with the onset of puberty, or later in secondary school or college, or later still? There are grounds to support all of these stages, but it seems likely that the most appropriate method will be different at different ages, possibly also with wide individual differences depending on previous experience and present attitudes.

The most difficult issue is that of transfer: how can we ensure that the outcomes of teaching thinking are applicable, and are actually applied, beyond the context in which they are learned? This is a classic problem in education and we are still far from resolving it. Perkins and Salomon (1988) suggest that we need to distinguish two forms of transfer: 'high road' and 'low road' transfer. Low road transfer is 'the automatic triggering of well-rehearsed schemata' (p. 25), as when the skill of driving a car is adapted to driving a van or a lorry, or when we move from one word processor to another. Teaching for transfer of such skills involves practising them until they can be applied unthinkingly: reading and number skills are examples. High road transfer is a more conscious, deliberative action: it involves 'active decontextualisation . . . the deliberate mindful abstraction of a principle and its application to a different context' (p. 25). Through 'bridging', the teacher 'mediates the needed processes of abstraction and connection making' to help high road transfer, pointing out principles and encouraging students to make generalizations. This is an important distinction: in teaching thinking, are we aiming at 'automatic triggering' or 'deliberate mindful abstraction of a principle'? It is tempting (but probably wrong) to suggest that low road transfer applies more to the early stages of education or to the skills-based approach, whereas infused thinking in the advanced stages can only be transferred by high road processes. Both forms of transfer are needed. The key is to know when each is appropriate.

It is always difficult to identify the most promising trends in current research, but perhaps the most interesting developments derive from a widening of the field, rather than a focus on specific issues such as those mentioned above. We have tended to treat thinking as exclusively intellectual and individual. But cognitive research must also take account of the affective and social aspects. To quote Resnick and Klopfer (1989): 'The Thinking Curriculum must attend not just to teaching skills and knowledge, but also to developing motivation for their use' (p. 6). Boekaerts (1988) distinguishes between 'awareness' and 'willingness': often we are aware of a strategy to use, but fail to make the effort involved. This willingness, or 'disposition' (Resnick, 1987), is developed in a social context: hence the use of cooperative learning and modelling and the role of the teacher or parent as mediator. 'Engaging in higher order thinking with others seems likely to teach students that they have the ability, the permission, and even the obligation to engage in critical analysis' (Resnick, 1987: 41). It is the social setting which shapes a disposition to engage in thinking. We learn from 'the company we keep' (Smith, 1992: 129). Thus, students' perceptions are all-important: their perceptions of the task, of the process and of their own competence, as well as their self-image. This leads us into the 'climate' of learning and brings in relationships and attitudes – and, thus, thinking (itself a big enough field) spills over into other fields.

CONCLUSION

How, then, does one sum up the current position on the teaching of thinking? Thinking, as used here, is an imprecise term covering problem solving, decision making, critical analysis, hypothesizing and creative imagination. Developing competence in thinking is a valid aim for education. This involves more than the acquisition of knowledge; it also requires strategies for retrieving relevant knowledge and applying it and these strategies are more readily learned and applied if they are made explicit, through teaching (or mediating, to use Feuerstein's concept) and metacognitive monitoring or self-regulation, and if they are practised in contexts which encourage transfer. Attitudes, self-image and the climate of learning are of crucial importance.

On the conflict between programmes and infusion, Baron and Sternberg (1987) suggested that 'the most profitable program of instruction will probably be one that combines the best elements of various approaches' (p. 5). To use a sporting metaphor of Perkins and Salomon (1988), the different approaches 'are not rivals: rather they are members of the same team that play in different positions' (p. 31). But since that was written, the balance has swung in favour of the infusion approach: Glaser and Bassok (1989), for example, conclude: 'Thinking skills are best cultivated in the context of the acquisition of domain knowledge' (p. 645). Teachers are wise in being suspicious of programmes which seem to offer a quick and easy route to thinking: 'how to teach thinking' tends to be seen as in the same category as other 'how to' books – 'How to make your first million dollars', or 'How to see Europe in ten days'. Instead, we have begun to work towards a thinking curriculum.

Thus, what we are proposing is a profound change of attitude to education, knowledge, teaching and learning – yet not really a change, rather a new form of the old principles of the progressive education movement. It is a movement which is developing strongly. Elsewhere (Nisbet, 1991) I have suggested that, before the century is out, no curriculum will be regarded as acceptable unless it can be shown to make a contribution to the teaching of thinking.

REFERENCES

Adey, P.S. Shayer, M. and Yates, C. (1989) *Thinking Science: the Curriculum Materials of the CASE Project*, London: Macmillan.

Baron, J.B. and Sternberg, R.J. (eds) (1987) *Teaching Thinking Skills: Theory and Practice*, New York: Freeman.

Barth, B.M. (1987) *L'Apprentissage de l'Abstraction*, Paris: Editions Retz.

Blagg, N. (1991) *Can We Teach Intelligence?*, Hillsdale, NJ: Lawrence Erlbaum Associates.

Boekaerts, M. (1988) 'Emotion, motivation and learning', *International Journal of Educational Research*, 12: 229–34.

Bransford, J.D. and Stein, B.S. (1984) *The IDEAL Problem-Solver*, New York: Freeman.

Bruner, J.S. (1974) *Beyond the Information Given: Studies in the Psychology of Knowing*, London: Allen & Unwin.

Caillot, M. and Dumas-Carre, A. (1989) 'Teaching decision making to solve textbook problems', in H. Mandl, E. De Corte, N. Bennett and H.F. Friedrich (eds), *Learning and Instruction*, Vol. 2(2): 67–84, Oxford: Pergamon.

Coles, M.J. and Nisbet, J. (1990) 'Teaching thinking in Europe: a brief review', *International Journal of Cognitive Education and Mediated Learning*, 1: 229–36.

Coles, M.J. and Robinson, W.D. (1991) *Teaching Thinking: a Survey of Programmes in Education*, (2nd edn) London: Duckworth.

De Bono, E. (1976) *Teaching Thinking*, London: Temple Smith.

De Corte, E. (1990) 'Towards powerful learning environments for the acquisition of problem solving skills', *European Journal of Psychology of Education*, 5: 5–19.

Demetriou, A. and Efkleides, A. (1987) 'Experiential structuralism and neo-Piagetian theories: toward an integrated model', *International Journal of Psychology*, 22: 679–728.

Donaldson, M. (1992) *Human Minds: an Exploration*, London: Allen Lane.

Employment Department (1992) *Flexible Learning: a Framework for Education and Training in the Skills Decade*, Sheffield: Employment Department.

Ennis, R.H. (1962) 'A concept of critical thinking', *Harvard Educational Review*, 32: 81–111.

—— (1989) 'Critical thinking and subject specificity: clarification and needed research', *Educational Researcher*, 18: 4–10.

Feuerstein, R., Rand, Y., Hoffman, M.B. and Miller, R. (1980) *Instrumental Enrichment: an Intervention Programme for Cognitive Modifiability*, Baltimore, MD: University Park Press.

Fisher, R. (1990) *Teaching Children to Think*, Oxford: Blackwell.

Glaser, R. and Bassok, M. (1989) 'Learning theory and the study of instruction', *Annual Review of Psychology*, 40: 631–66.

Langrehr, J. (1990) *Teach Thinking Strategies: Ideas for Teachers*, Melbourne: Longmans Cheshire.

Lawson, M.J. (1984) 'Being executive about metacognition', in J. R. Kirby (ed.) *Cognitive Strategies and Educational Performance*, New York: Academic Press.

Lipman, M. (1974) *Harry Stottlemeier's Discovery*, Upper Montclair: Institute for Advancement of Philosophy for Children.

—— (1982) 'Philosophy for children', *Thinking: The Journal of Philosophy for Children*, 3: 35–44.

MacFarlane Report (1992) *Teaching and Learning in an Expanding Higher Education System*, Edinburgh: Committee of Scottish University Principals.

Maclure, S. and Davies, P. (1991) *Learning to Think: Thinking to Learn*, Oxford: Pergamon, for OECD.

McGuinness, C. and Nisbet, J. (1991) 'Teaching thinking in Europe', *British Journal of Educational Psychology*, 61: 174–86.

McPeck, J. (1981) *Critical Thinking and Education*, Oxford: Robinson.

Marton, F., Hounsell, D. and Entwistle, N.J. (eds.) (1984) *The Experience of Learning*, Edinburgh: Scottish Academic Press.

Marton, F. and Saljo, R. (1976) 'On qualitative differences in learning', *British Journal of Educational Psychology*, 46: 4–11.

Marzano, R.J., Brandt, R.S., Hughes, C.S. Jones, B.F., Presseisen, B.Z., Rankin, S.C. and Schor, C. (1988) *Dimensions of Thinking: a Framework for Curriculum and Instruction*, Alexandria, VA: Association for Supervision and Curriculum Development.

Monoreo, C. (ed.) (1991) *Enseñar a Pensar a traves del Curriculum Scolar*, Barcelona: Editorial Casals SA.

Murris, K. (1992) *Teaching Philosophy with Picture Books*, London: Infonet.

Nickerson, R.S. (1988) 'On improving thinking through instruction', *Review of Research in Education*, 15: 3–57.

Nisbet, J. (1990) 'Teaching thinking: an introduction to the research literature', *Spotlight 26*, Edinburgh: Scottish Council for Research in Education.

—— (1991) 'Projects, theories and methods: the international scene', in M.J. Coles and W.D. Robinson (eds) *Teaching Thinking: a Survey of Programmes in Education* (2nd edn), London: Duckworth.

Papert, S. (1980) *Mind-Storms: Children, Computers and Powerful Ideas*, Brighton: Harvester.

Paul, R., Binker, A.J.A., Martin, D., Vetrano, C. and Kreklau, H. (1989) *Critical Thinking Handbook: 6th–9th Grades*, Sonoma, CA: Center for Critical Thinking and Moral Critique. (Also Paul *et al.* (1986) *K–3rd Grade*; and (1987) *4th–6th Grades*.)

Perkins, D.N. and Salomon, G. (1988) 'Teaching for transfer', *Educational Leadership*, 41, September: 22–32.

Presseisen, B.Z. (1986) *Thinking Skills: Research and Practice*, Washington, DC: National Education Association.

—— (1987) *Thinking Skills through the Curriculum: a Conceptual Design*, Bloomington, ID: Pi Lambda Theta.

Pressley, M., Borkowski, J.G. and Schneider, W. (1987) 'Cognitive strategies: good strategy users coordinate metacognition and knowledge', *Annals of Child Development*, 4: 89–129.

Ramsden, P. (ed.) (1988) *Improving Learning: New Perspectives*, London: Kogan Page.

Resnick, L.B. (1987) *Education and Learning to Think*, Washington DC: National Academy Press.

Resnick, L.B. and Klopfer, L.E. (eds) (1989) *Toward the Thinking Curriculum: Current Cognitive Research*, Alexandria, VA: Association for Supervision and Curriculum Development.

Rowe, H.A.H. (1985) *Problem Solving and Intelligence*, Hillsdale, NJ: Lawrence Erlbaum Associates.

Siegel, H. (1988) *Educating Reason: Rationality, Critical Thinking and Education*, London: Routledge.

Simons, P.R.J. (1989) 'Learning to learn', in P. Span, E. De Corte and B. van Hout-Wolters (eds) *Onderwijsleerprocessen*, Lisse, Swets & Zeitlinger.

Smith, F. (1992) *To Think: in Language, Learning and Education*, London: Routledge.

Sternberg, R.J. (1977) *Intelligence, Information Processing and Analogical Reasoning: the Componential Analysis of Human Abilities*, Hillsdale, NJ: Lawrence Erlbaum Associates.

Tomlinson, P. and Kilner, S. (1992) *The Flexible Approach to Learning: a Guide* and *The Flexible Learning Framework and Current Educational Theory*, Sheffield: Employment Department.

Valente, M.O., Gaspar, A., Salema, H., Morais, M. and Cruz, N. (1989) *Aprender a Pensar: metacognicao-Bibliografia tematica*, Lisbon: Departamento de Educacão, Universidade de Lisboa.

Voutilainen, T. (1991) 'The project FACE', in S. Maclure and P. Davies (eds) *Learning to Think: Thinking to Learn*, Oxford: Pergamon for OECD.

White, R. and Gunstone, R. (1992) *Probing Understanding*, London: Falmer Press.

Whitehead, A.N. (1932) *The Aims of Education*, London: Williams & Northgate.

Zimmerman, B.J. and Schunk, D.H. (eds) (1989) *Self-Regulated Learning and Academic Achievement: Theory, Research and Practice*, New York: Berlin and Heidelberg, Springer-Verlag.

Chapter 25

Situated cognition and the culture of learning

*John Seely Brown, Allan Collins
and Paul Duguid*

The breach between learning and use, which is captured by the folk categories 'know what' and 'know how', may well be a product of the structure and practices of our education system. Many methods of didactic education assume a separation between knowing and doing, treating knowledge as an integral, self-sufficient substance, theoretically independent of the situations in which it is learned and used. The primary concern of schools often seems to be the transfer of this substance, which comprises abstract, decontextualized formal concepts. The activity and context in which learning takes place are thus regarded as merely ancillary to learning – pedagogically useful, of course, but fundamentally distinct and even neutral with respect to what is learned.

Recent investigations of learning, however, challenge this separating of what is learned from how it is learned and used.[1] The activity in which knowledge is developed and deployed, it is now argued, is not separable from or ancillary to learning and cognition. Nor is it neutral. Rather, it is an integral part of what is learned. Situations might be said to co-produce knowledge through activity. Learning and cognition, it is now possible to argue, are fundamentally situated.

In this paper, we try to explain in a deliberately speculative way, why activity and situations are integral to cognition and learning, and how different ideas of what is appropriate learning activity produce very different results. We suggest that, by ignoring the situated nature of cognition, education defeats its own goal of providing useable, robust knowledge. And conversely, we argue that approaches such as *cognitive apprenticeship* (Collins, Brown, and Newman, 1989) that embed learning in activity and make deliberate use of the social and physical context are more in line with the understanding of learning and cognition that is emerging from research.

SITUATED KNOWLEDGE AND LEARNING

Miller and Gildea's (1987) work on vocabulary teaching has shown how the assumption that knowing and doing can be separated leads to a teaching method that ignores the way situations structure cognition. Their work has described how children are taught words from dictionary definitions and a few exemplary sentences, and they have compared this method with the way vocabulary is normally learned outside school.

People generally learn words in the context of ordinary communication. This process is startlingly fast and successful. Miller and Gildea note that by listening, talking, and reading, the average 17-year-old has learned vocabulary at a rate of 5,000 words per year (13 per day) for over 16 years. By contrast, learning words from abstract definitions and sentences taken out of the context of normal use, the way vocabulary has often been taught, is slow and generally unsuccessful. There is barely enough classroom time to teach more than 100 to 200 words per year. Moreover, much of what is taught turns out to be almost useless in practice. They give the following examples of students uses of vocabulary acquired this way:

Me and my parents correlate, because without them I wouldn't be here.

I was meticulous about falling off the cliff.

Mrs. Morrow stimulated the soup.[2]

Given the method, such mistakes seem unavoidable. Teaching from dictionaries assumes that definitions and exemplary sentences are self-contained 'pieces' of knowledge. But words and sentences are not islands, entire unto themselves. Language use would involve an unremitting confrontation with ambiguity, polysemy, nuance, metaphor, and so forth were these not resolved with the extralinguistic help that the context of an utterance provides (Nunberg, 1978).

Prominent among the intricacies of language that depend on extra-linguistic help are *indexical* words – words like *I, here, now, next, tomorrow, afterwards, this.* Indexical terms are those that 'index' or more plainly point to a part of the situation in which communication is being conducted. They are not merely context-sensitive; they are completely context-dependent. Words like *I* or *now*, for instance, can only be interpreted in the context of their use. Surprisingly, all words can be seen as at least partially indexical (Barwise and Perry, 1983).

Experienced readers implicitly understand that words are situated. They therefore ask for the rest of the sentence or the context before committing themselves to an interpretation of a word. And they go to dictionaries with situated examples of usage in mind. The situation as well as the dictionary supports the interpretation. But the students who produce the sentences listed had no support from a normal communicative situation. In tasks like theirs, dictionary definitions are assumed to be self-sufficient. The extra-linguistic props that would structure, constrain, and ultimately allow inter-pretation in normal communication are ignored.

Learning from dictionaries, like any method that tries to teach abstract concepts independently of authentic situations, overlooks the way understanding is developed through continued, situated use. This development, which involves complex social negotiations, does not crystallize into a categorical definition. Because it is dependent on situations and negotiations, the meaning of a word cannot, in principle, be captured by a definition, even when the definition is supported by a couple of exemplary sentences.

All knowledge is, we believe, like language. Its constituent parts index the world and so are inextricably a product of the activity and situations in which they are produced. A concept, for example, will continually evolve with each new occasion of use, because new situations, negotiations, and activities inevitably recast it in a new, more densely textured form. So a concept, like the meaning of a word, is always under construction. This would also appear to be true of apparently well-defined, abstract technical concepts. Even these are not wholly definable and defy categorical descriptions; part of their meaning is always inherited from the context of use.

Learning and tools

To explore the idea that concepts are both situated and progressively developed through activity, we should abandon any notion that they are abstract, self-contained entities. Instead, it may be more useful to consider conceptual knowledge as, in some ways, similar to a set of tools. Tools share several significant features with knowledge. They can only be fully understood through use, and using them entails both changing the user's view of the world and adopting the belief system of the culture in which they are used.

First, if knowledge is thought of as tools, we can illustrate Whitehead's (1929) distinction between the mere acquisition of inert concepts and the development of useful, robust knowledge. It is quite possible to acquire a tool but to be unable to use it. Similarly, it is common for students to acquire algorithms, routines, and decontextualized definitions that they cannot use and that, therefore, lie inert. Unfortunately, this problem is not always apparent. Old-fashioned pocket knives, for example, have a device for removing stones from horses' hooves. People with this device may know its use and be able to talk wisely about horses, hooves, and stones. But they may never betray – or even recognize that they would not begin to know how to use this implement on a horse. Similarly, students can often manipulate algorithms, routines, and definitions they have acquired with apparent competence and yet not reveal, to their teachers or themselves, that they would have no idea what to do if they came upon the domain equivalent of a limping horse.

People who use tools actively rather than just acquire them, by contrast, build an increasingly rich implicit understanding of the world in which they use the tools and of the tools themselves. The understanding, both of the world and of the tool, continually changes as a result of their interaction. Learning and acting are interestingly indistinct, learning being a continuous, life-long process resulting from acting in situations.

Learning how to use a tool involves far more than can be accounted for in any set of explicit rules. The occasions and conditions for use arise directly out of the context of activities of each community that uses the tool, framed by the way members of that community see the world. The community and its viewpoint, quite as much as the tool itself, determine how a tool is used. Thus, carpenters and cabinet makers use chisels differently. Because tools and the way they are used reflect the particular accumulated insights of communities, it is not possible to use a tool appropriately without understanding the community or culture in which it is used.

Conceptual tools similarly reflect the cumulative wisdom of the culture in which they are used and the insights and experience of individuals. Their meaning is not invariant but a product of negotiation within the community. Again, appropriate use is not simply a function of the abstract concept alone. It is a function of the culture and the activities in which the concept has been developed. Just as carpenters and cabinet makers use chisels differently, so physicists and engineers use mathematical formulae differently. Activity, concept, and culture are interdependent. No one can be totally understood without the other two. Learning must involve all three. Teaching methods often try to impart abstracted concepts as fixed, well-defined, independent entities that can be explored in prototypical examples and textbook exercises. But such exemplification cannot provide the important insights into either the culture or the authentic activities of members of that culture that learners need.

To talk about academic disciplines, professions, or even manual trades as communities or cultures will perhaps seem strange. Yet communities of practitioners are connected by more than their ostensible tasks. They are bound by intricate, socially constructed webs of belief, which are essential to understanding what they do (Geertz, 1983). The activities of many communities are unfathomable, unless they are viewed from within the culture. The culture and the use of a tool act together to determine the way practitioners see the world; and the way the world appears to them determines the culture's understanding of the world and of the tools. Unfortunately, students are too often asked to use the tools of a discipline without being able to adopt its culture. To learn to use tools as practitioners use them, a student, like an apprentice, must enter that community and its culture. Thus, in a significant way, learning is, we believe, a process of enculturation.

Learning and enculturation

Enculturating may, at first, appear to have little to do with learning. But it is, in fact, what people do in learning to speak, read, and write, or becoming school children, office workers, researchers, and so on. From a very early age and throughout their lives, people, consciously or unconsciously, adopt the behaviour and belief systems of new social groups. Given the chance to observe and practice *in situ* the behaviour of members of a culture, people pick up relevant jargon, imitate behaviour, and gradually start to act in accordance with its norms. These cultural practices are often recondite and extremely complex. Nonetheless, given the opportunity to observe and practice them, people adopt them with great success. Students, for instance, can quickly get an implicit sense of what is suitable diction, what makes a relevant question, what is legitimate or illegitimate behaviour in a particular activity. The ease and success with which people do this (as opposed to the intricacy of describing what it entails) belie the immense importance of the process and obscure the fact that what they pick up is a product of the ambient culture rather than of explicit teaching.

Too often the practices of contemporary schooling deny students the chance to engage the relevant domain culture, because that culture is not in evidence. Although students are shown the tools of many academic cultures in the course of a school career, the pervasive cultures that they observe, in which they participate, and which some enter quite effectively are the cultures of school life itself. These cultures can be unintentionally anti-thetical to useful domain learning. The ways schools use dictionaries, or math formulae, or historical analysis are very different from the ways practitioners use them (Schoenfeld, 1991). Thus students may pass exams (a distinctive part of school cultures) but still not be able to use a domain's conceptual tools in authentic practice.

This is not to suggest that all students of mathematics or history must be expected to become professional mathematicians or historians, but to claim that in order to learn these subjects (and not just to learn about them) students need much more than abstract concepts and self-contained examples. They need to be exposed to the use of a domain's conceptual tools in authentic activity – to teachers acting as practitioners and using these tools in wrestling with problems of the world. Such activity can tease out the way a mathematician or historian looks at the world and solves emergent problems. The process may appear informal, but it is nonetheless full-blooded, authentic activity that can be deeply informative – in a way that textbook examples and declarative explanations are not.

AUTHENTIC ACTIVITY

Our case so far rests on an undefined distinction between authentic and school activity. If we take learning to be a process of enculturation, it is possible to clarify this distinction and to explain why much school work is inauthentic and thus not fully productive of useful learning.

The activities of a domain are framed by its culture. Their meaning and purpose are socially constructed through negotiations among present and past members. Activities thus cohere in a way that is, in theory, if not always in practice, accessible to members who move within the social framework. These coherent, meaningful, and purposeful activities are *authentic*, according to the definition of the term we use here. Authentic activities then, are most simply defined as the ordinary practices of the culture.

This is not to say that authentic activity can only be pursued by experts. Apprentice tailors (Lave, 1988a), for instance, begin by ironing finished garments (which tacitly teaches them a lot about cutting and sewing). Ironing is simple, valuable, and absolutely authentic. Students of Palincsar and Brown's (1984) reciprocal teaching of reading may read elementary texts, but they develop authentic strategies that are recognized by all readers. The students in Miller and Gildea's (1987) study, by contrast, were given a strategy that is a poor extrapolation of experienced readers' situated use of dictionaries.

School activity too often tends to be hybrid, implicitly framed by one culture, but explicitly attributed to another. Classroom activity very much takes place within the culture of schools, although it is attributed to the culture of readers, writers, mathematicians, historians, economists, geographers, and so forth. Many of the activities students undertake are simply not the activities of practitioners and would not make sense or be endorsed by the cultures to which they are attributed. This hybrid activity, furthermore, limits students' access to the important structuring and supporting cues that arise from the context. What students do tends to be ersatz activity.

Archetypal school activity is very different from what we have in mind when we talk of authentic activity, because it is very different from what authentic practitioners do. When authentic activities are transferred to the classroom, their context is inevitably transmuted; they become classroom tasks and part of the school culture. Classroom procedures, as a result, are then applied to what have become classroom tasks. The system of learning and using (and, of course, testing) thereafter remains hermetically sealed within the self-confirming culture of the school. Consequently, contrary to the aim of schooling, success within this culture often has little bearing on performance elsewhere.

In the creation of classroom tasks, apparently peripheral features of authentic tasks – like the extralinguistic supports involved in the interpretation of communication – are often dismissed as 'noise' from which salient features can be abstracted for the purpose of teaching. But the context of activity is an extraordinarily complex network from which practitioners draw essential support. The source of such support is often only tacitly recognized by practitioners, or even by teachers or designers of simulations. Classroom tasks, therefore, can completely fail to provide the contextual features that allow authentic activity. At the same time, students may come to rely, in important but little noticed ways, on features of the classroom context, in which the task is now embedded, that are wholly absent from and alien to authentic activity. Thus, much of what is learned in school may apply only to the ersatz activity, if it was learned through such activity.

The idea that most school activity exists in a culture of its own is central to understanding many of the difficulties of learning in school. Jean Lave's ethnographic studies of learning and everyday activity (1988b) reveal how different schooling is from the activities and culture that give meaning and purpose to what students learn elsewhere. Lave focuses on the behaviour of JPFs (just plain folks) and records that the ways they learn are quite distinct from what students are asked to do.

Three categories primarily concern us here: JPFs, students, and practitioners. Put most simply, when JPFs aspire to learn a particular set of practices, they have two apparent options. First, they can enculturate through apprenticeship. Becoming an apprentice doesn't involve a qualitative change from what JPFs normally do. People enculturate into different communities all the time. The apprentices' behaviour and the JPFs behaviour can thus be thought of as pretty much the same.[3]

The second, and now more conventional, option is to enter a school as a student. Schools, however, do seem to demand a qualitative change in behaviour. What the student is expected to do and what a JPF does are significantly different. The student enters the school culture while ostensibly being taught something else. And the general strategies for intuitive reasoning, resolving issues, and negotiating meaning that people develop

Table 25.1 JPF, practitioner, and student activity

	JPFs	*Students*	*Practitioners*
reasoning with:	causal stories	laws	causal models
acting on:	situations	symbols	conceptual situations
resolving:	emergent problems and dilemmas	well-defined problems	ill-defined problems
producing:	negotiable meaning & socially constructed understanding	fixed meaning & immutable concepts	negotiable meaning & socially constructed understanding

through everyday activity are superseded by the precise, well-defined problems, formal definitions, and symbol manipulation of much school activity.

We try to represent this discontinuity in Table 25.1, which compares salient features of JPF, practitioner, and putative student behaviour.

This table is intended mainly to make apparent that, in our terms, there is a great similarity between JPFs' and practitioners' activity. Both have their activities situated in the cultures in which they work, within which they negotiate meanings and construct understanding. The issues and problems that they face arise out of, are defined by, and are resolved within the constraints of the activity they are pursuing.

Lave's work (1988b) provides a good example of a JPF engaged in authentic activity using the context in which an issue emerged to help find a resolution. The example comes from a study of a Weight Watchers class, whose participants were preparing their carefully regulated meals under instruction.

> In this case they were to fix a serving of cottage cheese, supposing the amount laid out for the meal was three-quarters of the two-thirds cup the program allowed. The problem solver in this example began the task muttering that he had taken a calculus course in college. . . . Then after a pause he suddenly announced that he had 'got it!' From then on he appeared certain he was correct, even before carrying out the procedure. He filled a measuring-cup two-thirds full of cottage cheese, dumped it out on the cutting board, patted it into a circle, marked a cross on it, scooped away one quadrant, and served the rest.
>
> Thus, 'take three-quarters of two-thirds of a cup of cottage cheese' was not just the problem statement but also the solution to the problem and the procedure for solving it. The setting was part of the calculating process and the solution was simply the problem statement, enacted with the setting. At no time did the Weight Watcher check his procedure against a paper and pencil algorithm, which would have produced ¾ cup × ⅔ cup = ½ cup. Instead, the coincidence of the problem, setting, and enactment was the means by which checking took place.
>
> (1988b: 165)

The dieter's solution path was extremely expedient and drew on the sort of inventiveness that characterizes the activity of both JPFs and practitioners. It reflected the nature of the activity, the resources available, and the sort of resolution required in a way that problem-solving that relies on abstracted knowledge cannot.

This inventive resolution depended on the dieter seeing the problem in the particular context, which itself was embedded in ongoing activity. And this again is characteristic of both JPFs and experts. The dieter's position gave him privileged access to the solution path he chose. (This probably accounts for the certainty he expressed before beginning his cal-culation.) He was thus able to see the problem and its resolution in terms of the measuring cup, cutting board, and knife. Activity–tool–culture (cooking–kitchen utensils–dieting) moved in step throughout this proce-dure because of the way the problem was seen and the task was performed. . . . Knowing and doing were interlocked and inseparable.

This sort of problem solving is carried out in conjunction with the environment and is quite distinct from the processing solely inside heads that many teaching practices implicitly endorse. By off-loading part of the cognitive task onto the environment, the dieter automatically used his environment to help solve the problem. His actions were not in any way exceptional; they resemble many ordinary working practices. Scribner (1984) records, for instance, how complex calculations can be performed by practitioners using their environment directly. In the case she studied, dairy loaders used the configuration of crates they were filling and emptying almost like an elaborate abacus. Nor are such problem-solving strategies limited to the physical or social environment. This sort of reliance on situations can be seen in the work of physicists, who see 'through' formulae by envisioning a physical situation which then provides support for inferences and approximations (de Kleer and Brown, 1984). Hutchins' (in press) study of intricate collaborative naval navigation records the way people distribute the burden across the environment and the group as well. The resulting cognitive activity can then only be explained in relation to its context. '[W]hen the context of cognition is ignored', Hutchins observes, 'it is impossible to see the contribution of structure in the environment, in artifacts, and in other people to the organization of mental processes'.

Instead of taking problems out of the context of their creation and pro-viding them with an extraneous framework, JPFs seem particularly adept at solving them within the framework of the context that produced them. This allows JPFs to share the burdens of both defining and solving the problem with the task environment as they respond in 'real time'. The adequacy of the solution they reach becomes apparent in relation to the role it must play in allowing activity to continue. The problem, the solution, and the cognition involved in getting between the two cannot be isolated from the context in which they are embedded.

Even though students are expected to behave differently, they inevitably do behave like the JPFs they are and solve most of their problems in their own situated way. Schoenfeld (1991) describes mathematics students using well-known but unacknowledged strategies, such as the position of a problem in a particular section of the book (e.g., the first questions at the end of chapters are always simple ones, and the last usually demand con-cepts from earlier chapters) or the occurrence of a particular word in the problem (e.g., 'left' signals a subtraction problem), to find solutions quickly and efficiently. Such ploys indicate how thoroughly learners really are situated, and how they always lean on whatever context is available for help. Within the practices of schooling this can obviously be very effective. But the school situation is extremely specialized. Viewed from outside, where problems do not come in textbooks, a dependency on such school-based cues makes the learning extremely fragile.

Furthermore, though schooling seeks to encourage problem-solving, it disregards most of the inventive heuristics that students bring to the classroom. It thus implicitly devalues not just individual heuristics, which may be fragile, but the whole process of inventive problem-solving. Lave (1988c) describes how some students feel it necessary to disguise effective strategies so that teachers believe the problems have been solved in the approved way.

Structuring activity

Authentic activity, as we have argued, is important for learners, because it is the only way they gain access to the standpoint that enables practitioners to act meaningfully and purposefully. It is activity that shapes or hones their tools. How and why remain to be explained. Activity also provides experience, which is plainly important for subsequent action. Here, we try to explain some of the products of activity in terms of idiosyncratic 'indexicalized' representations.

Representations arising out of activity cannot easily (or perhaps at all) be replaced by descriptions. Plans, as Suchman argues (1987), are distinct from situated actions. Most people will agree that a picture of a complex machine in a manual is distinctly difference from how the machine actually looks. (In an intriguing way you need the machine to understand the manual, as much as the manual to understand the machine.) The perceptions resulting from actions are a central feature in both learning and activity. How a person perceives activity may be determined by tools and their appropriated use. What they perceive, however, contributes to how they act and learn. Different activities produce different indexicalized representations not equivalent, universal ones. And, thus, the activity that led to those representations plays a central role in learning.

Representations are, we suggest, indexicalized rather in the way that language is. That is to say, they are dependent on context. In face-to-face conversations, people can interpret indexical expressions (containing such words as *I, you, here, now, that*, etc.), because they have access to the indexed features of the situation, though people rarely notice the significance of the surroundings to their understanding. The importance of the surroundings becomes apparent, however, when they try to hold similar conversations at a distance. Then indexical expressions become problematic until ways are found to secure their interpretation by situating their reference (see, for instance, Rubin, 1980, on the difference between speech and writing).

Knowledge, we suggest, . . . indexes the situation in which it arises and is used. The embedding circumstances efficiently provide essential parts of its structure and meaning. So knowledge, which comes coded by and connected to the activity and environment in which it is developed, is spread across its component parts, some of which are in the mind and some in the world much as the final picture on a jig-saw is spread across its component pieces.

As Hutchins (in press), Pea (1988), and others point out, the structure of cognition is widely distributed across the environment, both social and physical. And we suggest that the environment, therefore, contributes importantly to indexical representations people form in activity. These representations, in turn, contribute to future activity. Indexical representations developed through engagement in a task may greatly increase the efficiency with which subsequent tasks can be done, if part of the environment that structures the representations remains invariant. This is evident in the ability to perform tasks that cannot be described or remembered in the absence of the situation. Recurring features of the environment may thus afford recurrent sequences of actions. Memory and subsequent actions, as knots in handkerchiefs and other *aides memoires* reveal, are not context-independent processes. Routines (Agre, 1985) may well be a product of this sort of indexicalization. Thus, authentic activity becomes a central component of learning.

One of the key points of the concept of indexicality is that it indicates that knowledge, and not just learning, is situated. A corollary of this is that learning methods that are embedded in authentic situations are not merely useful; they are essential.

LEARNING THROUGH COGNITIVE APPRENTICESHIP

We have been working toward a conception of human learning and reasoning that, we feel, it is important for school practices to honour. Though there are many innovative teachers, schools, and programmes that act otherwise, prevalent school practices assume, more often than not, that knowledge is individual and self-structured, that schools are neutral with respect to what is learned, that concepts are abstract, relatively fixed, and unaffected by the activity through which they are acquired and used, and that JPF behaviour should be discouraged.

Cognitive apprenticeship (Collins, Brown and Newman, 1989), whose mechanisms we have, to some extent, been trying to elucidate, embraces methods that stand in contradistinction to these practices. Cognitive apprenticeship methods try to enculturate students into authentic practices through activity and social interaction in a way similar to that evident – and evidently successful – in craft apprenticeship. In this section, we examine briefly an example of mathematics teaching in an attempt to illustrate how some of the characteristics of learning that we have discussed can be honoured in the classroom. We use an example from mathematics in part because that is where some of the most innovative work in teaching can be found. But we firmly believe that this sort of teaching is not just possible in mathematics.

Lampert's teaching of multiplication

Lampert (1986) . . . involves her students in mathematical exploration, which she tries to make continuous with their everday knowledge. She has devised methods for teaching mathematics to fourth grade students that lead from students' implicit understanding of the world beyond the classroom, through activity and social construction in the culture, to the sort of robust learning that direct teaching of algorithms usually fails to achieve.

She starts teaching multiplication, for example, in the context of coin problems, because in the community of fourth grade students, there is usually a strong, implicit, shared understanding of coins. Next, the students create stories for multiplication problems, drawing on their implicit knowledge to delineate different examples of multiplication. Then, Lampert helps them toward the abstract algorithm that everyone learns for multidigit multiplication, in the context of the coin problems and stories the community has created. Thus, the method presents the algorithm as one more useful strategy to help them resolve community problems.

The first phase of teaching starts with simple coin problems, such as 'using only nickels and pennies, make 82 cents'. With such problems, Lampert helps her students explore their implicit knowledge. Then, in the second phase, the students create stories for multiplication problems (see Figure 25.1). They perform a series of decompositions and discover that there is no one, magically 'right' decomposition decreed by authority, just more and less useful decompositions whose *use* is judged in the context of the problem to be solved and the interests of the problem solvers.

The third phase of instruction gradually introduces students to the standard algorithm, now that such an algorithm has a meaning and a purpose in their community. The students' procedure parallels the story problems they had created. Eventually they find ways to shorten the process, and they usually arrive at the standard algorithm, justifying their findings with the stories they created earlier.

Through this method, students develop a composite understanding of four different kinds of mathematical knowledge: (a) *intuitive knowledge*, the kind of short cuts people invent when doing multiplication problems in authentic settings; (b) *computational knowledge*, the basic algorithms that are usually taught; (c) *concrete knowledge*, the kind of concrete models of the algorithm associated with the stories the students created; and (d) *principled knowledge*, the principles such as associativity and commutativity that

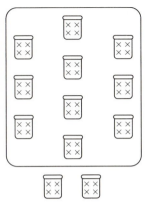

T: Can anyone give me a story that could go with this multiplication . . . 12 × 4?
S1: There were 12 jars, and each had 4 butterflies in it.
T: And if I did this multiplication and found the answer, what would I know about those jars and butterflies?
S1: You'd know you had that many butterflies altogether.
T: Okay, here are the jars. [*Draws a picture to represent the jars of butterflies – see diagram.*] The stars in them will stand for butterflies. Now, it will be easier for us to count how many butterflies there are altogether if we think of the jars in groups. And, as usual, the mathematician's favourite number for thinking about groups is?
S2: 10.
T: Each of these jars has 4 butterflies in it. [*Draws a loop around 10 jars.*] . . .

T: Suppose I erase my circle and go back to looking at the 12 jars again altogether. Is there any other way I could group them to make it easier for us to count all the butterflies?
S6: You could do 6 and 6.
T: Now, how many do I have in this group?
S7: 24.
T: How did you figure that out?
S7: 8 and 8 and 8. [*He puts the 6 jars together into 3 pairs, intuitively finding a grouping that made the figuring easier for him.*]

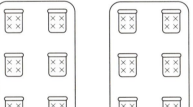

T: That's 3 × 8. It's also 6 × 4. Now, how many are in this group?
S6: 24. It's the same. They both have 6 jars.
T: And now how many are there altogether?
S8: 24 and 24 is 48.
T: Do we get the same number of butterflies as before? Why?
S8: Yeah, because we have the same number of jars and they still have 4 butterflies in each.

Figure 25.1 Story problems for teaching multiplication

underlie the algorithmic manipulations of numbers. Lampert tries to inculcate an inseparable understanding of these kinds of knowledge and the connections between them, and thus to bridge the huge gap that emerges from much conventional teaching between conceptual knowledge and problem-solving activity – between, as we characterized them at the beginning, knowing and doing.

This approach fosters procedures that are characteristic of cognitive apprenticeship:

• By beginning with a task embedded in a familiar activity, it shows the students the legitimacy of their implicit knowledge and its availability as scaffolding in apparently unfamiliar tasks.

- By pointing to different decompositions, it stresses that heuristics are not absolute, but assessed with respect to a particular task – and that even algorithms can be assessed in this way.
- By allowing students to generate their own solution paths, it helps make them conscious, creative members of the culture of problem-solving mathematicians. And, in enculturating through this activity, they acquire some of the culture's tools – a shared vocabulary and the means to discuss, reflect upon, evaluate, and validate community procedures in a collaborative process.

Figure 25.2 shows how, in the terms of cognitive apprenticeship, we can represent the process of the students from embedded activity to general principles of the culture. In this sequence, apprenticeship and coaching in a domain begin by providing modelling *in situ* and scaffolding for students to get started in an authentic activity. As the students gain more self-confidence and control, they move into a more autonomous phase of collaborative learning, where they begin to participate consciously in the culture. The social network within the culture helps them develop its language and the belief systems and promotes the process of enculturation. Collaboration also leads to articulation of strategies, which can then be discussed and reflected on. This, in turn, fosters generalizing, grounded in the students' situated understanding. From here, students can use their fledgling conceptual knowledge in activity, seeing that activity in a new light, which in turn leads to the further development of the conceptual knowledge.

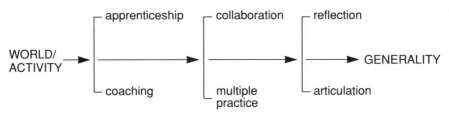

Figure 25.2 Students' progress from embedded activity to generality

. . . The threadbare concepts that initially develop out of activity are gradually given texture as they are deployed in different situations.

APPRENTICESHIP AND COGNITION

The development of concepts out of and through continuing authentic activity is the approach of cognitive apprenticeship – a term closely allied to our image of knowledge as a tool. Cognitive apprenticeship supports learning in a domain by enabling students to acquire, develop, and use cognitive tools in authentic domain activity. Similarly, craft apprentice-ship enables apprentices to acquire and develop the tools and skills of their craft through authentic work at and membership in their trade. Through this process, apprentices enter the culture of practice. So the term *apprenticeship* helps to emphasize the centrality of activity in learning and knowledge and highlights the inherently context-dependent, situated, and enculturating nature of learning. And *apprenticeship* also suggests the paradigm of situated modelling, coaching, and fading (Collins, Brown and Newman, 1989), whereby teachers or coaches promote learning, first by making explicit their tacit knowledge or by modelling their strategies for students in authentic activity. Then, teachers and colleagues support students' attempts at doing the task and finally they empower the students to continue independently. . . .

Cognitive emphasizes that apprenticeship techniques actually reach well beyond the physical skills usually associated with apprenticeship to the kinds of cognitive skills more normally associated with conventional school-ing. This extension is not as incompatible with traditional apprenticeship as it may at first seem. The physical skills usually associated with apprenticeship embody important cognitive skills, if our argument for the inseparability of knowing and doing is correct. Certainly many professions with generally acknowledged cognitive content, such as law, medicine, architecture, and business, have nonetheless traditionally been learned through apprenticeship.

In essence, cognitive apprenticeship attempts to promote learning within the nexus of activity, tool, and culture that we have described. Learning, both outside and inside school, advances through collaborative social interaction and the social construction of knowledge. Resnick (1988) has pointed out that throughout most of their lives people learn and work collaboratively, not individually, as they are asked to do in many schools. Lampert's work, Scardamalia, Bereiter, and Steinbach's teaching of writing (1984), and Palincsar and Brown's (1984) work with reciprocal teaching of reading all employ some form of social interaction, social construction of knowledge, and collaboration.

Within a culture, ideas are exchanged and modified and belief systems developed and appropriated through conversation and narratives, so these must be promoted, not inhibited. Though they are often anathema to traditional schooling, they are an essential component of social interaction and, thus, of learning. They provide access to much of the distributed knowledge and elaborate support of the social matrix (Orr, 1987). So learning environments must allow narratives to circulate and 'war stories' to be added to the collective wisdom of the community.

The role of narratives and conversations is perhaps more complex than might first appear. An intriguing role in learning is played by 'legitimate peripheral participation', where people who are not taking part directly in a particular activity learn a great deal from their legitimate position on the periphery (Lave and Wenger, in preparation). It is a mistake to think that important discourse in learning is always direct and declarative. This peripheral participation is particularly important for people entering the culture. They need to observe how practitioners at various levels behave and talk to get a sense of how expertize is manifest in conversation and other activities.

Cognitive apprenticeship and collaborative learning

If, as we propose, learning is a process of enculturating that is supported in part through social interaction and the circulation of narrative, groups of practitioners are particularly important, for it is only within groups that social interaction and conversation can take place. Salient features of group learning include:

- *Collective problem solving.* Groups are not just a convenient way to accumulate the individual knowledge of their members. They give rise synergistically to insights and solutions that would not come about without them (Schoenfeld, in preparation).
- *Displaying multiple roles.* Successful execution of most individual tasks requires students to understand the many different roles needed for carrying out any cognitive task. Getting one person to be able to play all the roles entailed by authentic activity and to reflect productively upon his or her performance is one of the monumental tasks of education. The group, however, permits different roles to be displayed and engenders reflective narratives and discussions about the aptness of those roles.
- *Confronting ineffective strategies and misconceptions.* We know from an extensive literature (diSessa, 1982, 1983, 1986; McCloskey, Caramazza and Green, 1980; White, 1983) that students have many misconceptions about qualitative phenomena in physics. Teachers rarely have the opportunity to hear enough of what students think to recognize when the information that is offered back by students is only a surface retelling for school purposes (the handing back of an uncomprehended tool, as we described it at the beginning) that may mask deep misconceptions about the physical world and problem-solving strategies. Groups, however, can be efficient in drawing out, confronting and discussing both misconceptions and ineffective strategies.
- *Providing collaborative work skills.* Students who are taught individually rather than collaboratively can fail to develop skills needed for collaborative work. In the collaborative conditions of the workplace, knowing how to learn and work collaboratively is increasingly important. If people are going to learn and work in conjunction with others, they must be given the situated opportunity to develop those skills.

... The increasing role of the teacher as a master to apprentices, and the teacher's use of authentic domain activity as a major part of teaching will, perhaps, once and for all dismiss George Bernard Shaw's scurrilous criticism of teachers, 'He who can, does. He who cannot, teaches.' His comment may then be replaced with Alexander Pope's hopeful 'Let such teach others who themselves excell'.

CONCLUSION – TOWARD AN EPISTEMOLOGY OF SITUATED COGNITION

Much research investigating situated features of cognition remains to be done. It is, however, already possible to begin serious reappraisal of the assumptions about learning that underlie current classroom practice (see, for example Resnick, 1988; Shanker, 1988).

One of the particularly difficult challenges for research (which exceptional teachers may solve independently) is determining what should be made explicit in teaching and what should be left implicit. A common strategy in trying to overcome difficult pedagogic problems is to make as much as possible explicit. Thus, we have ended up with wholly inappropriate methods of teaching. Whatever the domain, explication often lifts implicit and possibly even nonconceptual constraints (Cussins, 1988) out of the embedding world and tries to make them explicit or conceptual. These now take a place in our ontology and become something more to learn about rather than simply something useful in learning. But indexical representations gain their efficiency by leaving much of the context underrepresented or implicit. Future work into situated cognition, from which educational practices will benefit, must, among other things, try to frame a convincing account of the relationship between explicit knowledge and implicit understanding.

We have described here only a fragment of an agenda for a fully developed theory of situated cognition. There remains major theoretical work to shift the traditional focus of education. For centuries, the epistemology that has guided educational practice has concentrated primarily on conceptual representation and made its relation to objects in the world problematic by assuming that, cognitively, representation is prior to all else. A theory of situated cognition suggests that activity and perception are importantly and epistemologically prior – at a nonconceptual level – to conceptualization and that it is on them that more attention needs to be focused. An epistemology that begins with activity and perception, which are first and foremost embedded in the world, may simply bypass the classical problem of reference – of mediating conceptual representations.

In conclusion, the unheralded importance of activity and enculturation to learning suggests that much common educational practice is the victim of an inadequate epistemology. A new epistemology might hold the key to a dramatic improvement in learning and a completely new perspective on education.

NOTES

1 All work in this area is to a greater or lesser degree, built upon research of activity theorists such as Vygotsky, Leontiev, and others. . . . Anyone familiar with Jean Lave's work on learning, apprenticeship, and everyday cognition will realize at once that we are deeply indebted to her groundbreaking work.

2 The dictionary definitions that the students used in writing these sentences are as follows: *Correlate* – be related one to the other; *meticulous* – very careful; *stimulate* – stir up. They were given these definitions with little or no contextual help, so it would be unfair to regard the students as foolish for using the words as they did.

3 The JPF must, of course, have access to a culture and become what Lave and Wenger (in preparation) call a 'legitimate peripheral participant'. And, of course, an apprentice usually has to do a great deal of work. We are not trying to suggest that anything magical occurs in the process of enculturation. (Medical interns testify to how hard it can be.) But the process, we stress, is not qualitatively different from what people do all the time in adopting the behaviour and belief systems of their peers.

REFERENCES

Agre, P. (1985) *Routines*, MIT Al Memo.

Barwise, K. J. and Perry, J. (1983) *Situations and Attitudes*, Cambridge, MA: MIT Press.

Collins, A., Brown, J. S. and Newman, S. E. (1989) 'Cognitive apprenticeship: teaching the craft of reading, writing and mathematics', in L. B. Resnick (ed.), *Knowing, Learning, and Instruction: Essays in Honor of Robert Glaser*, Hillsdale, NJ: Erlbaum.

Cussins, A. (1988) *The Connectionist Construction of Concepts* (SSL Research Report), Palo Alto, CA: Xerox Palo Alto Research Center.

deKleer, J. and Brown, J. S. (1984) 'A qualitative physics based on confluences', *Artificial Intelligence Journal*, 24: 1–3.

diSessa, A. (1982) 'Unlearning Aristotelian physics: a study of knowledge-based learning', *Cognitive Science*, 6: 37–75.

—— (1983) 'Phenomenology and the evolution of intuition', in D. Gentner and A. Stevens (eds), *Mental Models*, Hillsdale, NJ: Erlbaum.

—— (1986) 'Knowledge in pieces', in G. Forman and P. Pufall (eds), *Constructivism in the Computer Age*, Hillsdale, NJ: Erlbaum.

Geertz, C. (1983) *Local Knowledge*, New York: Basic Books.

Hutchins, E. (in press) 'Learning to navigate', in S. Chalkin and J. Lave (eds), *Situated Learning*.

Lampert, M. (1986) 'Knowing, doing, and teaching multiplication', *Cognition and Instruction*, 3: 305–42.

Lave, J. (1988a) *The Culture of Acquisition and the Practice of Understanding* (IRL Report 88–00087) Palo Alto, CA: Institute for Research on Learning.

—— (1988b), *Cognition in Practice*, Boston, MA: Cambridge.

—— (1988c) 'Word problems: a microcosm of theories of learning'. Paper presented at AERA annual conference, New Orleans, LA.

McCloskey, M. Caramazza, A., and Green, B. (1980) 'Curvilinear motion in the absence of external forces: naive beliefs about the motion of objects', *Science*, 210: 1139–41.

Miller, G.A. and Gildea, P. M. (1987) 'How children learn words', *Scientific American*, 257 (3): 94–9.

Nunberg, G. (1978) *The Pragmatics of Reference*, Bloomington, IN: Indiana University Linguistics Club.

Orr, J. (1987) *Talking about Machines* (SSL Report) Palto, CA: Xerox Palo Alto Research Center.

Palincsar, A. S. and Brown, A. L. (1984) 'Reciprocal teaching of comprehension-fostering and monitoring activities', *Cognition and Instruction*, 1: 117–75.

Pea, R. D. (1988) 'Distributed intelligence in learning and reasoning processes'. Paper presented at the meeting of the Cognitive Science Society, Montreal.

Resnick, L. (1988) 'Learning in school and out', *Educational Researcher*, 16 (9): 13–20.

Rubin, A. (1980) 'A theoretical taxonomy of the differences between oral and written language', in R. J. Spiro, B. C. Bruce and W. F. Brewer (eds), *Theoretical Issues in Reading Comprehension*, Hillsdale, NJ: Erlbaum.

Scardamalia, M. Bereiter, C. and Steinbach, R. (1984) 'Teachability of reflective processes in written composition', *Cognitive Science*, 8: 173–90.

Schoenfeld, A. H. (1991) 'On mathematics as sense-making: an informal attack on the unfortunate divorce of formal and informal mathematics', in D. N. Perkins, J. Segal and J. Voss (eds), *Informal Reasoning and Education*, Hillsdale, NJ: Erlbaum.

—— (in preparation) *Ideas in the Air* (IRL Report 88–0011) Palo Alto, CA: Institute for Reaseach on Learning.

Scribner, S. (1984) 'Studying working intelligence', in B. Rogoff and J. Lave (eds), *Everyday Cognition: its Development in Social Context*, Cambridge, MA: Harvard University Press.

Shanker, A. (1988) 'Exploring the missing connection', *New York Times*, E7.

Suchman, L. (1987) *Plans and Situated Actions*, New York: Cambridge University Press.

White, B. (1983) 'Sources of difficulty in understanding Newtonian dynamics', *Cognitive Science*, 7: 41–65.

Whitehead, A. N. (1929) *The Aims of Education*, Cambridge: Cambridge University Press.

Notes on sources

Chapter 1 Original.

Chapter 2 Abridged from Thomas, N. (1989) The Aims of Primary Education in Member States of the Council of Europe, in Galton, M. and Blyth, A. (eds), *Handbook of Primary Education in Europe*, London: David Fulton, pp. 9–27.

Chapter 3 Abridged from Benavot, A., Cha, Y., Kamens, D.H., Meyer, J., and Wong, S. (1992) Knowledge for the Masses: World Models and National Curricula, 1920–1986, in Meyer, J., Kamens, D., Benavot, A., Cha, Y-K. and Wong, S. (eds), *School Knowledge for the Masses: World Models and National Primary Curricular Categories in the Twentieth Century*, London, Falmer. Original paper published in *American Sociological Review* 56 (1), February 1991, pp. 85–100.

Chapter 4 Abridged from Ball, S.J. (1993) Education, Majorism and the Curriculum of the Dead, *Curriculum Studies*, Vol. 1 (2), pp. 195–214, Triangle Journals, Cambridge.

Chapter 5 Alexander, R. (1992) The problem of good primary practice, in Alexander, R. *Policy and Practice in the Primary Curriculum*, London, Routledge, pp. 174–91.

Chapter 6 Original.

Chapter 7 Abridged from Street, B. and Street, J. (1991) The schooling of literacy, in Barton, D. and Ivanic, R. (eds), *Writing in the Community*, London: Sage, pp. 143–66.

Chapter 8 Gregory, E. (1992) Learning codes and contexts: a psychosemiotic approach to beginning reading in school, in Kimberley, K., Meek, M. and Miller, J. (eds), *New Readings: contributions to an understanding of literacy*, London: A & C Black, pp. 37–49.

Chapter 9 Bourne, J. and Cameron, D. (1988). Taken from Cameron, D. and Bourne, J. (1988) No common ground: Kingman, grammar and the nation, *Language and Education*, Vol. 2/3, Clevedon, Multilingual Matters, pp. 147–60.

Chapter 10 Abridged from Christie, F. (1990) Young children's writing: from spoken to written genre in Carter, R. (ed.), *Knowledge about Language and the Curriculum*, Sevenoaks: Hodder & Stoughton, pp. 234–47.

Chapter 11 Abridged from Derewianka, B. (1990) Rocks in the Head, in Carter, R. (ed.), *Knowledge about Language and the Curriculum*, Sevenoaks: Hodder & Stoughton, pp. 197–202.

Chapter 12 Original.

Chapter 13 Solomon, J. (1994) Constructivism and Quality in Science Education, in Paulsen, A.C. (ed.), *Naturfagenes Paedagogik*, Gylling, Denmark: Narayana Press, pp. 1–27.

Chapter 14 Driver, R., Leach, J., Scott, P. and Wood-Robinson, C. (1994) Young people's understanding of science concepts: implications of cross-age studies for curriculum planning, *Studies in Science Education* Vol. 24, pp. 75–100.

Chapter 15 Gott, R., Duggan, S., Millar, R. and Lubben, F. (1994) Progression in Investigative Work in Science. Paper presented 10–16 American Educational Association, New Orleans, USA.

Chapter 16 Howe, C. (1992) Learning about Physics through Peer Interaction. Paper presented to the Psychology Section of the British Association for the Advancement of Science, Southampton, 25 August 1992.

Chapter 17 Original.

Chapter 18 Commissioned for this volume.

Chapter 19 Abridged from McIntoch, A., Reys, B.J. and Reys, R.E. (1992) A proposed framework for examining basic number sense, *For the Learning of Mathematics*, Vol. 12 (3), November, pp. 2–8, FLM Publishing Association, White Rock, BC, Canada.

Chapter 20 Cobb, P., Wood, T. and Yackel, E. (1991) A constructivist approach to second grade Mathematics. In E. von Glaserfeld (ed.), *Radical Constructivism in Mathematics Education*, Kluwer: Dordrecht Netherlands, pp. 157–76.

Chapter 21 Abridged from Love, E. and Mason, J. (1992) Four frames for teaching, in Love, E. and Mason, J. *Teaching Mathematics: actions and awareness*, Monograph EM236, Milton Keynes, Open University, pp. 29–53.

Chapter 22 Original.

Chapter 23 Glaser, R. (1992) Expert knowledge and the processes of thinking, in D. Halpern (ed.), *Enhancing Thinking Skills in the Sciences and Mathematics*, Hillsdale, New Jewsey: Lawrence Erlbaum Associates, pp. 63–75.

Chapter 24 Nisbet, J. (1993) The Thinking Curriculum, *Educational Psychology*, Vol. 13 (3 and 4), pp. 281–90, Abingdon, Carfax.

Chapter 25 Brown, J.S., Collins, A. and Duguid, P. (1989) Situated Cognition and the Culture of Learning, *Educational Researcher*, Vol. 18 (1), pp. 32–42, Educational Research Association, Washington DC.

Author Index

Adey, P. S. 292
Agre, P. 311
Ainley, J. 253, 264
Alexander, R. 60
Anderson, A. B. 97
Anderson, C. W. 173
Anderson, J. R. 284
Andersson, B. 173–4
Armon-Jones, C. 239
Aronowitz, S. 35
Australian Education Council (1991) 219

Balacheff, N. 236–7
Baron, J. B. 291, 296–7
Bartholomae, D. 280
Barwise, K. J. 302
Bassok, M. 286, 298
Bauersfeld, H. 262
Beattie, A. 42
Berne, E. 253
Bernier, N. 97
Bernstein, B. 20, 94
Blagg, N. 292, 293–4
Bloom, A. 35
Boekaerts, M. 296
Bourdieu, P. 149
Bransford, J. D. 294
Brewer, W. F. 169–70
Bridwell, L. S. 281
Brook, A. 160, 162–5, 170
Brown, A. 285
Brown, A. L. 285, 306, 315
Brown, J. S. 99, 301, 311–12
Bruner, J. 211–12, 215, 293
Burstall, C. 10

Campione, J. 285

Carey, S. 163
Cazden, C. 96
Chase, W. G. 275
Chi, M. T. H. 276, 284
Christie, F. 115, 117
Clarke, K. 43–5
Cochran–Smith, M. 97
Cockcroft, W. H. 219, 254
Coles, M. J. 292
Collins, A. 99, 301, 311–12
Collins, B. 23
Council of Science and Technology
   Institutes (1993) 186
Crowley, Tony 110–11
Crowther 219
Cussins, A. 317

Davies, P. 291
De Bono, E. 291, 294
De Corte, E. 291–2, 296
Demetriou, A. 292
Department of Education and Science
   (1988) 45, 103, 107
Desautels, J. 152
Dewey, J. 44
Donaldson, M. 293
Driver, R. 144–5, 174–5
Duguid, P. 99
Durkheim, E. 21
Duveen, J. 151

Edwards, D. 213
Efkleides, A. 292
Egan, D. 275
Employment Department (1992) 294

Fairclough, N. 100
Feuerstein, R. 291, 294

Feyerabend, P. 147
Finley, F. 159–60
Fisher, Robert 292
Fishman, A. 77, 83
Flew, A. 37, 43
Flower, L. 281, 282
Foucault, M. 42, 93, 96
Freire, P. 90, 100
Fullan, M. G. 184

Geertz, C. 304
Ghilardi, F. 6, 7
Gibson, L. 96
Gilbert, J. 146
Gildea, P. M. 301, 306
Giroux, A. 100
Giroux, H. 35
Glaser, R. 284, 286, 298
Glaserfeld, R. von 151–2
Goodson, I. 31, 32
Greenfield, P. M. 213
Greeno, J. G. 285
Gregory, E. 97
Groot, A. de 274–5
Gunstone, R. 292

Hall, D. 40
Halliday, Michael 117, 123–5, 149
Hasan, R. 115
Hatano, G. 282
Heath, Shirley Brice 78
Hillgate Group 108
Hirsch, E. D. 35
HMI (Aspects of Primary Education) 271
Holding, B. 160–2
Holt, John 262
Hutchins, E. 309, 311

Inagaki, K. 282

Jameson, F. 41, 46
Jones, K. 35, 36

Kedourie, J. 41
Kelly, G. 145, 209
Klopfer, L. E. 296
Kuhn, T. 147, 154
Kulick, D. 77

Lampert, M. 312–14, 315
Langrehr, J. 292

Larkin, J. 276
Laroche, M. 152
Lave, J. 307–10, 315
Lawson, M. J. 292
Leach, J. 160, 165–6, 177
Lesgold, A. 275, 284
Lewis, H. D. 9
Lipman, M. 291, 295
Luckmann, T. 149

Macedo, D. 90, 100
McDermott, J. 276
McGuinness, C. 292
MacFarlane Report (1992) 289, 295
McLaren, P. 100
Maclure, S. 291
McPeck, J. 296
Mallinson, V. 10
Marek, E. A. 170
Marenbon, J. 108
Martin, J. R. 115, 121
Martin, N. 150
Marton, F. 292
Marzano, R. J. 291, 294
Mason, J. 216
Mathematical Association (1987) 264
Maybin, J. 212
Meek, M. S. 73
Mehan, H. 261
Mercer, N. 213
Merton, R. 154
Mickulecky, B. 76
Millar, R. 192
Miller, G. A. 301, 306
Monoreo, C. 292
Murris, K. 292

National Council for Teachers of Mathematics (1989) 219
Newell, A. 274
Newman, S. E. 301, 311–12
Nickerson, R. S. 291
Nisbet, J. 292, 298
Nunberg, G. 302

O'Hear, A. 38–9
Office for Standards in Education (1993) 184
Ogbu, J. 76, 78
Orr, J. 315
Oxenham, J. 73

Paige, J. M. 277
Palincsar, A. 285, 306, 315
Papert, S. 295
Pascall, D. 271
Paul, R. 291, 295
Paulos, J. A. 219
Pea, R. D. 311
Perkins, D. N. 296
Perry, J. 302
Piaget, J. 144–5, 158, 198, 209, 293
Presseisen, B. Z. 291
Pressley, M. 292

Ramsden, P. 292
Reid, A. 76
Resnick, L. B. 291, 296, 315, 317
Robinson, W. D. 292
Rorty, R. 152
Rosier, S. 174
Rothery, J. 121
Rousseau, J.–J. 44
Rubin, A. 310
Rudy, M. 82

Saljo, R. 292
Salomon, G. 296
Samarapungavan, A. 175
Sampson, G. 111
Schieffelin, B. B. 97
Schneider, W. 284
Schoenfeld, A. H. 284, 305, 309
Schon, D. 232, 239
Schunk, D. H. 293
Schutz, A. 149
Schwartz, B. 275
Scollon, B. K. 91
Scollon, R. 91
Scribner, S. 309
Scruton, R. 38–9
Shanker, A. 317
Silver, E. A. 220, 236, 242

Simon, D. P. 276, 277
Simon, H. A. 274, 275, 276, 277, 285
Smith, E. L. 173
Smith, F. 296
Solomon, J. 146, 148, 149, 155, 156
Springer, U. 22
Sternberg, R. 291, 296–7
Stokes, S. J. 97
Stroud, C. 77
Suchman, L. 310

Taylor, C. 152
Trench, D. 111

UNESCO (1987) 20

Valente, M. O. 292
Ventola, E. 115
Viennot, L. 174
Voigt, J. 236
Volosinov, V. N. 93
Vosniadou, S. 169–70
Voutilainen, T. 292
Vygotsky, L. S. 170–1, 198, 210–11, 263, 285–6

Walkerdine, V. 92–3, 96
Waller, W. 22
Westbrook, S. L. 170
White, R. 292
Whitehead, A. N. 289, 296, 303
Willes, M. J. 94
Williams, R. 112–13
Wittgenstein, L. 152
Wood, D. J. 212
Wynne, B. 156

Yin–yee ko, D. 76

Ziman, J. 154
Zimmerman, B. J. 293

Subject Index

Page numbers in **bold** refer to figures or tables.

achievement levels 11–14
activity: authentic 306–11;
   classroom 306–7; in context 308–9;
   and culture 304; embedded 314;
   instructional 232–3; structuring
   310–11
adult–child ratio, learning 213–14
aims, educational 5, 18
air, physical properties 162–5, 170
algebra, problem-solving 277
algorithms 220, 294
Amish communities, literacy 77–8
anthropology and learning 149
anthropomorphic reasoning 166
anti-intellectualism 45–7
apprenticeship: cognitive 301,
   311–16; and experts 306; learning
   128, 306, 307; reading 99–100
asking 260–6; enquiring 265–6;
   focusing 261–3; funnel effect 238,
   262–3; rehearsing 263–5
'Aspects of Primary Education' (HMI)
   271
assessment, educational 42–3
attainment levels 214
Australian Science Education Project
   158
authentic activity 306–11
authoritarianism 52
automaticity, competence 283

Baker, Kenneth 41, 102
beginning reading: children's
   expectations 96–100;
   interpretational context 91, 96–100;
   linguistic theory 91; psychosemiotic
approach 89–90; shared reading
94–6; situational context 91; textual
context 91–4
benchmarks, numerical 225–6
bilingual children 90, 96, 98–9, 107,
   108
Bransford, IDEAL algorithm 294

CASE project (Cognitive Acceleration
   through Science Education) 292
causation, experiential gestalt 173–4
checking up 264
chess problems 274–5
child-centred approach 43–4, 51
children: achievement 11–14;
   cooperation 244–7; educational
   rights 5–6; as individuals 5–14;
   misconceptions 155;
   non-school-oriented 89, 92, 95,
   96–7, 98; operational levels 158–9;
   as practical people 236–7;
   responsibility for learning 233–4;
   school-oriented 95, 96, 98; as
   scientists 147–8; social comparisons
   239; and teaching 60, **61**, 62;
   written genre 114
Children's Learning in Science
   Research Group, (CLIS) Leeds
   University 148, 160
chunks of information 275–6
citizenship and nationhood 107–10
Clarke, Kenneth 36, 43–5
classics, studying 111, 290
classification activity, mode, tenor and
   field 131–3
classroom: activity 306–7;

adult–child ratio 213–14; organization 233–5; and personal experience 118, 120; problem solving 237–49; roles of teacher/pupil 125–7; social dialogue 238–42; social obligations 243–4; spoken discourse 114; strategy 66; tasks specified 118–20; tenor 125–7; themes and discourse 117–18
CLIS project, Leeds 148, 160
Cockcroft Report 219, 254
cognitive apprenticeship 301, 311–16
Cognitive Research Trust (CoRT) 291, 294
cognitive theory of thinking 293–4
collaboration 68–9, 316
common sense 45–7, 170, 173–4
community: cultural, racial and religious make–up 16; and literacy 78–9, 86
competence 274; automaticity 283; teaching implications 283–6; in writing 279–82
Componential Training Program 291
computational settings 222, 228–30
computers, teaching of thinking 295
concepts, spontaneous/scientific 170–1
conceptual trajectories 168–72
conceptual understanding 155; development 285; good primary practice 64–5, 67; science 188–9, 191–2; and tools 303–4; trajectories 168–72
conjecturing 258–9, 260
constructivism: education 144; learning 147–8; mathematics 207–8, 209, 232, 235–6; personal 144–6; radical 151–3; science 151–2, 154–6; social 150–1; and teaching 147–8; teaching thinking 293–4
content, primary practice 60, 61
context: in authentic activity 308–9; primary practice 59, 61, 62
cooperation in working 244–7
Council of Europe: children as individuals 5–14; primary education aims 17–18; primary education programme 6–11; requirements and constraints of society 14–16

Council of Science and Technology Institutes 186
Critical Thinking Handbooks (Paul) 291
cross-age studies 159–68
cultural popularism 45–6,
cultural practices, home/school 92–4
cultural restorationism 35; geography 40–1; history 41–2; music 38–40; policy influences 36–8
curriculum: balance 13; core categories 26, 30; formal content 21–2; functionalism 23, 31; fundamentalism 42; hidden 18; ideology 22; research 23; science 15, 22–3, 141–3, 158; and societal development 21, 22–3; subject-based ix–xi, 26, 271–3; and timetabling 18, 27, 29; see also National Curriculum; thinking curriculum
curriculum genre 114, 115–16, 117, 120–2
curriculum integration 68
curriculum planning 172, 175–9
curriculum sequencing 159, 176–8

data handling 174–5, 190, 194
decomposition/recomposition 224–5
deep learning 289, 292
dialectical teaching 295
Dimensions of Thinking (Marzano) 291, 294
domain-specific reasoning, conceptual trajectories 168–71
domains of knowledge x, 148–9, 159

ecology 165–6, 176–7
education: aims 5, 18; compulsory 7–8; constructivism 144; for democratic process 185; for the masses 110–12; nostalgia 45–6, 112–13; objectives 5, 18; range 6–11; vocational 26; for work-force 185; worldwide standardization 23, 28, 30–2
Education Reform Act (1988) 36–7, 38
Egan, Fran 123
elitism 108, 109

enculturation 304, 305, 314–15, 318 (n3)
engineering, evidence and data 187–8
English teaching 102–3, 105–6, 107–8, 110–12
English Working Group 102–3
enquiring 265–6
epistemological commitments 174–5, 177, 179
ethnic minorities 16, 107–8
ethnocentrism 108
Evening Standard 45
evidence: concepts **190**, 191–2; engineering 187–8; and investigation **191**; physics 187–8; primary practice 64–9
experiential structuralism 292
experimenting, mode, tenor and field 133–4
expertise 274, 279–82, 285, 286
experts: and apprentices 306; knowledge structures 277–8; pattern perception 275, 276; unfamiliar territory 278–9
explaining 256–8, 259–60
exposition 253, 255–6, 259

fantasy 152
flexible learning 289–90, 294–5
focusing, in asking 261–3
functional grammar 123
functionalism, curriculum 23, 31
fundamentalism, curricular 42
funnel effect, asking 238, 262–3

genre, defined 115–16
geography, restorationist 40–1
goal orientation 282
good primary practice: *see* primary practice
grammar 102–5; anti–prescriptivists 104–5; functional 123; social significance 104
group settings, learning 285–6

Harry Stottlemeier's Discovery (Lipman) 291
health education 26, 28, 30
heuristics 279, 284
hidden curriculum 18
historicism, curriculum 23, 31
history, restorationist 41–2

HMI (Her Majesty's Inspectorate): 'Aspects of Primary Education' 271; French primary education 45; good primary practice 53–4, 55, 57–8, 62; restorationism 36
home environment, non-school-oriented 89, 92, 95, 96–7, 98
home/school culture 92–4
Human problem solving (Newell and Simon) 274

IDEAL algorithm 294
ideology: and curriculum 22; and writing 115
indexical words 302
individual learning 68, 167–8
individuality 5–14
information, chunking 275–6
infusion 294, 297–8
INSET programmes 271
instructional activities, problem-solving 232–3
Instrumental Enrichment Program (Feuerstein) 291, 294
integrated day 69
inter-subjectivity 150–1, 152
investigation, and evidence 188–92

Jenkins, Simon 103
Joseph, Keith 62

Kingman Committee's Report 102–3; common culture 112–13; English teaching 105–6, 107–8, 110–12; grammar 103–5; Standard English 109–10
knowledge: declarative to procedural 188–9, 191–6, 215, 286; domains x, 148–9, 159; everyday/school 215; and experts 277–8; indexing the world 303, 311; integrated 280–1; learning 301–5; and mass populations 20–1; observable data 174–5; personal 152; procedural and conceptual 188–9, 191–2; in science 158, 171–5; situated 301–5; social construction 150; sociology of 20; and teaching 60, **61**, 62
knowledge claims, warranting 174–5
knowledge-in-action 239

labelling, pupils 266

language: and action 127–9; and
    ambiguity 146; field 124, **126**;
    indexical words 302; national 16;
    objectified 80–3; register 123, 127;
    in school 84–5; and self-awareness
    80; variations 106
language programming 123; and
    action 127–9; classification activity
    131–3; context planning 123;
    experimenting 133–4; field 124;
    and learning 123; mode 124–5; in
    practice 127; recount 129–31; tenor
    125–7
language teaching 9–10, 26, 27–8, 30;
    see also English teaching
learning: activity, concept and culture
    304; cognitive apprenticeship
    311–16; and constructivism 147–8;
    context planning 123; deep/surface
    289, 292; as enculturation 304,
    305; field 124, **126**, 127–9;
    first/second hand 7; flexible
    289–90, 294–5; group setting
    285–6; individual 68, 167–8; and
    knowledge, situated 301; and
    language 123; mode 124–5, **126**,
    127–9; peripheral participation 315;
    problem-solving 232–7; procedural
    188–9, 191–6, 215; rote 289; and
    social class 81; social context
    210–11, 236, 285–6, 315;
    structured 81–2; and telling 254–5;
    tools 303–4
learning theories, and course planning
    158–9
'Learning to think: thinking to learn'
    (OECD) 291
Leeds Primary Needs Programme
    (1985) 51–2, 53, 56–7, 58, 69 (n1)
light, knowledge domain 168–9, 172
linguistic diversity 106
linguistic knowledge 280
linguistics, and learning 149
literacy: Amish 77–8; autonomous
    model 79–80, 83; ethnographies
    86–8; formal 7–8, 12; homogenized
    86–7; meaning and uses 75;
    missionary 77; New Guinea 77–8;
    pedagogization 79–80; procedures
    79–80, 85–6; schooled 78–9, 81–2,
    87; outside school 76–9, 81–2; and
    social class 78; as social process 87;

UNESCO definition 73–4; women
    76
literature, and thinking 295
LOGO 291–2, 295

MacFarlane Report (1992) 289, 295
Major, John 36, 52
mathematical facts 257–8
mathematics: algorithms 220;
    computation **222**, 228–30, 313;
    concrete knowledge 313; construc-
    tivism 207–8, 209, 232, 235–6;
    intuitive knowledge 313; mathemat-
    ical properties 227–8; multiple
    strategies 229; multiplication
    312–14; operations **222**, 226–8;
    patterns of discourse 238; principle
    knowledge 313; time spent on 28
Maths Talk (Mathematical
    Association) 264
matter: conservation of 172–3, 177;
    cycling of 176–7; structure 160–2,
    172
measurement, evidence **190**
metacognitive awareness 292, 295
misconceptions 155, 170, 316
modelling 155–6, 174, 215, 295, 314
motor control 10–11
multiplication teaching 312–14
music, restorationist 38–40
Music Teacher 39

National Curriculum 37–42;
    conceptual framework 62; core
    subjects 15; data and study 24–32;
    English language 102–3; geography
    40–1; history 41–2; music 38–40;
    science 185, 192; subject divisions
    50; uniformity 105–6; see also
    Kingman Committee's Report
National Curriculum Council 36–7,
    38–40, 54–5, 192
national educational institutions 20–1
New Guinea, literacy 77–8
New Zealand, personal constructivism
    145–6
Newbolt Report (1921) 111–12
nostalgia, educational 45–6, 112–13
number sense 218, 219, 220–1, **222**;
    framework 221–30; numbers,
    operations and computational
    settings **222**, 223, 226–8;

decomposition/recomposition
224–5; facility with 223–6
numeracy 7–8, 12, 219

objectives, educational 5, 18
Observer 104
OECD conference (1989) 291
ontological entities, constructed 172–3
oral procedures, literacy 85–6

PACKS project (Procedural and
Conceptual Knowledge in Science)
185, 192, **193**
Parent's Information Committee 82
pattern perception 275, 276
pedagogy 43–5; and literacy 75–6,
79–80; process 59, **61**, 62
peer interaction: computer-based tasks
200–2; conflict/partial truths 198;
physics 197–200; preconceptions
197–8, 202–3; writing 133
peer relationship 133
peripheral participation, learning 315
Personal Construct Theory 145–7
personal constructivism 144–6
personal experience 118, 120–2
Philosophy for Children movement
291, 295
physical development 10–11
physical phenomena 172
physics teaching 187–8, 197–200
Piaget, J. 144–5, 158, 198, 209, 293
Plowden Report 50–1, 53, 57, 62
political changes 16
popularism 45–6, 112–13
practice, and proficiency 283
preconceptions 197–8, 202–3
primary curriculum: *see* curriculum
primary education: *see* education
primary practice: authority appeals
53–5; conceptual framework 59–62;
content 60, **61**; context 59, **61**, 62;
empirical considerations 65, **67**;
imperatives 62–4; invisible criterion
55; management 60, 62; pedagogic
process 59, **61**, 62; planning 54;
political factors 65, **67**, 68; practice
criteria 57; practitioner views 50–3;
quality criteria 56–7; and relativism
67; values and evidence 64–9
principled performance 284–5
principles, and procedures 284

problem solving: chunking of
information 275–6; classroom
examples 237–49; classroom
organization 233–5; collective 316;
consensus 242–3; development
process 235; everyday/school 215;
instructional activities 232–3; and
learning 232–7; mental models
276–7; pattern perception 275,
276; pause-times 276; research
emphases 235–7; science **189**; small
group interactions 242–9; unfamiliar territory 278–9; whole class
interactions 237–42
procedural understanding, science
170–1, 188–9, 191–6, 215
process science 187
proximal development zone 211, 212,
263, 285–6
public information 185–6
pyramid building task 212

questions 260–6

radical constructivism 151–3
Rae, John 104–5
reading: and mastery of words 99; as
metaphor 96; tasks 89–90; teaching
of 315; *see also* beginning reading;
shared reading
reading recovery 214
reasoning development 171–5
register, language 123, 127
rehearsing 263–5
relativism **67**, 147
religious education 26, 28, 30
representation, writing 281–2
restorationism 35; assessment 42–3;
pedagogy 43–5; and UK policy
influence 36–45
revision 281–2
rote learning 289
routines 311
Royal Society (1985) 186

scaffolding learners 209, 210–13, 216,
314
school: culture 92–4, 97; procedures
84–6; sign systems 84; space
labelling 83–4; *see also* classroom
Schools Council Integrated Science
Project 159

Schools Examination and Assessment
    Council (SEAC) 36, 55
'Science: a Process Approach' 159
science: children's conceptions
    159–68; conceptual and procedural
    understanding 188–9, 191–2;
    cross-age studies 159–68; in
    curriculum 15, 22–3, 141–3, 158;
    and employment 186–7;
    investigative work 184, 188–92;
    knowledge acquisition 158, 171–5;
    model for 189; process science 187;
    reasoning development 171–5; skills
    186–7; and society 153–4, 185–7;
    spontaneous concepts 170–1;
    validity 191
Science 5–13, UK 158
Science Curriculum Improvement
    Study 158
science education, constructivism
    151–2, 154–6
self-monitoring 284
shared reading: contexts 90–4;
    interpretational context 91, 96–100;
    modelling 94–6; situational context
    90, 91, 93, 95; textual context
    91–4
sign systems, in school 84
situated cognition 301, 317
situated knowledge and learning
    301–5
social class: and learning 81; and
    literacy 78; and mass education
    111–12
social constructivism 150–1
social context of learning 210–11,
    236, 285–6, 315
social development 8–9
social modelling 155–6
social setting: learning 210–11, 236,
    285–6; telling 253; thinking 297
society: individual needs 60;
    requirements and constraints 14–16;
    and teaching 60, 61, 62
sociologists of knowledge 152
sociology of education 20
Somerset Thinking Course 292
space labelling 79, 83–4
spiral curriculum 178
Spotlight (Nisbet) 292
Standard English 103, 109–10
story-reading 91–2

strategies for thinking 292, 316
stroking, social interaction 253
structuralism, experiential 292
structured learning 81–2
subject-based curriculum ix–xi, 26,
    271–3

tasks: modelling 215; monitoring 282;
    pyramid-building 212; specified in
    classroom 118–20; structure 203–4
teacher-pupil interactions 125–7, 252
teacher-training 58
teachers: asking 260–6; and
    attainment levels 214; as authority
    240–1, 243, 249, 256; and
    children's achievement 11–14; and
    classroom tenor 125–7; and
    discourse 120; as evaluator 115; as
    expert 135; as funnel for
    information 238; modelling tasks
    215; non-evaluative 234–5;
    scaffolding 215; telling 252–60
teaching: constructivism 147–8, 150;
    dialectical 295; implicit/explicit
    content 317; intuitive 212–13; and
    knowledge 60, 61, 62
Teaching Children to Think (Fisher)
    292
teaching thinking 289–91;
    constructivism 293–4; methods
    294–5; research 296–7
Teaching Thinking Skills: Theory and
    Practice (Baron and Sternberg) 291
Teaching Thinking (De Bono) 291
telling 252–60; conjecturing 258–9,
    260; explaining 256–8, 259–60;
    expounding 255–6, 259; learning
    254–5
terminology, everyday/specific 128–9,
    130–1, 134
text talk, mode, tenor and field 134–5
Thatcher, Margaret 38
thinking: American studies 291;
    Australian studies 292; cognitive
    theory 293–4; domains 148–9;
    European studies 291–2;
    process/content 296; skills and
    strategies 290–1; studies 291–3;
    teaching methods 294–5; teaching
    of 289–91, 296–7; transfer of skills
    296–7
thinking curriculum 289–90;

cognitive theory 293–4; methods 294–5; research 296–7; review of work 291–3
Thinking Skills Network 292
Thinking, journal 291
timetables 18, 24
tools, and learning 303–4
topics 178–9

understanding 152; procedural 170–1, 188–9, 191–2; in science 188–9, 191–2; *see also* conceptual understanding
UNESCO, literacy 73

value factors, educational practice 65–6, **67**
variables, and evidence **190**, 194–5
verbal interactions, telling 252–60
vocabulary learning 302
vocational education 26
Vygotsky, L. S. 170–1, 198, 210–11, 263, 285–6

Welsh language 107–8
words, situated 302–3
work skills, collaborative 316
'Working Scientifically', Australia 185
writing: beginning 114; experts/novices 281–2; ideology 115; representation 281–2; skills 279–82; and thinking 295
writing in curriculum: classification activity 131–3; context 123–7; experimenting 133–4; practice 127–9; recount 129–31; texts 134–7; *see also* language programming
written genres 115–16; and curriculumgenre 115–16, 120–2; examples 116–20

zone of proximal development 211, 212, 263, 285–6